Churchwarden ALEC DICKINSON, DAVID BAINES the author and PETER BATES a descendant of an old Offley family at Offley Church in July 1993. Photo: J.Bates

# "TWO COATS COLDER"

## CHRONICLES OF OFFLEY

### IN

### HERTFORDSHIRE

by

D.C. Baines

1994

Dedicated to Jacquie, my wife, without whose t.l.c., encouragement and assistance this book would not have been written.


Sold in aid of the Offley Church Restoration Fund.


Published by D.C. Baines, 1994
8, West Lane,
Great Offley,
Hitchin.
Herts.
SG5 3AL.


ISBN  0 9524279 0 7


Printed in Great Britain by
Antony Rowe Ltd, Chippenham, Wiltshire


Copyright D.C. Baines.

# CONTENTS  PAGES

| | |
|---|---|
| ILLUSTRATIONS, MAPS & PLANS | (iii) |
| INTRODUCTION | 1 - 3 |
| MISTS, MYTHS and MAY-BEs | 4 - 6 |
| GOOD MANORS | 7 - 11 |
| THE CHURCH AND the CHURCH | 12 - 24 |
| RECTORS AND VICARS | 25 - 38 |
| OFFLEY PLACE & ITS RESIDENTS | 39 - 56 |
| OTHER PROPERTIES AND PERSONALITIES | 57 - 90 |
| THE VILLAGE SCHOOL | 91 - 100 |
| AG LABS AND STRAWPLAITERS | 101 - 107 |
| THE MISSUS | 108 - 111 |
| THE POOR | 112 - 118 |
| LAW AND ORDER | 119 - 123 |
| ROADS AND RETICULATIONS | 124 - 129 |
| WARS AND THE WAR MEMORIALS | 130 - 135 |
| SOURCES OF REFERENCE | 136 - 149 |

Appendix "A" - Names on Memorials inside
and outside the Church. 150 - 164

Appendix "B" - Supplementary information on
the War Memorial Names. 165 - 184

Appendix "C" - Schedules of Owners and
Occupiers of Offley Place
from 1554. 186 - 187

INDEX 188 - 191

## ACKNOWLEDGEMENT OF THE ORIGINS OF THE ILLUSTRATIONS.

From drawings by Mrs J.A. Baines - Items 1 & 21.

From "Domesday Book" edited by John Morris & published by Phillimore & Co. Ltd (See Source 13) - Item 4.

From the Gatty Collection held by the Hertfordshire County Record Office - Item 5.

From photographs in St Mary Magdalene Church, Offley - Items 7, 8 & 9.

From the Hughes family albums held by Dr H. Clough - Items 10, 12, 13, 14, 16 & 20.

From the Lay Subsidy Rolls held by the Public Record Office - Item 18.

Available from a number of sources but owner not known - Item 24.

The remainder are from the private collection of the Author.

| | ILLUSTRATIONS | PAGES |
|---|---|---|
| 1. | Church of St Mary Magdalene, Offley. | Cover |
| 2. | Churchwarden Dickinson, David Baines and Peter Bates a descendant of an old Offley family. | Frontispiece |
| 3. | Sketch Maps of Great Offley 1890 and 1990. | (iv) & (v) |
| 4. | A page from Domesday Book. | 9 |
| 5/6. | The Church circa 1903 and 1993. | 21 |
| 7. | Rev. P.E. Gatty    - Vicar 1900 to 1924. | 33 |
| 8. | Rev. A.T.S. Henry  - Vicar 1925 to 1946. | 34 |
| 9. | Rev. J.M. Courtenay - Vicar 1949 to 1955. | 34 |
| 10. | Offley Place - West side circa 1880. | 53 |
| 11. | - Rose Garden Gates 1993. | 53 |
| 12. | H.G. Salusbury Hughes & family circa 1887. | 54 |
| 13. | Anne Salusbury Hughes & family circa 1896. | 55 |
| 14/15. | Offley Place 1880 and 1993. | 56 |
| 16. | Wellbury House under the Goslings circa 1900. | 60 |
| 17. | Lych Gate Memorial to the Goslings. | 60 |
| 18. | Extracts from the Lay Subsidy Rolls of 1314-15. | 71 |
| 19. | Recreation Club, Church, Offley Place and the Cricket Pavilion. | 80 |
| 20. | Peter Burgess - An old labourer of Offley. | 103 |
| 21. | Strawplaiting Equipment. | 106 |
| 22. | The old road through Offley. | 126 |
| 23. | The road to Charlton. | 127 |
| 24. | The opening of the Well in 1897. | 127 |
| 25. | Plan of Offley Church & Churchyard Memorials. | 150/151 |
| 26. | The Village War Memorial. | 182 |

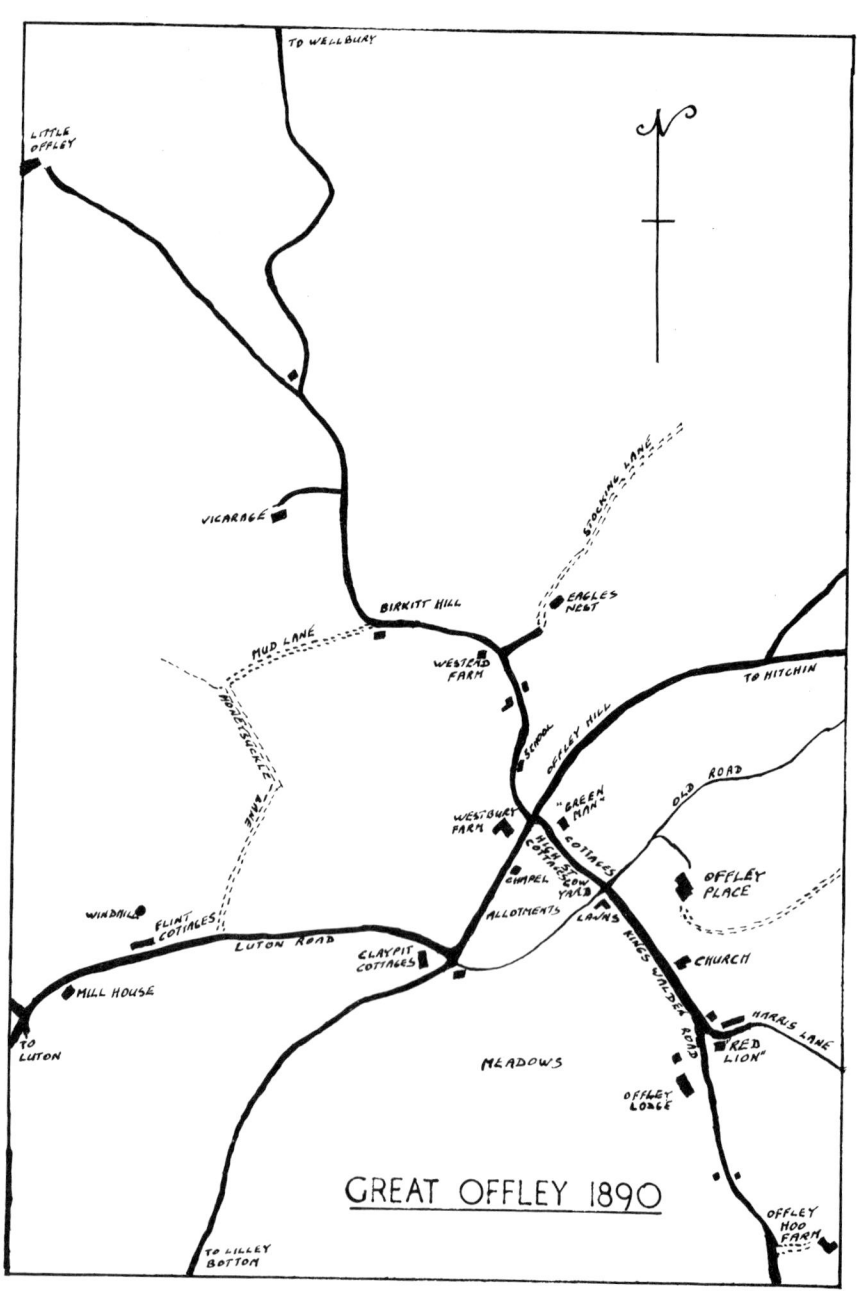

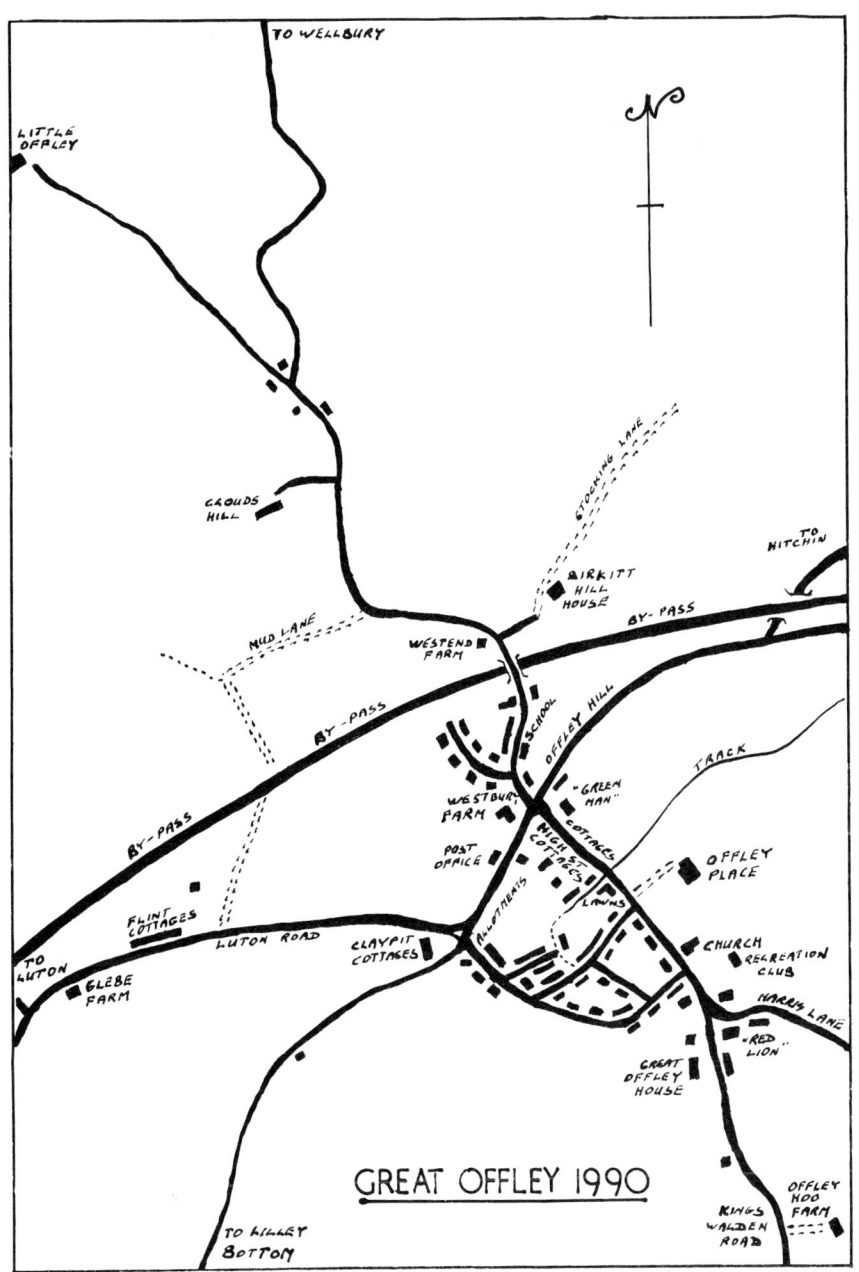

# INTRODUCTION

*"The coatless antiquary in his unemblazoned cell, revolving the long line of a Mowbray's or De Clifford's pedigree, at those sounding names may warm himself into as gay a vanity as those who do inherit them".*
*(Charles Lamb 1775-1834).*

The name of Offley village appears to be derived from King Offa, sometimes called the Terrible, sovereign of the Anglo Saxon Kingdom of Mercia, and was certainly well established by the time of the Domesday survey in 1086. Situated on a ridge high in the chalk downs of north west Hertfordshire, the village is said to be "Two coats colder" than the rest of the district, meaning that a person needs warmer clothing to live in Offley, a saying well-founded in the writer's experience. Its population of approximately 1,000, depending upon the method used to assess it, has changed little over the past 150 years, but the inherent feudal agricultural economy gradually disappeared in the 1920s and the village is now a dormitory for most of its working population and a retirement village for most of the rest of us. As so often happens in rural villages, there tends to be a conflict of interests between many of the older people plus the "Uitlanders" who would not wish a stone to be turned in this the village of their choice and the needs of the younger people, tradesmen and even the landowners who require a progressive living village.

The village has five public houses or restaurants, a fine recreation club and adjacent grounds for cricket, football and tennis. A small bleak village hall, which curiously enough was once described by a well-britched retired vicar as "cosy", serves all manner of social activities including the Women's Institute, Children's Play Group and the occasional public meeting. The village is fortunate in that a School for Junior and Mixed Infants survives and even more fortunate in these lawless times to have a resident police officer. There is a post office cum general store, a butchery and a number of small businesses for building work of all kinds and even a monumental mason.  Traffic through the village reduced dramatically with the opening of the A505 by-pass between Luton and Hitchin some years ago, but public transport to the towns of Hitchin, Luton and elsewhere is good if expensive.  A full range of public utility services is available with the exception of gas.

The 13th Century parish church of St Mary Magdalene, helped by a few dedicated souls, struggles with the ravages of time and the effects of small congregations.  The Wesleyan chapel succumbed to the latter in 1983 and was converted to dwellings.

The principal landowners are the North Hertfordshire District Council in respect of the dwellings and the Kings Walden Estates for the agricultural land.  The fields surrounding the village are mostly hedged and there are many small woods.  Although the land is almost all privately owned, there are a reasonable number of footpaths and bridleways, effectively allowing access to most of the area.  The agricultural use is mainly for wheat, barley, oil seed rape, linseed, sheep grazing and pheasant shooting.  Fortunately mining and quarrying are absent, though an array of high voltage electricity pylons are an eyesore and the proximity of real and model aircraft vie with each other in causing periodic irritation to the villagers.

A pleasant village, sufficiently off the beaten track for the enjoyment of the countryside, but near enough to the towns to avoid any feeling of isolation.

The volume you are about to read is an attempt to record something of the people and events making some recognisable impression on the village during the thousand years and more of its existence.  The information has been culled from many sources indicated by brackets ( ) and listed in the Sources of Reference Chapter.  They range from Domesday Book to the Minutes of the modern Parish Council and from the ancient writings of the Anglo Saxon Chronicler to the present day recollections of many of the villagers.  I have pried into the lives of people whose memorials are still legible in church and churchyard, but many others are mentioned, some centuries old, who have made an impact in one way or another.  In the course of this research it is inevitable that anomalies and discrepancies appear between the various sources of reference and on occasions I am sure to have sacrificed historical accuracy when choosing the most likely course of events.  This is quite apart from my own errors of transcription and interpretation, but hopefully the reader will not call to mind too frequently "Little we write is read as little we read is right".

The story contains hardly any material which could be considered as original, but is a wide-ranging compilation, hence the long list of sources and I am grateful to all their owners and custodians as well as to all those whose memories and speculations have contributed to this work.

It is, of course, sad that many worthies and probably a few villains cannot be mentioned, either because they have no memorials or their deeds have faded with time, though solace can be found in that lovely Eighth Verse of Chapter xliv of Ecclesiasticus, which we sang so long ago at the Grammar Schools Annual Founders Day Service in the ancient parish church of St Mary at Hitchin, whose precincts may well have been the original religious house of King Offa.

> "And some there be, which have no memorial; who
> are perished as though they had not been,
> and are become as though they had not been born;
> and their children after them.  But these were
> men of mercy, whose righteous deeds have not
> been forgotten.  With their seed shall remain
> continually a good inheritance; their children
> are in their testaments.  Their seed standeth fast,
> and their children for their sakes.  Their bodies
> were buried in peace, and their name liveth to all
> generations.  Peoples will declare their wisdom,
> and the congregation telleth out their praise".

# MISTS, MYTHS AND MAY-BEs

*"Yet ever and anon a trumpet sounds*
*from the hid battlements of eternity*
*those shaken mists a space unsettle, then*
*round the half-glimpsed turrets slowly wash again".*
*(Francis Thompson 1859-1907).*

It was difficult to resist the temptation to start this first chapter with "Once upon a time" as the origins of the village of Offley are as lost in the mists of time as, to this day, a traveller can be in the mists surrounding the village. Apart from odd scraps, the earliest written mention of Offley is about the year 758 in the writings of the St Alban's monk Matthew Paris. It must be remembered that Matthew Paris was writing in the 1230s embracing the writings of Roger of Wendover along with other fables and legends handed down through the ages (1), which must have been akin to a present day person writing a history of the Wars of the Roses relying on the hearsay of elderly relatives and friends. To reduce the chances of historical accuracy still further, Matthew Paris wrote in Latin, the translation of which is prone to differences of interpretation. However, we have to make a start somewhere so let us try to gaze through those mists until the picture becomes clearer.

It seems to be reasonably certain that the southern route of the ancient Icknield Way passed through Hitchin and Luton. This was not a road as we understand it but rather a broad generally east/west trail for traders, drovers and those engaged in predatory raids on other tribes. Arriving in the vicinity of what is now Offley on the high ground above and to the west of Hitchin, it would make sense for a halt to be called to refresh humans, horses and cattle at the natural ponds which occur along the ridge, yet at the same time to be tolerably safe from sudden attack. This is of course pure speculation, but it cannot be unreasonable to suppose that small semi-permanent settlements may have been established in the area along the ridge to serve those travellers from very ancient times. A further possible indication of ancient occupation of the Offley area is to note the occurrence of the word "Hoo" from an Anglo Saxon word variously meaning a spur of land, a burial ground or a homestead as in Offley Hoo, Lilley Hoo nearby and Sutton Hoo in Suffolk.

Now we come from dense fog to thick mist. In the year 758, Matthew Paris tells us that the Anglo Saxon Chieftain Offa marshalled his forces at Hitchin and fought the Mercian usurper Beornred at Pirton, Pegsdon and finally at Offley where Beornred was vanquished. Offa was then elected King of the Mercians and decided to build a palace and a religious house on the site of his victory, staying at Hitchin while the work progressed. The site is said to have "stood between the stream and the Ickening Way", a description which fits Hitchin perfectly but not Offley which has no surface running water. It has however been suggested that such chieftains often built their palaces a few miles from their minsters (2) which could mean that the religious house was in Hitchin and the palace at Offley was on the high ground three miles away. The religious house in Hitchin built by Offa was a Benedictine monastery on the site of what is now the parish church of St Mary and was founded in AD 792. That Offa did have influence over the area can be inferred from the discovery of a silver coin in 1923 on a cart track between Hitchin and Offley near "Foxholes" and bearing the inscription OFFA/REX on the obverse and VULF/HAR on the reverse (3).

The name Offley is thought to be derived from "Offa" whose "leag" or meadowland it was but, although probable, it is impossible to be certain that this refers to the Mercian King Offa (4,5 & 6). Sir Henry Chauncy, the noted Hertfordshire antiquary writing about 1700, convinced himself that it was the same person stating "This Vill received its appelation from Offa, that great King of the Mertians, who was the Lord hereof, resided often here, and in this Place resigned his Soul to the Disposal of God; this Parish derived its name from him, for in the Saxon Language it signified the Land of Offa" (7).

On the 7th July 795 King Offa was "gathered to his fathers", having died at Offley according to Matthew Paris "in villa Offeleia noncupatur junta multorum opinionem diem (Offa) clausit extremum" (8). His body was apparently not buried at Offley but taken for burial to a chapel at the side of the River Ouse at Bedford, which may support the view that there was no religious house at Offley. At some later time the chapel was washed away and the burial place lost.

Over the centuries claims were made to substantiate a contention that Offa was in fact buried at Offley. The most interesting of these claims arises from a tablet placed over two reverse encaustic tiles on the south wall of the south aisle in Offley church stating "These tiles were found within this church 1777 which proves that King Offa was buried here". They had been unearthed by John Jeeves, a Hitchin bricklayer, when he was digging a new vault at the west end of the church or chancel and he came across a tomb covered with encaustic tiles and it was thought that they had the name "Offa" inscribed on them. There was also a skeleton seven and a half feet long apparently surrounded by honesty and rosemary leaves. At the instigation and expense of Dame Sarah Salusbury, of whom we shall learn a great deal later, Isaac Duncalt a stonemason and antiquary of Hitchin had two of the tiles affixed to the wall of the south aisle with the inscription attributing them to the burial of King Offa. Cussans discovered nearly a century later that what had been deciphered as "Offa" was in fact "ossa" meaning bones and that the tiles are from a set of four making a circular band. Such tiles were frequently used in churches for paving and these date from circa 1350 and carry the inscription in reverse as they were master tiles for imprinting (10). Letters of 1861 and 1864 from eminent authorities said that they had no more to do with King Offa than with Mr Gladstone (9). Percy Gatty, vicar of Offley during the first twenty five years of the 20th Century, wrote that another tile is inscribed "ono confido" meaning in the Lord put I my trust (8).

After the death of King Offa, the power of the Mercians gradually declined and the Danish invaders took control spreading from the east. The consequent separation of English Mercia from the Danelaw meant that by the year 886 the southern route of the Icknield Way had declined in importance (2). Matthew Paris wrote that after the death of King Offa, "Offley descended to Aethelgiva who in her Will left it to Leoffius for the rearing of pigs on condition that for three days in every year he shall feed the whole congregation of St Albans" (11). Chauncy tells us that Offley remained in the possession of the Crown after the death of King Offa, descending eventually to King Edward the Confessor and King Harold prior to the invasion by the Normans in 1066. The mists descended again.

# GOOD MANORS

*Domesday is near; die all, die merrily.*
*(William Shakespeare 1564-1616).*

The story of Earl Harold being shipwrecked off the French coast in 1064 and his solemn oath to Duke William of Normandy to renounce all rights or designs upon the English Crown is familiar to us from the Bayeux Tapestry. In fact it is almost certain that had he not made those promises he would never have seen either crown or England again (12). However, the promises given, he was released back to England, but following the death of Edward the Confessor in January 1066 Harold was crowned King of England, contending that the promises had been made under duress and by false pretences. Duke William, not surprisingly, did not consider this much of an excuse and promptly invaded and defeated the Saxon English at the Battle of Hastings, killing King Harold in the process.

On Christmas Day 1066 William was crowned King of England. The host of mercenaries and buccaneers he had brought with him took possession of manors and counties across the land, each being rewarded according to his status and contribution. The Saxon English gentry and their families were mostly evicted or murdered and the population terrorised into submission. Even the Archbishop of Canterbury, Stigand, was ousted by 1070. This wholesale re-apportionment of the land resulted in endless feuding and disputes over titles and in 1086 William commissioned a survey of most of the shires of England to establish what he had and who held it. It is at this time that the history of Offley becomes more certain and the mists referred to in the previous chapter recede, as the village can be readily identified in this great survey of 1086 known to us as the Domesday Book.

We learn from the Domesday Book (13) that in the Half Hundred of Hitchin there were several holdings but it is not easy to identify precisely the individual Manors. Cussans studied the problem in some detail circa 1870 (4) and came to the conclusion that they could be identified to the following :-

(a)  *In (Offelei) Offley William Delemere holds 8 hides (a hide was approximately 120 acres) and 8 acres from William of Ecu. Land for 16 ploughs. In lordship 4; 16 villagers with a priest and 3 men-at-arms have 9 ploughs; a further 3 possible. 8 smallholders; 4 cottagers; 8 slaves. Pasture for the village livestock; woodland, 12 pigs. Total value £11; when acquired £8; before 1066 £15. Alstan of Boscombe, a thane of King Edward's, held this manor.*

This was the Manor of Offley De La Mares (Delemere) later Great Offley later Westbury. Chauncy (7) links it to the Manor of Poderich (Puttridge). The De La Mares continued to hold it to the time of Henry IV.

(b)  *King William holds (Offelei) Offley. It answers for 2 hides. Land for 9 ploughs. 5 Freemen held it before 1066; they now hold from King William. 8 ploughs a ninth possible. 2 villagers; 17 smallholders; 3 cottagers; 3 slaves. Meadow for 1 plough; pasture for the livestock; woodland, 120 pigs; wood for fences. In total the value is and always was £4-4s. They also held from Earl Harold; they could grant or sell, but the jurisdiction always lay in Hitchin, and they found 2 cartages and 2 escorts. In the same village Edward of Pirton holds 3 virgates (about 30 acres). Land for 2 ploughs; half there one and one half possible. 1 villager. Wood for fences. Value 5s; when acquired 6s 8d; before 1066 10s. Alwin, Archbishop Stigand's man held one half hide of this land and a man of Earl Harold's. named Abo, had 1 virgate; they could grant and sell their land. the jurisdiction remained in Hitchin.*

The Manor of Offley, later Offley St Leger, from the family of that name, and still later Offley Park or Place.

(c)  *King William holds in the other (altera Offelei) (Little) Offley 1 Freeman holds 1 hide. Land for 2 ploughs; 1 there; another possible. 1 villager; 1 smallholder; 1 cottager. Wood for fences. The value is and always was 26s 8d. The present*

Rex . W . ten̄ OFFELEI . p . II . hid̄ se desd̄ . Tr̄a . ē
IX . car̄ . Quinq; sochi tenuer̄ . T.R.E. 7 m̄ tenet
de rege . W . Ibi sun̄t . VIII . car̄ . 7 IX . pot̄ fieri.
Ibi . II . uilli 7 XVII . bord̄ . 7 III . cot̄ . 7 III . serui . Pt̄u
. I . car̄ . Pasta ad pecun̄ . Silua CXX . porc̄ . Nem̄ ad
sepes . Int̄ tot̄u ual 7 ualuit sēp . IIII . lib̄ 7 IIII . sot.
Istimet tenuer̄ de Heraldo . 7 dare 7 uend̄e potuer̄.
Soca ū jacuit sēp in Hiz . 7 II . Aueras 7 II . inwardos
In ead̄ uilla ten̄ Eduuard̄ de Periton   inuener̄.
III . uirḡ . Tr̄a . ē . II . car̄ . Ibi . ē dimid̄ . 7 una 7 dim̄
pot̄ fieri . Ibi . ē . I . uilts . 7 Nem̄ ad sepes . Val . V . sot.
Qdo recep̄ . VI . sot 7 VIII . den̄ . T.R.E. x . sot.
De hac tr̄a dimid̄ hidā tenuit Aluin hō Stigand
Archiep̄i . 7 un̄ hō Heraldi | . I . uirḡ habuit . Isti
7 dare 7 uend̄e tr̄a suā potuer̄ . soca remansit in hiz.
In altera Offelei ten̄ un̄ sochs . I . hid̄ . Tr̄a . ē . II .
car̄ . Ibi . ē una . 7 alia pot̄ fieri . Ibi un̄ uilts . 7 I . bord̄
7 I . cot̄ . Nem̄ ad sepes . Val 7 ualuit sēp . XXVI . sot.
 7 VIII . den̄.

Isd̄e qui n̄c ten̄ tenuit T.R.E. de Heraldo . 7 uend̄e
potuit . Soca remansit in hiz . Auerā 7 inward redd̄.
Hc sochm 7 V . sup̄iores de Offelei . apposuit Ilbt̄
de Hertford in hiz.
In WELLE ten̄ . I . sochs . I . hid̄ . Tr̄a . ē . V . car̄ . In
dn̄io . ē . I . 7 II . pos̄ fieri . Ibi . IIII . bord̄ hn̄t . I . car̄.
7 alia pot̄ fieri . Pasta ad pec uillæ . Nem̄ ad sepes.

Part of Offley in the Domesday Book

holder also held it from Earl Harold before 1066; he could sell. The jurisdiction remained in Hitchin. He paid cartage and escort. Ilbert of Hertford placed this Freeman, and the 5 above from (Great) Offley, in Hitchin.

The Manor of Little Offley which originally seems to have passed with Wellbury and to which it later paid a fee-farm rent.

(d) *King William holds in (Welle) Wellbury 1 Freeman holds 1 hide. Land for 5 ploughs. In lordship 1; 2 possible. 4 smallholders have 1 plough; another possible. Pasture for the village livestock; wood for fences. In total value 26s 8d; when Peter acquired it 40s; before 1066 60s. Leofeva held this land from Earl Harold; she could sell. Ilbert placed it in his manor of Lilley while he was Sheriff. After he lost the sheriffdom, Peter of Valognes and Ralph Tallboys took it from him and placed it in Hitchin, as the whole Shire testifies; it did not lie there before 1066 nor did it pay any customary dues.*

The Manor of Welle later Wellbury.

The confusion is made worse by the fact that at various times the Manors were in common ownership or portions were leased to each other and varied considerably in area over the centuries.

The translations make it clear that William of Ecu held a large part of Offley and King William held the remainder including Little Offley and Wellbury. It also seems that there was a priest in William Delemere's holding. After examining entries relating to other villages and towns it does not seem that any conclusion can be drawn by the absence of mention of a church.

King William died in 1087, at which stage William of Ecu who owned part of Offley engaged in a plot to advance Robert Duke of Normandy to the English throne. This proved unsuccessful and William of Ecu came to England and offered his services to the now King Rufus. He then conspired with the Earl of Northumberland to murder Rufus in a wood. The attempt failed and William of Ecu was accused and challenged to a duel which he lost. King Rufus, like his father King William the Conqueror, was apt to be heavy-handed and to signify his displeasure Rufus promptly had William's eyes pulled out and "his privy members cut off" (7). Offley thereby lost one of its new landowners.

What happened then for a hundred years is not known, as the next event recorded for the village is the indictment of Geoffrey De La Mare in 1198 (14) for making a ditch to the injury of the free tenement of Thomas De La Mare, which rather suggests that two brothers had decided to lock horns. The records make no mention of the outcome.

Not many years later in 1221 and only six years after Magna Carta, Geoffrey de St Leger owned the Manors of Offley and Cockernhoe and Cussans (4), quoting the Annals of the Priory of Dunstable, records that the Steward of the Earl of Gloucester and an armed force destroyed his house by fire. The reason for the expression of displeasure is not known but this was at the height of the barons wars so that any pretext was more than ample.

About this time, that is in 1220, we first have mention of a village church and the story continues by tracing its development down the ages. This is close followed by mention of those worthy clerics who have served the faithful, and the unfaithful, throughout that same long period in the parish. After that long saga, we will revert to following the fortunes of the various owners and occupants of the several manors.

# THE CHURCH AND the CHURCH

*"What is a church - Our honest Sexton tells,*
*It's a tall building with a tower and bells".*
*(George Crabbe 1754-1834).*

Reference was made in the previous chapter to a priest at Offley at the time of the Domesday survey in 1086 but no mention of a church. We first learn of a church in 1220 when Amicia de Mare gave it to the Priory of Bradenstoke in Wiltshire, a grant confirmed much later in the reign of Edward III (8 & 10), although by 1238 local control seems to have been reasserted by the advowson being granted to William St Leger by Simeon the Prior of Bradenstoke (9). This means that the church probably existed prior to 1220 and the list of Rectors shows a Henry de Gravel instituted in 1214 (8).

Without becoming too involved in architectural detail it seems that the church of the 1220s consisted of a nave connected to north and south aisles by arcade piers, a chancel, a large porch and probably a stone tower. The arcade piers lean considerably from the vertical but this seems to have been deliberate and not the result of ground settlement. With the exception of the rebuilt chancel and tower, the structure is practically the same today. The church does not face due east as might be expected but is some 20 degrees north of east. Clerestory windows were added about 1380. The church is dedicated to St Mary Magdalene, whose festival is on the 22nd July, but whether it has always been dedicated to this Saint is not known. A hundred years later the font, of Totternhoe stone, arrived with its rose-tipped arches and window tracery of the time. It is said to be the most beautiful in Hertfordshire of its age and was fortunate to be spared the mutilation such as was inflicted by Cromwell's soldiers on the font in St Mary's Hitchin (10). The font cover is Jacobean.

A new development came in 1399 when Sir Nigel Loring directed in his Will the foundation of the Chauntrey of Chalgrave in the County of Bedford and Offley was annexed to the foundation. This was confirmed in 1411 by Apostolic letters from John, Bishop of Rome (7) and Offley remained in the possession of the Chauntrey for well over a hundred years. The main purpose of a Chauntrey seems to have been as a place where prayers were constantly said for its deceased benefactors.

A curious inscription was cut in the stone of the most easterly window in the north aisle in 1416 which reads as follows :-
*Dedicatu fuit istud altar(e) in festo sti (sancti) ---? epi. AO DM MCCCCXVI et. Regis Henrici V (Quarto) belley.* (This Altar is dedicated on the festival of St ---? Bishop in the year of our Lord 1416 and of King Henry V in the fourth year of his reign). The Bishop's name has not been resolved and the signature at the end is probably that of the Offley priest (9).

The church only has two brasses and portions of these are missing. One dates from 1529 and refers to John Samwell, his wives Elizabeth and Joane plus one son. A further effigy of two children has been stolen. The other brass is of the same period and refers to an unknown person and shows him with his three wives and eight daughters and one son. The brasses were originally on the floor of the north aisle but, due to wearing, the brass insets were removed and placed on the slate slabs and hung on the north wall in 1906 at a cost of £6 (4,9 & 15).

In 1534 John Friday obtained a lease of the advowson of the church for 43 years at an annual rental of £30. Strangely enough he was permitted to enjoy it until the expiration of the term despite the dissolution of religious houses and their annexation to the Crown by King Henry VIII (8). The dissolution of the Chauntry of Chalgrave itself took place in 1547 along with many other religious houses (7).

An inventory of church goods was delivered into the hands of Richard Derman of Offley in 1553 and consisted of the following :-

Various Vestments.
An old clock of iron.
A Saune bell.
Three bells in the steeple.

An additional note states that "their chalice was stolen and now they minister with a glass" (9). Some things change but little!

When these old bells were removed is not known and it may have been in stages, but a large new bell was installed in 1583 inscribed "John Dier made me 1583" and is the oldest of the present-day bells. It is thirty four and a half inches in diameter and weighs nine and a half hundredweight (15) and has been ringing now for over four hundred years.

Not long after this two further bells were installed in 1618 and are still in the bell tower today. One is inscribed "Richard Shepeheard and Thomas Field churchwardens. Thomas Bartlett made me 1618", weighing eleven and a half hundredweight and having a diameter of thirty two inches. The other is inscribed "God be my good speed 1618. Thomas Bartlett" weighing seven hundredweight and having a forty-one inch diameter. It is interesting to note that the word "speed" at that time meant success or prosperity and was not related to acceleration or rapidity as understood today. Another bell was added the following year inscribed "Richard Shepeheard churchwarden. Thomas Bartlett made me 1619" weighing eight and a half hundredweight with a diameter of thirty eight inches.

This accounts for four of our present bells and a fifth was included in 1632 and inscribed "Jesvs be ovr speed 1632", weighing sixteen hundredweight, made by William Oldfield and having a diameter of thirty and a half inches. The sixth and last bell was not added until 1803 and is inscribed "John Briant Hertford fecit 1803. Thomas Bates Warden" weighing six hundredweight and having a diameter of forty four and a half inches (9 & 15).

The installation of five bells round about 1600 must indicate a period of relative prosperity for the village or at least for its leading landowners and farmers and it certainly coincides with the Spencers building of Offley Place. However, the village must still have been quite small as a Terrier (a record of land holdings) was issued in 1638 showing a total of thirteen and a half acres for church glebe land and a further half acre for the churchyard.

The Civil War years of the 1640s must have been trying times for the majority of villagers whose energies must have been almost totally absorbed in feeding themselves and their families. North West Hertfordshire was fortunate in not being fought over to any great extent but troops of both sides moved through the towns and villages, most of them living off the land to the detriment of the inhabitants. The people of the area generally including many of the prominant landowners, were supporters of Parliament rather than of the Royalists, but on the 7th February 1645 the vicarage at Offley was deserted by Thomas Read, it having been sequestered from him for "various misdemeanours and for his malignancy against the Parliament" (16). Even the execution of King Charles in 1649 does not seem to have caused the revulsion in the area noticed in other parts of the country.

A most important event in the history of the parish occurred on the 22nd September 1653 as a result of the "Barebones Parliament" changing the responsibility for keeping parish registers from the clergy to a Parish Registrar (17). John Deremer of Offley was appointed to that office and the same year the Offley registers for baptisms and marriages began, with the register for deaths commencing the following year. Most of the records have survived though some are difficult to read and others decidedly muddled. Reginald Hine, the Hitchin historian, wrote in the 1920s that he believed that earlier records are held at Lincoln but the accuracy of this has not been tested (18).

Acts of 1666 and 1678 were designed to encourage the wool trade by requiring that a deceased person should only be wrapped in wool for burial and an affidavit had to be made by a relative or clergyman before a Justice of the Peace certifying that this had been observed. It is interesting in that it remained as a custom long after the Act was repealed in 1814 (17) and even to quite recent times. Gertrude Elizabeth Foster who was born on the 23rd July 1870, died on the 27th November 1952 and was buried on the 3rd December 1952 directed that she wished to be "buried in wool" and kept clothing suitable for the occasion (19).

On the death of the Offley vicar Richard Willowes, "barbarously murdered as he came home from Hitchin" (20) in 1698, the patron of the church changed from Gravely Norton to the Richard Helder of Little Offley whose tombstone and others of his family are still to be seen on the floor at the east end of the chancel. Only twenty years later the patronage changed yet again to Sir Henry Penrice of Offley Place and remained with his descendants, their numerous monuments and tombstones bearing testimony to their influence on the village.

In 1730 the church received its only valuable pieces of silver plate. They are inscribed "Eliza Chamber. wid, dedicated this to God and the Church of Offley, A.D. 1730" (see also Church Memorial

10). The items consist of a chalice ten and a quarter inches high and very thick at the lip; the cover with a stem to serve as a paten five and three quarter inches in diameter; a large paten of ten and a one eighth inches diameter which was probably intended for use as an alms dish and a very large flagon eleven and a half inches circumference, fourteen and a half inches high. At the Church History Exhibition of 1905 it was described as a fine set typical of the period. Each piece bears a coat of arms in a lozenge and the sacred monogram (I.H.S.) surmounted by a Cross with three nails below, in a medallion surmounted by rays and the inscription noted earlier. The items bear the mark "A N" which was that of Antony Nelme who was a goldsmith of Ave Maria Lane, a mark first entered at Goldsmith's Hall in 1697. Antony died in 1722 and was succeeded by Francis Nelme in 1722 who adopted the same mark until 1739 when he changed it to "F N" (8).

Even in the days when theft from churches was virtually unknown, the plate was kept in a box in a chest with three locks and in 1749 was stated to be valued at £60. At this same time Thomas Ringer the vicar and Cornelius Hill the sole churchwarden certified that "There be no benefactions given in land or money, that we know of, towards the repairs, utensils or ornaments of our church". Security of the plate was still necessary in 1831 as on the 20th February the churchwardens paid four shillings for a horse and cart to take the church plate to the church on Sacrament Days (22). Today the silver plate is rarely on display and quite a good case could be made for disposing of it. It has to be kept in a bank vault for safety and is not seen from one year to the next.

The 1700s seem to have been the heyday in the fortunes of the church. Hester Salusbury, of whom we shall learn more in the Chapter concerning Offley Place, wrote a long poem entitled " Offley Park 1761" in which she refers to a new chancel as "This sacred structure" (10). This could only have been commissioned by Sir Thomas Salusbury in memory of his wife Anna Maria nee Gore who had died in 1759 and was probably to house the memorials to the Spencer family of which Anna Maria had been so proud to be a descendant. The exact nature of the alterations commissioned by Sir Thomas is not known but in 1774, the year after his death, his widow (Dame Sarah his second wife) commissioned the rounded alcove at the east end of the chancel, probably to his memory.

Two years later more ambitious plans were put in hand. On the 29th May 1776 a licence was granted to Dame Sarah, now very much the Lady of the Manor at Offley Place, by the Archdeaconry of Huntingdon and the Diocese of Lincoln for the Sir Henry Penrice and Sir John Spencer Memorials to be moved, removal and replacement of sundry floor stones, the beautifying of the chancel and increasing the chancel entrance from 4ft 11ins to 11ft 8ins to the size of the alcove at the east end (76). The work was completed the following year and part of the beautification was to cover the old walls of the chancel internally and externally leaving no windows except in the east end alcove and raising the height of the chancel above that of the nave. A vault was also constructed under the chancel as a private mausoleum. The general effect of the new chancel is best summarised by a later vicar, Percy Gatty writing "The chancel is completely out of character with either nave or tower, presents a striking irregularity in being carried higher than the body of the church and being devoid of windows on the north or south sides, it has pinnacles at the angles and is altogether about as incongruous a piece of work as it would be possible to devise" (8). Most viewers would probably agree that it looks better from the inside than from the outside and it has all the hallmarks of being to the glory of Dame Sarah Salusbury and little else.

By this time the village was clearly expanding, as in 1810 the Bishops were paid £8-5s-8d for consecrating another half acre onto the churchyard, making an acre in all. The land had been given by the Rev. Salusbury Burroughs who was now the occupier of Offley Place next door to the church (22). The churchyard was not extended again until 1870 when a piece of land one rood eleven perches was consecrated by the Bishop of Rochester. Part of this was to be reserved for the then owners of Offley Place George Edward Hughes and his wife but in practice it was not used for them (23). After that the churchyard was not increased again until 1929 when the Bishop of St Alban's consecrated one rood and 27 perches on the 25th July after a gift from the family of Guy Hughes the grandson of George Edward Hughes, bringing the churchyard to its present size (24). The names on the Memorial stones and their positions both inside and outside the church are shown at Appendix "A". It should perhaps be mentioned that not everyone regards the churchyard as an entity. Alice Jones (Churchyard Memorial 168), who died on the 4th May 1992 aged 87 years had specified that she did not wish to be buried alongside her husband Walter (Churchyard Memorial 233) as "It is too cold and wet at that end of the churchyard".

In 1814 it was decided that the old stone tower and steeple were in a dangerous condition and had to be pulled down, the churchwardens receiving £10 from the surveyor of roads for the 200 loads of stone from the demolition (22). The churchwardens borrowed £1,000 at 5% per annum interest from Thomas Kidman, a farmer probably of Offley Grange and levied a rate of 1/- in the £1 on the parish to pay for it (15). It did not take long to build as it is recorded that early in 1815 the bells were rung for the first time in the new tower. At the same time that the tower was being built, a new roof of lead was put on the church which was to survive until sections were stolen in 1957. A small portion of the old lead roof survives and has been placed on the floor at the west end of the north aisle and bears the inscription "Thomas Bates churchwarden October 13 1814 A & I Newton plumbers". Most of the lead was replaced by copper in 1957 at a cost of £2,243 and was intended to last a hundred years, but by 1993 was so corroded that another replacement became necessary, this time with stainless steel.

A curious incident took place on the 28th June 1826 when Charles Lane, a batchelor, aged 51 years was buried. It is stated in the Burial Register (33) that not being baptised the funeral service was not performed. The Rev. Lynch Burroughs at his autocratic best or worst.

The next major change at the church was the addition, in 1836 of a singing gallery at the west end (8) and the following year the installation of an organ which had been presented by John Dickie (25), the father of the Rev. Lynch Burroughs second wife.

Also in 1836 a stone coffin (Churchyard Memorial 053) was found buried in the church. It was rediscovered in 1875 under the seats of the south aisle. At this later time it was opened and found to contain bones which rapidly crumbled and the coffin was placed outside where it remained until 1905 when it was placed in the chancel (8). Much amusement was created in the village when five parishioners were moving it again from the chancel into the open in 1966 using rollers as it weighs nearly a ton and one of the workers said "I'm glad I wasn't an undertaker in those days!" (9). It must have been for a person of distinction as it is finely tooled and the stone is not from within a fifty mile radius of Offley (8). It is however extremely narrow at the shoulders. A great pity that the bones were destroyed.

In 1860 the church came within the Diocese of Rochester Archdeaconry of St Albans and about this time an amusing incident occurred when the Hertfordshire historian Cussans was visiting the church looking for inscriptions and he pulled back the matting covering the chancel floor and started to sweep the dust away. Immediately a cloud of fleas settled on his lavender coloured trousers and he "retired into the vestry (which I used in quite the opposite manner than the word imports it was devised for) and subsequently continued my archaeological researches in the costume of Adam before the Fall. And in this fearful place, unswept for years, the school children of Offley are expected to sit quietly, and attend to the Service" (26 & 27).

1876 was an eventful year for the old building. The singing gallery had not been a success and was demolished (8), the "old-fashioned" pews and the tall pulpit were removed and "modern" benches and a pulpit with a reading desk were installed (28). The previous year the organ had been altered and given new pipes and stops and was moved from the west end of the church into the chancel and stalls fitted there for the choir (22). It is almost certain that at that time the wrought iron screen was removed from the chancel steps to become the entrance to the rose garden at Offley Place. Ground fixing dimensions of the gates correspond exactly to the filled holes on the chancel steps. As the costs of the alterations were largely carried by Mrs Hughes of Offley Place and Mr Richard Marsh of Little Offley perhaps Mrs Hughes felt entitled to a modest quid pro quo.

A vexacious subject was raised by the vicar, the Rev. Northey, at a Vestry meeting on the 10th April 1882. All over the country, pew-rents were gradually being abolished and the vicar felt that Offley should consider a similar abolition. The matter was debated at length but no decision reached.  It needs no great imagination to gauge the reaction of the local landowners, tenant farmers and tradespeople and especially their wives, to a suggestion that they give up their private pews so that all members of the congregation could sit where they liked.  At about that time the church could seat 300 persons of which 139 were free places (30).  Such changes in Offley are not reached lightly and it was not until the 30th April 1917 that pew-rents were abolished and annual contributions sought in quarterly instalments using sealed envelopes on specified Sundays (29).  Human nature being what it is, it must be unlikely that the contributions were sustained to the level of the pew-rents and this must have aggravated the affect on church finances caused by the disenchantment towards religion of so many people as a direct result of their experiences in the Great War of 1914-18.

Another subject guaranteed to keep the villagers in a heated frame of mind, if frozen in church, was the question of warming the ancient pile.  The matter seems to have been raised initially at a meeting of parishioners on the 17th October 1883 when, after much discussion, it was decided "that further heating of the church is necessary and that it is advisable to effect this by adopting hot water apparatus".  Again, Offley was in no hurry to incur the expense of the said hot water apparatus and it was finally installed in 1915 by Mr Fred Foster (29).  Prior to that there seems to have been a tortoise stove in each of the nave and the chancel (9).  Heating the church has been a perpetual problem ever since.  The "hot water apparatus" was troublesome and expensive with the underground boiler room flooding and blowing up from time to time although in 1930 the vicar recorded that "All the money needed for the new boiler has been freely given. There is no debt. Thanks be to God".  In much more recent times the bottled gas heaters proved to be smelly and the latest electric heaters warm the bats in the belfry but not the faithful on the floor.

The advantages of having a wealthy vicar were felt in 1907 when the Rev. Gatty gave the church a new organ from monies left to him by his mother's Will.  It was supplied by Thomas Jones organ builders of Upper Holloway and had 574 pipes and cost £315 plus £330 for the oak case and a further £60 for an extra diapason. Part of the north chancel wall had to be cut away to accomodate it

South side of the Church circa 1903

South side of the Church 1994
Note the removal of plaster from the porch

and it was then that the old chancel wall was found together with a window all dated circa 1310 and sandwiched between the walls built in the 1700s (9).

A new clock was started by the Squire, Mr H.G. Hughes, on the 22nd June 1911 to mark the Coronation of King George V and the same clock is still working and still has to be wound manually. Even as far back as 1553 the church had a clock and the churchwardens accounts of the 19th Century mention several payments to maintain it. However, prior to 1911 the clock may have been inside the church and the time indicated externally by a bell ringing, as old photographs of the outside of the church do not show a clock.

1912 and 1913 were years of gifts to the church. Claude Miller of Hoo Farm presented an oak litany desk left by his brother, a processional cross was donated by the vicar and a funeral bier was purchased from a legacy given by Mrs Phillips whose husband had tutored the Hughes children at Offley Place. The bier could be hired for 2/6d per funeral and was ultimately given to the Hitchin Museum where it remains to this day but now sadly in very poor condition.

The 8th April 1920 marked the first Annual Meeting of the Parochial Church Council. Eight persons were elected from Offley and four from Cockernhoe excluding the clergy and churchwardens. Such Councils were established about this time by Act of Parliament and substantially took over the work of the Vestry. Two years later the first Diocesan Quota was paid and remained at an average annual payment of about £30 for twenty six years (29). Since then the rate of increase has gone up in leaps and bounds until now, with the small congregations, it is almost impossible to meet.

A facility which we take for granted today came in 1933 when the North Metropolitan Electric Company brought electricity to the church. Up to that time the church lighting came from oil lamps which had to be lowered for filling and then raised again. Later, in 1949 with £100 coming from Mr Brown and his friends at the "Red Lion", came an added advantage when the organ was fitted with an electric blower and the hand pump, which for generations had made unseemly noises at the wrong moments, could be discarded.

The panel picture originally showing twenty three coats of arms of various families at the east end of the north aisle has had a chequered career. When it was originally installed is not known, but by 1907 the number of panels had been reduced to one. At some time later it was smashed to pieces but in 1939 the remnants were pieced together and the panel replaced. The panel remains to this day with the rest of the window being clear glass.

The 1950s was a decade when a number of valuable and useful gifts were made to the church. In 1952 an interesting and beautifully bound copy of Beza's Bible more commonly known as a "Breeches Bible" was presented by Mr Clough Park to commemorate his sister's marriage which had taken place at Offley on the 2nd September 1950. The book is in three parts containing the Book of Common Prayer printed in 1607, the Bible of 1597 and the Book of Psalms of 1612. In the same year a new altar rail of English oak was installed to the memory of Arthur George Brown, Mrs Pilkington presented an illuminated "Our Parish Aim" and Mrs Curley gave a number of books for the childrens corner of the church. Other gifts later in the decade were a pair of churchwardens staves presented by David Lord Lloyd and two vases for the altar by Mrs Dorothy Hughes (9).

Another gift with an interesting story came in May 1964 when the vicar collected a parcel from Hitchin railway station which contained a watercolour of the church. Miss Townend had set out from Folkstone in 1957 to attend her uncle's (Algernon Cyril Townend, A.F.C.) funeral bringing the picture with her. On the way, the train caught fire and the picture was lost in the upset. The vicar had the glass repaired and the picture still hangs in the church (9).

When thinking of gifts, we should also pay tribute to all those worthy souls who, despite the experience of Cussans, have striven through the ages to keep the church clean. Let us remember those such as Mary Bates who in 1834 was paid 2/6d by the Churchwardens for washing the church and Annie Jane Day (Churchyard Memorial 196) known as "Mrs Church" Day who cared for the old building for some 37 years, at the end of which on the 11th September 1961 a presentation was made to her and the comment "She did her work quietly and unostentatiously and was ever ready to help vicar or layman" (9).

Major restoration work was necessary by 1966 and much of the interior cleaning and painting was done by the vicar and parishioners, probably the last time that the villagers engaged in communal effort. Mrs Pilkington paid for the replacement of pipes stolen from the organ and the following year a faculty was granted for the organ to be moved from the chancel back to the west end of the nave (9).

At the time of writing the ancient church is in a poor state of repair and needs vast sums of money to maintain it. Sadly it is no longer the centre of village life as it was in earlier generations and it might be argued that the sums of money needed could be used to some better effect, though to see this part of our heritage decay to a heap of stones would surely be the ultimate piece of vandalism by our generation.

# RECTORS AND VICARS

*"Who will free me from this turbulent priest."*
*(Attributed to Henry II 1133-1189)*

Having spent some time examining the development of the church we must now turn to look at the long schedule of Rectors and Vicars who have cared for our souls and bodies over the centuries. The prime source of information has been a schedule prepared by the Rev. Gatty at the beginning of the present century (8), though unfortunately it contains very little biographical detail. Where he obtained the information from is not known, but, where it can be checked, rarely has he been found to have made material errors. Information has also come from the Diocesan Office at St Albans and various other sources as noted.

## RECTORS

Little is known of these early Rectors of the Parish.

| Bishop | Rector | Instituted | Patron |
|---|---|---|---|
| Wells | HENRY de GRAVEL | 1214 | |
| Wells | LAWRENCE de STANEWYK (one part) | 1217 | |
| Wells | RICHARD DANY (one part) | 1217 | |
| Wells | ADAM de OGARD | - | Prior & Convent of Bradenstoke |
| Grosthead | JOHN de STOKE | 1238 | " |
| Grosthead | HENRY de BADLESMERE | - | " |
| Gravesend | HENRY de MALOLACU | 1276 | " |
| Gravesend | THOMAS SUDYNGTON | 1295 | " |
| Sutton | JOHN de GRUNDEWELL | 3 July 1299 | " |

| Dalderly | ROBERT ARUNDEL (Acolitus) | 4 Mar 1305 | " |
| --- | --- | --- | --- |
| Burgherst | JOHN DELAWELD | 7 Oct 1332 | " |
| | | | |
| Burgherst | JOHN de WALDA | 1343 | " |
| Beck | WILLIAM de LYNHAM | 1345 | " |
| Gynewell | JOHN de STRATTON | 10 Aug 1361 | " |
| Gynewell | RICHARD de STRATTON | 6 Nov 1361 | " |
| Buckingham | RICHARD de ECCLESHALL | 16 Jul 1381 | " |
| | JOHN atte GATE | 5 Nov 1381 | " |

## VICARS

| Grosthead | JOHN de SHRYVENHAM | 1249 | Rectors of Offley |
| --- | --- | --- | --- |
| Gravesend | WILLIAM de OFFLEY, pbr | 3 Aug 1276 | " |
| Sutton | RICHARD de EYCOTE, cap | 2 Feb 1295 | " |
| - | WILLIAM de WALDA | 6 May 1343 | " |
| Beck | JOHN de NORWICO | 12 Feb 1345 | " |
| Gynewell | LAWRENCE de WELL | 8 Apr 1351 | " |
| Repington | THOMAS atte GATE | 28 Feb 1410 | Master & Fellows of the Chauntry of Chalgrave |
| - | JOHN THIRNSTON | - | |
| Chedworth | JOHN LYSTER, pbr | 9 Nov 1463 | |
| - | THOMAS TRYLLE | - | |
| Rotherham | RICHARD LORCHYN | 25 Mar 1479 | " |
| Russell | JOHN WULBOROUGH, pbr | 6 May 1485 | " |
| Russell | WILLIAM HUDSON | 20 Sep 1490 | " |
| Russell | WILLIAM WALLS | 31 Aug 1493 | " |
| - | RICHARD MALPAS | - | " |
| Smith | RICHARD WHYTE, cap | 1 May 1506 | " |
| Longland | THOMAS CALLEWARD | 24 Oct 1521 | " |
| Longland | JOHN KNIGHT, cap | 15 Mar 1534 | John Franke and Robert Rose, Citizens of London |
| Longland | JOHN NICKS, cap | 1 Aug 1545 | John Franke Clothworker |

| | JOHN TURNER | 1556 | |
|---|---|---|---|
| Cooper | ROGER HENLEY<br>In 1576 he was described as<br>"Ad concionandum habilis" (16). | 1582 | Queen<br>Elizabeth |
| Chadderton | OLIVER PERKYNS | 6 Aug 1603 | Luke Norton |
| Chadderton | FULK ROBERTS, S.T.B. | 1606 | " |
| Chadderton | WILLIAM SHERLOCK<br>(Rector of Lilley) | 19 Jan 1608 | " |
| Neal | WM CHAUNTRELE Clk MA | 28 Sep 1614 | " |
| Neal | THOMAS READ, Clk, D.D.<br>He became a non-conformist and deserted<br>as a result of his "malignancy against<br>the Parliament" and other misdemeanours (16).<br>This seems to have occurred in 1645. It was<br>in the 1640s that the Long Parliament turned<br>out 2000 incumbents for siding with Charles I<br>and Archbishop Laud (77). | 16 Apr 1617 | " |
| Williams | THOMAS ASPIN<br>He was in fact the curate. His churchwardens<br>were Henry Tylers (who signed with an "x")<br>and John Collins (32). | 1637 | |
| - | JOHN NORTON<br>He may also have been a curate. | 1640 | |

THOMAS WHOTTAN
He took over when Thomas Read deserted.
He was "a godly and orthodox Divine" (16).
Strangely his name does not appear on the
Rev. Gatty's schedule of vicars.

| - | RICHARD SWIFT 1650
He was Chaplain to Sir Brocket Spencer and tutor to his sons. He left Offley in 1656. In 1662 he was ejected from Edgware for non-conformity (16). |

- EDWARD WARREN 1657

- JOHN BAKER 1657
On the 18th November 1656 he was given a £50 augmentation "for his better encouragement" by order of the Lord Protector (Oliver Cromwell) and the Councell (16).

- PHILIP OSBALDESTON 1657
He was also given an annual £50 augmentation on the 8th July 1658 (16).

Saunderson RICHD WILLOWES Clk, BA  4 Nov 1661  Graveley
He conformed (16).                                Norton
"A person of very pious and inoffensive life" he was "barbarously murdered by highwaymen as he came home from Hitchin" (20). Buried on the 30th November 1698 (33).

Gardiner  WILLIAM THOMAS Clk, B.A  7 Sep 1699  Robert
His presentation, in Latin, still                 Helder
exists at the Herts C.R.O.
The Patron is described as Ricus Spicer alias Helder de Offley Parva.

Gibson    THOMAS DANE Clk, B.A.   26 Feb 1719  Sir Henry
He must have been a person of some              Penrice &
firmness & courage taking legal                 Elizabeth
action against the Piggot family                his wife
to secure payment of a bequest to
the vicarage and the village
children made by Alice Piggot.

|  |  |  |  |
|---|---|---|---|
|  | See the Village School Chapter.<br>Possibly he was backed by Sir Henry. |  |  |
| Reynolds | THOMAS OSBORN LL.B. | 19 Oct 1729 | Sir Henry Penrice |
| Reynolds | GEORGE AULT Clk, LL.B. | 9 Oct 1732 | " |
| Reynolds | THOMAS RINGER Clk, M.A. 22 Dec 1735 "<br>He was presented on the 27th Oct 1735 upon the resignation of George Ault. He was ordained priest on 21st Dec 1735, was instituted on 22nd Dec 1735 and inducted into the full possession on 26th Dec 1735 (34). |  |  |
| Thomas | THELWALL JT SALUSBURY 29 Apr 1755 Sir Thomas<br>He was originally recruited at Salusbury<br>Cambridge as the curate for Thomas Ringer who was old & sick. He was a distant cousin of a part of the Salusbury family not in favour with those at Offley & they did not wish him to live in Offley so instead he boarded at Hitchin. Ringer had wanted him to marry his daughter but she "drowned herself for spite".<br>Nevertheless Ringer left him his books, money, house and the vicarage.<br>His face was marked by the Kings Evil (scrofula). He befriended the Radcliffe family of Hitchin (35) and took over Offley on the death of Thomas Ringer. According to the Will of Sir Thomas Salusbury (36) by 9th April 1772 he was already vicar of Graveley.<br>In July 1788 he was granted dispensation to hold the vicarage at Weston in addition to Graveley with |  |  |

Chivesfield (37). On the 6th March 1798 a daughter married a Mr Telford of York (37). He died on the 17th July 1803 (35 & 37).

Green      GERVAS JONES M.A.      7 Mar 1775      The King by reason of a lapse
He arrived when Thelwall Salusbury resigned but according to the Will of Sir Thomas Salusbury (36) who had left him £100 in his Will, by 10th February 1773 he was already vicar of Offley. He died at Offley on the 18th February 1784 and his tombstone in the church states "by his desire this stone never to be removed". He was also rector of Holwell and minister of the donative of Kings Walden (37).

Pretyman      THOMAS DOVE Clk, LL.B.      25 Mar 1784      Dame Sarah Salusbury
He was appointed on the death of Gervas Jones but Dame Sarah encouraged him to resign as she wanted Lynch Salusbury in the position. After his resignation he became a Justice of the Peace and adjudicated at the realignment of the Offley to Hitchin road in 1807 (38 & 47). He adjudicated in favour of Lynch Salusbury which seems to indicate that he did not bear any ill will.

Pretyman      LYNCH SALUSBURY M.A.      21 Dec 1787      "
He took office on the resignation of Thomas Dove whose curate he had been (26). Later to comply with his Patron's Will, he changed his name to BURROUGHS. His story is told in the Chapter dealing with the Offley Place occupants.

| | | | |
|---|---|---|---|
| | JOHN THOMAS THELWALL SALUSBURY M.A. | 4 Dec 1835 | Rev. Lynch Burroughs |

He was born on the 28th June 1801 and took office when Lynch Burroughs, his uncle, resigned. His wife was named Elizabeth Anne and they had at least two sons and two daughters. They lived in some style at the Vicarage (now Clouds Hill) (39). He died at Hitchin Railway Station on the 9th December 1880 (40).

His curate, J.W. Sawyer, had been very well thought of in the village, but resigned in 1881, shortly after the vicar had died (28). Sawyer had been born in 1844 and was lodging at Little Offley as he was probably related to the Sheppard/Marsh family who lived there (39).

| | | | |
|---|---|---|---|
| Claughton | ALFRED EDWARD NORTHEY M.A. | 1880 | Mrs Salusbury Hughes |

He was an Old Harrovian. His father was ex-Eton and of a county family in Kent, had been a Queen's page at Windsor and a Colonel in the Guards. His son was therefore well equipped socially to mix with the local gentry of Offley. He gave generously to the parish poor. He moved to a parish at Rickmansworth and took Coulton, his curate, with him (41). He died 24th January 1911 at Torquay aged 72 years (9).

| | | | |
|---|---|---|---|
| Claughton | CHARLES ROBERT WILLIAM HARDY B.A. | 1885 | Mrs Salusbury Hughes |

Born in 1846, he graduated at Oriel College, Oxford. By 1891 he was living

at the Vicarage (now Clouds Hill) and
had two daughters and two sons (39).
He left Offley to go to Canewdon in Essex
where he died after a long illness in
September 1922 at the age of 76 (9).

| Festing | PERCIVAL EDMUND GATTY M.A. | 14 Oct 1900 | Mrs Salusbury Hughes |

One of the greatest and the last of
the "feudal" vicars who were of
considerable private means. His
interests and achievements were so
great that he has been included in the
Chapter dealing with the vicarage where
his work for the village is considered
at greater length. He resigned in 1924,
left in 1925, died on the 30th December
1937 and was buried at Offley on the
3rd January 1938. His wife Alice wrote
"He rests where his heart had always been".
She died on the 25th February 1944 and her
ashes were interred in the same grave as
her husband (33), near the south west
corner of the church. Two of his curates
were Mr Jordan and Alfred Robert
Ashton (42). Ashton was buried at Offley
on the 26th June 1928.

| ALEXANDER THOMAS STEWART HENRY B.A. | 1926 | Trustees of the late Mrs Hughes including Guy Hughes |

He was born in 1874 and studied at
Selwyn College, Cambridge (30).
He came to Offley from Walsall
and although not a countryman he
grew to love the village. He reflected
the strongly pacifist views of his day
writing "Thanks be to God for the
deliverance from war" and "There is a

Rev. P.E. GATTY
The last of the "feudal" Priests
Vicar 1900 - 1924

Rev. J.M. COURTENAY
2nd W.W. Soldier and P.O.W.
Vicar 1949 - 1955

Rev. A.T.S. HENRY
A pacifist of his time
Vicar 1925 - 1946

stronger will among the peoples to labour for Peace", at the time of Munich when Czechoslovakia was abandoned to the Nazis by Great Britain led by Neville Chamberlain, and Lord Halifax, and by France.
When war did come he gave up much of his new vicarage to accomodate evacuees (9). Apparently he regularly went to sleep in the pulpit (19). He was a tall well-dressed man who wore glasses (43). He left Offley on the 29th August 1946 having resigned "as I am growing old" (9). He moved to Church St, Folkestone but was buried at Offley on the 12th March 1964. There was a muffled peal of bells and a memorial service on the 15th March 1964. For some reason not known he wished to be buried as far from the church as possible and not next to his wife Margaret who had died on the 19th January 1952 (44).

CHARLES GEOFFREY HOW   5 Oct 1946
He was born on the 4th April 1900. He was very much the left wing radical Anglican priest who enjoyed a drink in the "Red Lion" (45) although he was High Church to the extent of using incense. He started a Youth Club in the Offley Working Mens Clubhouse (19). He lived with his mother who had been a widow for over 40 years. He resigned in April 1949 to go to Bloxham School (9).

JOHN MANIFOLD           2 Sep 1949
COURTENAY
He had been a Captain in the 60th Rifles during WW2 before being ordained and had been a P.O.W. at Colditz in Germany having

been captured at Calais in 1940. He was
ordained at Liverpool and was curate at
Warrington before coming to Offley. He
retired from Offley at the end of 1955 but
resumed duties as Chaplain of St Edmunds
School Canterbury and died in the 1980s (9).

HOWARD SENAR             25 Jan 1956 Mrs Hughes
Prior to coming to Offley he had been
vicar of Haigh with Aspull near Wigan
for 9 years and prior to that was a
curate at Wigan. He was made vicar of
Offley and rector of Lilley on the 11th
November 1958 (9). He refused to have
ladies in the church choir (46). He
left Offley on the 31st December 1961 to
go to the Rectory of Little Gaddesden.
He wrote a thesis on Offley Church but it
has not proved possible to obtain a copy
of it (46).

DARREL ERIC JOHN HODGE 2 Mar 1962   Mrs Hughes
He was married with one son. He had had
curacies in Cheshire and Cornwall. In
1935 he was Chaplain at Singapore Cathedral
and in 1940 had a living in Ceylon and
later in South Africa. He returned to
England in 1948 to two parishes in the
Canterbury Diocese, then to Adisham as
rector. He also guided visitors at
Canterbury Cathedral (9). His induction
here was to the combined benefice of Offley
and Lilley (9). He did not prove to be a
popular figure especially in Lilley and
was made to feel unwelcome (44). By his own
admission he was of decidedly low church
persuasion (38).

CYRIL GUY HEPHER    1963    Mrs Hughes
His wife's name was Evelyn. He wrote some very interesting and detailed parish magazines. He had been Vicar of Castle Hedingham in Essex from 1936-1941 (9.) He took his duties of caring for the sick very seriously. He seems to have suffered from poor health especially bronchitis. In 1966 he presented the church with a small chalice and paten for regular use, a set that he had used as an army chaplain on the African and Italian fronts, in dug-outs, caves, holes in the ground and even in Lutheran churches in Austria. The chalice was re-silvered and gilded inside from the Captain Vaughan legacy given in the time of the Rev. Hodge (9). The set was still in use in 1993. He was keenly interested in the church history and repair of the fabric (9). Led by his own example, he mobilised the villagers to clean and repaint the church.

ALBERT GEORGE    1969    Mrs Hughes
GRANSTON RICHARDS
He had been curate to Mr Bradley the vicar of St Peter's, St Alban's (9).
He did much good work visiting the sick and rode round the village on a bicycle (44).

## Informal Group with King's Walden, Lilley, Whitwell and Pirton

JOHN CHANNING ABDY    Oct 1972

| | |
|---|---|
| PETER G. BANHAM<br>Left after Sep 1977 | 20 Mar 1974 |
| PATRICK FORBES | Jun 1978 |
| KENNETH MARTIN<br>(Kings Walden) | 8 Oct 1979 |
| Interregnum | 30 Aug 1988 |

## Combined Benefice of Offley, King's Walden and Lilley

| | |
|---|---|
| IVOR NICKLIN | 15 Sep 1989 |
| Interregnum | 1 Jan 1993 |

# OFFLEY PLACE AND ITS RESIDENTS

*"Why so large cost, having so short a lease,
Dost thou upon thy fading Mansion spend."
(William Shakespeare 1564-1616).*

Having considered the people and fabric of matters spiritual, we will revert to matters temporal and in particular the owners and occupiers of the Manor of Offley which became Offley St Legers (from the family of that name) and still later Offley Park or Place.

We have already come across the unfortunate Geoffrey de St Leger having his house destroyed in 1221 by the Steward of the Earl of Gloucester and robber barons of this ilk continued to plague the country until Edward I took effective control in 1273. Whether the St Leger's house stood where Offley Place now stands is not known but it is unlikely to have been far distant.

When Edward I returned from the Holy Land in 1273, he found that the people were being subjected to all manner of oppression by the nobility and gentry and, more importantly to Edward, he discovered that revenue was being witheld from the Crown, such as the fees which accompanied rights of free warren. He therefore caused an Enquiry to be made in each of the Hundreds (an administrative area within the Shires) to ascertain the rights and liabilities of all concerned in a mini form of the Domesday Survey. Hitchin, Lilley and Kings Walden are all mentioned in the Enquiry but not Offley. Perhaps the gentry of Offley had not taken advantage of the lawlessness of the period, were innocent of any oppressions of the people or abuses of revenues due to the Crown and paid all their lawful taxes without demur, but that hardly seems likely. Certainly by 1294 the St Legers appear on the Subsidy Rolls which were taxes on moveable property (68) and in 1301 John St Leger, the son of Geoffrey St Leger, and John's wife Isabel were granted the right of free warren which in effect meant that they could keep and kill rabbits and hunt other game. It is interesting to note that as late as 1761 there was a herd of deer and a stag in the park adjacent to Offley Place (35).

Time marched on and Isabel was to marry again and into the De Hoo family and the Manor of Offley St Leger descended to them. The De Hoo family held courts at Offley in the mid 1400s as did the Bullens when the male line of the De Hoos failed. It is interesting to note that the Will of Sir Godfrey Bullen, an ancestor of Queen Elizabeth I, gave pensions in 1455 to some of his servants at Offley and Cockernhoe (7). The Bullens seem to have gradually lost interest in Offley as by careful marriages they were moving up the social scale, starting with Sir Godfrey's son marrying the daughter of the Earl of Wiltshire and Ormond.

The next we know is the Manor of Offley St Legers being sold to Richard Farmer, a Merchant of the Staple in 1543. The Staple was a Crown controlled monopoly organised for the wool trade to fix prices and raise taxes, which meant that its members were both influential and wealthy. Not that our Richard was without his problems, as three years earlier he had fallen foul of Henry VIII due to denial of the King's supremacy in ecclesiastical matters (4). This was Henry exercising Richard II's Great Statute of Praemunire enacted in 1393 making it a capital offence to assert that the Pope had supremacy in England (77), which Henry found useful when trampling opposition to his ecclesiastical aspirations. Richard Farmer must have atoned for his sins otherwise he would have been hard put to keep his head on his shoulders, but his problems were resolved early in 1547 when Henry VIII died and four years later Richard was granted the Manor of St Legers in Offley by a Royal Charter dated 17th November 1551. Sadly, Richard Farmer was not to enjoy his Offley property for very long as he died the following year and his son John promptly sold it in 1554 to Sir John Spencer of Althorp, for what was to prove a momentous development in the life of the village.

The Spencers were a wealthy and sometimes unscrupulous family of sheepfarmers from Warwickshire and later at Althorp in Northamptonshire. Sir John Spencer had four sons and three daughters and lines of descent lead eventually in our own times to Sir Winston Churchill (48) and Princess Diana. Estates were settled on all four sons, the youngest, Sir Richard Spencer, receiving Offley Manor in 1577. After Sir John died in 1586, Sir Richard Spencer set about building the mansion at Offley which we know as Offley Place. It was completed about 1600 but such have been the alterations over four centuries that it is difficult to know what it looked like, what is left of the original or whether there was an earlier building on the site. Without doubt it created considerable employment in the village both during construction and as a working estate.

A succession of Spencers inherited the Manor during the 1600s (see Appendix "C") which neither the Civil War nor a riot in the village in 1665 (49) (see the Law & Order Chapter) seem to have disturbed. Lady Mary Spencer was keeping a diary over a three year period about 1683 in which she gives a clear indication of her interest in the manor, the church and the village, but much of her time was spent looking after her son Jack, later also a Sir John Spencer, who was delicate and needed much nursing care. At one stage he was taken to London to be "touched for the King's Evil", a disease called scrofula characterised by glandular swellings and probably a form of tuberculosis, but the "touching" was unsuccessful (50 & 51). He eventually died in 1699 having inherited the estate on his father's death in 1687 and his mother, now married to Sir Ralph Radcliffe, paid for an anniversary sermon on the birthday of her son, the minister to have forty shillings, the clerk ten shillings and about £4 to be given to poor families at a crown apiece (52). In memory of the Spencer succession at Offley she also caused a large memorial to be erected which is attributed to Stanton & Nost and depicts two figures in Roman attire with a large marble plaque underneath, at the west end of the south aisle.

Yet another Sir John Spencer took over the estate, this time the uncle of the sickly lad who had just died. The last of the Offley Spencers to bear that distinguished name, Sir John soon became a magistrate on the Hitchin Bench but attendance was not always easy for him. He wrote to his fellow magistrates on the 5th January 1708 that he had not been able to go in his "charriot" to Hitchin because of gout and "our ways are almost impracticable". Nevertheless, he seems to have been keenly supportive of law and order by improving the quality of the constables and meting out heavy punishments to local malefactors (5). He was not long for this world and died a batchelor on the 16th November 1712 aged 67 years. Mortality also seems to have afflicted several of his sisters in rapid succession at about this time including Alice Pigott nee Spencer of Abington Pigotts and Bassingbourn, of whom we shall learn more in relation to the village school. The estate ended up in the hands of Alice's niece, Elizabeth Gore, who, having married an astute sea lawyer in 1714 named Sir Henry Penrice, seems to have made some judicious purchases from the aunts estates, bringing the whole of Offley Place under her control. The complexities of the succession can be seen clearly in the schedules to Appendix "C".

By 1726, Sir Henry Penrice L.L.D. was firmly in control of Offley Place, his wife Elizabeth having died. He was clearly an eminent personage as his elaborate memorial on the north side of the chancel (Church Memorial 16) so eloquently states *Judge of the High Court of Admiralty, Chancellor of the Diocese of Glocester, and official of Middlesex, which employments he long discharged with honour and integrity. When the University of Cambridge sent deputies to compliment Frederick First King of Prussia on his foundation of the University of Francfort upon the Oder 1705 he was the civilian chosen on that occasion. He loved hospitality, encouraged industry and increased the ancient estate of the Spencer family.* This epitaph is not completely in accord with another contemporary comment that although a literary man he was a famous miser (35). He was undoubtedly a "Hanging Judge". Writing on the 1st March 1736 to the Rev. Ringer, vicar of Offley, he said "I have lately been very busy and made my report yesterday to the King of four persons condemned for murder and piracy at the Sessions of Admiralty; which will suffer the Law next week and be hanged in chains" (51).

Sir Henry's only son, Spencer Penrice, died in 1739 aged only 20 years which must have been a great blow to the old man now in his sixties. However he had also been blessed with a daughter, Anna Maria, who was to prove one of the great ladies of the manor. Young Anna Maria must have been quite free with her favours and not necessarily within her social station, as we read in a letter to Edward Radcliffe dated January 1734 when Anna Maria was only sixteen "It is rumoured that a young tit up on the hill has shown some inclination to be trading with your coachman, some of your servants thought to confide. I hear doctor goes for London next Sunday. It must be allowed we live in a forward age" (53).

However, involvement with a coachman did not warrant a shotgun wedding and Anna Maria was not to marry until the 20th November 1751. Her choice was Thomas Salusbury, another lawyer of a good if impecunious family, whose financial circumstances improved immeasurably with his marriage. Old Sir Henry was far from enthusiastic and would not give his approval until he had manipulated both the Admiralty and his future son-in-law into taking over his position as a Judge of the High Court of Admiralty due to his own age and sickness. He was also undoubtedly instrumental in Thomas becoming a Knight two days before his marriage (37), and gave £10,000 as a dowry on their wedding day on condition that the happy couple undertook not to leave him (35). Fortunately for their peace of mind, old Sir Henry did not last much longer and he died on the 10th August 1752, leaving his whole estate valued at £150,000 to Anna Maria. Sir Thomas was duly confirmed in Sir Henry's stead, with rather curiously worded "Letters Patent under the Great Seal of Great Britain dated 19th December 1752 granted to the Right Worshipful Sir Thomas Salusbury Knight Doctor of Laws for the Office of Judge of the High Court of Admiralty of England so long as he shall behave himself, with a salary of £400 per annum" (58). Some might consider that there would be advantages in using a similar wording when appointing judges in modern times.

The next few years must have brought great happiness to Anna Maria. We have quite good descriptions of her even if they view her from different perspectives. She was highly educated with a keen interest in Romance languages, especially Italian and Spanish (55) and Offley Place became noted for its hospitality and gaiety. She was a woman of great piety, charity and general benevolence and had a strong cultured mind. However this doesn't seem to have stopped her from being coarse mannered, frequently as drunk as her husband and not famous for her temperance in eating (25).  She was fair and plump, had a fine complexion, an epileptic and at times the stammer in her speech made her almost unintelligible.  She was keenly interested in the village church and its memorials to her Spencer ancestors of whom she was intensely proud and her husband was instrumental in having two tablets erected in the church (Church Memorials 41 & 42) listing all the Spencers from the 1500s.  Another of her interests came in 1757 when she was made a Trustee of the new Hitchin to Shefford to Bedford Turnpike (5).

After marriage she did not become pregnant and did not want to be (35) but she and her husband found a substitute on whom to lavish their affection.  This was a vivacious Hester Lynch Salusbury who was the daughter of Sir Thomas's brother John, a man noted for his shortage of money and willingness to sponge on anyone in the family who would put up with his arrogance and bad-temper.  Hester stayed with her uncle and aunt at Offley Place for some years and even at an early age became a lady of letters and poetry.  She wrote "Sir Thomas had no joy except his dogs, his horses and myself" (56).  She was also adored by her aunt Anna Maria who assisted Hester to learn classics and foreign languages.  Hester revelled in the attention bestowed upon her and understood that she was the Offley Park heiress.  Both Anna Maria and Hester dearly loved the mansion and park at Offley, so much so that Hester was to write a poem concerning a huge ash tree, a favourite of Anna Maria, which fell in a great storm the year after Anna Maria died and a further long poem lauding the beauty of the estate and  entitled "Offley Park 1761"

Circumstances conspired against Hester, that is if they were ever favourable in the first place.  Firstly Anna Maria died in 1759 at the early age of 41, then at the end of 1762 there was a violent quarrel between Sir Thomas and his brother John, Hester's father, as a result of which John, his wife and daughter left Offley Place for ever.  Finally, Sir Thomas met a local widow and they were married on the 8th November 1763 and this wrecked any chance that Hester might inherit Offley Place, as the new lady of the manor formed an instant and passionate hatred of and vindictiveness towards Hester, no doubt aggravated by Hester becoming Mrs Thrale three days later (10) having wrung a £10,000 dowry from Sir Thomas.

We must now meet this new and most notable lady of the manor, vigorous, determined and strong-willed who did so much for the church, the village and her estate, though not necessarily in that order.  She was born Sarah Burroughs in 1722 and by 1763 was the widow of the Hon. William King of Wellbury.  The most romantic legend (4) we know of in the history of Offley is that Sir Thomas Salusbury and Sarah King were engaged to be married but some misunderstanding arose by which the match was broken off.  A short time afterwards, they both, though unknown to each other, sought shelter during a shower under the same tree.  They quickly discovered the awkwardness of their situation; but as the rain continued to fall retreat was impossible.  The result of the meeting was an adjustment of the differences which had existed between them and when the shower was passed, they were once more betrothed to each other.  The actual tree was still standing at Wellbury in 1907 (8) and a coarse representation of it forms the background to the enormous and disproportionate memorial of the two lovebirds, at that time aged 55 and 40 respectively, which stands on the south side of the chancel (Church Memorial 22).

They were devoted to each other and were to have ten years of happiness together, but by that time Sir Thomas Salusbury was bloated with hard drinking and loaded with fat and he died of apoplexy (stroke) at Offley on the 28th October 1773 (33 & 37).  It is interesting to note at this stage, that whatever Hester Thrale's expectations, she was not left even a penny piece in Sir Thomas's Will.  Dame Sarah in the meantime had busied herself with Wellbury which she had inherited from her father (4) and consolidations of land ownership which were made possible by the first Act of Inclosure for Offley of 1767 and which no doubt gave full reign to her capacity for "rapacious avarice" (35) to use Hester's fine choice of phrase.  After Sir Thomas had died, Dame Sarah had full control of Offley Place and Wellbury and by 1777 had acquired Westbury from the Byde family of Ware Park.  She may also have owned the substantial property opposite Offley Place known today as "The Lawns", as her initials appear on garden gates and on a drainage cover there.

Thus she had three out of the four Offley manors and few could have been in doubt as to her status in the community and certainly the last twenty five years of the 1700s formed a highpoint in the fortunes of the estate. She commissioned alterations in the church and especially the chancel (see the Church Chapter) which to this day bears her initials "SS 1777" and she is said to have done much for the village (50). She also successfully sued Hester Lynch Salusbury now Mrs Hester Thrale for £6,000 in respect of a debt Hester's late father was said to have owed the late Sir Thomas Salusbury and which Hester maintained had been a gift some twenty years earlier (35 & 59). Years later in 1801, Hester, who had become a famous socialite, lady of letters and a great friend of Doctor Samuel Johnson, tried to make peace with Dame Sarah by sending a copy of her book "Retrospection", but it was returned by a servant without a message.

However, we are aware that this formidable lady did have other and more generous characteristics. She reciprocated kindness and loyalty as evidenced by her generosity to Mrs Maude (Church Memorials 14 & 27), her companion of forty eight years and to whom she intended to leave her personal estate. Sadly, Mrs Maude died before her mistress but Dame Sarah's generosity extended to Mrs Elizabeth Hawkes who was left £20 per annum "in remembrance of her tender behaviour to my dearest friend" (60). Like so many of the English gentry of the time, who may not have been unmindful of the effects of the French Revolution, she did consider the distressed in the village and made codicils dated 1795 and 1797 to her Will leaving £1,000 for the benefit of the poor.

Not having any children and determined that Hester Thrale should not be in a position to inherit the estate, Dame Sarah put in hand a series of devious ploys. Firstly as patron of the church she encouraged the resignation of the Rev. Dove in 1787 and had his curate, the Rev. Lynch Salusbury, appointed in his stead. Lynch was the product of another impecunious branch of the Salusbury family (see Appendix "C") and did not find favour with

Dame Sarah until his prospects improved by his acquaintance with William Offley, a rich port wine importer and whose daughter, Jane, he was to marry in 1790. In her somewhat convoluted Will, she left all her real and personal estate to Lynch for his use during his lifetime provided that he agreed to change his name to Burroughs and refrain from using the surname Salusbury. Dame Sarah was without doubt a keen student of human nature and knew how to manipulate her man. Due to conditions in the late Sir Thomas's Will she could not include Offley Place or the land in her bequest as this had been left to the Salusbury family (36). However, in the event this was not an obstacle, as when Lynch's elder brother Sir Robert Salusbury inherited, he did not have the cash from Dame Sarah's personal fortune to run the estate and was virtually forced to sell to Sarah's executors, who in turn gave it to the use of Lynch Salusbury, now Burroughs, with the rest of Sarah's assets. Dame Sarah's final touch was to place a male entail on the estate which meant that it could only be inherited by a male and this was to cause a frightful problem over a quarter of a century later. Even in what we would now call environmental matters, Sarah took an interest and her Will provided that the estate timber was only to be used for necessary repairs. Dame Sarah died at her house in Harley Street in London on the 24th June 1804 and her Will ordered that her body be buried in the chancel she had erected to the memory of her husband (60). Thus passed a great and forceful lady the like of whom will not be seen again in the parish of Offley.

Her protégé, now calling himself the Rev. Lynch Burroughs, installed himself at Wellbury until the Salusburys sold Offley Place to Dame Sarah's executors in 1806, having done their best to bankrupt themselves and pillage the estate with their excessive hospitality. With the need for timber as a result of the Napoleonic Wars there must have been a great temptation for them to denude Offley Park of its famous oaks and one was felled in 1805 yielding 396 cubic feet of timber (75).

With effective control of Offley Place with its 2,000 acres of land, Wellbury, Westbury, the Church, the Vicarage as well as being the Parish Vicar and Lord of the Manor, Lynch soon became a benevolent despot. Cussans (26) tells two delightful stories of

Lynch's younger days when he first came to the parish. As an impoverished cleric he lived in the curate's house near the church when, on a dark winter's night in 1784/5, the post-chaise of wealthy William Offley had broken down nearby. Lynch invited him into his humble lodging where they shared a bed for the night which led to William inviting Lynch to his grand home in London's Great Ormond Street where before long he was sharing the bed of William's daughter Jane. A few years later, on the 15th July 1789, William died and in accordance with his wishes, his body was brought from London to Hitchin churchyard for burial. An argument ensued between the undertaker and the Hitchin vicar over the fee, but rather than take the body back to London in the hot July sun eleven days after its death, Lynch offered to bury his late future father-in-law at Offley for nothing. This was readily accepted to the annoyance of the avaricious Hitchin vicar and William Offley lies in the Offley chancel to this day (Church Memorial 20).

We must now get back to the work of Lynch Burroughs at Offley Place which he occupied from 1806. He soon found that the volume of traffic on the road (now Old Plantation Road and West Lane), passing through the village and adjacent to Offley Place, was excessive and arranged for it to be diverted to its present position (47) and he probably took advantage of the Inclosure Act for Offley of that year to assist with the alteration (64). The traffic was probably disturbing the pheasantry which was at the corner of what is now the High Street and the lane opposite West Lane, but the increased gradient for road users on Offley hill does not seem to have been worthy of consideration. In 1808 he rebuilt the front of Offley Place in Gothic style at a cost of £9,000 (61) though various accounts seem to indicate that he preferred to live at Wellbury House rather than Offley Place. He was also active in his secular role by creating Corn Rents (66) to the benefit of the benefice in 1814 and in the same year organised the rebuilding of the church tower.

He was certainly one of the more benevolent of the village despots. In 1825 he gave land on which to build a new workhouse for the paupers of the village and he built new cottages in the village and established both Sunday and Day schools. With the legacies from Dame Sarah's Will and his own contributions, he endowed the village schools with £2,000 to put them on a permanent basis. However, he did believe in exercising the utmost rigours of the law and in 1832 four men, convicted of stealing four of his rabbit traps, were sentenced to transportation.

His first wife, Jane Offley, had died in 1815 and of their four children only Elizabeth Mary was still alive at the time of her father's death in 1837. Lynch had in fact married again, to Ann Dickie in 1821, but there were no children from that union. He died at Wellbury House on the 10th August 1837 and Church Memorial 23 records *"This monument is erected by his widow as a small tribute of affection to the memory of a husband justly beloved and deservedly lamented"*.

Elizabeth Mary, the only surviving daughter of the Rev. Lynch Burroughs formerly Salusbury, in 1834 had married (62) Sir Thomas Robert Salusbury, the son of the Sir Robert Salusbury who had wasted the estate and sold it to Dame Sarah's executors back in 1806. Sir Thomas Robert died at Wellbury within a year of the marriage leaving his widow, now Dame Elizabeth Mary Salusbury. She never really recovered from her husband's death. She would not permit his name to be mentioned and everything of his was sacred and kept out of sight. Dresses she had worn before his death never saw the light of day again until after her death (51).

A storm was not long in erupting on the peace of Offley Place. On her father's death in 1837 Elizabeth fully expected to inherit all the estates occupied by her father but to her horror discovered Dame Sarah's male entail and that she was not therefore the rightful heir. The estates rightly belonged to the Morley family in the person of the 13th Marquess of Winchester and in order to secure the estates Elizabeth had to pay him the formidable sum of approximately £77,000. To do this she had to raise substantial mortgages on the estate (63 & 65) which may have had the effect of undermining its future, as Offley Place was never again to achieve its former glory. She never did obtain Wellbury which was purchased by her step-mother from the good Marquess and of course the vicarage and its glebe lands went to the new incumbent. However, there were still some 2,000 acres and a large house to be administered with all its problems of tenant farmers, servants, maintenance and cash flow.

It must have been a most traumatic period for her, especially as she had no children of her own and having recently lost her husband. She sought solace by adopting Anne Steward who had been born in 1831, the motherless child of her first cousin's daughter (see Appendix "C"), Anne's mother having died in childbirth. Anne lived at Offley Place and grew to love it as much as Elizabeth and the two women were devoted to each other. Time passed, Anne grew up and married George Hughes in 1852 and they both came to live at Offley Place.

George Hughes was an interesting person. He was a London barrister born at Uffington in Berkshire in 1822 the son of John Hughes of Doddington Priory Berkshire. He was a great athlete and stroked the "Glorious Seven" to a victory of Oxford over Cambridge at Henley. He was a quiet reserved man very knowledgeable in the ancient history of Greece and Rome (28). His brother was Judge Thomas Hughes who wrote "Tom Brown's Schooldays" and "Memoir of a Brother" the subject of the latter being George. However, George did not share his brother's political beliefs and saw no reason why he should wear ill-fitting boots just because they were made by Christian Socialist workers (38). In later life, besides caring for the Offley estate, he was the local Commissioner of Taxes, and was on the Hitchin Bench as a magistrate where it was said that he always leaned towards mercy. He died on the 2nd May 1872 from a chill caught whilst playing golf and he was buried in the family vault which had recently been built (Churchyard Memorial 003). One of the few relics of the family left in the house today is a bust of George Hughes which stands forlornly on the floor in a corner of the entrance hall where once he roamed as master of the house.

In the meantime, the redoubtable and kindly Dame Elizabeth Mary Salusbury shuffled off this mortal coil at the end of 1867 leaving Offley Place to Anne (70 & 71) and the sons Anne was to present to her husband George Hughes. Anne had a long reign and was to remain in control of the estate until her death in 1903 (Churchyard Memorial 003). Towards the end of her life she seems to have suffered much ill-health and photographs show her confined to a wheel chair. She was a person "kindly, full of sympathy and ready with practical help" and although for "many years had spent a very retired life but never lost interest in the village and welfare of its people" (9). A great tribute to a grand old lady.

As Anne grew older she seems to have relied more and more on her eldest son Herbert George Salusbury Hughes who was born in 1853. By 1871 she had three sons living at Offley Place, Herbert, Reginald who later occupied Westbury Farm and Edward. Edward was to die tragically in 1881 at Barn Elms in a riding accident when his horse "Skit" fell and crushed him (28).

Herbert was the archtype village squire of his time and continued in that position until his death in 1926. He was a Master of Arts, a Justice of the Peace sitting on the Hitchin Bench, a strong and striking personality with the nickname "Stosher", was a lifelong friend of W.G. Grace the famous cricketer and a lifelong enemy of the Offley vicar the Rev. Gatty, all of which give quite a definite impression of the man. He made a good marriage on the 11th May 1881 to Henrietta Louisa Beale of Brettenham Park in Suffolk and it was said that when they returned to Offley from honeymoon "nearly every house was profusely decorated with flags, flowers and evergreens and the church bells rang merrily" (40). In due time Henrietta seems to have inherited at least a share of Brettenham Park but by 1899 it was sold "the family regretted that circumstances had arisen which necessitated their leaving Brettenham" though what those circumstances were is not known. Under Herbert the estate seems to have had mixed fortunes. Up to the late 1800s it seems to have been expanding with purchases from the Little Offley estate (69) but by 1910 matters seem to have gone into reverse and he was selling to the Harrison family of Kings Walden and by the time of his death the whole estate was ready for sale and the long family succession at an end. What caused the problem has not been unravelled, death duties, collapse of other investments, poor management, cash flow, too many family and servants mouths to feed, the possibilities are legion but whatever it was, it brought the end of an era.

Herbert's eldest son Guy Salusbury Hughes sold the estate two years after his father's death and moved to "The Lawns" opposite, storing much of the magnificent furniture and pictures in an outbuilding there. Offley Place was purchased by Colonel Acland an executive of W.H. Smith the booksellers in 1928. He proceeded with a number of alterations including the removal of the tower but was not to stay long and by 1939 had moved to Ware and let the mansion to the Froebel Institute of Education. They purchased it in 1943 for use as a teachers training college and in 1953 it was acquired by the Hertfordshire County Council for educational purposes.

We should also not forget the many servants who toiled for all those generations at Offley Place, making the beds, cleaning the floors, washing the clothes, ironing, cooking the meals, washing up, lighting the fires, house-keeping, gardening and the thousand other tasks involved in keeping the family in the manner to which it was accustomed. People such as Magdalene Palmer (Churchyard Memorial 134) who died on the 14th December 1852 aged 69 years "She was for many years the faithful and esteemed servant of Lady Salusbury of Offley Place by whom this stone is erected as a tribute of respect to her memory". A delightful story told by Mrs Daisy Ruffet who, about 1920, was a kitchen maid at Offley Place, concerns her attempts to light the kitchen fire one cold dark morning. In tears she knelt among the blackened ashes when one of the more senior servants came and asked her what was the matter. On being told he said that when he had that trouble he always made the sign of the cross over it to drive the devil out. Daisy tried it and, without fail, it works to this day!

Apart from a couple of inferior framed prints and the bust of old George Hughes in a corner, there is little trace of the family that had ruled supreme for so long. It could now be any hotel with a large transitory population and furniture to match. There was no feeling of the busy family home, the stability, the gaiety and indeed the sadness which it must have seen in its long history. Just a poor tired old lady whose joys are only in her past.

Front or West Side of OFFLEY PLACE - Circa 1880

The Entrance Gates to the Rose Garden at OFFLEY PLACE.
Until Circa 1875 they formed the Screen on the Chancel
steps in Offley Church.

HERBERT GEORGE SALUSBURY HUGHES
Husband

HENRIETTA LOUISA SALUSBURY HUGHES nee BEALE
Wife

GUY SALUSBURY HUGHES
Son

JACK SALUSBURY HUGHES
Son

Circa 1887

ANNE SALUSBURY HUGHES nee STEWARD (in the wheelchair)
HERBERT GEORGE SALUSBURY HUGHES her son (to Anne's left)
HENRIETTA LOUISA SALUSBURY HUGHES nee BEALE his wife (to Anne's left)
JACK SALUSBURY HUGHES his son (seated front left with cap)
GUY SALUSBURY HUGHES his son (seated front right)
Others not known
Circa 1896

South Side of OFFLEY PLACE - Circa 1880

South Side of OFFLEY PLACE - Sep 1993

# OTHER PROPERTIES AND PERSONALITIES

*"It's all so boring."*
*(Author's daughter when aged thirteen)*

For those readers who would share my daughter's views, though these were not confined to history, let us change at least one chapter from a chronicle to a journey through the village commenting as we go (see the 1890 & 1990 Sketch Maps). We will start from Wellbury in the north to Offley Hoo in the south and then from Grange Farm in the east to Glebe Farm in the west. The story inevitably becomes fragmented as much has been either lost or needs more research to discover, but hopefully we shall include most of the more interesting places and the people associated with them.

## Wellbury

This was the original Manor of Welle mentioned in the Domesday Book (see Chapter on Good Manors), held by William the Conqueror and worth 26s-8d having depreciated from 60s. The Anglo-Saxon Shire Reeve (sheriff) had been evicted or murdered with a Frenchman and a Quisling placed in his stead. Everything was therefore quite normal. By 1370 we know that it was possessed by John de Vere the Earl of Oxford (52) and another long period elapsed before we learn that a Sir John Gates was attainted for high treason by Queen Mary in 1554 and forfeited Wellbury among his other estates (4). However, the following year the Crown granted it to Sir Henry Gates, Dame Lucy his wife and their heirs, reserving a yearly fee-farm rent of £9-2s-1d. From the Gates it passed to Richard Spicer alias Helder, of whom we shall read more in connection with Little Offley, who later sold off parts of the estate to various people including a William Crawley. When the latter died in 1595 and his son Richard inherited, it is stated that he held it in capite for the Crown. Curiously enough the same annual sum for the fee-farm rent was still being paid in 1934, part by Wellbury Farm and part by Wellbury House (7).

Another hundred years passed until, in 1700, we find Wellbury flourishing with water supplied in leaden pipes from a conduit leading from a spring in an adjacent hill. This fits closely to the name "Wellbury" as indicated in the "Place Names of Hertfordshire" (96). The "well" means a "spring" and Fuller's "Worthies of England" reads *"surely no county can shew so fair a bunch of berries for so they term the fair habitations of gentlemen of remark which are called Places, Courts, Halls and Mannors in other Shires"*. By this time the estate had been divided, the farmhouse and barns valued at £374 to Sir Ralph Radcliffe well-known in Hitchin gentry circles, part (probably land) to Richard Helder of Little Offley and the Manor House and "chiefest" part to Mr Henry Dolerne. We learn that the house "is much improved by good husbandry and neatly adorned with walks which shows the ingenuity of the owner and the delight he takes in his habitation" (7 & 53).

Mr Dolerne for all his interest and care does not seem to have occupied the house for very long, as by 1763 we know it to have been occupied by the formidable Sarah King whom we know as Dame Sarah Salusbury of Offley Place, she having inherited it from her father Samuel Burroughs. It must still have been a most desirable home, as there are indications that both Sarah and her successors preferred it to Offley Place until well into the 1800s. The house and the farming activities seem to have stayed separately from each other though whether the farmers were tenants or owners has not been established. In 1851, Thomas Smoothy (Churchyard Memorial 067) was farming 381 acres and employing eleven labourers and three servants at Old Wellbury according to the Census of that year which suggests a flourishing enterprise.

By 1840 Wellbury House and park had been purchased by Ann Burroughs, widow and second wife of the Rev. Lynch Burroughs formerly Salusbury, from the Marquess of Winchester following the debacle over the male entail in Dame Sarah's Will. When Ann died in 1856 Wellbury went to her sister Maria Newbury of Clapham Rise, Surrey who shortly afterwards leased it to the most celebrated of its occupants, Francis Gosling.

The Goslings were certainly at Wellbury by 1860 (83) but do not seem to have purchased it until 1872 (4). Francis Gosling was a banker and even today his name is perpetuated by a branch of Barclays Bank at Temple Bar in London's Fleet Street called Goslings Bank. There were few constraints with money and he set about creating a country mansion fitting his position as a leading banker. It was described at the time as a spacious mansion standing in a park of 324 acres. Additionally, in his spare time, Francis was in 1877 the appointed Overseer of the Poor for Offley (29) and, for a time, was the Master of the Hertfordshire Hounds arising from which he kept some twenty horses on the estate (104). Although Wellbury had its own chapel, the family of thirteen and the majority of its dozen servants were expected to go to Offley church regularly each week arriving in wagonettes, with the family sitting in the front pew on the south side of the nave.

Francis was probably the greatest of village benefactors and his wife Katherine and their eight daughters were all expected to distribute food and clothing to the poor of the village. He also had three sons who no doubt also had to do their share of "good works". They were justifiably popular in the village and probably the most tangible evidence of their kindness was paying for the first public well, some 300 feet deep on the village green, in 1897. Prior to that there was no water available except from the pond, the occasional water cart from Hitchin or from privately owned wells and cisterns. Francis died on the 24th February 1910 and the Parish Magazine recorded "Offley never had a truer or better friend keenly interested in all that was for the welfare of the village". His grave (Churchyard Memorial 004) is a neglected and broken stone cross to the north of the church, but a more appropriate memorial is the handsome lych gate (Churchyard Memorial 001) to both Katherine and Francis which was dedicated on the 4th May 1918 and it was said of her "Her work in the parish was extensive and well known and will long be remembered". Fitting tributes to a family who took their responsibilities very seriously.

Shortly after Francis had died much of the land at Wellbury was sold so that by 1914 the park had been reduced to 100 acres (18) and the buildings were never to recover their former glory as a private mansion. It became a private school by 1919 with extensive alterations including the pulling down of the Elizabethan wing and a new classroom built over the site. It is interesting to note that in 1927 Mary Ann Muddle, the owner of Wellbury Farm which had been part of the estate many years earlier, applied to have her

WELLBURY HOUSE under the GOSLINGS - Circa 1900

THE CHURCH LYCH GATE
A Memorial to FRANCES AND KATHERINE GOSLING

liability to the vicar of Offley for £13-17s-1d per annum under the Corn Rent Act discharged (67).

By 1933 Wellbury had recovered, if in a different role, and was now 130 acres of park and woodland for a select Roman Catholic Preparatory School for Boys complete with a Roman Catholic Chapel. It was all owned by the Headmaster, Mr Bernard Evelyn Kenworthy-Browne, who was proud of the fact that he was Lord of the Manor of Wellbury. No doubt erroneously, but the name and the remoteness of the school somehow evokes a Dickensian impression of Mr Wackford Squeers of Dotheboys Hall in "Nicholas Nickleby". The private school continued when Mr Solly took over as headmaster in 1955 but it closed in 1965 (79). The buildings stood empty for some long time and eventually another school was opened, this time by the St Christopher's Fellowship dealing with disturbed boys, initially from London but later from a wider area. This lasted until 1988 and the following year the old house was purchased by the Tarah Chessed Group as a seminary for an ultra-orthodox Jewish sect. Unfortunately, time and circumstances have not looked kindly on the old mansion and by 1994 it is in a sorry state and the public authorities have questioned whether it is even habitable. An even sadder story to that of Offley Place.

### Little Offley

We will divert from the direct road from Wellbury to Offley to tell the much happier story of the Manor of Little Offley. This was also held by the King at the time of the Domesday survey and by Earl Harold before him, the value "is and always was 26s-8d".

We then have a long gap in its history until 1556 when it was granted by the Crown to Richard Spicer alias Helder, although for about a hundred years it had already been in the possession of the Helders but on long leases from the Crown (7). This suggests that it had not parted from the Crown in the five hundred years from Domesday. There was a hamlet in the vicinity which Richard now set about demolishing until there was only the one house and a few outbuildings. The foundations of some of these early buildings were still visible in 1700 (7). A delightful story (42) related some years ago by the village raconteur George Pearman (Churchyard Memorial 288) was that the hamlet was called "Little Hitchin" and that an ancient tapestry in the house depicted the hamlet as an enclosed village, but the present owners (80) cast doubt on the historical accuracy of the tale. The main house was originally a small 16th Century homestead but there was much rebuilding in 1696 when a clocktower was removed, a lead rainwater head bearing that date (81). There is also a fine carved wooden overmantel in a ground floor room (14).

Through failure of the male line, the family name changed to Sheppard and still later and for the same reason changed to Marsh. Numbers of Helders, Sheppards and Marshs are to be found in both church and churchyard. A personal touch was in the 1745 Will of Ann Sheppard "To Sarah Baldock my servant, my nightgown" (18). Other homes, probably those of employees, reappeared in the vicinity and at the Quarter Sessions and before the Archdeacon of Huntingdon on the 21st July 1761, the house of John Marshall at Little Offley was being used by Protestant Dissenters (82).

The family continued to own the estate until it was sold in 1912 thus ending an occupation of over five hundred years. Curiously enough the first two decades of the 20th Century seem to have marked the sale of most of the three Offley manors, the fourth having long lost its independence. Little Offley was purchased by C.E. Johnston who was soon to take part in the Great War of 1914-18, at the end of which he was Lieut Colonel C.E. Johnston M.C.,D.S.O. Shortly after the war, in 1922, "Amid a sense of loss to the Parish" (29), Colonel Johnston was drowned at Bude in Cornwall attempting to rescue a friend (40). Shortly thereafter the property was sold to Thomas Rupert Clutterbuck and it remained in the Clutterbuck family until sold again in 1966. During that time it must have been leased from time to time, as it was certainly occupied in the 1930s and early 1940s by Hubert and Ruth Pilkington and their four sons two of whom were to be killed in military operations during the Second World War.

Today, the operation and administration of a large estate must be incredibly difficult in the face of modern "stop-go" agricultural policies and we can only hope that the present fine-looking and well-loved appearance of Little Offley will continue for the delight and admiration of future generations interested in our heritage.

## Clouds Hill formerly The Vicarage

We rejoin the road from Wellbury and before long we see a large white house through the trees. This was formerly the Vicarage and, in the days before cars, the vicars must have found it quite a penance making the mile or so journey to church on a winter's morning. Although Offley ceased to have Rectors from about 1400, when looking at old books and documents we find reference to a rectory and it is questionable as to whether we are referring to the vicarage, though the glebe lands seem to have been in the locality we could expect. We know that curates homes were usually nearer the church, but the vicars do seem to have been rather remote from their flock, but maybe they preferred it so.

An early reference is in 1575 when the rectory was leased by Queen Elizabeth I to George Bredyman for twenty-one years and the fee simple was later acquired by George Graveley. He died in 1600 leaving as heir his daughter Lettice the wife of Luke Norton and we notice from the schedule of vicars that Luke was patron of the church. Seven years later an interesting document was prepared and which still exists at the Hertfordshire County Record Office being the "Deed of Assignment by Ralph Radcliff Esq of Hitchin to Luke Norton Esq his half-brother of the advowson of Offley Vicarage". Through marriage it descended to a William Angell of London (7), the Norton's having disposed of the greater part of the tithes and glebe on the lands by several people paying fees in substitution (7). After that, nothing more is heard until 1698 when the rectory passed from William Angell to Richard Helder who lived on the adjacent estate at Little Offley and was the patron of the church. All this suggests that this rectory is the same dwelling that we call the Vicarage or more recently Clouds Hill and as there appears to be no further descent after 1698 it may have been acquired as part of the patronage of the church, as we notice that from 1719 it was in the gift of the Lord or Lady of Offley Place who had become the patrons.

Fifty seven years later we find that on the death of the Rev. Thomas Ringer, he leaves his books, money, house and vicarage to the Rev. Thelwall Salusbury and thereafter the vicarage seems to have been available for occupation by successive vicars. About 1830 it was rebuilt or extended on a Queen Anne cottage in Regency

Gothic style (84) and by 1839 it consisted of a vicarage house and two cottages (63) but whether they were all together is not known.

In 1900 the last and greatest of what might be called the wealthy "feudal" vicars arrived in the person of Percival Edmund Gatty. Throughout his twenty five years in the village he lived at the vicarage though he frequently complained of its deteriorating condition. His wife Alice Mabel Wellwood was married to him the year before they came to Offley and he was to have a son named Hugh and a daughter Margaret. He had not worked in a country parish before, having previously been in Leeds, Brighton and, immediately before coming to Offley, as a curate at Biggleswade.

In his dealings with people he had pronounced likes and dislikes and his dislike of the Squire, Herbert Salusbury Hughes, was well-known. Otherwise he was "of a retiring and rather shy disposition, slow at making friends, but once made they were lifelong". He interested himself in every aspect of the parish and was instrumental in founding a new church at Cockernhoe which he had named St Hugh's after his son. A great traditionalist, a strict disciplinarian and hard-working, he tried to instil thrift into his parishioners as well as a sense of community. He was not a good preacher but was a very good man (42). He loathed collecting subscriptions saying "It is not conducive to edification for the Parish Priest to be a chronic beggar" (9). Until he obtained the services of a curate about 1905 he tottered on the verge of a nervous breakdown. A fluent speaker of French, during the Great War he went to France taking his chauffeur and personal car with him as an ambulance and transported wounded French soldiers for three months in each of 1915 and 1916.

In 1924 he wished to purchase the vicarage in order to release money so that future incumbents of Offley did not have to be of independent means and also so that he could own the property and thereby spend substantial sums on alterations to make it more suitable to his requirements. He offered £700 over the value as assessed by Jackson's the local Auctioneers, but this was not acceptable to the Church Commissioners who wanted more, no doubt egged on by the patron Herbert Hughes. In consequence he withdrew his offer, resigned the living and left the village in 1925. He predicted that what he was proposing would in due time happen and indeed it did ten years later. He was buried on the 3rd January 1938 at Offley (Churchyard Memorial 013), cricketers carrying his body to the grave, and his wife wrote "He rests where his heart had always been". He left a legacy of £200 to keep the churchyard in repair and £500 for the poor, sick, aged and infirm of Offley (9). Salute the memory of him as you pass his grave to the left of the path leading from the churchyard gates to the church porch.

The next incumbent, the Rev. Henry, struggled on at the vicarage as its condition gradually deteriorated until eventually a decision was made to sell the property. Some idea of the problem can be gained from the papers of the Rev. Henry (67) which show his net annual income as £237-2s-5d, with which he was expected to keep himself and his family in an old and enormous vicarage. In 1935 the property was sold and a new dwelling which will be discussed later, built near the church.

The vicarage passed into private ownership to George, Lord Lloyd of Dolobran on the 24th June 1935. Accounts vary as to the amount paid for it. A letter from the Queen Anne Bounty Office dated 20th July 1936 shows it as £2,776 (85), a biographer of Lord Lloyd states it at just under £4,000 (86) and a note of the Rev. Henry's shows it as £3,750 (67), which even for those times seems a small sum with ninety acres of land included. The house was renamed Clouds Hill from Lawrence of Arabia's cottage of that name. He had been killed in a motor-cycle accident on the 13th May 1935 and had been a great friend of Lord Lloyd's in the Middle East where they had served together.

At the instigation of Blanche, Lady Lloyd, considerable demolition, restoration and extensions of wings to the house took place in the next few years and a further purchase of land took place in 1937 to "guarantee their privacy". According to Lord Lloyd she "was preoccupied by domesticity or horticultural details in respect of Clouds Hill and regarded it as her nest" and after the incessant wanderings with her husband this is not really surprising. Lord Lloyd was an inveterate traveller and diplomat, an enthusiastic Frankophile, pro Arab and a keen supporter of rearmament which brought him into close association with Winston Churchill (87). Lady Lloyd wrote of Clouds Hill "It has no particular architectural distinction, its proportions are pleasant to the eye, it has a situation of charm and an atmosphere of gentle and happy repose" (40). Lord Lloyd made desperate efforts, on instructions from Winston Churchill, attempting to keep the French in the war in 1940 but to no avail. Early in 1941 Lord Lloyd died and his son David succeeded to the title.

Since that time, nothing has really changed. Clouds Hill is still with the Lloyd family and a place of gentle and happy repose.

### Bucketts or Birkitt Hill

A short distance after leaving Clouds Hill on the right on our way to Offley we come across a sharp left hand turn and rise in the road. This was known as Bucketts Hill and in 1891 (39) had two old cottages on the right hand side between the two ponds (one now landscaped) which were used for domestic water. The cottages have long since been demolished though the location can be seen by the position of the hedgerows, but photographs of the cottages still exist (40). One was occupied by Jabez Robinson and his wife Mary Ann both Offley born and the other by Henry and Eliza Jenkins and their three children. Both men were agricultural labourers. To the right is a rising muddy track appropriately named Muddy or Climber Lane which leads to Honeysuckle Lane where, in World War II, the Royal Observer Corps had a post known as "Able One" (27).

### West End Farm

Proceeding onwards, we pass West End Farm on our right. Whether it was named after a man named West many hundreds of years ago as suggested in "Place Names of Hertfordshire" (96),or was at the end of Westbury or regarded as being at the west end of the village could be argued indefinitely. This was the site of a fearful tragedy to the Handley family and an aircraft crew in 1944 when a British bomber crashed into the old farmhouse, demolishing the building and killing several of the occupants, but we will deal with this in greater detail in the War Chapter. Earlier, in 1839, the farm was tenanted by William Olney (63) who also tenanted "The Lawns" and in 1891 the farmhouse was occupied by Sibble Stoten a farm foreman, his wife Carrie, three sons and a daughter. The farm was owned as part of the Offley Place estate and was probably included in Westbury Farm. Nearby, in 1912, was a substantial brick-built water tower with an elevated tank, which supplied water to West End Farm, Westbury Farm and the then Eagles Nest. It was demolished by explosives in the 1970s, after a bulldozer failed to make any impression on it, to make way for the A505 by-pass.

## Eagles Nest now Birkitt Hill House

On a site exposed to the elements down a lane to the left of the Wellbury to Offley road, we come across a large house known as Eagles Nest, more recently renamed Birkitt Hill House, the core of which is 18th Century with Victorian, Edwardian and modern alterations and extensions. It was part of the Offley Place estate in 1838 (63) but at that time consisted of a cottage, garden and orchard with no specific name. About 1855 the house was developed, possibly by Anne and George Edward Hughes (Churchyard Memorial 003) who, as newly weds, probably wanted a home of their own rather than live at Offley Place. We know that by 1868 it was owned by George Hughes (71) but in 1871 it was occupied by a farm bailiff and his wife, William and Mary New and in 1881 by a gamekeeper and his wife, Thomas and Jane Foster both families probably as caretakers (39). By 1891 Mary Wilkinson, who was related to the family at Little Offley and her daughter plus three servants were living there. Mary (Churchyard Memorial 005) was a clergyman's widow and described herself as "living on her own means" (39). She took a keen interest in the school and presented a cricket bat annually to the "best boy" of the year.

Mary Wilkinson died in 1911 and the following year Thomas Fenwick Harrison, who had purchased it from Herbert Salusbury Hughes, leased Eagles Nest to Henry Grey Tylecote for twenty one years at an annual rent of £80 plus a share of the water pumping costs. The lease included five acres of land and a motor garage. Mr Tylecote took an active part in village events especially the school and did not leave until April 1931 at which time John Fenwick Harrison leased the property to Maud Heath Rosselli at £133 per annum for fourteen years.

The occupation changed yet again in 1938 with Mr J.F. Harrison leasing the property to Georgina Tennant at an annual rental of £150. This included the middle of three cottages at Bean Close Cottages in the centre of the village occupied by Harold Woodfield who was not to be disturbed for three years. The reference to

Harold should in fact have been to Hubert Woodfield, as Hubert and his wife (Churchyard Memorial 227) were chauffeur and parlourmaid at Eagles Nest. The value of Eagles Nest for insurance purposes at that time was £2,500, but the land seems to have shrunk to about three acres having lost a strip at the far end of the property (100).

Some long time after the Second World War, Mr Harrison decided to sell the property to Mrs Ruth Honor Pilkington (Churchyard Memorial 239) whom we have already met with her husband and sons at Little Offley. She had moved firstly to Great Offley House after the death of her husband and two sons in 1942, then to Eagles Nest which she said was the first property she had owned. She probably stayed at Eagles Nest until her death in 1975.

Since then it has been sold again and had its name changed to Birkitt Hill House.

## Hunters Moon

We now pass over the bridge towards the village and view an enormous cutting on the left where, in 1891, stood three cottages occupied by two families of Marlow and a family named Woodfield. These dwellings were demolished long ago, but about 1950 a substantial dwelling was built nearby known as "Hunters Moon". This was owned by Mrs Eileen Sheppard (Churchyard Memorial 100) who originally came to the village in 1921, the widow of Lieut Colonel Samuel Gurney Sheppard Commanding Officer of the 1st/1st Herts Yeomanry who had been killed at Gallipoli in 1915 (116 & 117). This tall and autocratic lady did a great deal for the village and was especially interested on all matters connected with the church. We shall read more of her when we come to Great Offley House. Eileen was not to enjoy her new home for long as she died in 1955 and shortly afterwards it was decided to build a by-pass to the village and as the roadway was scheduled to go through the middle of the house, the house was demolished. All trace of the house and even the land it stood on has disappeared and nothing is left except some fine views towards Hitchin and Letchworth.

## The Old Workhouse

We are now into School Lane and leaving the bridge on our way into the village, the first dwellings on the right were originally parts of the Old Workhouse. Now three dwellings, sections of these buildings must be quite ancient but the alterations and modernising make it difficult to date. The buildings probably ceased being a workhouse when the new workhouse at Claypits corner was built in 1825. It may even have been a dwelling before it was a workhouse, as it was not until Knachbull's Act of 1723 that individual parishes were allowed to hire premises for use as workhouses and also it is possible to see where windows were bricked up possibly to avoid the window taxes of 1696 onwards. Other evidence suggests that it was not a workhouse until as late as 1815 as this is the year that the Churchwardens Accounts first mention payments for removing coal and straw to it (22). It was part of the Offley Place estate in 1838 (63) and in 1868 (71) was occupied by Samuel Chapman and others. In 1891 it was described as four cottages part of the old workhouse, occupied by people named Arnold, Chapman (including a Samuel), Bond and Armitage, mostly middle aged or elderly folk. In the 1960s the buildings had had no permanent occupiers for some time and it is thought that vagrants caused the serious fire which occurred, following which it was substantially re-built (40 & 42).

## Council Houses

In front of us we see a Council House development which started in 1922 when the first twelve were completed (40). Our old friend the Rev. Gatty campaigned long, hard and successfully to have each house fitted with a rainwater tank as there was still no other water supply (9). Six more were built in 1930 and still more, in what is now known as Meadow Way, were commenced in 1936.

## The School

On the left we see the village school and this deserves a chapter of its own but a few comments concerning the buildings are appropriate at this stage. The school was endowed in 1839 and founded in 1841 and it is noticeable that the 1838 plan of the Offley Place estate shows the school area as "Cottages and Gardens" (63) whereas a similar plan of 1868 shows it as "The School" (71). Whether there was a cottage as well as the school is difficult to know, but by 1876 there was a dwelling for the schoolmaster as he was given a furnished house, garden and coals (88). At the turn of the century one of the reasons given by Mr Paine for resigning as schoolmaster was the poor condition of the buildings, but nothing much seems to have happened until 1929 when it is said that a cottage which had stood between the school itself and the schoolmasters house was demolished and reconstructed as a purpose built classroom (40 & 42). Since that time there have been numerous alterations to the fabric.

## Westbury Farm

At the end of School Lane on the right at the crossroads is the Manor of Westbury which according to Domesday Book (13), was the "Offelei" of the Delemere family who were in occupation until the time of Henry IV and their name appears on the Lay Subsidy Rolls (a tax on moveable property) of 1314-15. It was certainly by far the largest of the Manors as in 1085 it was 8 hides in extent which is nearly 1,000 acres. According to Chauncy it was linked with the Manor of Poderich (Puttridge) and we learn that in 1412 Sir George Darell, Knight, died "seized of Puttridgebury and part of Westbury" (7). Chauncy states that thereafter Westbury closely follows the descent of Offley Place, though this does not appear to be correct as according to Salmon (52) it was owned by a Mr Byde in 1728. Clutterbuck (75) confirms this by his mention that Westbury was purchased by Dame Sarah Salusbury round about 1777 from Thomas Hope Byde (the Ware Park family).

From that time it did follow as part of the Offley Place estate usually having tenant farmers. One of the best known was Thomas Bates (Churchyard Memorial 069) who was occupying it by 1807 (47), was paying rates for it in 1815 (22) but died in 1823 describing himself in his Will as a Yeoman (89). He presented the last of the bells to the church, was an active churchwarden and is mentioned in the Church Chapter. His wife Sarah bore him twelve surviving children and direct descendants exist to this day.

By 1839 Westbury Farm was tenanted by Daniel Marsh who is probably the person of that name, related to the Sheppard and Marsh family at Little Offley, who died in 1866 (Churchyard Memorial 055) having moved earlier to Kings Walden. By 1851 the tenancy had changed yet again to Charles Davis (Churchyard Memorial 126) and at that time he was farming 475 acres, employing eleven labourers

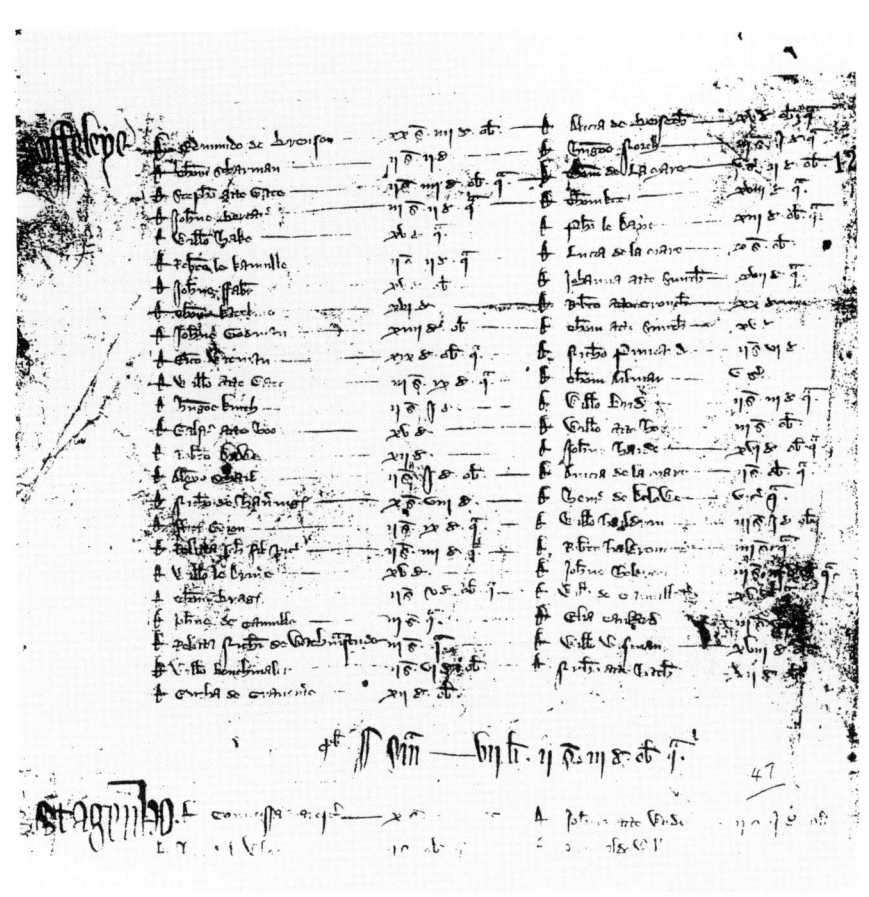

THE LAY SUBSIDY ROLLS 1314-15 FOR OFFLEY
NOTE THE NAMES "De La Mare" and "atte Hoo"

and six boys (39). It stayed tenanted by the Davis family until 1888 when William Davis died (Churchyard Memorial 127).

The Census of 1891 shows Westbury occupied by Walter John Mansfield Hughes. He was described as a farmer having been born at Pau in France and was the brother of Herbert George Hughes, the squire at Offley Place. He was not to stay long as by 1903 Westbury was tenanted by A.W. Sturgeon farming 277 acres at a rental of £210 per annum (90) which suggests that some of the land had been sold.

By 1910 the tenancy had changed again and was now with Daniel Hall (Churchyard Memorial 167) who also tenanted West End Farm and was a cattle dealer and butcher. Daniel, an enormous man over six feet tall and weighing eighteen stones, was a popular figure in the village. Generous to employees and being of a musical temperament, he arranged concerts and parties for the villagers in one of his barns at West End or Westbury and, at harvest time, weighed and bought the gleanings they had gathered in the fields.

By the end of the war yet another change had been made and it was tenanted by Alexander Fraser and his wife (Churchyard Memorial 101). These were people in their sixties and it is probable that the land had been separated from the dwelling with Dan Hall continuing to farm the lands. This is confirmed by December 1921 when John Fenwick Harrison, who had by this time purchased the property from the Salusbury Hughes, leased Westbury Farm House, outbuildings and orchard to Lieut Colonel Reginald Salusbury Hughes, another brother of Herbert Salusbury Hughes at Offley Place, for 21 years at an annual rental of £60 (100).

The farmhouse dates from late Tudor times i.e. late 1500s but underwent substantial alteration in the 18th Century and a wing was added in the 19th Century (14). The brick dovecote in the yard dates from the 17th Century and is constructed of brick nogging on a timber frame. It was used to provide cheap fresh pigeon meat especially during the winter months and there are few examples of such a structure left in Hertfordshire. Other buildings in the vicinity consist of massive agricultural barns.

About 1970 the farmhouse was used as flats (79) but in 1993 the villagers were shown proposals to convert the area to dwellings and offices, though the intention was for much of the existing configuration to be retained. It is in such proposals we see conflicts of interests between those who would not wish to see a single stone turned in a time-capsule of a village and those, especially the younger generation, commercial people and the landowners themselves, who require economic development in a living village.

## The Pubs

Leaving Westbury Farm we are at the village crossroads and it will be appropriate to deal with the public houses in one section. Crossing into the High Street towards Kings Walden we see on the left the largest of the pubs, the "Green Man". Parts of the building date back some 300 years but the alterations, especially in modern times, have been such that it is difficult to identify its original appearance. In 1839 Mary Bates (Churchyard Memorial 048) was the licencee (30) with ownership in the hands of the Offley Place estate. No doubt business improved when the well was installed on the village green just outside the "Green Man" when massive thirsts developed after winding up buckets 300 ft and, as the water had to be taken home, the thirsts had to be quenched elsewhere. Several other dwellings and barns were in this area until recent times including a blacksmiths shop and cottage which in the 1890s (83) was run by George Swain (Churchyard Memorial 075) and by Henry Watts in the 1930s. It remained a sleepy village pub until the 1980s when it was expanded to include a licenced restaurant catering mainly for people outside the village. The blacksmiths shop disappeared after the Second World War.

The second of the public houses is just across the High Street and currently called the "Lobster Tail". The building dates from the 17th Century on land formerly known as "Abdells" and owned by the Offley Place estate certainly until 1903 (90). The public house was called "The Cock" in 1839 and in 1869 George Foster was the licencee, the parish clerk and a carpenter (83). A series of tenants followed until 1971 when it became the "Crusty Loaf", a licenced restaurant (91) and changed again circa 1988 to the "Lobster Tail".

A little further down the road we can next slake our thirst in the "Bull". When husbands arrived home late it is possible that this was the origin of "the Cock and Bull" story. Another ancient structure, it was a bakery as well as a public house until circa 1920

(42) and had a yard on the opposite side of the road still known as Bakers Close. The licence was restricted to a beerhouse in former times, as we notice that in 1891 Charles Clarke was the beer retailer and baker at the "Bull" (39) and in both 1926 and 1933 (83) Frederick Clare (Churchyard Memorial 179) was described as a "Beer Retailer". Fred Clare was a generous man and gave prizes to the village school for the best kept garden (88). Another popular licencee was Robert Waugh (Churchyard Memorial 108) who had been chauffeur to Lady Ashley Cooper of Hexton Manor (44) before coming to the "Bull" and when he finally retired in 1964 the Morris Men performed a serenade for Bob and his wife Florence (9).

Immediately next door to the "Bull" towards what is now the "Lobster Tail" there used to be another beerhouse coupled with a grocery shop called the "Carpenters Arms". In 1898 it was sold freehold having been owned by the late Richard Marsh of Little Offley (69). It has been a private dwelling for many years.

Past the church, on the Kings Walden road where it joins the lane to Charlton is yet another pub named the "Red Lion". This was also owned as part of the Marsh estates of Little Offley and sold freehold as a public house and grocery shop in 1898 (69). The lane to Charlton and Hitchin, now called Harris Lane, had far greater significance in the early 1900s and this, coupled with the substantial cluster of cottages in the vicinity of the "Red Lion" until the 1950s and another blacksmiths and public well nearby, must have all tended to provide a useful drinking trade. With all these aspects having declined or disappeared the trade has switched to that of a small hotel and licenced restaurant as well as a public house.

The last of the named pubs is a short distance along the road to Luton from the village crossroads and next to the former Chapel. In 1891 (39) it was a public house known as Simpsons Cottages, possibly after the local brewer of that name and the licencee was James Bardin who lived there with his wife and family. Later it became known as the "Gloucester Arms" and after closure for several years, re-opened in the late 1980s as a licenced restaurant and public house called the "Prince Henry".

There were also two or three small named and unnamed beerhouses in or near the village so that all in all there was little need for the villagers or weary travellers to go thirsty.

## Pond House, Grocer's and Butcher's Shops

We now cross over the Luton to Hitchin road into the High Street and the first dwelling on the right is Pond House. As its name suggests, it was adjacent to the village pond which was filled in some years ago and now forms a small public garden. Pond House itself is of considerable age and in 1891 was part dwelling and part tiny grocery shop where the Olneys, who were already there in 1807, and the Lakes lived and worked. Later it was occupied by the Halls whom we have mentioned as tenants of Westbury farm on the other side of the road. Daniel and his son John also operated the butcher's shop next door to Pond House and its shop. In the 1920s the butcher's shop had 6ft high iron palings in front of it (42) which probably dated from the time that animals were kept in the adjacent butcher's yard awaiting slaughter. The palings disappeared early in the Second World War for conversion to armaments.

An interesting event took place on the 23rd May 1920 when a serious fire broke out in the roof of Miss Lake's shop which spread to Pond House and threatened the butchers shop. Fortunately, the redoubtable Offley fire engine was able to check it for the half hour it took for the Hitchin Brigade to struggle up Offley Hill with their new "steamer". Then another half hour went by and the Luton Fire Brigade arrived on the scene. Fortunately the damage, although severe, was all insured and it was said that Dan Hall did much good work to save the properties (9 & 28).

Terror by fire was not unknown to Pond House as it was customary at the beginning of this century on Guy Fawkes Night for the lads of the village to roll a barrel of flaming tar through the village ending by rolling it into the village pond next to Pond House. It was said that the girls of the village were locked up on that evening (19) in case their long dresses should catch fire (if for no other reason).

Finally, in this section we should mention a notable resident of Pond House, John Hall (Churchyard Memorial 167), who was the son of Daniel Hall. He was born on the 12th September 1899, attended the village school and later went to the Hitchin Grammar School (88) and was a great favourite of some of the village girls (101). He succeeded his father as tenant farmer at Westbury and also built the local garage. He served in World War II as an R.A.F. officer and afterwards was Treasurer of the Offley Branch of the British Legion. Later he became a County Councillor and worked hard to secure the Offley by-pass (46). He died on the 4th April 1974 his home being shown as Pond House (33).

## Chapel Yard and The Chapel

Curiously enough the two are some distance from each other. Offley has a long Non-Conformist tradition (16) and the Chapel was originally next to the "Green Man". When the Chapel moved in 1887 the cottages in the vicinity remained as Chapel Yard, though now even the cottages have disappeared and the name lost. The "new" Wesleyan Chapel was opened the same year on a new site along the Luton road but financial problems forced it to close in 1983 and it was converted to four cottages (44). Typically keen chapel people were Mary Alice and her husband Charles Walker (Churchyard Memorial 225) who were married at Offley in 1907 (9) and who both died in the 1960s. He was a carter of soot from London for use on the land and was later a roadsweeper.

## Vine Cottage and the Old Post Office

Further down the road from the "Green Man" towards the church we arrive at two ancient dwellings. The first is called "Vine Cottage" and for many years was the home, workshop and yard of the village wheelwrights, the Cannon family. In the early 1900s the frontage was covered by a large vine, hence the name. On the 4th September 1914 a fire broke out which destroyed sheds, timber, wheels and a cart and only with difficulty was it prevented from spreading to the thatch of the Post Office nearby. The Hitchin Fire Brigade "was summoned by the use of the telephone" (9) and apparently the village policeman was very worried that the blaze might attract German Zeppelins (42).

The Old Post Office, which was originally thatched, is of great antiquity and is probably the oldest building in the village. It also has the name of the "Old Court House" and may have been the building where Richard Farmer of the Staple and maybe Henry VIII held courts in 1527 and 1543 respectively (4 & 7). It is interesting to notice that it faces into Old Plantation Road now very overgrown, which, until 1807, was the main road through the village from

Hitchin to Luton. In the 1920s and 1930s Bessie Wilmot (Churchyard Memorial 140) kept the post office and shop where "a strange mixture of smells, from foodstuffs to paraffin, greeted the shopper on entering her shop" (92).

## Cowyard and Crawleys Alley

In 1891 Cowyard was a collection of assorted cottages opposite Vine Cottage mainly, if not all, owned by the Offley Place estate. Some were scarcely habitable and demolished in 1938 (9) while others were substantial homes, the rents from which were used to maintain the school. At one end was Crawleys Alley which was a wide drive leading to the allotment gardens but in part is now a single footpath. At the corner of Crawleys Alley where it joined the High Street was a shed used to house the village fire engine and where the Goslings of Wellbury parked their carriages when the family went to church. At the other end is West Lane, an unmade public footpath and private road owned by "The Lawns". Apart from one dwelling called "Rosemary Cottage", the rest of the site was redeveloped in the 1960s for eight Georgian-style terrace houses.

The fire engine must be mentioned as it served the village long and faithfully for many years and was even sent to combat Hitchin fires on occasions. It is said to have had a board on it inscribed "Bristow fecit" meaning Bristow made me and a date 1693. Certainly fire engines were made by a Mr Bristow but a little later into the 18th Century. The machine had two 5" plungers and had pump handles sufficient for eight men to operate and was said to be able to throw water in leather hoses 70-80 feet with enough force to knock a man over (103). The fire brigade had three practices a year. When water was not readily available by hose the machine was filled at each end with water from pails. The Churchwardens accounts mention maintenance costs on the 4th December 1830 for example when we read that the engineers were paid £2 for "proveing the ingine and replacing it again" (22). The machine still exists and in 1993 was owned by the Hitchin Museum but on loan to the Shuttleworth Collection at Old Warden.

At the back of Cowyard are Garden Fields. These were owned by the Offley Place estate and in existence in 1868 (71) as rented garden allotments. The area had previously appeared in the 1838 (63) plan of the estate as Hare Field. When a parish meeting was called on the 7th February 1908 to receive applications for land under the Smallholders and Allotments Act (93) there were no applicants as all who wanted allotments already had them.

## The Lawns

The continuation of the High Street after crossing West Lane is the Kings Walden Road and the first dwelling on the right is known as "The Lawns". Of substantial size both in buildings and land, it formerly had a number of large barns round it as it seems to have been a farm. A large adjacent meadow of some forty acres also bore the same name. A wrought iron gate to the walled garden has a metal plaque with a coat of arms and inscribed "S.S. 1778" which are undoubtedly the initials of the famous lady of Offley Place, Dame Sarah Salusbury. A drain cover near the house has the same initials. The next we know comes in 1807 when the map giving details of the proposed move of the road through the village from West Lane to its present position (47) shows "The Lawns" as being tenanted by Richard Oakley. By 1839 Richard Oakley had left, possibly as early as 1813 when he purchased the Manor of Cockernhoe from Lynch Burroughs (50 & 51) and it was tenanted by the William Olney who also tenanted West End Farm.

The next occupant we know of was Charlotte Hale an elderly lady probably related to the Hale family of Kings Walden. In 1871 at the age of 83 she was living at "The Lawns" in some style with six servants including a page (39). By 1891 she had departed and an 82 year old widow, Mrs Symons, was in occupation with her 51 year old daughter and a mere three servants. Although the Census only mentions mother and daughter, there must have been two other daughters, as in 1900 the Parish Magazine regrets the three daughters leaving the village after "many years of willing and greatly valued work in the parish".

Nothing more of note seems to have happened until 1928 when Guy Salusbury Hughes, having sold Offley Place and remarried, moved to "The Lawns". This he continued to occupy until he shot himself in the house in 1955 (Churchyard Memorial 012). Later the property was sold to Dr & Mrs Clough (38).

### Gosling Ave and Salusbury Lane

These are mainly large Council property developments, portions of it for elderly people but with part in private ownership, all having taken place since 1950 (93). Much of the development has been on the large meadow formerly known as the Lawns.

### Recreation Club

Though it does not have a permanent occupant, the Recreation Club is of importance to the village and deserves to be mentioned. As far back as 1904 A.W. Sturgeon as tenant of Westbury Farm and H.G. Salusbury Hughes as owner of the land, agreed a lease on four and a half acres of Sowdell Field (behind Claypit Cottages) at a rental of £9 per annum for its use as a recreation field. This continued as a football field for many years and in 1948 the tenant farmer, Mr Sutton, was at variance with the Parish Council as their request that he refrain from grazing his cattle there during the football season prompted a demand for a reduced fee (93).

Meantime the cricketers fared rather better by having Colonel Acland, who had purchased Offley Place in 1928, provide them with a fine ground between Offley Place and the Church. A pavilion was erected in 1931 and a concrete pile inscribed "1931-A" can still be seen. In 1938 Major Harrison gave the Offley Recreation Ground to commemorate the Coronation of King George VI. Whether this was the Sowdell football field or the cricket field near Offley Place is uncertain though probably the former. In 1977 a Clubhouse was erected on the site near Offley Place and the Church and with the grounds is large enough for football, cricket and tennis, not to mention those who only exercise their elbows. A fine brick built extension was added to the Clubhouse in the late 1980s to provide a lounge, bar and upstairs committee room.

### The Old Vicarage

Going along the Kings Walden road past the church we see a large house on the right called the "Old Vicarage". This of course adds to our confusion over vicarages, as it should perhaps be more correctly described as the "Old New Vicarage". When the true "Old Vicarage" was sold to Lord Lloyd in 1935 as predicted by the Rev. Gatty ten years earlier, a site for a new vicarage was provided by Guy Salusbury Hughes (Churchyard Memorial 012) and his family

THE RECREATION CLUB AND PART OF THE GROUNDS,
THE CHURCH, OFFLEY PLACE AND THE OLD CRICKET PAVILION
1993

Trustees in agreement with the Governors of the Bounty of Queen Anne and the Rev. A.T.S. Henry the incumbent at the time. The Purchase Deed states "....to hold unto the Incumbent and his successors for ever as and for a site for a parsonage house for the residence and occupation of the Incumbent and his successors...." (94). The idea was to provide a reasonable vicarage or parsonage "it should be possible for any priest without private means to accept the benefice of Offley in the future" (9).

The new dwelling was not completed until August 1939, at a cost of £3,022. The incumbent, the Rev. Henry, was not to enjoy it for long as war was declared the very next month and he allowed much of his new home to be used by evacuees.

The house continued to be used by the Offley vicars until the 1970s when the Church Commissioners decided to sell it. How they were able to persuade themselves that it was right and proper to sell in view of the clearly expressed intention in the Purchase Deed, will probably never be known. It probably joins the loss of £500 million which was the subject of an administrative enquiry appointed by the Archbishop of Canterbury (77) into the Commissioners property speculations.

The sale has proved a disaster to the village in that a vicar can no longer be accomodated in the village at any affordable price, the very reason for which it was built in the first place. The effect is that Offley is most unlikely ever again to have a resident priest caring for souls and sharing the problems of his flock on a day to day basis. This is quite apart from the near impossibility of the widely separated parishes of Lilley, Kings Walden and Offley with three Patrons, three Parochial Church Councils and six Churchwardens ever agreeing anything, especially the suitability of an incumbent who also has to be approved by the Diocese and be willing to accept the combined benefice.

## Angels Farm

On the same side of the road as the Old Vicarage and beyond the "Red Lion" we see a house set way back from the road with farm buildings behind it. It was built in Victorian times probably between 1871 and 1891. In 1898 it was sold under the name of "Great Offley Farm" with a rental value of £40 per annum and consisted of

139 acres with many barns. From the early 1900s the dwelling has usually been leased separately from the farm lands and buildings. The house at that time was used by the curate and known as "Donnington House" (42). This may have been taken from "Donnington Priory" the home of John Hughes the grandfather of the house owner Herbert Salusbury Hughes. Not long after, about 1914, the property was purchased by Thomas Fenwick Harrison later becoming part of Kings Walden Estates.

The lands which gave the farm its name of Angels, have had various tenants including the White family of Grange Farm. A lease dated 25th August 1914 shows Mary White (Churchyard Memorial 102) of Offley Grange Farm leasing Angels Farm of 275 acres from Thomas Fenwick Harrison at an annual rent of £186-10s-0d. Later Walter John Carter (Churchyard Memorial 219) was the tenant in the 1930s (83). In 1993 it is included in the Kings Walden Estates.

## Great Offley House

This is a large three storey house next to Angels Farm. It has a Georgian frontage but much older portions exist at the rear and there are several ancient farmbuildings scattered about the property. It was probably the original farmhouse for Angels Farm but was separated from farming activities at some time in the 19th Century when tenants living elsewhere operated the lands as part of larger farms. In 1898 it was sold freehold having been owned by Richard Marsh (Churchyard Memorial 062) of Little Offley who had died in 1893. It consisted of an Upper Floor of two servants bedrooms, a First Floor of eight bedrooms, box room, bathroom with hot and cold water laid on, W.C., front and back staircase, a Ground Floor of dining room with open and tiled hearth, garden morning room, library, drawing room, entrance hall, conservatory, kitchen, larder, dairy, coalhouse, two capital cellars and two W.Cs. Gardens were one and a half acres and the grounds eight acres in all (69). It was purchased at auction by Herbert Salusbury Hughes of Offley Place for £1,600, the annual rental value said to be £110. About 1912 it was sold again, like so much of the Offley Place estate at that time, to Thomas Fenwick Harrison.

The earliest reference found so far was in 1816 when Richard Sheppard of Little Offley was paying rates for it (22). By 1891 it was still owned by the family at Little Offley but occupied by a retired Indian Army Lieut Colonel and his wife, two daughters, six boarding scholars, governess, nurse, cook and housemaid (39). On the 11th September 1913 Mr T.F. Harrison leased it to Alfred Egerton Maynard Taylor for 14 years at an annual rental of £100 plus £1-10s-0d for £1,590 of fire insurance. Mr Maynard Taylor worked in London and was taken to Hitchin Station each day by pony and trap (42). The property had by this time shrunk to approximately three acres. Significantly, the lessee undertook not to destroy or molest foxes.

In 1920 Mr Maynard Taylor disappeared from the scene and enter the formidable Mrs Eileen Mary Winchester Clowes Sheppard. We have already met her in her later years as owner of "Hunters Moon" on School Lane. Her husband Lieut Colonel Samuel Gurney Sheppard had been killed at Suvla Bay Gallipoli in 1915 and it was said that she kept his uniform in her bedroom for many years after (95). He had been a friend of T.F. Harrison at Kings Walden who leased Great Offley House to Eileen at the nominal annual rental of £17-10s-0d. Eileen, described as tall and autocratic (46), quickly involved herself in village activities, was Vicars Warden from 1928-40 and generally did much good work throughout the parish and especially for the church. During the war she was Commandant at St Paul's Waldenbury and active in Hitchin Hospital matters and left the village returning to her new home at "Hunters Moon" in 1952.

A little mystery surrounds her place of burial, which took place on the 24th January 1955 (Churchyard Memorial 100). Many years earlier, an elderly lady of 78 years with the curious name of Hamilton Burns was a guest at Great Offley House and died on Sunday the 24th August 1924. She was buried in Offley Churchyard. When Eileen's turn came to join the dear departed, it was specified that she was to be buried alongside Hamilton Burns. The Burial Register is noted accordingly and the inscription to Eileen appears on one side of the stone and that to Hamilton Burns daughter of Archibald Burns of Perthshire appears on the other side but there is no mention of the relationship.

## Offley Hoo Farm

The last house along the Kings Walden road out of the village is currently known as Offley Hoo and has for many years been part of the Kings Walden Estates and home for the Farm Manager. Otherwise known as Hoo Farm the farmhouse is three storeys high and several hundred years old with numerous additions and alterations having taken place over the centuries. Substantial barns are nearby, some of considerable age.

It is tempting to relate Offley Hoo Farm with the 15th Century De Hoo family of Offley St Legers (see Offley Place Chapter) and to ruminate on whether the farm was the family homestead long before Offley Place was built. Unfortunately, there is no evidence to support such a link other than the name, that the farm is undoubtedly ancient and that it was part of the Offley Place estate as far back as can be ascertained. As mentioned in the first chapter the word "Hoo" variously means a spur of land, a homestead or a burial ground (96) and therefore is not especially helpful in establishing the antiquity of the site.

The first certain mention is in 1807 when we find Richard Oakley, who also tenanted "The Lawns" paying rates on Offley Hoo Farm (22) and it must be borne in mind that rates were paid by the tenant not necessarily by the owner. Richard purchased the Manor of Cockernhoe in 1813 and by 1814 Offley Hoo Farm was occupied by Daniel Chapman a relation by marriage to the Marsh family of Little Offley (Churchyard Memorial 061) and friend of the Salusbury family at Offley Place (22). A Richard Marsh described as a gentleman farmer of Offley Hoo died in 1838 (33) and the following year a Valuation of the Offley Place estate (63) shows Lavinia Marsh (Church Memorial 01), who became Mrs George Bates, as the tenant of Offley Hoo Farm.

By 1851 the Marshs and Bates' had left and the tenant was John Sworder. He was farming 416 acres and employing 24 labourers and to look after his personal needs he had two servants and a lady companion (39). John Sworder moved among the gentry and in 1863 was found guilty of trespass on Lilley Hoo by holding horse races there on the 11th December 1862. The action was brought by Col. Thomas Sowerby who claimed it as Lord of the

Manor of Lilley. Sowerby was awarded one shilling plus costs (97). John Sworder was gathered to his fathers on the 5th November 1869 at the early age of 53 years and was buried in the family vault at St Mary's churchyard in Hitchin.

His successor as tenant of Offley Hoo Farm was Henry Miller (Churchyard Memorial 059). By 1871 he was farming 386 acres and employed 12 men, 4 boys and had 3 servants (39). He was not only a highly competent and respected farmer but he found time to take an interest in village matters. At various times he was Overseer of the Poor, Clerk of the School and was a Churchwarden for forty years. When he died in 1910 it was recorded that "he always gave of his best to the church that he loved" (9).

His son Claud Harrow Miller took over the farm on the death of his father, his initial lease being with Herbert George Salusbury Hughes of Offley Place for 405 acres at a yearly rental of £366 on the 15th March 1911, the lease being very specific concerning the use of the five course system of crop rotation. Shortly after, Hughes sold the land to the Harrisons of Kings Walden. However, Claud was not as successful as his father and within a few years the farm was in marked decline, so much so that in 1918 the Government Inspectors, who were interested in food production as part of the war effort, recommended that the tenancy be cancelled, which had duly happened by September 1920. Poor Claud blamed the wet autumn of 1917 as well as mange on the horses but the problem really lay with his lack of ability as a farmer.

At the termination of the tenancy, John Fenwick Harrison decided to interest himself in the farm and so did not find another tenant but instead appointed a Farm Manager, a practice which has been continued to the present day. In 1931 the Farm Manager received an annual salary of £250 and it remained at that level for at least a decade. A Guernsey dairy herd was developed which provided about 50% of the farm revenue and costs and continued until 1974 when it was dispersed. Pig farming was also a feature of the farm and this ceased about 1969. The concentration altered to arable and sheep farming, though a pedigree flock of Jacobs sheep was disposed of in 1970. The area has increased considerably since the 405 acres of Claud Miller's day as tenancies over the land holdings gradually terminated and Offley Hoo Farm currently operates at nearer 1750 acres whilst the Farm Manager, Alec Dickinson, instead of having 24 employees as in John Sworder's time, has only 3 employees besides himself. It would be difficult to find a better, or worse according to the point of view, example of the machine taking over a labour intensive industry.

Having completed our visit from north to south let us journey to some of the more interesting properties from east to west.

## Offley Grange

This flourishing and ancient farm lies about a mile to the north east of Offley village off the main road between Offley and Hitchin with buildings identified as dating from 1530 (98). It seems to have been part of the Offley Place estate for a very long time and we read that in 1815 the rates were paid by Thomas Crawley (22). By 1839 the tenancy had changed to William Cox who died at the early age of 31 years the following year. He was buried in a vault constructed in the churchyard (Churchyard Memorial 063) with an enormous headstone still in the correct place, but the footstone was moved some distance away in the clearances of the 1960s.

1845 brought a proposal which must have lifted the hearts of the landowners but plunged the Kidman family as the tenants into despair. It was proposed to build a railway to link Cambridge to Oxford and the suggestion was that the line should go through the middle of Offley Grange from Hitchin, passing Offley village roughly where the bridge over the A505 is today (99). Fortunately for the Offley Grange tenants the idea was abandoned due to the cost of tunnelling through the hills in the vicinity of Offley and Lilley.

By 1903 the tenancy had changed again, this time to our old friend John Hall whom we met at Pond House and he was now leasing the 468 acres of Offley Grange at an annual rental of £346-16s-0d though he probably did not live there (90). By 1906 John had relinquished it and Herbert George Salusbury Hughes had leased its then 454 acres to Harry J. White at an annual rental of £394. At the same time a new farmhouse was built nearer the road for Harry, his wife and family and the old farmhouse was occupied by Jack

Bliss their foreman (90). Harry died in 1912 (Churchyard Memorial 102) and his widow Mary negotiated a lease with the new landowner Thomas Fenwick Harrison for the addition of Angels Farm.

In practice it was Mary's son Stanley who was the farmer and it was a flourishing enterprise even at that time. In 1912 Offley Grange alone had arable land, 12 horses, 400 sheep, 35 beef cattle, 6 breeding sows and employed 12 men. Stanley rode to hounds with the Hertfordshire Hunt and his sheep branding iron is still to be found in a collection of agricultural bygones at Flamstead (90).

Harry Burr was the tenant in the early 1930s (83) but another tenant was required in 1939 and the lease was taken up by Matthew Park (Churchyard Memorial 240). Similar to the situation of the Whites, it was Matthew's son Clough who took the main interest in the farm which soon became M.C. Park & Son. Matthew was primarily a motor engineer who had driven at Brooklands Racing Circuit and who became a test driver and later Chief Inspector at Vauxhall Motors in Luton (98). The farm continues in the tenancy of the Park family to this day.

### Lodge

Leaving Offley Grange we rejoin the road but before ascending Offley Hill go past the row of Grange Cottages on the right and look among the trees to the left. You will see a gateway, near which used to stand a Lodge. This was at the end of the private drive leading to Offley Place. The public road was moved to its present position in 1807 and the Lodge was possibly a toll house for traffic wishing to use the easier gradient of the old road. A board of tariffs was found when the house was demolished circa 1950 (40).

### Garage

Proceeding up Offley Hill to the village, we pass over the cross-roads and to the left are a complex of motor trade buildings set back from the road. It was here that the first Offley petrol pump was established by John Hall of Westbury and Pond House fame round about 1920. The man who operated the pump was Beauchamp Vaughan Wright, who had been in the Royal Welch Fusiliers and spent nine years in India and attended the Great Durbar of 1911 (Churchyard Memorial 201). Nowadays the motorist can buy, sell or have his car serviced or repaired, but no petrol!

## Village Hall

A little further and we can pass down a narrow lane to the left between the "Prince Henry" and the Old Chapel. Here we come across the Village Hall which was opened on the 21st October 1936. In one of his rare moments of exaggeration or perhaps in an unaccustomed attempt at droll humour, the Rev. Gatty on a visit to Offley described it as a "cosy hall" (9) which, though hard to believe, maybe it was by the standards of the day. Today, the most kindly description is that it is functional.

## Claypits

Turning left on rejoining the road, we may see in front of us a block of five cottages at the beginning of a broad sweep in the road to the right. Visibility is not always good as large trucks and impedimenta massed in front tends to obscure the view. Originally the road was almost straight and a distinct turn had to be made onto the minor road to the right but now that minor road is the main road to Luton.

Having dealt with that complexity let us ponder the cottages at Claypits. They were built in 1825 as the new Poor House to replace the workhouse in School Lane, at a cost of £1,000 on land given by Lynch Burroughs of Offley Place (22). £900 of the cost was borrowed from Mr Kidman at an annual 3% rate of interest. Mr Kidman seems to have had plenty of cash as it was he who lent the £1,000 for the rebuilding of the church tower eleven years earlier. The building was constructed by Offley builder Samuel Lane (Churchyard Memorial 105). It was not used as a workhouse for very long though the name "Workhouse Corner" has stuck and by 1841 it had been converted to six cottages with the rents used to finance the village school. Some time later, during the third quarter of the 1800s, part was used by William Hull to make ropes and one of the cottages is still called Ropewalk Cottage. One hundred and fifty years later the cottages still exist though it is doubtful whether, if still tenanted, the annual rents are the £5 per cottage which they were at the turn of the century (9).

## Glebe Farm, the Mill and the Flints

Our last stop is about half a mile out of the village on the road to Luton where we find on the right a small cluster of buildings now usually known as The Flints. This takes its name from the several cottages made of dressed flint but there are several other dwellings scattered in the vicinity including a turkey farm owned by Richard (Dick) Foster whose ancestors provided Offley with carpenters and builders from time immemorial. At intervals, various small businesses have appeared in the area and vanished, notably Arthur Dyer's printing press in the 1920s and about the same time a petrol pump was installed operated by William Dyer whose wife Eliza ran a little grocery shop in the vicinity.

An interesting building was the Offley Windmill which was set back from the road behind the Flints. The earliest reference to a windmill in Offley is in 1644 when a payment release for millstones is recorded and it is probable that the mill was on the same site as in more recent times (119). It had very little iron in it but instead had wooden wheels with wooden cogs made of crab-apple wood which is apparently harder than oak or hornbeam (41). It was five storeys high and had a revolving cap (40) and, according to the 1881 Ordnance Survey Map, was a corn mill. The cap had a gallery round it and a fantail high above the rear edge of the cap. There were four double-shuttered patent sails which operated four pairs of millstones (119). It appears on the 1834 Ordnance Survey Map but is not mentioned on the 1838 Ground Plot of the Offley Place estate. It was almost certainly on vicarial land with the rents providing an income for the vicar. In 1851 the miller was William King aged 34 years (39) but no family is mentioned. A family named Ingle occupied it in 1871 but by 1891 it was back in the King family with James King as probably the last of the millers. His wife Elizabeth is commemorated on Churchyard Memorial 139. The mill ceased production about the turn of the century (83) due to severe damage by gales and in 1926 was cut down to two storeys, re-roofed and has been used as a shed ever since (102).

On the other side of the road and a little further from the village is the site of a dwelling which in the 1881 Ordnance Survey Map is called "Mill House" which was presumably the home of the miller. A "Mill House" is referred to in the Act of Inclosure of 1767 which indicates that there was a mill and probably a miller at that time. This later became a farm known as Glebe Farm which again stresses the ecclesiastical connection. This must have changed at some time early in the 20th Century as on the 15th March 1911 we find H.G. Salusbury Hughes leasing Mill House and its meadow, garden and pasture, a total of 15 acres, to John Stuart Sutton of Glebe Farm at an annual rental of £36-15s-0d (28) and the farm continued to be tenanted by the Sutton family for much of the century. It is possible that Salusbury Hughes was acting in his capacity as Patron of the Church for the purposes of this lease. In 1945 a devastating explosion virtually demolished the buildings and they had to be re-built but this will be commented upon in the War Chapter.

This concludes our journey through the village. We have not, of course, been able to visit every building in the village and have hardly touched on the many old dwellings which have been demolished during the last hundred years and especially after the Second World War, but an interesting account of them can be found in Angela Hillyard's "Images of Old Offley".

# THE VILLAGE SCHOOL

*"Better build schoolrooms for "the boy"
than cells and gibbets for "the man."*
*(Eliza Cook 1818-1889).*

This little homily has a very similar inference today as it had when compiled in the 19th Century and Offley was fortunate in having benefactors who, for whatever reasons, altruistic or egotistic, provided an opportunity for the education or advancement of children whose family circumstances would otherwise have kept them in the hopeless grinding poverty traps of those days. This Chapter will only deal with the Village School, not the schools, colleges and seminaries which at various periods were associated with such places as Offley Place, Wellbury and Great Offley House.

The first of the known benefactors came from an unlikely source, yet her generosity has stood the test of two hundred and fifty years albeit now providing a negligible sum. It all started with Alice Spencer who was the daughter of Sir Brocket Spencer and his wife Susanna of Offley Place. Alice grew up at Offley in the mid 1600s and like so many of the ladies at the Manor, formed a great love of the village. She was later to become the second wife of Granado Pigott of Abington Pigotts and Bassingbourn in Cambridgeshire, his first wife having been buried on the 8th August 1701. During her marriage she directed that "having a concern for the good of Offley and the meanness of the maintenance of the vicars there and the need for them to instruct the poor children of the parish and for putting them out as apprentices", £20 per annum should be paid for the augmentation of the vicarage of Offley and a further £10 per annum for putting out two apprentices (boys or girls), the money to come from the rentals of "certain land of the Manor of Symonside in the parish of Bishop's Hatfield in the county of Hertford". Alice Pigott died in 1713 but her husband was in no hurry to fulfil his late wife's wishes by making the payments. The new Offley vicar from 1719 thought otherwise and took action against him in the Court of Chancery and it was decreed on the 25th

May 1721 that the payments must be made. More delays took place due to the death of Pigott in 1723, but the persistence of our vicar, the Rev. Thomas Dane, no doubt egged on by Sir Henry Penrice at Offley Place as sharp a sea-lawyer as was likely to be found in the Kingdom, prevailed and a son by the first marriage, also a Granado Pigott, "By Indenture of Bargain and Sale dated 18th July 1724" arranged for the payments to commence and so they have continued to this day.

By 1724, Offley therefore had the vicar being paid £20 per annum to teach the poor children of the parish with "the principles of religion as by law established" and a further £10 per annum available to apprentice out boys or girls (75). Bless the memories of a dear generous lady Alice Pigott and of our persistent and worthy Rev. Thomas Dane. They were making the first small hesitant steps towards equality of opportunity, though they would certainly have been appalled at such a radical concept.

Having read of such an extreme in progress, do not expect too much to happen in Offley for the next hundred years. We wait until the year 1804 when that seemingly indestructible Lady of the Manor, Dame Sarah Salusbury, is finally placed under the chancel of the church and it is discovered that in codicils to her Will dated 1795 and 1797 she has left two amounts of £500 for the benefit of the poor of Offley, to be disposed of at the discretion of the Rev. Lynch Salusbury (60). Lynch, who now became Lynch Burroughs in order to qualify for the benefits of Dame Sarah's Will (see the Offley Place Chapter) decided to establish Day and Sunday Schools which continued until his death in 1837.

By 1839 the dust had begun to settle following Lynch Burrough's death and it was found that he and his second wife Ann (Church Memorial 23) had made arrangements for the substantial sum of £2,000 to be made available to endow a village school and to this was added the £1,000 from Dame Sarah's bequest (38). Two years later, in 1841, came the Foundation of Offley Schools by a Deed (enrolled) of Endowment. It was a Charity School and was founded for "the education of the children of the poor parishioners of Offley in the Established Religion, and in such other skill, learning and knowledge as should for the time being be thought useful or proper for boys and girls in their respective situations in life". The

Trustees had the power to "deprive and remove, or to suspend the Schoolmaster or Mistress, or to expel any of the said poor children". The boys and girls had separate rooms and their ages had to be not less than five years. A sum of money was invested, together with the rents from five cottages, three small barns, a shoemaker's shop and a tailor's shop all at Old Cow Yard, two tenements used as School Rooms plus two cottages adjoining with three barns and gardens, an acre of ground being a corner piece between roads leading from Offley to Luton and Cockernhoe bounded on the west by land owned by Lynch Burroughs and in addition the former Workhouse which had been converted to six cottages with sheds and outbuildings, thereby providing for the upkeep of the building and it was from this endowment that the School received its name "Offley Endowed School" (88).

In establishing a village school we were level with our neighbours at Pirton and Ickleford whose schools started in 1841 and 1839 respectively (105) but well in advance of nearby Lilley where schooling was not commenced until 1865 (97). Offley school was certainly operating by 1851 as we learn from the Decennial Census that John Church was the schoolmaster aged 52 years with his wife Phebe, a bonnet sewer. Seven years later the school became more formalised and on the 14th June 1858 the Charity for the school was regulated by a Scheme of the Court of Chancery whereby income from Consols valued at £2,467-1s-8d was applied to the endowment (38).

John Church had retired by 1871 (39) and in 1876 Julius B. Whicker was appointed master of the Offley Schools including Mrs Whicker for the infants and for sewing. The salary for the two of them was £70 per annum plus half the school fees plus half the Government grant plus a furnished house, garden and coals (88). This may be compared to the agricultural labourer's annual wage of about £37 with harvest bonus. There were approximately 100 children on the registers and the method of remuneration was designed to stimulate the schoolmaster into ensuring maximum attendance by his pupils. It should also be remembered that in those days there was considerable social status in being the schoolmaster and it was a vocation rather than a job. He lived and worked among the people and by his contacts he knew virtually all the happenings in the village and, after the Squire and the Vicar, was undoubtedly the most influential and respected person in the community.

Despite his efforts and the affect on his pay, poor Mr Whicker struggled with attendance. We read in the school log that in May 1876 "briskness in the (straw)plaiting trade" reduced attendance by the older children. In the following month the boys were away "carlot-pulling". Charlock was a considerable pest as a weed on arable land reducing the cereal yield and also harbouring flies and beetles harmful to crops, all at a time when pesticides were virtually unknown. The only method of controlling the weed was by manually pulling it up which was a job for boys. The school was also closed for over four weeks during harvest as most of the children took part either gathering it or gleaning the fields afterwards. Then again at the end of October 90% of the children were absent due to measles and scarlet fever. It must have been difficult to carry out any programme of teaching. However he did try to maintain standards both for the children and himself. In 1878 several children were sent home because their parents hadn't paid the school fees on which his income depended. One suspects that it was more likely to have been a case of couldn't rather than wouldn't. In the following year Charles Day was sent home because he was not wearing boots (88).

The school fees were listed in the school log of 1889 and make quite interesting reading with regard to social divisions, family numbers and amounts. The following were the rates per week with the Vicar's decision final :-

Children of :-

| | | |
|---|---|---|
| Tradespeople | - First Child | = 4d |
| | Second Child | = 3d |
| | Third Child | = 2d |
| | Fourth Child | = 1d |
| Head-gardeners, Bailiffs | - First Child | = 3d |
| Coachmen and Keepers | Second Child | = 2d |
| | Others | = 1d |
| Labourers | - First Child | = 2d |
| | Second Child | = 2d |
| | Others | = 1d |

By Act of Parliament charges to parents ceased in 1891 and the school received a Government Grant on the following basis :-

Principal Grant 12/6d per head on the average attendance
Discipline 1/6d  "  "  "  "  "  "
Singing 1/-  "  "  "  "  "  "
English 1/-  "  "  "  "  "  "
Geography 2/-  "  "  "  "  "  "
Needlework (girls) 1/-  "  "  "  "  "  "

The allowances were far from automatic and regular checks were made on the attendance register and on the standards of the individual subjects though teaching was not confined to those listed. The school was expected to teach the three "Rs" of reading, writing and reckoning (arithmetic). Also, being a church school, further inspections were carried out by the church authorities with particular regard to religious instruction.

By 1895 both Mr Whicker and his successor Mr Hutchinson had left and Mr A.S. Paine and his wife Elizabeth were appointed in charge of the school. The 21st October of that year was a notable date for the infants. At long last backs were fitted to the seats in the infants gallery "adding much to their comfort and ease" (88). Repeatedly, Government Inspectors also complained that the seats were too far from the desks in the gallery but this fell on deaf ears. The criticisms they made of the lack of attention by the infants to their lessons should hardly have been a matter of surprise to anyone when the poor mites were made to sit on seats without backs and with desks too far forward from the seats.

It was possibly against this background that trouble arose in 1897 between Ethel Sharp, a pupil teacher, and the redoubtable Thirza Read (Churchyard Memorial 129) a character well known for a willingness to lock horns with anyone. The newspaper report (107) of the Petty Sessions makes fascinating reading "Thirza Read the wife of a labourer was charged with assaulting Ethel Sharp of Offley on October 8th 1897. The complainant who is a pupil teacher of the elementary school at Offley said she saw the defendant on the road and was asked by her "Why did you keep my child in at school" to which she replied "Because she deserved it". Thereupon the defendant struck her on the mouth saying "Take that". The defendant said she did not ask why her child had been kept in. She asked why the complainant had beaten her child. The witness said she had repeated as far as she could remember the words used. Mr Paine, the master of the schools, said that the defendant had given trouble before. The defendant said that it was quite true that she had struck the complainant and she was sorry that she did not hit her harder. She struck the blow because her little girl had been assaulted by the pupil teacher. She was fined £1 including costs or in default fourteen days imprisonment. Mrs Read said that she would go to prison".

The poverty in the village was still as bad as ever and the school log of the 2nd February 1898 reads "Nearly twenty away sick. The weather being a little cold, so many of them are so weakly (being underfed) that they are very quickly affected by the cold and heat". This represented about one quarter of the school.

By 1901 Mr Paine had had enough and resigned, having done a great deal in six years to raise the standard of teaching and having become very frustrated in the process. Among the complaints which he recorded were that he only had two pupil teachers for forty four infants with one of those teachers "wearing a short skirt", that the local farmers encouraged boys to take time off from school to go farming and game beating especially H.G. Hughes whom he thought should know better as a magistrate and being on the school board and finally that the school building and his house were in such poor condition. The reference to the short skirt undoubtedly meant that the forward miss was showing part of her ankle below her dress.

A schoolmaster who was to give thirty years of splendid service to the children of the village arrived in 1903. A strong disciplinarian, Mr Charles W. Mears would have found the absence of many children to attend Buffalo Bill's visit to Hitchin on the 24th June 1904 a considerable trial. Never a schoolmaster shy of using his cane, the punishment book records that he gave Walter Stokes (Churchyard Memorial 131) four strokes for playing truant on the 18th October 1907 (88).

A most appalling tragedy occurred on the 14th December 1906. Florence Lawrence aged six and the daughter of a farm labourer at Wellbury climbed over the school fireguard, which was only twenty inches high, whilst playing hide and seek, when her pinafore and then her flannelette dress caught fire and she was badly burned about the head, face, neck and arms. The burns were then covered, as was customary at the time, in oil-soaked lint which certainly did not help and two and a half hours later the screaming child was taken to Hitchin Hospital where she died on the evening of the following day. An Inquest (106) brought in a verdict of accidental death and no one was blamed, this despite the fact that the fireguards had been criticised in earlier Government Inspectors reports. An unsupervised six year old, in a room containing an open fire with an unsuitable fireguard, was deemed responsible for her own actions. A most interesting difference to social attitudes ninety years later.

Illness was as prevalent as ever and early in 1908 the school was closed as there were thirty cases of diphtheria, one of which proved fatal.

At that time the education of children centred around obedience, duty, responsibility and discipline and this was to continue until the 1950s when a new breed of educator gradually changed the ethos to the concepts of rights, freedom from restraint and that the world owes us a living which the State must provide. A good example of the now long outdated pride of nation was on the 14th June 1910 when Mr T.F. Harrison presented the schools with "a large map of the British Empire expressing the hope that it would remind them of the duty and responsibility towards that Empire" (9). That the children of Offley were faithful to such a charge can be seen by their contribution to a determined nation in two World Wars, curiously the results being sufficiently decisive for the abandonment of the very attributes which had made it possible.

During the first World War hundreds of eggs were collected by the children and sent to the hospitals for wounded soldiers and sailors. Many put their names and addresses on the eggs and there were several delightful if jingoistic letters in reply from individual recipients (9). Food shortages by 1917 inspired the school to have school gardens to grow vegetables to help the war effort and these continued long after the war teaching the children the benefits of gardening. The day after the war ended, a procession took place at 5.30pm from the schools with the "pre-historic" fire engine, the children in fancy dress. They stopped at the Well for an address by

Mr Tylecote, then on to Hall's field for fireworks and a bonfire. It was recorded that there were no casualties and the event concluded with the singing of "Rule Britannia" and "God save the King" (9).

All was peaceful at the school until 1930 when, in the summer of that year, the old infants room which had been a cottage, was demolished and a purpose-built classroom constructed in its stead. In the same year the first school cook in the county was appointed and commenced her duties at Offley. This was Gertrude Beatrice Harley (Churchyard Memorial 223) and she was to stay in the job for twenty four years some of which, particularly in wartime, must have been extremely trying.

An interesting sign of the times had occurred four years earlier when the children commenced listening to wireless broadcasts. Another technological development came in November 1932 when electric lighting was put into the school. Up till then oil lamps had been the only source of lighting.

Further changes towards equal opportunity were made in the 1930s to enable the brighter children to be screened at age eleven for subsidised scholarships at Grammar Schools. Unfortunately this did not always function fairly or uniformly and tended to create a second class image of the village schools.

More celebrations came on the 6th May 1935 on the occasion of the Silver Jubilee of King George V. The event was held at Offley Place, courtesy of Col. Acland who also gave the children Jubilee beakers and Major Harrison gave them Jubilee medals. They also released balloons given by Mrs Pilkington some of which were later returned from France (9).

On the 29th September 1938 the war clouds were looming once again and the headteacher was engaged in a billeting census so that evacuee children from areas such as London could be accomodated in the event of war. Later the children were allocated trenches in case of bombing and were given gas-mask drill (88) as were the evacuees when they arrived shortly after war declared in September 1939. School work was interrupted in 1940 by constant air raid warnings but fortunately there was little damage in the vicinity.

A most important event took place in 1942 and one which we have forgotten fifty years later. It was in that year that the school children were first innoculated against diphtheria, a disease which had been a major killer of children for generations.

The 27th July 1945 was the last day of the All Standard School and thereafter it became a Primary School. The country was now to experience the ultimate in equal opportunity with every child having the right to achieve its potential in comprehensive schools with all the problems that has created, especially the unsuitability of much of the schools output for any wealth-creating job.

Five years later, on the 31st August 1950, Mr Thomas Halliwell the headmaster of the school, retired after seventeen years of distinguished service much of it through very troublous times. An excellent photograph of him is to be seen on Plate 60 of "Images of Old Offley". The following year Mrs Curley, who had been on the staff for twenty one years (9) also left and, on leaving, gave a number of books to the church for use in the children's corner.

A change in the way the school was funded came in 1964 with the formation of "The Salusbury and Burroughs Educational Foundation" by the Department of Education and Science and the Charity Commissioners (9). This combined the former charities for the educational benefit of Offley and Cockernhoe with the income split two thirds to Offley and one third to Cockernhoe. By this time, the only property held was the School House, the remainder having been sold (the Cow Yard property conveyed on the 24th July 1964).

The Trustees consisted of the Vicar (ex officio) and

(a). A Parochial Church Council Representative.

(b). A Parish Council Representative.

(c). A Herts County Council Representative.

(d). A Representative of the Managers of the Cockernhoe Endowed Church of England Primary School.

(e). Three co-opted members of the Church of England appointed by resolution of the other Trustees.

The co-opted members were Mr Peck the Luton solicitor, Dr Jonas of Cockernhoe and representing that village and Mr Clough Park representing the village of Offley.

The school, catering for junior and mixed infants, has changed but little since then. Even though Lilley has now been included with Offley, numbers have reduced from the one hundred of a century ago to about seventy and the school is bedevilled by the shortage of funds. These aspects certainly threaten its longer term future, but at least we still have our village school for the moment and long may it continue, as the community will be the poorer without it.

# AG LABS AND STRAWPLAITERS

*"The glories of our blood and state
Are shadows, not substantial things:
There is no armour against fate
Death lays his icy hand on kings:
Sceptre and crown must tumble down
And in the dust be equal made
With the poor crooked scythe and spade"
(James Shirley 1596-1666).*

It is time that we looked at the principal occupation over countless generations for most of the males of the village, followed by similar consideration of a 19th Century occupation for a large proportion of the village females keeping many a family from starvation. These two occupations were as Agricultural Labourers and as Strawplaiters.

A typical agricultural labourer was Peter Burgess whose photograph, which comes from the private albums of the Hughes family (38), appears in this book. Peter was born at Offley in 1813 just before the Battle of Waterloo and he died early in the 1900s. In his later years he lived in a thatched cottage in West Lane now known as the "Old Cottage".

When Peter was eight, by which time he would have already started working in the fields, of the 165 families in the parish 143 were in agriculture (22). This proportion gradually diminished as time marched on but Peter, having married and raised a family, remained an agricultural labourer. He was not to be given the vote until quite late in his life when the 1884 Act effectively enfranchised the agricultural labourers. Let us have a look at a life which can only be described as one of unremitting toil.

Work started shortly after 5.00am and went on for a twelve hour day, with an hour's break at midday, for six days per week. Holidays were on Sundays, Christmas Day and Good Friday afternoon (90). Pay was about 13/- per week for a labourer with an extra two shillings per week for special skills such as horsekeepers and shepherds, all plus a flat £4 for the harvest month.

On his head our agricultural labourer wore a flat cap which was as much a social distinction as a protection against the weather. Other clothing consisted of a collarless open-necked shirt of thick striped oxford shirting to which a stiffened collar could be attached with studs for Sunday wear. This was worn next to his skin except in winter when he may have worn a thick prickly woollen vest. Over his shirt he wore a long-sleeved weskit (waistcoat) and over that a heavy jacket. He wore corduroy trousers secured by a wide leather belt and braces but was unlikely to have worn underpants (90). His legs were wrapped with strips of rick canvas or paper like bandages or puttees and tied with binder string or strips of leather. This was not to keep out rats and mice but for warmth and to try to keep the wet out. Paper was often stuffed under the shirt front and back for the same purpose. He wore heavy hobnail boots which he would spend seemingly endless time packing and repacking with straw and paper ready for a day working in the fields in the pouring rain.

The great event was Largesse Day when the men were given a day off at the end of harvesting. This was a Tuesday (market day in Hitchin) and usually in September when the men and their families went to Hitchin to buy clothes for the next twelve months. Most of them headed for Hawkins the Outfitters, still in existence in 1994, where strong cheap clothing could be purchased and then on to Lucas the Brewers who supplied free beer for the day.

For all his humble station he would have been a proud man and if given a task, however long and arduous, he would not brook interference and such was the system with the presence of several tenant farmers and rented cottages in the village that if a labourer, known to be reliable, had a disagreement with one farmer, he could usually find work with another without losing the roof over his family.

Peter Burgess has been used as an example but there were many others. A little later, but living in the same house, was Fred Pedder (Churchyard Memorial 180) who in addition to being an agricultural labourer also thatched the hay and straw ricks, a very skilled task. In his spare time Fred had yet another source of

Peter Burgess -
an old labourer at Offley -

income as he used to cut his neighbours hair, using candle and comb in one hand scissors in the other (42).

Towards the end of the 19th Century, machinery was making an ever greater impact on agriculture in the form of binding machines, steam operated ploughs and elevators. Gradually fewer and fewer men were required to work the farms and the onset of the 1914-18 War meant that men were in short supply thereby making the need for machinery all the greater. This trend was not reversed after the war and the arrival of tractors, combine-harvesters and a whole array of other equipment decimated the numbers of men required for work on farms. There has been no let up in this trend so that Hoo Farm of 416 acres needing the tenant farmer and 24 labourers in 1851, by the 1990s only required a farm manager plus three men to farm 1750 acres. Fortunately the favourable aspect is that the farm manager and his three men enjoy an appreciably higher standard of living than their predecessors, due to the need for them to be skilled not only in basic agricultural crafts but in a whole range of engineering, marketing, chemical, conservation and financial matters not dreamt of by their forefathers.

*"It makes the poor saucy, and no servants can be procured, or any field work done".*
*(Arthur Young circa 1800).*

It is not easy to sympathise with this opinion given by a leading agriculturist of his day, that strawplaiting caused a shortage of domestic servants and those, mainly women, who did the menial tasks in the fields such as weeding and gathering stones.

Let us now take a look at this source of income which saved many a family from the extremes of poverty in North Hertfordshire during periodic agricultural depressions and was to give women a status in the community not usually found in the 19th Century and which was only due to the substantial contributions they made to the family income.

Strawplaiting developed in the 1700s with the demand for straw hats and its heyday came after the Napoleonic wars of the early 1800s. The industry had spread from the South East Midlands to various parts of the country including Northern Ireland, but eventually concentrated in North Hertfordshire and South Bedfordshire adjacent to the hat manufacturing industry of Luton. The industry flourished in the middle of the century but collapsed towards its end due to the import of cheap plait from Italy, China and Japan. From the Offley Census we learn that of the 530 villagers there were 160 in the strawplaiting trade in 1851 (39). By 1871 out of 685 villagers there were 85 in the strawplaiting trade and the corresponding numbers for 1891 were 840 villagers with 120 strawplaiters. By the commencement of the 1914-18 War strawplaiting had virtually ceased but, in general, so had the grinding poverty of the preceeding Century.

Let us look at the process. Firstly the plaiter purchased the straw in bundles from travelling dealers or from the markets in Luton or Hitchin. At this stage either the dealer or the strawplaiter would cut it into lengths of about nine or ten inches and ensure that there were no knots or defects. The straw was then split into a number of splints, using a metal tool or splitter according to the fineness of the required plait. The splints were then passed through a hand-operated mill to flatten them. The straw needed to be damp in order to be flexible and it was soaked in water and during the actual plaiting the splints were usually held across the mouth and moistened with the lips. Following plaiting, the product was put through another hand-operated mill to flatten it throughout its length. After being put through the plait mill, all the ends of the splints were carefully clipped away and it was then looped in loose coils and put in a box with a small piece of brimstone on a hot coal for some hours in order to bleach the plait lightly and to impart a brighter appearance. The standard measure was a score which amounted to a length of plait twenty yards long, earning an average of one shilling when sold to the travelling dealers or at the plait markets in Luton or Hitchin. A good plaiter could make ten score i.e. 200 yards of plait in a week though quality varied considerably as did the various types of plait e.g. whole straw, whipcord, plain, purl, etc and of course the price paid for the work varied accordingly (108). Offley, Lilley and Breachwood Green tended to specialise in plain and twist wholestraw.

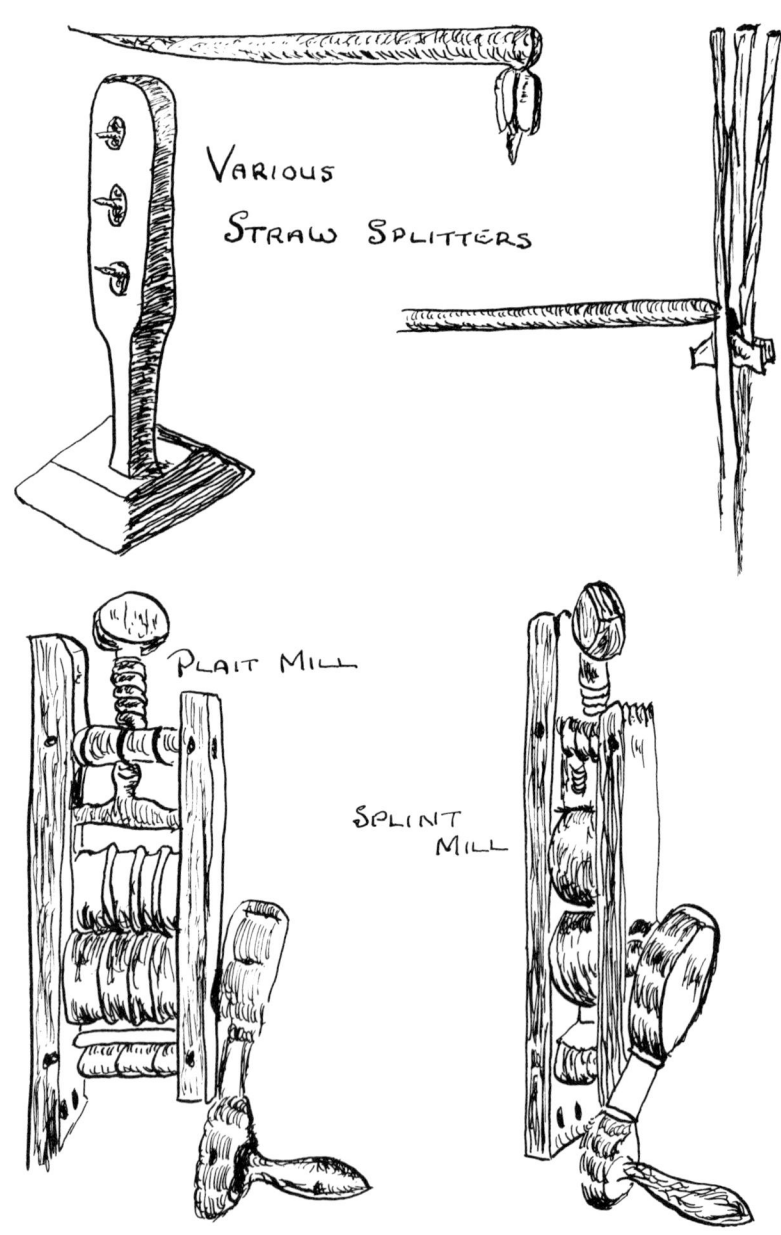

For a skilled plaiter the probable average earnings throughout the year was in the region of five shillings per week, though there were very marked seasonal variations so that even twenty one shillings in one week was not unknown. In spring and summer the earnings were double those of autumn and winter. When work was slack the plaiters would make flowers, dolls and other ornaments known as corn dollies, a craft which still exists in a small way today. The men would also participate if work was slack on the farms.

Very often as soon as a child could walk it was sent to a plaiting school where it was set a task to produce so much plait per day. A child of eight could be expected to earn in the region of 9d per week. Whilst there is no mention in the Offley Censuses of plaiting schools in the village, they almost certainly existed though they do not seem to have received the opprobrium of the Pirton schools "Close and crowded places. Nurseries of moral and physical disease" (105).

Offley Churchyard Memorial 020 is to the memory of James and Sophia Hawkes. He was an agricultural labourer and Sophia, who died in 1867, was a strawplaiter as was their daughter Harriet (Churchyard Memorial 046) in 1851. Another family was that of Alfred Day (Churchyard Memorial 078) who in 1851 was living with his seven brothers and sisters and their parents Samuel and Ann who were farm labourer and strawplaiter respectively.

In addition to the strawplaiters themselves, there was a cottage industry for the sewing of bonnets and in 1851 the wife of the village schoolmaster, Phebe Church who originated from Luton the centre of the industry, was such a sewer. A similar trade was that of a straw hat manufacturer and in 1891 we find Clara Smith, an unmarried 23 year old, stating this as her occupation. This work was often done in large Luton factories but there was also a strong cottage industry. The village also had at least one strawplait dealer in Arthur William Claridge (Churchyard Memorial 144) as late as 1898.

Useful though it was in its time, we must be thankful that the need is no longer there but it is strange that a whole industry should develop and virtually disappear in a little over one hundred years.

# THE MISSUS

*"Is this the silent woman?"*
*"Nay, she has found her tongue*
*since she was married"*
*(Ben Jonson 1573-1637).*

Having looked at an agricultural labourer's life of about one hundred years ago, let us now pry into the life of his "Missus". It would be difficult to argue convincingly that old Offley constituted "the good old days" for these people. What a time it must have been for the married woman trying to bring up a family and keep house under such conditions, although her problems started long before marriage. Such a person was Julia Simpkins who was born in 1857 at Offley, married circa 1870 to Frederick Morley who was four years younger and they had five children by 1891. She was a strawplaiter and he an agricultural labourer and shepherd. She died in 1927 and he in 1932.

Throughout childhood daughters would usually be regarded as inferior to sons as she would not have the same potential as an income for her parents in their old age. The sooner she could be married off at modest cost the better and in the meantime it was her duty to learn from and help her mother with the household chores. In Offley this usually included learning straw-plaiting from an early age, an occupation which to some extent could be performed whilst moving around doing other duties. This did not stop our girl from going to school and, as she was not taken out of school for farming activities as frequently as the boys, she often ended up more capable of reading and writing than her brothers. As a young woman she had to take care "not to lose her reputation", as the social standards of the time, especially in villages, could be very severe. Not that these sanctions prevented the births of illegitimate children, as the Baptismal Registers of the Parish amply show.

During the marriage ceremony she promised "to love, cherish and to obey" which fairly clearly established her status in the partnership. However, careers for working women were almost non-existent in country districts and in any event employers paid women substantially less than the equivalent male, on the grounds that they were less capable physically and emotionally and likely to be absent due to pregnancy and other family commitments. A woman therefore had to bear in mind her future security as much as her attraction to her potential husband. If she made the wrong choice, divorce was hardly an option due to the cost and although she could leave her husband, this raised the almost insuperable problem of how to live, probably with children to support, without an income from husband or State.

Weddings were often held on Christmas Day which was one of the few days when the men did not have to work. Without any hastening circumstance manifesting itself, the couple would be married usually in their early twenties. Our happy couple were very likely to have come from the same village, as transport, other than on foot, was not easy for working people and this accounts for the high rate of family intermarriages so noticeable in Offley. Our agricultural labourer's bride is unlikely to have had a special wedding gown and she certainly would not have had a honeymoon away from the village. Most of her energies would have been engaged in setting up her home, probably consisting of a single rented room in one of the village cottages and hopefully not with the in-laws. In time and probably after the arrival of their first or second child and provided that her husband could keep in work and she could keep up with the straw-plaiting, they would probably rent at least part of a village cottage.

What changes could our young modern-day wife expect to experience if she was suddenly transported back to the Offley of one hundred years ago. There would be no water taps and she would have to carry all water in pails from the pond or from a rainwater cistern, as one hundred years ago (1894) only the gentry had wells. There would be no sewerage system and buckets would be emptied from privies into the cottage or communal cesspits, hence a constant smell over the village. No electricity but instead candles and oil-lamps with cooking done on a wood and coal burning range. No washing machine or tumble-drier, but if fortunate she would have the use of a wood-burning iron copper for boiling the clothes and a mangle with wooden rollers, probably shared with a number of other families. No detergents, but she would have a scrubbing-board, bars of soap and plenty of elbow-grease on which she would rub the clothes to get them clean and would have a basin in which to mix the starch to stiffen the two collars for her husband's Sunday shirt. A bath would be unknown but a wash in a tin bath placed in front of the fire would be a periodic luxury along with the clothes being dried or aired. The floors, mostly of stone but some of earth and upper floors of wood, would have to be swept and scrubbed, as would the deal kitchen table on which would be done the ironing using two flat-irons heated on the range.

At the end of her day, she could look forward to hand-sewing repairs to the children's clothes, darning her husband's woollen socks if he was fortunate enough to have any, and making her own clothes by candle or oil light. She would not have been able to afford a sewing machine.

No car, no buses, unable to afford a pony and trap or even a bicycle, shanks pony would be her only reliable means of transport. No super-markets as food and other supplies would have to be bought at one of the little grocery shops in the village or carried from Hitchin. Tuesdays and Saturdays were the market days in Hitchin and she would walk there and back taking her strawplait for sale and carrying home her domestic purchases, though sometimes she would purchase straw and sell plait with the village dealers such as William Claridge of Claypit Cottages.

The huge families of the earlier years in the 1800s were on the decline and she would be more likely to have five or six children than the nine or ten of former years. However, there was no "pill" or contraceptive measures to help her avoid pregnancy so that induced abortions were commonplace with all the medical risks entailed. During childbirth or should she or her family experience some serious medical problem, there was no doctor or hospital facility in Offley, the nearest being at Hitchin. This meant that in the absence of telephones in the village, either the patient had to be taken to town or someone sent to Hitchin to ask the doctor to come to Offley, all of which cost money which was unlikely to be available. Hence the women tended to pool their knowledge and experience with "Old Wives Tales" to deal with most family ailments.

Our young wife would have had little entertainment there being no radio, television or cinemas, but occasionally the vicar's wife might organise an afternoon cup of tea in the Vicarage garden where she would be instructed on such matters as the virtues of a frugal life and the need to avoid indolence. Public houses were for men's recreation and our young wife would not risk her reputation by visiting such premises except infrequently with her husband. She might reasonably expect him to come home at least once a week having had too much to drink, but this was virtually his sole escape from the drudgery of his all weather work in the fields six days per week. She had no such relaxation, no holidays, just the constant worry of keeping her home and family together.

# THE POOR

*"It's the same the 'ole world over*
*It's the poor wot gets the blame*
*It's the rich wot gets the pleasure*
*Ain't it all a blooming shame."*
*(Anon Soldiers Song 1914-18).*

Care for the poor has been a part of the social conscience of the nation throughout the ages, though what constitutes "the poor" has been less well defined and seems to have been related to the wealth of the rest of the community. For example, it is difficult to compare the starving old couple with only the rags they stood up in, evicted from a 19th Century hovel and sent to separate parts of the workhouse, with the modern unmarried woman living in a flat with one or more children on income support, who considers it her right to be provided with a television, a car and an annual holiday abroad all at the taxpayers expense. Yet both, in their separate times, are considered to be the poor and deprived.

Until the last fifty years, the culture was that most of the poor were in their situation because they were either idle or improvident and the sifting out of people in these categories dominated the thoughts of those who were concerned to pay for them. As early as 1601, a Poor Law was passed setting principles (1) which were to last until 1834 :-

(a). That National uniformity was essential.
(b). That the most suitable unit of administration was the parish.
(c). That the funds were to be provided by compulsory rates locally assessed and collected.
(d). That the able-bodied must be put to work and the idle punished.

This was added to in 1662 by a Settlement Act which was designed to hinder the migration of paupers from their places of birth or settlement. This had the effect that the spearhead of local action became the removal of paupers back to their settlement parishes. This in turn made the ratepayers take a considerable interest in encouraging the idle to work and to discourage the creation of yet more paupers. One of the problems was, however, that working class people tended to regard a large family as a basis for security in old age as state pensions were unknown.

Offley certainly had its share of these problems and Hester Lynch Salusbury later Thrale wrote (35) that in 1760 the poor of the village came to Offley Place twice per week for milk and broth. Every week an ox was killed and the cuttings made into an immense pie and on Sunday mornings the village poor came to the front of the church and were given portions of the pie which they fried "pudden and all together". The Lord and Lady of the Manor at Offley Place also clothed seventeen poor boys and girls who went to church on Sundays in their uniforms.

The problem was aggravated by the creation of larger numbers of poor people by the passing of the "Inclosure Acts", the first of which for Offley was at the relatively early date of 1767 (4). "An Act for inclosing the common fields, the commonable lands and grounds, in the Parish of Lilley and Offley, in the County of Hertford, except a certain sheepdown called Lilley Hoo, in the said parish of Lilley, and certain lands, part of the common fields, lying south east of West Lane End, the Mill House and Cole's Cross, North End of the town of Offley". This meant that the land previously divided into strips on the "open field" system was consolidated into blocks of land owned by individuals. As might be expected, the larger landowners came out best, as those with strips too small to be consolidated and too poor to take legal action, found themselves dispossessed and totally dependent on finding work from an employer which, with the periodic agricultural depressions, was not always possible.

The French Revolution had a major impact on the thinking of the English aristocracy and gentry on the basis that if the masses could rise in France they could in England and reformers by the beginning of the 1800s recognised that something must be done to aid the poor and considered that the answer was to create workhouses to accomodate those needing relief. In Offley the position was not helped by further Inclosure Acts of 1801 and 1807.

The old workhouse and possibly pesthouse in School Lane was probably established during this period mainly to help the old and sick, with the system trying to make up wages to a living level for those who were able-bodied and who could live elsewhere than in the workhouse. Such "outdoor" relief was related to the price of grain. Assisted passages were given to those who were prepared to emigrate (109) and any destitute persons passing through the village were moved on as fast as possible before they could become a burden on the parish. We read in the Churchwardens Accounts of a small sum being paid to a disabled soldier from the Napoleonic wars in effect to move elsewhere. A little earlier, in 1810, the churchwardens even paid four shillings "for removing a man (bit with a dog) to Stopsley" rather than risk keeping him at Offley's expense. The first we know of an actual workhouse in Offley was the mention in the Churchwardens Accounts (22) of May 1815 that payments were made for removing coal and straw to it.

The School Lane workhouse was either unsuitable or inadequate and in 1825 a new Poor House at what is now called Claypits Cottages or Workhouse Corner was built at a cost of £1,000 on land given by the Rev. Lynch Burroughs of Offley Place. The building included an area later used as a ropewalk and originally may have been utilised by the inmates for picking oakum which was the unpicking of old ropes into loose fibres for caulking and plugging leaks. This was an unpleasant task but one much favoured by the Overseers of the Poor and the Workhouse Masters, as it produced a useful revenue.

By 1834 the authorities recognised that the effect of making up the wages of able-bodied men in order to avoid putting whole families in the workhouse resulted in depressed wage levels so that the non-agricultural rate-payers were subsidising the farmers and landowners. The Poor Law Amendment Act was therefore passed which had the effect of :-

(a). Providing central control thereby bringing greater uniformity of standards.
(b). The provision of institutional relief even for the able-bodied.
(c). Grouping Parishes together into Unions.
(d). Parishes continuing to bear the financial responsibility.

The amendments created even greater hardship to individual paupers but gave greater uniformity across the country and brought order into the management of the poor in country districts (1). Offley became part of the Hitchin Union along with several other villages in the area and the Offley workhouse was closed and had been converted into cottages by 1841.

An examination of the 1851 Census (39) of the Hitchin Union discloses that out of 175 pauper inmates, there were only three who were Offley born :-

John Davis aged 77 a former grinder
James Plowman aged 75 a former agricultural labourer
John Gillhams aged 56 a former agricultural labourer

To administer the poor, parishes appointed various functionaries according to the number of persons concerned. This was usually done by the Vestry which was a meeting of the parish priest as chairman, the churchwardens and respected householders of the parish. In the case of Offley the Vestry appointed Guardians of the Poor who were usually minor gentry who ensured that no major irregularities took place, an Overseer of the Poor who was usually a tenant farmer or tradesman who supervised an Assistant Overseer of the Poor who did the work. The Guardians and the Overseer kept careful note as they had a vested interest as ratepayers whereas the Assistant Overseer was salaried. For example, Richard Marsh landowner of Little Offley (Churchyard Memorial 062) was a Guardian of the Poor in 1864 and on the 13th April 1868 William Olney was appointed Assistant Overseer of the Poor at a salary of £20 for the ensuing year with Rhoda Olney (Churchyard Memorial 029) who could not write, and Charles Davis (Churchyard Memorial 126) being the bondsmen (29). The following year the Vestry Minutes defined the duties of the Overseers of the Poor, Thomas A.B. Smoothey (Churchyard Memorial 067) and John Lake (Churchyard Memorial 044), and the salaried Assistant Overseer as :-

(a). To make out and correct the Poor Rates for the Parish and collect the same.
(b). To keep the papers and other documents belonging to the Parish.
(c). Attend the Vestry and keep the Minutes in a book to be provided.
(d). To carry into execution all orders of removal and such other business as the Overseers direct.
(e). To call a meeting of ratepayers every quarter and produce accounts for inspection.

By 1891 the position had worsened possibly due to the introduction of mechanisation on farms, the agricultural depressions and the decline of strawplaiting following cheap foreign imports. It is also noticeable that there were at least eight public houses and beerhouses in the village and such a high concentration curiously enough usually indicates considerable poverty in an area. This time there were six Offley-born paupers in the Hitchin Union out of a total of 140 inmates :-

Thomas Lawrence aged 85 former agricultural labourer
James Summerfield aged 64 former coal carter
Roger Chapman aged 31 former agricultural labourer
Isaac Burgess aged 71 former agricultural labourer
Samuel Pearce aged 69 former thatcher
Joshua Thrussell aged 71 former carpenter

The year 1894 was the last mention in the Vestry Minutes of nomination of Overseers of the Poor, as by the Local Government Act of that year the civil functions of the Vestry were taken over by local councils. Apart from the Assistant Overseer, it is unlikely that anyone mourned the loss of the unpleasant tasks involved.

About this time great help was given to the poorer people of the village by the provision of a district nurse, the nearest hospital and doctor being at Hitchin. The cost had to be borne by the parish ratepayers as the services to cottagers was free. Patients were invited to contribute but the amounts received were negligible and a source of bitter complaint. Nevertheless there was no shortage in the demand for the services of the nurse and we learn that in 1900 Nurse Stoten paid 1,586 visits, attended 110 cases of illness and only eight of her patients died (9). Infant mortality, which as the registers show, had been a scourge for centuries was on the decline. From 1900, only in 1911 were there as many as six infant deaths and three of those were the Stevens triplets George 10 hours, Ethel 2 days and Jessie 36 hours (33). It must have been a terrifying task for a nurse working without medical supervision having to deal with every conceivable type of accident, illness and condition with her very limited skills and virtually no equipment available. Fortunately at that time people were only too grateful to have any help and the nurse was unlikely to land up in court on charges of negligence if the patient did not recover. In 1905 Nurse Stoten left and Nurse Bunn commenced and the rules for the nurse were re-stated and included that she was to "be an example of order, neatness and helpfulness and must avoid gossip". One cannot help sensing the pen of the vicar, the Rev. Gatty, in this pronouncement.

Probably the greatest of the District Nurses was Lilian Mabel Nash (Churchyard Memorial 118) who lived from 1889 - 1975 and was the nurse for Offley and Lilley from 1924 - 1950. In the early years she used a bicycle for transport but in 1936 she was provided with an Austin motor car. As might be expected, the perception of her varied considerably. To some, she was unsympathetic and had a narrow view of morality. This is perhaps typified when in 1948 she asked that the Parish Council lock the children's recreation area on Sundays. To others, probably the majority, she was extremely popular and did much good work. In 1966 she received a letter from Muriel Bodsworth "Dear Nurse, I thought you would like to see an account of Carolyn's wedding, as you were responsible for bringing her into the world. We had a lovely day for the wedding and are so pleased about it all, with best wishes" (9). What a delightful tribute to a great lady.

Of less significance but nevertheless worthwhile for the poorer people was the provision of Clubs for various commodities, notably coal. For example, in 1901 the Offley Coal Club had 42 depositors who each paid 10/- over a number of months and received 13 hundredweight of "excellent quality coal". The wealthier residents were cajoled into making donations to the Club so that more coal could be purchased than the contributions would permit and two of these people would usually go to Franklins, the coal merchants of Hitchin, to negotiate the bulk purchase.

It seems that by the beginning of the 20th Century although there was still real poverty among many of the village families, it was not quite as desperate as in earlier years. However, benefactors such as the Goslings of Wellbury were popular in the village on account of their "good works" in distributing food and clothing to needy families in the first decade of the century. As the decades passed, Governments made steadily increased and wider benefits for the less fortunate in the community, including old age pensions, unemployment pay, medical treatment, subsidised rents and a host of other provisions. By the 1990s the stage has been reached whereby it has become almost impossible politically to put any curb on such costs, as huge numbers of voters are living "on benefit" as a way of life. The "poor" with knowledge of how "to work the system" are frequently better off than the taxpayers who pay for them and the trend is to penalise the provident for the benefit of the improvident. No doubt, with time, the pendulum will swing again but let us hope that it does not swing back as far as the poverty of the "poor" of previous centuries.

# LAW AND ORDER

*"Order is not a pressure which is imposed on society from without, but an equilibrium which is set up from within."*
*(Jose Ortega Y Gasset 1883-1955).*

As might be expected, the village has seen an incredible variety of happenings in its long history but the changes in attitudes to law and order, reflected in the quotation above, are perhaps the most extraordinary of all. The problems for William of Ecu, one of our early Norman Overlords, in having his eyes pulled out and "his privy-members cut off" for merely planning an attack on the King's person in 1096 have been described in the first chapter. Today, a criminal can gain access to the Queen's bedroom without fear of anything much more than an admonition and the rest of us risk imprisonment if, even in our own homes, we dare molest the burglar armed with gun, knife or cosh.

We can be quite certain that, although the records are sparse, Offley had its share of the troublesome throughout the ages. It must be remembered that the English have been traditionally arrogant, aggressive and violent, a people feared even by their own rulers, a people who built the greatest empire the world has ever known and which only fell apart after the Second World War when they lost their national pride. In many cases we can sympathise with the actions of those troublesome people of old and certainly with the punishments inflicted on them, but care has to be exercised in judging standards in different ages. The Peasants Revolt of 1381, when the peasants of Hertfordshire rose against the powerful and hated Abbey of St Albans and marched on London headed by Jack Straw, was brought about by wage restrictions in the Statute of Labourers, conditions of villein tenure of land and an inequitable poll tax (12), the first and last of which may seem familiar. However, the demonstrations at that time were considered a threat to the State and the ringleaders were hanged, drawn and quartered, whereas in today's society similar demonstrations, often with far greater violence than exercised by the Hertfordshire peasants, are tolerated as part of the democratic right of vocal minorities.

At the less organised level, Offley had its share of crime. In 1427 Ralph Wettenale alias John Rand broke into the close and houses of Thomas atte Hoo of Offley and stole money, gold rings, an ornamented belt, towels and a pound of pepper (5). To respect the gentle reader, his punishment is not stated.

The location of Offley no doubt attracted malefactors of various sorts and kinds. From the earliest times the well-wooded steep slopes near the village must have been a haven for highwaymen, footpads and other persons determined to create all manner of havoc. Certainly on the 30th September 1622 one of the minor gentry of the village, William Crawley gentleman, was taken to task by a presentment to the jury of the Hundred of Dacorum the Half Hundred of Hitchin at the Hertford Sessions "for harbouring rogues and vagabonds" (49) and for a great many years the lane between Charlton and Offley was notorious for gangs of ruffians. Perhaps it was this that made Edmund Papworth of Charlton in 1656 "make a ditch lying at the back of his orchard which is a great annoyance to people passing from Hitchin to Offley and that he also erected a brick wall upon part of the highway leading from Hitchin to Offley". By the end of the century, as has been seen in the Chapter on Vicars, the situation had become so bad that even our inoffensive vicar Richard Willowes was "barbarously murdered by highwaymen" and as far as we know the perpetrators were never found.

Petty crime and sheer annoyance to neighbours seems to have been as prevalent in bygone centuries as today. "William Dawes of the parish of Offley has thrown a heap of mould into the highway leading from Lilley Street in Lilley into the common fields there so that no passengers or carriages can pass that way" was dealt with at the Hertford Sessions in 1649. Another on the 1st May 1671 was the appearance, at the Sessions, of John Cawdell of Offley who had "hedged and ditched and enclosed part of the common and has built a messuage thereupon". Maybe some of these cases were the result of the vigilance of Thomas Dearman the Offley petty constable.

More serious was on the 30th August 1665 when Sir Brocket Spencer Bart of Offley Place and Thomas Docwra Esquire issued a writ to the Sheriffs of the County to summon a jury to meet at the sign of "Le George" at Ickleford at nine in the morning to enquire into certain riots at Offley (49). The cause of the riots is not known but at the time the plague was at its height and there was serious political unrest throughout the country (118).

By 1701, it is noticeable that not only were Offley residents expected to obey the laws affecting secular activity but had laws spiritual added to their burdens. On the 28th April of that year was the presentment at the Sessions of Edward Swayne of Offley for working his team on the fast day and for not going to church or any other place of worship for one month. No doubt the elderly residents of the parish considered that the country was going to the dogs!

By the 19th Century we begin to have a clearer picture of the severity of punishments for what today would be regarded as trivial crime. James Curry, an Offley labourer, was ordered to be imprisoned for a month in the bridewell (the local lock-up) and publicly whipped for stealing a pair of leather boots in 1817. On the 25th July 1827 at the Hertford Assizes Joseph Sinfield and William Worsley were sentenced to death for burglary of the house of Thomas Bates a farmer of Offley living at Westbury Farm. Worsley was wounded in the affray but this did not save him as the sentences do not appear to have been commuted. Today the authorities would do their best to have the burglars cautioned and Farmer Bates jailed.

In 1832 we come across the first of several transportations of the Offley criminal fraternity to Tasmania and Australia. Here again the sentences seem extremely severe but were probably against the background of the agricultural riots which rocked north Hertfordshire in 1830. On the 27th November 1832 John Lavender, James Clarke, James Goodge and Charles Tarryer were convicted of stealing rabbit traps the property of the Rev. Lynch Salusbury of Offley Place and Wellbury. Lavender received a life sentence and was transported on the "Isabella" and the others received seven year sentences and may have been transported. The "Isabella I" of 579 tons, sailed from Plymouth on the 28th July 1833 arriving at Hobart Tasmania on the 14th November 1833 with 300 prisoners of whom six died on the voyage.

The year 1833 was to see the conviction of Samuel Parker and Felix Swainston aged 30 and 26 years respectively for stealing a quantity of carpenters tools from John Hack and Samuel Foster of Offley. Both thieves were sentenced to be transported for seven years. Parker was sent on the "Henry Tanner" a barque of 388 tons which sailed from London on the 1st July 1834 arriving at Sydney on the 26th October 1834 with 218 men, two having died on the voyage. Swainston was transported on the "Roslin Castle" of 450 tons sailing from London on the 27th May 1834 arriving at Sydney on the 15th September 1834 with 227 men, three having died on the voyage. Descendants of Swainston are still living in Australia.

Further severe sentences for theft were to follow. On the 28th February 1838 at the Hertford Assizes, Matthew Marlow aged 25 years and James Walker aged 29, labourers of Offley, were sentenced to fourteen years transportation for stealing a mattock and a spade the property of John Pearman, plus a pig and other articles. They went to Sydney from Portsmouth on the "Earl Grey" (110). Yet only two weeks gaol was given to William Roberts aged 22 years for stealing a pair of boots from George Cole at Offley Grange in March 1841. Sentencing was as unpredictable then as it is at the present time.

Two years later Thomas Davis, aged 23 years, of Offley was lucky to escape with his life when he and John Pitts, aged 22 years, of Pirton robbed William Huckle of £4-19s-0d on the road between Offley and Hitchin. Both were sent to Gibralter initially but confirmation is lacking as to whether they went to Australia. Fortunate was Ellen Bygrave in 1845 to be acquitted of receiving stolen goods from her sister Mary Ann Bygrave. Mary Ann was convicted of stealing a thimble, a pair of gloves, a yard of linen and other articles the property of Miss Eliza Bates and her sisters at Lilley Hoo Farm for which she was sentenced to a twelve month gaol sentence, but was acquitted of setting fire to the house of John Bates of Lilley (111).

The last of the transportations came in 1852 following the conviction on the 25th February of David Claridge aged 15 years, a labourer of Offley, for arson to barns belonging to Richard Oakley of Offley. Claridge apparently went to Australia on the "Stag". If this is correct, he was kept in prison or in the hulks for a long time, possibly on account of his age, as the next sailing of the "Stag" as a convict ship was from London on the 5th February 1855, taking until the 23rd May 1855 to arrive at the Swan River (Fremantle) in Western Australia. The barque "Stag" was of 678 tons and on the voyage held 225 convicts of whom only one died during the passage (110).

Offley has been fortunate in having a resident police constable for several hundreds of years. Until well into the 1800s the Vestry (29) seems from time to time to have appointed a constable of the "inner part" and a constable of the "outer part" dealing respectively with the village and the area surrounding it, although some of these constables were either not resident in the parish or were part time. As far back as the 12th July 1686 we find "John Bates sworn petty constable of Offley in place of John Arnold" (49). A constable is also mentioned in each of the Censuses from 1851 (39). Perhaps because they had their policeman to keep them relatively safe from villains, the inhabitants were not willing to pay for oil lamps in the village streets and those venturing out at night were prepared to take their chances with slipping into one of the deep drainage ditches or, even worse, falling into one of the numerous cesspits.

In more recent times, as mentioned in the Chapter on the Church, theft of parts of the lead roof on the church took place in 1957 and theft of some of the church organ pipes in 1966. Since then, theft of and from vehicles and from homes has become a regular occurrence and seldom does a week go by without some act of theft or vandalism. Our police constable fights a losing battle, as without effective deterrents to wrongdoers and with the law on the side of the criminal rather than the victim, ordinary villagers have little protection from the State and are penalised should they attempt to defend their families, property or themselves.

# ROADS AND RETICULATIONS

*"One may not doubt that, somehow, good
shall come of water and of mud
and sure, the reverent eye must see
a purpose in liquidity."*
*(Rupert Brooke 1887-1915).*

The roads around the village must have been a talking point from the time that permanent settlement began as, until the present century, they were nothing more than muddy tracks and virtually impassable in winter. We have already noted Sir John Spencer complaining in January 1708 that he had not been able to go out in his "charriot" not only because of his gout but "our wayes are almost impracticable" (5).

One hundred years later the situation was unchanged. At the Hertford Quarter Sessions in 1812, there were three presentments that the inhabitants of Offley ought to repair the roads within the parish between Hitchin and Pirton, Mill House Lane and the Hoo Road between Offley and Kings Walden. No doubt the difficulties for traffic were made worse by moving the main road through the village to an alignment with a steeper gradient in 1807 so that Offley Place and its pheasantry could enjoy less noise. It must be remembered that the parishes themselves were responsible for road maintenance, usually controlled by the Parish Vestry with the work being performed by the numerous labourers available in the vicinity. However, Offley did take some notice, as in 1814 the churchwardens received £10 for 200 loads of stone from the Surveyor of Roads following the demolition of the old church tower and at some time tolls were charged and collected at the Lodge at the bottom of Offley Hill. In addition to the main road through the village, for many hundreds of years there has also been a lane from Charlton near Hitchin across the fields to Offley terminating near the "Red Lion". There must have been a serious attempt at some stage to upgrade this route, probably during the first two decades of the

20th Century, as the cutting built to reduce the gradient can still be clearly seen.

By 1863 the Vestry Minutes (29) record that an Offley Highway Rate was assessed at 6d in the £1 to pay for highway expenses. Relief came to the parish in 1893 when negotiations were concluded for the taking over of the main road through the village from Offley Cross to Holly Bush Hill by the County Council. This left the Parish with only the minor roads to consider but these gave problems enough. By this time the roads seem to have improved slightly, as we learn that roads generally were made of brazil-nut sized pieces of granite covered by gravel, watered and rolled flat. The rolling was done by steam-rollers. There were few gullies and drains but ditches were constructed at the sides of the roads. It must also be remembered that, in the absence of motorised traffic, there were quantities of horse manure everywhere especially along the centres of the roads (42).

Real improvement did not come till as late as the 1930s when gradually the roads were surfaced with tarmac and the drainage improved. Even then, buses struggled up Offley hill and frequently the passengers would be asked to alight, walk up the hill and get in again at the top of the hill. Motorised traffic gradually built up, especially on the main road through the village, until by the post Second World War years it developed into a non-stop roaring monster. The Offley crossroads became notorious throughout the area as a "blackspot" for serious traffic accidents. A long and arduous campaign was conducted by John Hall (Churchyard Memorial 167), who became a County Councillor, for the building of a by-pass the construction of which, through the hills, was a major engineering enterprise. Sadly, John was not to see the work completed as he died on the 4th April 1974 whereas the by-pass was not opened until the 25th November 1974, but it remains a tribute to his perseverance and love of his village.

The Luton to Hitchin Highway through Offley until 1807. Facing West from the High Street in 1994.

The Luton to Hitchin Highway through Offley until 1807. Facing East from the High Street in 1994.

Old road from Charlton to Offley in 1994.

OPENING OF THE FIRST PUBLIC WELL
near the "Green Man"
22nd JANUARY 1898
Francis & Katherine Gosling with
their son Charles on the carriage.

Of even greater importance to the villagers than roads was water. Until the end of the 19th Century there were a few wells, pumps and elevated tanks for the larger houses such as Offley Place, Westbury and Eagles Nest whilst Wellbury had a conduit of lead pipes from a spring in the nearby hillside. For the majority there were no such luxuries and the villagers had to rely either on water they could obtain from the private wells, rainwater from the roofs stored in tanks, the ponds or from the occasional watercart which came from Hitchin.

Progress came in 1896 when the Hitchin Rural District Council recommended that wells be dug near the "Green Man" and the "Red Lion". Francis Gosling (Churchyard Memorial 004) offered to sink one of them at his own expense if the other was supplied by public subscription (9). Mrs Gosling turned the first sod at noon on the 20th July 1896 and the well was opened at noon on the 22nd January 1897. It was 300 ft deep and it took seven minutes to raise a bucket to the surface. It was operated by a windlass, chains and two huge buckets so that as one went down the other came up. Each bucket had the capacity to fill three domestic pails. It was considered a great improvement to life in the village and as time went on, a higher roof was made, the sides were shuttered and an elevated tank, a lean-to for a pump and a tap were installed (112). Due to lack of financial support the well near the "Red Lion" was not sunk immediately and it was not until 1910 that it was constructed at the expense of Mr H.G. Salusbury Hughes of Offley Place.

In 1926 water in lead pipes was supplied to Offley Place and "The Lawns" from a pump station near a pond to the west of what is now Salusbury Lane. The foundations of the pump house are still visible (1994). The pipes were removed when Gosling Ave was built but some of the piping is still in position underground at "The Lawns" (38 & 44).

Thus matters stood until 1937 when the first boring for a new water scheme commenced (9) and a water works was installed the following year. However, the scheme consisted of standpipes to various places in the village, such as near to the Chapel and the "Red Lion", not pipes into each house. The latter had to wait until after the 1939-45 war and in 1945 the Parish Council noted that the well water was undrinkable but the engine and pump were in good condition but in need of re-leathering the pipes (93). By 1969 water reticulation had been completed throughout the village and a public meeting decided that the old 1897 well should be filled in. It seems probable that it was not in fact filled in but a heavy concrete cover placed over it, as its site can still be seen quite clearly.

Obviously, until piped water was available to each household, there could be no water-borne sewerage system. The Rev. Gatty (Churchyard Memorial 013), as perspicacious as ever, wrote in 1921 "Our sewage is interred as it has been since the Conquest, no doubt, within a stone's throw of our back doors. We have no lamps - not even a solitary oil lamp. We have no public baths or wash-house - no water supply" (9).

Twenty five years went by. On the 23rd October 1946 Mr Handscombe reported to the Parish Council that it would be five to ten years before Offley had a sewerage system as the new satellite town of Stevenage had to come first (93). He was not far out. It was March 1955 when the Parish Magazine (9) was able to report that the sewerage system had been installed.

Electricity came to Offley in 1932 via the reticulation system of the North Metropolitan Electricity Company. "The Lawns" was connected on the 6th February and it is interesting to note that the electricity consumption then was about 50 units per quarter compared to a quarterly consumption in 1992 of about 1,600 units per quarter. By the end of the year electricity had reached the church and the school so that the oil lamps, which had served for so long, were discarded. Eventually electrically powered street lights were to reach Offley but that is another story and one that is not resolved to this day. It is unfortunate that many of the splendid vistas from the parish are spoiled by the intrusion of hideous high voltage pylons but most progress seems to have its environmental price.

You may ask about the supply of gas to the village. Unfortunately it is all uphill and the North Sea is a long way away!

# WARS AND THE WAR MEMORIALS

*"The Saxon is not like us Normans.
His manners are not so polite,
but he never means anything serious
till he talks about justice and right.
When he stands like an ox in the furrow,
his sullen set eyes on your own,
and grumbles "This isn't fair dealing"
My son, leave the Saxon alone."
(Rudyard Kipling 1865-1936).*

There is little information concerning the participation of Offley men in the many wars the country has been involved in over the centuries, but we can be sure that the village has been represented in a good proportion of them if the contribution to the two great wars of the 20th Century is any guide.

During the Civil War of the 1600s Offley does not seem to have been notably disturbed. The area, like much of East Anglia, was strongly for the Parliamentarians and no doubt some Offley men found themselves recruited into Cromwell's New Model Army. Likewise with the Napoleonic Wars, a few of our agricultural labourers were sure to have escaped the drudgery of their lowly station for the prospect of excitement and booty with the army. The attraction of the latter does not seem to have extended to our gentry as soldiers among them are few and far between.

The first war of which we have any real knowledge involving the men of the village is the South African (Boer) War of 1899-1902. On the 4th June 1902, seven Offley men, probably in the Militia, returned from Hertford having received their medals there. Mr Gosling drove them in his brake to the top of Offley hill where a triumphal arch had been erected. The horses were then removed and the brake was dragged to the church by the villagers for a Thanksgiving Service. After that, the brake was dragged to Wellbury House, the Gosling's home, for a party. Lieutenant Gosling was given a similar welcome when he returned on the 27th

September (9). The seven were probably in the 42nd (Hertfordshire) Company of the Imperial Yeomanry formed in December 1899 which landed in Cape Town in March 1900. They were used mainly on patrol duties based at Krugersdorp in the Transvaal until the end of April 1901. They would have done little fighting but, like the rest of the army, suffered considerably from sickness. The Company left South Africa in May 1901 (113) and were disbanded at Hertford. This means that there is a year's discrepancy between the account in the parish magazine and the story of the Hertfordshire Soldiers (113) and unfortunately it has not yet proved possible to establish the individual names and units of the Offley contingent. The only name we know of was William Dyer (Churchyard Memorial 192) who lived from 1880 to 1949 and was partly paralysed from wounds he received during the Boer War and who later operated the filling station at the Flints while his wife ran the little shop nearby (19 & 92).

The war clouds loomed once again and, in August 1914 the mincing machine of the Great War commenced. It was undoubtedly a popular war and the nation entered into it with a show of patriotism which is difficult to comprehend eighty years later. We have already seen in earlier chapters how the village policeman was worried that a fire in Cannon's yard would attract Zeppelins, how the Rev. Gatty went off to France with his car and chauffeur to help wounded French soldiers and that the children sent eggs to soldiers in the hospitals. The threat of bombing from Zeppelins was taken quite seriously and it was decided to insure the church against damage by aircraft from 1916-1918. Shortages created long queues at the shops but a rural community was cushioned to some extent by local produce from allotments and gardens and the keeping of chickens, rabbits, pigs and other animals. The farmers were placed under fairly strict surveillance to ensure that they did their best for the war effort and we have already seen the problems of Claud Miller at Hoo Farm losing his tenancy as he was unable to reach the required standard.

The men of the village responded to Kitcheners's call for New Armies and some 128 joined the armed forces during the war, mostly in the army and of those, 18 were to die as a result of active service. All those known to have been in the forces are mentioned in Appendix "B" together with any information known about their service. Most of them were in the category of private soldiers in the P.B.I. (Poor Bloody Infantry) but there was one very senior officer, Brigadier General Charles Gosling the son of Francis Gosling, who was killed in action on the 12th April 1917. One man who died as a result of war service and was buried at Offley was Private Robert Stanley Bird (Churchyard Memorial 081) who died in 1919. His Commonwealth War Graves Commission stone still stands but was unfortunately placed circa September 1967 some yards north of his actual resting place (44). A second man, Alfred James Smith, died in the military hospital at Colchester and was buried at Offley on the 8th August 1922 presumably of injuries sustained during the war. Memorials to all the other men are in foreign fields as was the custom in the British forces. An elegant village War Memorial was unveiled on the 7th March 1920 by the Lord Lieutenant of the County, Lord Hampden.

That was the war to end all wars and the men came home supposedly to a home fit for heroes. In fact they came home to the same virtual feudal state little better than that of their forefathers, with similar poverty and even greater difficulties in finding work. However, along with the rest of the country, they did not want to accept that they would have to fight again when, in the 1930s, the rise of Nazi Germany again threatened the peace of Europe. As we have seen, the Offley vicar the Rev. Henry, said in 1938 at the time of Munich "Thanks be to God for the deliverance from war" and this was the view of the majority of people at that time. A classic example of how wrong people can be, even collectively as a nation.

When Hitler marched on Poland on the 1st September 1939 it became apparent to nearly everyone that we could no longer hide by throwing the smaller countries into the Nazi maw and war was declared on the 3rd September 1939 and was to last until the Japanese were crushed by the 15th August 1945. It was obvious that in England this was going to be a war with a difference and the first event was huge numbers of children being evacuated from the larger towns in the south to be billeted in the country towns and villages. The cultural gap between these children and the locals was enormous. Few of them were absorbed into the local community and in fact most went back home within a year, but Offley did its best to welcome them, led by the vicar who gave up much of his new home to accomodate them. A second shock to the villagers was having to appoint one of their number, Mr Frederick Harper (Churchyard Memorial 109), to take away all the unnecessary iron and steel for conversion into tanks and guns. In this way the butcher lost the railings and gates in front of his shop and the churchyard lost most of its railings (Churchyard Memorials 003 & 055).

Throughout 1940 there were numbers of air raid warnings and invasion was expected at any moment. An Observer Corps post was established at the top of Honeysuckle Lane to report the presence of enemy aircraft (120). In September and October about 30 bombs were dropped in the parish but fortunately there was little damage. A stick of 10 bombs struck the area from north west of Old Wellbury to the south east on the 20th October. Another stick of 9 bombs was dropped from the vicinity of Glebe Farm to the south, one of them hitting the road shortly beyond Guys Plantation on the 22nd October. A cluster of incendiaries was found between Offley Grange and Offley bottom on the 10th November and a single bomb struck about a quarter of a mile north east of Eagles Nest on the 16th October (114). It is unlikely that any of these were aimed at Offley but rather enemy aircraft jettisoning their deadly cargoes on the way home from targets in the Midlands. A little later an enemy plane crashed just over the parish border towards Preston and, having buried itself some fifteen feet deep, has been a source of historical research in more recent times.

In 1944 came an appalling tragedy at West End Farm which brought the whole violence of war close to home. The Daily Mail of the 19th June 1944 described the scene "The ruins of a burned-out farmhouse at Offley, Hertfordshire were still being searched last night for the bodies of the farmer's wife, Mrs George Handley, and their daughters Elsie aged 23 and Mary aged 36, who were killed when an R.A.F. plane crashed on the house in the morning of the 18th June. Mr Handley and his two sons were milking cows in a shed, but they could not get near the house for the flames. It is feared that six airmen were killed. The plane, with one engine in flames, circled over Offley village before crashing. It hit some trees, then a field and ricocheted on to the farmhouse". At the time Elsie was home on leave from the A.T.S. and the long arm of coincidence extended even further in that one of the airmen killed in the tragedy came from Hitchin.

Six months later on the 8th January 1945 another war related incident took place. An American vehicle, loaded with bombs, was in collision with another lorry and caught fire beyond the Flints on the main road out of the village towards Luton. Two people were killed and several injured in the blast which left a crater 25 ft across and 25 ft deep. The driver, an exceedingly brave man, managed to warn villagers nearby before the explosion occurred. At the Inquest, the evidence was conflicting but all agreed that the road had ice and snow on it at the time (115). A number of cows were killed at Glebe Farm and the farm buildings were demolished. The schoolchildren had been taught to dive under their desks and "behaved splendidly" according to the school logbook. The school lost glass and had a damaged chimney (88) and there was a considerable amount of similar minor damage in the village (44).

As in the previous war, men marched away some never to return. This time many of the casualties were incurred whilst serving in the Royal Air Force but there were two who died in the horrors of the Japanese prisoner-of-war camps in the Far East. Thus another 14 names had to be added to the War Memorial and Appendix "C" gives as much information as could be found regarding each of them. On the 11th November 1951, Mrs Pilkington had a lantern installed under the Lych Gate with mirrors so positioned that they directed beams of light onto the War Memorial on the other side of the road (9). This was in memory of her two sons and her husband (Churchyard Memorials 001 and 239), all of whom died in 1942.

The last, and we must hope final, incident in this history of war came on the 21st November 1969 when the Lord Lieutenant of Hertfordshire, Major General Burns, unveiled in the chancel of the church, the two handsome green Westmorland slate plaques (Church Memorial 15) with the names of the fallen from the two world wars etched in gold lettering (9). Part of the cost was contributed by the British Legion but most of it was due to the generosity of David, Lord Lloyd. Curiously, the names on the plaques and on the War Memorial outside do not exactly tally and no really satisfactory explanation has been forthcoming to account for the differences.

After the Second World War, National Service continued for men until well into the 1950s but was then abolished. Historically, the English, after their experience with Oliver Cromwell, have never favoured keeping a large standing army and, like our gentry of old, there are few instances of young Offley people being attracted to service with the armed forces.

# SOURCES OF REFERENCE

*"I presume you're mortal, and may err"*
*(James Shirley 1596-1666).*

The Numbers are shown in the text of the Chapters in brackets e.g.(14).

1. Chambers Encyclopaedia.

2. "King Offa in Hitchin" by Clifford Offer.

3. "Note on Finds - Offley". East Herts Arch. Soc. Transactions Vol VII Part 1 1923.

4. "History of Hertfordshire" by J.E. Cussans. Published in 1874. Volume III.

5. "History of Hitchin" by Reginald Hine.

6. "Relics of an Uncommon Attorney" by Reginald Hine.

7. "Historical Antiquities of Hertfordshire" by Henry Chauncy who was writing after 1700 but who died in April 1719. The copy examined was a reprint made in 1826 and had been given to Lord Lloyd at Clouds Hill by Mr B.E. Kenworthy-Browne of Wellbury on the 11th July 1937 and has pencilled notes made by Mr Kenworthy-Browne regarding the Wellbury fee-farm rent. Chauncy's book is probably the most wide-ranging available and his work has been much used by later writers.

8. "Sketch of the History of Offley and its Church" by Percy Gatty (circa 1907). Copy held at the Herts County Record Office.

9. Parish Magazines 1896, 1900-1965 held by the Herts County Record Office. 1917 (May only) held by Angela Hillyard.

10. "A Short Account of the Church of St Mary Magdalene, Offley" by Ron Pigram.

11. Offley Paper by the Rev. Dr Griffiths held by the Herts County Record Office.

12. "A History of the English Speaking Peoples" by W.S. Churchill.

13. "Domesday Book". Reproduced by kind permission from the Phillimore edition of DOMESDAY BOOK (General Editor John Morris), volume 12 HERTFORDSHIRE (County Editors Margaret Newman and Sara Wood), published in 1976 by Phillimore & Co. Ltd., Chichester, West Sussex.

14. "History of Hertfordshire", "Victorian England" Series edited by Page.

15. "Offley Monumental Inscriptions" compiled by Valerie Hawkes for the Hertfordshire Family & Population History Society in 1985. This includes extracts taken from the original manuscripts of W.B. Gerish who noted the inscriptions prior to the First World War.

16. "Memorials of Non-Conformity in Herts" by William Urwick M.A. 1884.

17. "Dictionary of Genealogy" by T.V.H. Fitzhugh.

18. Notes of Reginald Hine held at the Hitchin Museum.

19. A personal discussion with Mr Brian Limbrick in 1993

and a talk given by him at the Offley Harvest Supper in October 1991.

20. "Confessions of an Uncommon Attorney" by Reginald Hine.

21. Schedule of Books, Vestments and Vessels of Offley Church in the Archdeaconry of Huntingdon dated 15th April 1749 held by the Herts County Record Office under reference AHH 11/1.

22. Churchwardens Accounts held by the Herts County Record Office.

23. Consecration document dated 27th July 1870 extending the churchyard, held by the Herts County Record Office under reference DSA 1/5/143.

24. File of correspondence from Lawrence Graham & Co (Solicitors) concerning the churchyard extension dated 1928 held by the Herts County Record Office under reference DSA 1/5/143. The correspondence mentions that portions of the Offley Place estate had been sold.

25. "Guide to Hertfordshire" by an Old Inhabitant 1880. Copy with the Herts County Record Office.

26. "A Professional Hertfordshire Tramp" by J.E. Cussans.

27. Article concerning the village of Offley. Hertfordshire and Bedfordshire Express dated 27th May 1955 Page 5.

28. Lawson Thompson Scrapbooks held by Hitchin Museum.

29. Offley Vestry Minutes 1863 - 1992.

30. Pigot's National & Commercial Directory September 1839.

31. Offley Parochial Church Council Minutes.

32. "Glebe Lands of Offley". Church Terrier 27th June 1638. Herts Genealogist and Antiquary Vol 3 1899.

33. Offley Parish Burial Registers 1653-1734 : 1732-1812 : 1813-1868 : 1868-1908 (Microfilm 359) and the original Register 1908-1985 all held at Herts County Record Office.

34. Offley Parish Marriage Registers held by the Herts County Record Office, mostly on microfilm.

35. "Thraliana 1776-1809". The Diary of Mrs Hester Lynch Thrale nee Salusbury later Mrs Piozzi. Published in 1942 in co-operation with the Huntington Library.

36. Transcript of the 1773 Will of Sir Thomas Salusbury held by the Public Record Office Chancery Lane Prob 11/992 Page 356 et seq.

37. Gentlemen's Magazine    xxi 524
    xxiv 483
    lxxiii 697
    Herts Entries 1731-1800

38. Dr Harry and Mrs Sally Clough - School Foundation, Hughes family photographic albums, extracts from "A History of Hertfordshire" page 44 quoting Cussans but Author Unknown, an early Northmet Electricity card for "The Lawns", a copy of the plan moving the main road (see also 47 below) and various discussions.

39. Decennial Censuses of Offley 1841-1891.

40. "Images of Old Offley" by Angela Hillyard.

41. "Fourscore Years" by G.G. Coulton.

42. Video recording of a commentary given at Great Offley House Barn by George Pearman on Saturday 8th November 1986 using modern photographic slides made from the Rev. Gatty's original lantern slides which had been taken between 1900 and 1925, plus Mr Pearman's own slides of a later period. The recording is held (1993) by Mr J. Perkins of Great Offley House.

43. Discussion with Mr Stanley and Mrs Eugenie Baker.

44. Discussions with Mrs Daisy Ruffet.

45. Discussions with Mrs Lily Monk.

46. Discussions with Mr James & Mrs Eileen Ganderton.

47. Plan and Justices of the Peace Decision concerning realignment of the road through Offley dated 26th September 1807 in the possession of Dr. H. Clough.

48. "Winston S. Churchill - Vol I - Youth" by Randolph S. Churchill.

49. Quarter Sessions Books and Sessions Rolls held by the Local Studies Department at Hertford.

50. "History of Offley Place" compiled by S.E. Joan Fraser.

51. "The History of Offley Place" by Guy Salusbury Hughes or possibly his father H.G. Hughes (Churchyard Memorial 012). Copies held at the Hertfordshire County Record Office and the Hitchin Museum. Notes of Reginald Hine at the Museum seem to indicate that Guy received considerable assistance in the compilation.

52. "The History of Hertfordshire" by N. Salmon. Copy seen was published in 1728.

53. "The Radcliffes of Hitchin Priory" by Ron Pigram.

54. "Offley Church needs help" by Ron Pigram. Hertfordshire Countryside January 1980.

55. "Hester Lynch Piozzi (Mrs Thrale)" by J.L. Clifford.

56. Hertfordshire Countryside Jan 1992 Page 16.

57. Autobiography of Mrs Thrale edited by A. Hayward.

58. Birrell's Admiralty Reports.

59. "Onlooker in Offley - Historical Background" by Denis Bidwell. Hertfordshire Countryside Vol 44 No.368 Dec 1989.

60. Transcript of the 1804 Will of Dame Sarah Salusbury (Church Memorials 22 & 26) held by the Public Record Office, Chancery Lane Prob 11-1412 Page 59 et seq.

61. Newspaper cutting in the Offley Folder at Hitchin Museum.

62. A Statutory Declaration by the Revd Thelwall John Thomas Salusbury on the family of the late Revd Lynch Burroughs dated 8th January 1858 held by the Herts County Record Office under reference D/ELg.T24.

63. Abstract of the Valuation of the Offley Estate in the Parishes of Offley, Lilley and Kings Walden in the County of Hertford made in 1839 and the Ground Plot and Plan of the Indenture, both held by the Herts County Record Office under reference D/Elg.T24.

64. Bill of Inclosure 1807 - 47 Geo III. In its final form the Bill became the Inclosure Act 1807 47 Geo III Sec 2 C.25.

65. An Agreement between Dame Elizabeth Mary Salusbury and the Marquess of Winchester dated 11th October 1840 held by the Herts County Record Office (Diocesan Records Section).

66. Return under the Tithe Act 1925 for Corn Rents made by the Rev. A.T.S. Henry dated 18th Feb 1927 lodged with Herts County Record Office.

67. File of correspondence held by the Herts County Record Office concerning the vexacious subject of the Corn Rents under the Tithe Act 1925.

68. Lay Subsidy Rolls 1294-5, 1307-8 and 1314-15 from Public Record Office E179/120/5, E179/120/8 and E179/120/10 all of which are extremely difficult to read.

69. Particulars Plan and Conditions of Sale of Freehold Properties Wednesday 6th July 1898 held by the Herts County Record Office under reference D/ELg.T.37.

70. Dame Elizabeth Mary Salusbury's (Churchyard Memorial 003) 18 page Will plus codicils dated 23rd December 1856. Copy held by the Herts County Record Office under reference D.ELg.T.25.

71. Offley Place Estate Map and Schedule dated 1868 held by the Herts County Record Office under reference D/ELg.P1.

72. Transcript of the 1712 Will of Susanna Nelson (Church

Memorial 33) held by the Public Record Office, Chancery Lane Prob 11 534 Page 26/27.

73. (a). Grant of Administration of the goods of Alice Piggott (Church Memorial 42) to Granado Piggott in 1714, held by the Public Record Office, Chancery Lane Prob 6/90 Page 87.

    (b). Grant of Administration of the goods of John Spencer (Church Memorial 24) to Elizabeth Penrice (Church Memorial 28) in 1716 held by the Public Record Office, Chancery Lane Prob 6/91 Page 75.

    (c). Letter from the Public Record Office, Chancery Lane dated 8th September 1993 advising that (a) above was cancelled as were Letters of Administration for Susanna Nelson and Anne Meredith when (b) above was granted.

74. Parish Registers of Bassingbourn and Abington Pigotts held by the Cambridgeshire Record Office.

75. "History & Antiquities of the County of Hertford" by Robert Clutterbuck Published 1815-1827 in three volumes.

76. Licence to alter the Offley Chancel dated 29th May 1776 from the Archdeaconry of Huntingdon and Diocese of Lincoln to Dame Sarah Salusbury held by the Herts County Record Office (Diocesan Records Section).

77. "The Church of England - A Portrait" by M. De-La-Noy.

78. Offley folder in the Reference Section at Hitchin Public Library containing copies of articles and information regarding various facets of Offley and its history including :-

(a) An account of Wellbury House.

(b) Letter to a magazine concerning the well buckets.

(c) Article from Hertfordshire Countryside Vol 23 No.112 dated August 1968 concerning the Rookery.

(d) "Offley's Charming Manor House". Extract probably from Herts Express 25th January 1913.

79. Discussions with Mr Ron and Mrs Pat Sayer.

80. Discussions with Mr Martin French.

81. Country Life Magazine February 24th 1947 article entitled "A small Country House of the XVIIth Century" by Messrs Lucas & Lodge.

82. W.B. Gerish Collection held by the Hertfordshire County Record Office.

83. Kelly's Commercial Directories 1860, 1890, 1898, 1899, 1926, 1933 & 1937.

84. Discussions with Lady Lloyd.

85. "Sale of the Old Vicarage" papers held by the Hertfordshire Record Office.

86. "Lord Lloyd and the Decline of the British Empire" by John Charmley (1987).

87. "Second World War" by Winston S. Churchill.

88. Offley School Log, Attendance and Punishment Books.

89. The Will of Thomas Bates dated 28th December 1823.

90. "Farming in a Hertfordshire Village circa 1910-1914" and various maps prepared by Angela M. Hillyard in July 1977 and discussions in 1993.

91. "Eating at the Crusty Loaf". Hertfordshire Countryside Vol 36 No.262 Feb 1981.

92. Discussions with Mrs Margaret Pearman.

93. Offley Parish Council minutes held at the Hertfordshire County Record Office.

94. Purchase Deed dated 24th April 1936 between Guy S. Hughes, family Trustees, Governors of the Bounty of Queen Anne and the Rev. A.T.S. Henry for the provision of the vicarage site out of the Lawns meadow opposite the Rookery. Deed held by the Herts County Record Office under reference DSA 1/8/81.

95. Discussion with Mr Richard (Dick) Foster.

96. "Place Names of Hertfordshire" by J.E.B. Gover.

97. "Between the Hills". The story of Lilley by Roy Pinnock.

98. Discussion with Mr Clough Park.

99. Plan of part of the 1845 proposed railway route between Hitchin and Luton, held by the Bedfordshire County Record Office.

100. Old Lease and other Agreements held by various people but mainly by the Herts County Record Office.

101. Discussion with the late Miss Elizabeth Hares.

102. "Windmills of Hertfordshire". Hertfordshire Countryside Magazine.

103. Article in the Pictorial Newspaper circa 1930 showing a photograph and detailing the wooden manual Fire Engine of Offley now (1993) housed in the Shuttleworth Collection at Old Warden. A copy of the article is held by Mr J. Ganderton.

104. Wellbury School Magazine 1934 held at the Hitchin Museum.

105. "A Foot on Three Daisies - Pirton's Story" by a Local History Group.

106. Hertfordshire Express - 22nd December 1906, Page 2.

107. Hertfordshire Express - 16th October 1897, Page 7.

108. "Luton and the Hat Industry" by Charles Freeman published by the Luton Museum and Art Gallery.

109. "Poor Law Union Records" by Jeremy Gibson, Colin Rogers & Cliff Webb.

110. "The Convict Ships 1787-1868" by C. Bateson (1985).

111. Hertford Assizes Records 1780-1853 relating to transportations. Letter from Ken Griffin of Hertford dated 13th July 1993.

112. Hertfordshire Countryside November 1966.

113. "Hertfordshire Soldiers from 1757" by J.D. Sainsbury.

114. Map in an oak picture frame hanging in the church belfry, prepared by Mr Jim Marlow, indicating bombs, incendiaries, plane crash and vehicle explosion in the parish during the Second World War.

115. Hertfordshire Express 16th January 1945 - Page 2.

116. "To what end did they die - Officers died at Gallipoli" by R.W. Walker.

117. "Hertfordshire Yeomanry & Artillery Roll of Honour" compiled by Maj. J.D. Sainsbury 1972.

118. The Diary of Samuel Pepys - 1665 edited by Latham.

119. "Hertfordshire Windmills" by Cyril Moore.

120. "Observers Trail". The story of Group 17 of the Royal Observer Corps.

OTHER SOURCES CONSULTED

Visual examination of the stones in the churchyard and the inscriptions within the church as seen by D.C. Baines in November 1992 and updated in 1993.

Plan and schedule of the old portion of the churchyard compiled by M.G. Limbrick in June 1961.

Schematic plot plan of the new portion of the churchyard compiled by Frank Thurston in May 1991.

Discussions with : -
Mr Trevor & Mrs Joanna Aldridge
Mr Peter & Mrs Jan Bates of South Wales
Mr Jack Claridge
Mr Colin Day of Letchworth
Mr Alec & Mrs Margaret Dickinson
Mr Aubrey Dyer
Mr Bill Harley of Hitchin
Mr Peter Harper
Miss D. Harrison

Mr Reg Hart
Mr Doug Hodgson.
Mr David Marlow
Mr Jim Marlow
Mr David & Mrs Pauline Prutton
Mrs D.G. Sheppard of Ashwell
Mr David & Mrs Lesley Watters

Article by Howard Swain. Hertfordshire Countryside May 1971.

Architectural and Archaelogical Society publication listing Church Plate.

Article by Bill Wigmore. Evening Post 22nd January 1968 Page 7.

Offley Church Faculties held by the Hertfordshire County Record Office.

Ecclesiastical Parishes of Offley and Lilley - 1958. Held by Offley Parish P.C.C.

Photograph of the well being opened on the Green on 18th January 1897 (22nd January according to 88 which is more reliable). It appeared in the November 1966 edition of the "Hertfordshire Countryside". Identification of a number of people was by Elsie M. Burgess (Churchyard Memorial 245) and recorded in the Parish Magazine of December 1966 though her identification of the incident and date of the photograph are faulty!

"Hertfordshire" by Arthur Mee.

"Three Stories of Offley" by John Lee. Hertfordshire Countryside Vol VII 1952/53.

"19th Century Miracle of Offley" by Eve Nash. Hertfordshire Countryside Vol 22 No.101 Sep 1967.

"Mrs Thrale's Hertfordshire Childhood" by Margaret Turner. Hertfordshire Countryside Vol 26 No.148 Aug 1971.

"Offley Place - Great Offley" by F. Hook. Hertfordshire Countryside Vol 19 No.76 Feb/Mar 1965.

"A Will from Offley - Samuel Lane". Hertfordshire People No.2 Autumn 1977 taken from Herts C.R.O. 88HW21.

"Particulars and Conditions of Sale of Tankards near Luton and Breachwood Green August 1879". Herts Local Studies Office Pamphlet H.728.6.

"Clan gathering of the Offleys in Offley Village Hall". Express August 6th 1987.

Baptismal Certificate dated 19th September 1837 from the Parish of Denbigh in the County of Denbigh relating to Lynch Salusbury, held by the Herts County Record Office under reference D/Elg.T15.

Extract from the Book of Baptisms of St Andrews, Holborn dated 25th October 1819 relating to Sarah Burroughs, held by the Herts County Record Office under reference D/Elg.T15.

Information on the Offley Family held by Jack Russell Richards of Codicote, Herts.

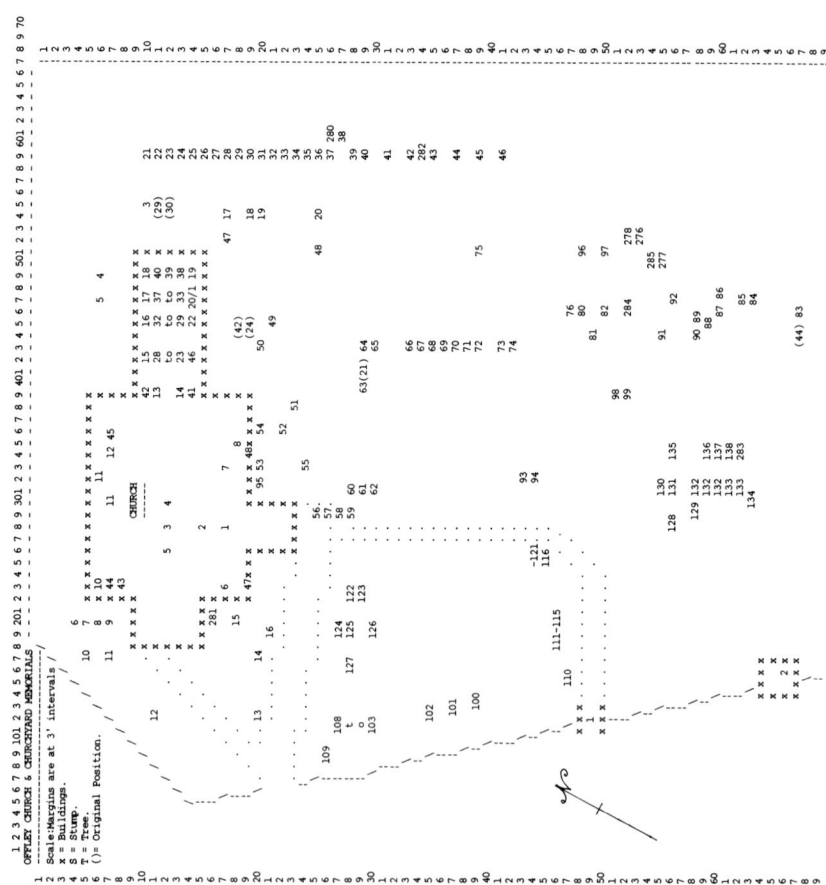

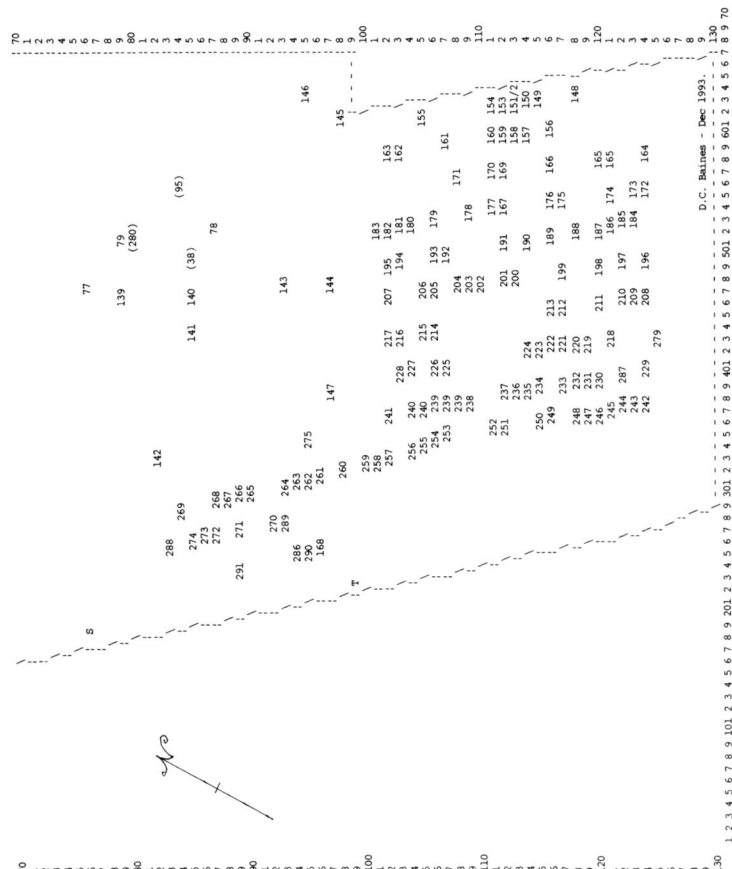

APPENDIX "A"
------------

INDEX OF PERSONS from the
MONUMENTAL INSCRIPTIONS of
OFFLEY CHURCH & CHURCHYARD
--------------------------

Note 1 - Dates are as stated on the Memorials except for the year born
where, if the age is stated, the year born is a simple
subtraction from the year died and is therefore an approximation.

Note 2 - References refer to the numbers on the church & churchyard plan

Note 3 - Numbers in brackets refer to the original position of the stone

| SURNAME | FIRST NAMES & OCCUPATION | | YEAR BORN | YEAR DIED | AGE | REFCE |
|---------|--------------------------|---|-----------|-----------|-----|-------|
| Allen | George | Head Cowman | 1877 | 1963 | 86 | 175 |
| Allen | Lucy | | 1873 | 1946 | 73 | 175 |
| Almond | Isaac | | 1842 | 1922 | 80 | 082 |
| Almond | Mary Ann | | | 1931 | | 082 |
| Altham | Alice | | | | | C41 |
| Altham | James, Sir | | | | | C41 |
| Altham | Mary | | | | | C41 |
| Anderson | Alice | | | | | C41 |
| Anderson | Henry, Sir | | | | | C41 |
| Anderson | Mary | | | | | C41 |
| Appleby | Duncan Charles | | 1951 | 1985 | 34 | 255 |
| Arnold | Sarah | Launderess | 1830 | 1901 | 71 | 038 |
| Asprey | Norman | | 1917 | 1973 | 56 | 237 |
| Aylott | Hannah Maria | Strawplaiter | 1858 | 1935 | 77 | 153 |
| Aylott | William | Ag. Labourer | 1854 | 1935 | 81 | 153 |
| Ayres | Lewis | | 1880 | 1935 | 55 | 149 |
| Backler | Ivy | | 1901 | 1981 | 80 | 247 |
| Bailey | Pamela Jean | | 1923 | 1974 | 51 | 116 |
| Bailey | Peter Raymond | | 1920 | 1972 | 52 | 116 |
| Bamber | Alison Elizabeth | Nurse | 1875 | 1944 | | 181 |
| Barker | Alice | | 1888 | 1951 | 63 | 183 |
| Barker | William Herbert | Car Worker | 1893 | 1978 | 85 | 183 |
| Baron | Annie | School Cleaner | 1903 | 1975 | | 235 |
| Baron | Horace | | 1901 | 1977 | | 235 |
| Bates | | | | | | 070 |
| Bates | | | | | | 068 |
| Bates | Elizabeth | | 1808 | 1837 | 29 | 047 |
| Bates | Hannah | | 1779 | 1848 | 69 | 105 |
| Bates | Harriet | | 1792 | 1868 | 76 | 065 |
| Bates | John | | | | | 019 |
| Bates | John | Innkeeper | 1786 | 1869 | 83 | 065 |
| Bates | Lavinia Harriet | | 1803 | 1854 | 51 | C01 |
| Bates | Lydia | Seamstress | 1787 | 1867 | 80 | 066 |
| Bates | Mary | | 1781 | 1839 | 58 | 066 |
| Bates | Mary | Publican | 1799 | 1883 | 84 | 048 |
| Bates | Rebecca | | 1783 | 1861 | 78 | 066 |
| Bates | Thomas | | | | | 047 |
| Bates | Thomas | Churchwarden & Farmer | | | | C49 |
| Bates | Thomas | Churchwarden & Farmer | | | | C43 |
| Bates | Thomas | Churchwarden & Farmer | 1750 | 1823 | 73 | 069 |
| Bates | William | | | | | 047 |

| | | | | | | |
|---|---|---|---|---|---|---|
| Bates f Forster | Jane | | 1749 | 1834 | 85 | 019 |
| Beale | T.B. | | | | | 012 |
| Bigge | Mary | | | | | C07 |
| Bigge | Thomas | Gentleman | 1617 | 1701 | 84 | C07 |
| Bird | Dennis Roy Mechanic | | 1924 | 1983 | 59 | 257 |
| Bird | Dorothea Alexandra | | 1903 | 1963 | 60 | 209 |
| Bird | Florence Annie | | 1884 | 1955 | 71 | 205 |
| Bird | Frank Reginald | | 1904 | 1969 | 65 | 209 |
| Bird | George | | 1880 | 1952 | 72 | 205 |
| Bird | Robert Stanley | | | | | C15 |
| Bird | Robert Stanley | Soldier | 1899 | 1919 | 20 | 081 |
| Botha | Sarah Catherine | | 1869 | 1950 | | 191 |
| Bowen | Glaslyn Thomas | Soldier | 1912 | 1991 | | 271 |
| Brocket | Susanna | | | | | C41 |
| Brockett | Hellen | | | | | C41 |
| Brockett | John, Sir | | | | | C41 |
| Brockett | John, Sir | | | | | C06 |
| Bunker | Hubert Samuel | | | | | C15 |
| Burchell | Phoebe Maria | | 1875 | 1957 | 82 | 216 |
| Burgess | Elsie Maud School Mistress | | 1892 | 1981 | 89 | 245 |
| Burns | Archibald | | | | | 100 |
| Burns | Hamilton | | 1846 | 1924 | 78 | 100 |
| Burroughs | Ann | | 1787 | 1856 | 69 | C23 |
| Burroughs | Gwen | | 1796 | 1812 | 16 | C46 |
| Burroughs | Jane | | 1767 | 1815 | 48 | C46 |
| Burroughs | Lynch, Revd Clerk Holy Orders | | | | | C46 |
| Burroughs | Lynch, Revd Clerk Holy Orders | | | 1837 | | C23 |
| Burroughs | Lynch, Revd Clerk Holy Orders | | | | | C18 |
| Burroughs | Samuel | | 1795 | 1815 | 20 | C46 |
| Burroughs | Samuel,L.L.D.,Master of High Court | | 1695 | 1761 | 66 | C13 |
| Burroughs | William | | 1811 | 1852 | 41 | C46 |
| Burrows | Mabel | | 1895 | 1967 | 72 | 213 |
| Burrows | Edmund (Bob) | | 1895 | 1961 | 66 | 213 |
| Cain | Harold Walter | | | | | C15 |
| Cannon | Agnes Mary | | 1878 | 1953 | 75 | 202 |
| Cannon | Emily | | 1874 | 1943 | | 171 |
| Cannon | Frederick George | | 1898 | 1923 | 25 | 284 |
| Cannon | George | | 1880 | 1962 | 82 | 202 |
| Cannon | Joseph Wheelwright | | 1845 | 1929 | | 094 |
| Cannon | Mary Ann | | 1846 | 1915 | | 094 |
| Carew | Nicholas, Sir | | | | | C41 |
| Carew | Susanna | | | | | C41 |
| Carr | Alec | | 1899 | 1978 | 79 | 231 |
| Carr | Alice | | 1895 | 1978 | 83 | 231 |
| Carrier | Mary | | 1722 | 1769 | 47 | 281 |
| Carrier | William Coachmaker | | 1717 | 1782 | 65 | 281 |
| Carter | Ellen | | 1896 | 1968 | 72 | 219 |
| Carter | Harry Tenant Farmer | | 1914 | 1990 | 76 | 289 |
| Carter | Monica Nancy | | 1921 | 1992 | 71 | 289 |
| Carter | Walter John Tenant Farmer | | 1903 | 1968 | 65 | 219 |
| Castle | Barry Michael Schoolboy | | 1941 | 1946 | 5 | 177 |
| Chamber | William Esquire | | 1700 | 1728 | 28 | C10 |
| Chamberlain | Ernest William Farm Labourer | | 1872 | 1949 | 77 | 150 |
| Chamberlain | Hannah Elizabeth | | 1873 | 1935 | 62 | 150 |
| Chamberlain | William | | 1699 | 1728 | 29 | C12 |
| Chapman | Daniel Tenant Farmer | | | | | 061 |
| Clare | Bernice Julia | | 1881 | 1944 | 63 | 179 |
| Clare | Frederick Publican | | 1884 | 1963 | 79 | 179 |

| Surname | Forename(s) | Occupation | Born | Died | Age | Ref |
|---|---|---|---|---|---|---|
| Claridge | Agnes | | 1865 | 1957 | 92 | 199 |
| Claridge | Arthur William | Strawplait Dealer | 1864 | 1953 | 89 | 144 |
| Claridge | Mary Ann | | 1860 | 1931 | 71 | 144 |
| Claridge | Sidney John | Tenant Farmer | 1871 | 1957 | 86 | 199 |
| Clark | Ernest George | Postman | 1914 | 1977 | 63 | 114 |
| Clark | Grace | | 1893 | 1933 | 40 | 147 |
| Clark | Henry | | | | | 147 |
| Clark | William | | | | | C15 |
| Clarke | Clara | | 1879 | 1962 | 83 | 188 |
| Clarke | Ellen | | 1886 | 1959 | 73 | 215 |
| Clarke | George | Soldier | 1885 | 1960 | 75 | 215 |
| Clarke | Nellie | | 1883 | 1954 | 71 | 188 |
| Clough | Clara | | 1887 | 1972 | | 106 |
| Clowes | Winchester | | | | | 100 |
| Coles | Arthur | Head Horsekeeper | | 1940 | | 143 |
| Coles | Emma | Housewife | | 1910 | | 143 |
| Collins | Ada | | 1886 | 1935 | 49 | 151 |
| Collins | Albert | | | 1979 | | 092 |
| Collins | Cecil | | | 1964 | | 228 |
| Collins | Ivy May | | 1909 | 1927 | 18 | 092 |
| Collins | Thomas Leslie | | 1913 | 1983 | | 152 |
| Collins | William Henry | | 1876 | 1945 | 69 | 178 |
| Cooper | Kathleen | | 1918 | 1944 | 26 | 182 |
| Corbett | Donald | | 1905 | 1961 | 56 | 211 |
| Cox | Constance | | 1915 | 1985 | 70 | 263 |
| Cox | George | Hairdresser & Bellringer | 1910 | 1984 | 74 | 263 |
| Cox | Henry | | 1833 | 1902 | 69 | 063 |
| Cox | Mary | | 1805 | 1838 | 33 | 063 |
| Cox | William | | 1809 | 1840 | 31 | 063 |
| Cox | William Walker Rood | | 1831 | 1909 | 78 | 063 |
| Coxall | Florence | | 1896 | 1988 | | 267 |
| Coxall | Sidney | | 1892 | 1986 | | 267 |
| Crockford | Alfred | | 1895 | 1981 | 86 | 248 |
| Crockford | Alice Elizabeth | | 1897 | 1990 | 93 | 248 |
| Crockford | Donald Arthur | | 1932 | 1955 | 23 | 185 |
| Culling | Mabel | | 1892 | 1981 | 89 | 249 |
| Davis | Ann | | 1794 | 1880 | 86 | 125 |
| Davis | Charles | Farmer | 1824 | 1895 | 71 | 126 |
| Davis | Eliza | | 1822 | 1875 | 53 | 126 |
| Davis | Elizabeth | | 1723 | 1805 | 82 | 124 |
| Davis | Frederick | | 1897 | 1937 | 40 | 163 |
| Davis | George | | 1895 | 1947 | 52 | 163 |
| Davis | John | | 1718 | 1800 | 82 | 124 |
| Davis | Martha | | 1857 | 1921 | 64 | 127 |
| Davis | William | | 1791 | 1857 | 66 | 125 |
| Davis | William | Farmer | 1853 | 1888 | 35 | 127 |
| Davis | Charles | | | | | C15 |
| Day | Alfred | | 1851 | 1900 | 49 | 078 |
| Day | Alice | | 1885 | 1965 | 80 | 173 |
| Day | Ann | | 1916 | 1972 | | 115 |
| Day | Annie Jane | Church Worker | 1887 | 1967 | 80 | 196 |
| Day | Arthur James | | 1915 | 1986 | | 115 |
| Day | Bertie William | | 1894 | 1949 | 55 | 193 |
| Day | Elsie Maud | | 1894 | 1974 | 80 | 193 |
| Day | George Alfred | | 1879 | 1947 | 68 | 173 |
| Day | Lewis Henry | Shepherd | 1885 | 1958 | 73 | 196 |
| Day | Mary | | 1849 | 1929 | 80 | 089 |
| Day | Nellie Smith | | 1908 | 1973 | | 103 |

| | | | | | | |
|---|---|---|---|---|---|---|
| Day | Stanley | | | 1914 | 1974 | 103 |
| Dean | Joseph | Servant | | 1755 | 1791 | 36 122 |
| Deller | Albert | Bricklayer & Footballer | | 1912 | 1980 | 68 243 |
| Deller | Jack | Road Sweeper | | 1918 | 1981 | 246 |
| Demetriadi | Michael | | | | | 181 |
| Demetriadi | Patricia | | | | | 181 |
| Dewitt | Simon Patrick | | | 1969 | 1975 | 6 238 |
| Dovey | John | | | 1902 | 1993 | 91 208 |
| Dovey | Marjorie Gwladys | | | 1898 | 1963 | 65 208 |
| Drewett | Frank | | | 1895 | 1922 | 27 080 |
| Dunkley | Elizabeth Agnes | | | 1871 | 1949 | 78 074 |
| Dunkley | William Ernest Butcher's Asst(1891) | | | 1865 | 1928 | 63 074 |
| Dyer | Edward | | | | | C15 |
| Dyer | Eliza | | | 1880 | 1970 | 90 192 |
| Dyer | William | Shop-Keeper | | 1880 | 1949 | 69 192 |
| Elborn | Rosa Kate | | | 1871 | 1970 | 99 279 |
| Ephgrave | Millicent Grace | | | 1909 | 1991 | 274 |
| Ephgrave | Percy William | Baker | | 1910 | 1983 | 274 |
| Ewington | Edward George | | | | | C15 |
| Exton | George | | | | | 006 |
| Exton | Harriett | | | 1779 | 1829 | 50 006 |
| Fairbanks | Benjamin | | | 1912 | 1976 | 64 234 |
| Fairbanks | Jessie | | | 1917 | 1988 | 71 234 |
| Field | Noel | | | 1924 | 1982 | 58 250 |
| Fleckney | George Frederick | | | | | C15 |
| Fleckney | Sidney Thomas | | | | | C15 |
| Fone | Robert | | | 1941 | 1984 | 43 261 |
| Forster | Charlotte | | | | | 017 |
| Forster | Samuel | | | | | 019 |
| Forster | William | | | 1808 | 1833 | 25 017 |
| Forster | William | Wheelwright | | | | 017 |
| Forster 1 Bates | Jane | | | 1749 | 1834 | 85 019 |
| Foster | Charles | Carpenter | | 1837 | 1912 | 75 142 |
| Foster | Christina Josephine | | | 1879 | 1961 | 82 141 |
| Foster | Eliza | Shopkeeper | | 1835 | 1932 | 97 142 |
| Foster | Frederick Thomas | Builder | | 1873 | 1952 | 206 |
| Foster | Gertrude Elizabeth | | | 1870 | 1952 | 203 |
| Foster | Jane | | | 1878 | 1954 | 206 |
| Foster | Marjorie Christina | | | 1907 | 1909 | 2 141 |
| Foster | Mary Ann | | | 1833 | 1914 | 81 095 |
| Foster | William | | | 1879 | 1956 | 77 141 |
| Fowler | Alice Maud | | | 1876 | 1930 | 54 072 |
| Fowler | David John | | | 1963 | 1987 | 24 253 |
| Fraser | Alexander | | | 1844 | 1919 | 101 |
| Fraser | Eliza Jane | | | 1850 | 1919 | 101 |
| French | Joseph Cullen | | | 1868 | 1939 | 71 161 |
| French | Olive Rose | Housekeeper | | 1909 | 1947 | 38 164 |
| Frost | Henry Fletcher (Jim) | Farmer | | 1925 | 1984 | 262 |
| Gatty | Alice Mabel Wellwood | Mrs | | 1879 | 1944 | 013 |
| Gatty | Percival Edmund | Vicar of Offley | | 1866 | 1937 | 013 |
| Goodall | Arthur | Design Engineer | | 1917 | 1992 | 75 286 |
| Goodall | Edward | | | | | 042 |
| Goodall | Elizabeth | | | | | 042 |
| Goodall | Elizabeth | Servant | | 1831 | 1866 | 35 042 |
| Goodge | George | Farm Labourer | | 1824 | 1885 | 61 077 |
| Goodge | Mary Ann | Strawplaiter | | 1827 | 1894 | 67 077 |
| Gore | Elizabeth | | | | 1726 | C42 |
| Gore | Elizabeth, Dame | | | | 1709 | C42 |

| Surname | Given | Occupation | Born | Died | Age | Ref |
|---|---|---|---|---|---|---|
| Gore | Elizabeth, Dame | | 1638 | 1709 | 71 | C29 |
| Gore | Humphrey, Sir | | | | | C42 |
| Gorringe | Bertha | | 1899 | 1955 | 56 | 187 |
| Gosling | Archibald Hugh | | | 1961 | | 212 |
| Gosling | Charles | Professional Soldier | | | | C15 |
| Gosling | Francis | Banker | | | | 001 |
| Gosling | Francis | Banker | 1836 | 1910 | | 004 |
| Gosling | Henrietta | | | | | 001 |
| Gosling | Violet Mabel | | | 1950 | | 207 |
| Greenleaf | Ronald | | 1912 | 1985 | 73 | 265 |
| Hailey | Elsie Maud | | 1914 | 1988 | 74 | 205 |
| Hall | Daniel | Butcher & Cattle Dealer | 1868 | 1945 | | 167 |
| Hall | Daniel George | | 1891 | 1979 | | 167 |
| Hall | Ellenor Ann | | 1869 | 1949 | | 167 |
| Hall | Helen Eugenie | | 1896 | 1962 | | 167 |
| Hall | Helen Eugenie | | 1896 | 1962 | 66 | 159 |
| Hall | Jane | | 1836 | 1917 | 81 | 275 |
| Hall | John Leslie | Farmer | 1899 | 1974 | | 167 |
| Hall | William | | 1834 | 1915 | 81 | 275 |
| Hancock | Leslie W. | Storeman | 1912 | 1989 | | 269 |
| Handley | Alice | | 1877 | 1944 | 67 | 165 |
| Handley | Barbara Dorothy | | 1914 | 1982 | 68 | 252 |
| Handley | Elsie | | 1920 | 1944 | 24 | 165 |
| Handley | Elsie | | | | | C15 |
| Handley | George | Tenant Farmer | 1872 | 1949 | 77 | 165 |
| Handley | Mary | | 1908 | 1944 | 36 | 165 |
| Handley | Roy | Farmer | 1913 | 1982 | 69 | 256 |
| Handley | Sydney | Farmer | 1917 | 1982 | 65 | 252 |
| Hardwick | Charles William | | 1914 | 1965 | | 226 |
| Hares | Albert | Tailor | 1883 | 1939 | 56 | 160 |
| Harley | Emily | | 1860 | 1927 | 67 | 073 |
| Harley | George Arthur | Bricklayer & Soldier | 1893 | 1966 | | 223 |
| Harley | Gertrude Beatrice | School Cook | 1892 | 1968 | | 223 |
| Harman | William | | | | | 026 |
| Harper | Clara | | 1904 | 1989 | 85 | 112 |
| Harper | Edward | | 1908 | 1973 | 65 | 112 |
| Harper | Frederick | | | | | C15 |
| Harper | Frederick | | 1901 | 1964 | 63 | 109 |
| Harper | Sarah Ann | | 1868 | 1945 | 77 | 076 |
| Harper | William David | | | 1949 | | 076 |
| Harper | William Edward | | 1835 | 1921 | 86 | 076 |
| Harrington | Alice | | 1886 | 1967 | 81 | 222 |
| Harrington | Herbert | | 1885 | 1968 | 83 | 222 |
| Harris | Frederick John Anthony | | 1913 | 1984 | | 260 |
| Harrison | Arnold Frederick | | 1906 | 1980 | 74 | 121 |
| Harrison | Violet | | 1906 | 1986 | 80 | 121 |
| Hart | Francis | | 1903 | 1976 | 73 | 119 |
| Hawkes | Ann | | 1930 | 1993 | 63 | 293 |
| Hawkes | Harriet | Strawplaiter | 1834 | 1894 | 60 | 046 |
| Hawkes | James | | | | | 046 |
| Hawkes | James | Agricultural Labourer | 1797 | 1883 | 86 | 020 |
| Hawkes | Sophia | | | | | 046 |
| Hawkes | Sophia | Strawplaiter | 1803 | 1867 | 64 | 020 |
| Helder | Mary | | 1670 | 1750 | 80 | C39 |
| Helder | Mary | | | | | C40 |
| Helder | Richard | | | | | C39 |
| Helder | Richard | | | | | C40 |
| Helder | Richard | Esquire | 1659 | 1718 | 59 | C38 |

| Surname | Forename(s) | Occupation/Notes | Born | Died | Age | Ref |
|---|---|---|---|---|---|---|
| Helder | William | Gentleman | 1693 | 1714 | 21 | C40 |
| Henman | William | | 1884 | 1918 | 34 | 278 |
| Henry | Alexander Thomas Stewart | Vicar | 1874 | 1964 | | 145 |
| Henry | Margaret Sheckleton | Wife of Vicar | 1868 | 1952 | 84 | 162 |
| Hill | Lewis Albert | | | | | C15 |
| Hodgson | Stanley Maurice | Builder | 1929 | 1983 | | 259 |
| Holton | Ellen Sylvia | | 1901 | 1972 | 71 | 107 |
| Horwood | Herbert | Soldier | 1883 | 1952 | | 204 |
| Horwood | Jane | Strawplaiter | 1845 | 1919 | 74 | 097 |
| Horwood | Victor | Soldier & Ploughman | 1890 | 1975 | | 204 |
| Horwood | Emma | | 1860 | 1939 | 79 | 097 |
| How | Charles Geoffrey | Vicar | 1900 | 1986 | | 194 |
| How | Georgina Madeleine | Vicar's Mother | 1867 | 1947 | | 194 |
| Hughes | Anne Salusbury | Landowner | 1831 | 1903 | 72 | 003 |
| Hughes | Dorothy Ivy Salusbury | Mrs | 1906 | 1971 | | 012 |
| Hughes | Edward M. | | 1856 | 1881 | 25 | 003 |
| Hughes | Edward Reginald Graham | | | | | C15 |
| Hughes | Edward Reginald Graham | Soldier | 1896 | 1915 | 19 | C08 |
| Hughes | George Edward | Barrister | 1822 | 1872 | 50 | 003 |
| Hughes | Guy Salusbury | Landowner | 1882 | 1955 | | 012 |
| Hughes | H.G. Salusbury | Landowner | 1853 | 1926 | | 012 |
| Hughes | Henrietta Louisa Salusbury | | 1856 | 1914 | | 012 |
| Hughes | Kendrick Salusbury | | 1910 | 1943 | | C15 |
| Humphries | William David | | | | | C15 |
| Jeffrey | William | | 1910 | 1980 | | 242 |
| Jones | Alice | | 1905 | 1992 | 87 | 168 |
| Jones | Gervas | Clerk Holy Orders | 1731 | 1784 | 53 | C44 |
| Jones | Walter | | 1903 | 1977 | 74 | 233 |
| Kayser | Frank | Soldier | 1872 | 1954 | 82 | 189 |
| Kidman | Ann | | 1727 | 1793 | 66 | 064 |
| Kidman | Edward | | | | | 045 |
| Kidman | Elizabeth | | 1794 | 1864 | 70 | 027 |
| Kidman | Sarah | | 1750 | 1776 | 26 | 064 |
| Kidman | Susan | | 1842 | 1900 | 58 | 045 |
| Kidman | Thomas | Farmer | 1720 | 1782 | 62 | 064 |
| King | Amelia Russell | | | 1942 | | 277 |
| King | Elizabeth | | 1840 | 1892 | 52 | 139 |
| King | James | | 1867 | 1925 | 58 | 277 |
| King | James | Miller | | | | 139 |
| King | James, Lord Baron of Kingston (Ire) | | | | | C13 |
| King | Sarah | | | | | C13 |
| King | William | | | | | C13 |
| Lake | Ann | | 1835 | 1904 | 69 | 044 |
| Lake | John | | 1826 | 1903 | 77 | 044 |
| Lane | Emma | Strawplaiter | 1805 | 1882 | 77 | 099 |
| Lane | Hannah | | 1779 | 1848 | 69 | 105 |
| Lane | Samuel | Carpenter | 1769 | 1826 | 57 | 105 |
| Lane | Samuel | Carpenter,Baker,Flour Dealer | 1806 | 1886 | 80 | 105 |
| Lane | William | Blacksmith | 1802 | 1861 | 59 | 099 |
| Lee | Martha | | 1703 | 1779 | 76 | C45 |
| Litton | Robert, Sir | | | | | C41 |
| Mace | Jeffrey Arthur | Soldier | 1912 | 1939 | 27 | 157 |
| Marlow | Albert Charles | | | | | C15 |
| Marlow | Bertie George | | | | | C15 |
| Marlow | Cicely Joan | | 1919 | 1985 | 66 | 264 |
| Marlow | Dorah A. | | 1883 | 1929 | 46 | 087 |

| | | | | | | |
|---|---|---|---|---|---|---|
| Marlow | Gerald G. | | 1914 | 1991 | 77 | 087 |
| Marlow | Sidney J. | | 1884 | 1952 | 68 | 087 |
| Marsh | Ann | | 1772 | 1829 | 57 | 061 |
| Marsh | Daniel | | 1802 | 1866 | 64 | 055 |
| Marsh | Frances Louisa | | 1803 | 1866 | 63 | 055 |
| Marsh | Harriet Elizabeth | Landowner | 1833 | 1898 | | 062 |
| Marsh | Helen | | 1850 | 1929 | 79 | 055 |
| Marsh | Richard | Farmer & Landowner | 1827 | 1893 | | 062 |
| Marsh | Richard | Gentleman Farmer | 1797 | 1838 | 41 | 060 |
| Marsh | Richard | Gentleman Farmer | 1773 | 1813 | 40 | 061 |
| Marsh | Richard Sheppard | | 1837 | 1866 | 29 | 055 |
| Marsh | William | | 1800 | 1863 | 63 | 060 |
| Marsh | William | | 1829 | 1912 | 83 | 055 |
| Marshall | Beatrice Anne | | 1920 | 1991 | 71 | 273 |
| Matson | Ivy | | 1907 | 1975 | 68 | 158 |
| Maude | Daniel | Esquire | | | | C14 |
| Maude | Elizabeth | | 1723 | 1796 | 73 | C14 |
| Maude | Elizabeth | Mrs | 1723 | 1796 | 73 | C27 |
| Maynard | John, Sir | Knight | | | | C06 |
| Mellor | Abel | Madras Civil Servant | | 1878 | | 132 |
| Mellor | Laura Anne | | 1832 | 1913 | 81 | 132 |
| Mellor | Wilfred | | 1852 | 1917 | | 133 |
| Meredith | Ann | | | 1714 | | C36 |
| Meredith | Anne | | | 1714 | | C42 |
| Meredith | Roger | | | | | C42 |
| Meredith | Roger | Esquire | 1637 | 1700 | 63 | C36 |
| Miller | Frederick | | 1859 | 1911 | 52 | 059 |
| Miller | Henry | Tenant Farmer | 1824 | 1910 | 86 | 059 |
| Miller | Marianne | Farmer's Wife | 1832 | 1915 | 83 | 059 |
| Mobbs | Richard Frederick | | 1947 | 1982 | 35 | 251 |
| Monk | Charles | Carpenter | 1860 | 1948 | 88 | 166 |
| Monk | Dorcas Emily | | 1885 | 1967 | 82 | 220 |
| Monk | Doris Elizabeth | | 1906 | 1993 | 87 | 268 |
| Monk | Emma | | 1860 | 1944 | 84 | 166 |
| Monk | Francis William | | 1904 | 1987 | 83 | 268 |
| Monk | Frederick | | 1869 | 1939 | 70 | 156 |
| Monk | Gladys Adah | | 1909 | 1981 | 72 | 244 |
| Monk | Herbert | Car Worker | 1904 | 1972 | 68 | 113 |
| Monk | John | | | | | C15 |
| Monk | Mary | | 1872 | 1945 | 73 | 156 |
| Monk | Reginald | Churchwarden | 1906 | 1991 | 85 | 244 |
| Monk | Robert John | | 1905 | 1978 | 73 | 230 |
| Moody | William Henry | | | | | C15 |
| Morley | Frederick William | Shepherd | | 1932 | | 086 |
| Morley | George, | Bishop of Winchester | | | | C13 |
| Morley | Julia | Strawplaiter | 1857 | 1927 | 70 | 086 |
| Morley | Sarah | | | | | C13 |
| Morley | Thomas, | Sergeant at Law | | | | C13 |
| Musselwhite | Annie Lily | | 1912 | 1980 | 68 | 232 |
| Musselwhite | Walter Charles | | 1904 | 1978 | 74 | 232 |
| Musters | Anne, Dame | | | | | C06 |
| Musters | John, Sir | | | | | C06 |
| Musters | John, Sir | | | | | C34 |
| Musters | John, Sir | | | | | C42 |
| Musters | Mary | | | | | C34 |
| Musters | Mary | | | | | C42 |

| | | | | | | |
|---|---|---|---|---|---|---|
| Nash | Francis | | | 1778 | 1825 | 47 007 |
| Nash | George | | | | | 008 |
| Nash | George | | | 1732 | 1796 | 64 009 |
| Nash | George | | | | | 010 |
| Nash | George | | | | | 007 |
| Nash | George | | | | | 011 |
| Nash | Lilian Mabel | District Nurse | | 1889 | 1976 | 118 |
| Nash | Mary | | | | | 010 |
| Nash | Mary | | | | | 011 |
| Nash | Mary | | | 1767 | 1786 | 19 008 |
| Nash | Mary | | | 1763 | 1852 | 89 011 |
| Nash | Penelope | | | 1770 | 1848 | 78 011 |
| Neal | Dinah | Lacemaker | | 1800 | 1877 | 77 083 |
| Neal | John | Coachman | | 1799 | 1880 | 81 083 |
| Neal | William | | | 1834 | 1879 | 45 083 |
| Negus | George Herbert | | | | | C15 |
| Nelson | Abraham | | | | | C42 |
| Nelson | Abraham | Esquire | | | | C33 |
| Nelson | Susanna | | | 1640 | 1712 | 72 C33 |
| Nelson | Susanna | | | | 1712 | C42 |
| O'Flaherty | Derrick | | | | | C15 |
| Oakley | Ann | | | 1758 | 1790 | 32 123 |
| Offa | King of Mercia | | | | | C09 |
| Offley | Charles | | | 1822 | 1857 | 35 137 |
| Offley | Charles | | | 1822 | 1857 | 35 C20 |
| Offley | Elizabeth | | | 1770 | 1811 | 41 C19 |
| Offley | Elizabeth | | | 1740 | 1803 | 63 C19 |
| Offley | Harriet | | | | | C47 |
| Offley | John | | | 1773 | 1812 | 39 C19 |
| Offley | John Henry | | | | | C47 |
| Offley | Mary | | | | 1868 | C20 |
| Offley | Mary | | | | | C47 |
| Offley | William | | | 1776 | 1847 | 71 137 |
| Offley | William | | | | | C47 |
| Offley | William | | | 1810 | 1852 | 42 137 |
| Offley | William | | | 1810 | 1852 | 42 C20 |
| Offley | William | Esquire | | 1734 | 1789 | 55 C19 |
| Offley | William | Esquire | | | | C20 |
| Offley | William | Esquire | | 1776 | 1847 | 71 C20 |
| Offley | William, M.D. | Surgeon | | | | C19 |
| Olding | William Thomas | | | 1873 | 1947 | 74 172 |
| Olney | James | General Shopkeeper | | 1802 | 1858 | 56 029 |
| Olney | Sarah | | | 1772 | 1842 | 70 030 |
| Olney | William | Butcher | | 1770 | 1848 | 78 030 |
| Olney | Rhoda | | | 1804 | 1870 | 66 029 |
| Orchard | Agnes Vincent | | | 1922 | 1980 | 58 229 |
| Orchard | Lewis Henry John | | | 1893 | 1970 | 77 241 |
| Orchard | Lilian | | | 1897 | 1985 | 88 241 |
| Page | Florence | | | 1886 | 1973 | 87 104 |
| Palframan | Ronald | Fitter | | 1916 | 1977 | 120 |
| Palmer | Magdalene | Servant | | 1783 | 1852 | 69 134 |
| Park | Margaret | | | | 1991 | 291 |
| Park | Matthew | Car Test Driver | | 1888 | 1971 | 240 |
| Park | May | | | 1891 | 1970 | 240 |
| Patten | Hannah | | | 1732 | 1809 | 77 049 |
| Patten | William | | | 1735 | 1809 | 74 049 |

| Surname | Name | Occupation/Title | Born | Died | Age | Ref |
|---|---|---|---|---|---|---|
| Payne | Charles Gillies, Sir, | Baronet | | | | C17 |
| Payne | Charles Gillies, Sir, | Baronet | 1793 | 1870 | 77 | 136 |
| Payne | Charles, Sir, | Baronet | | 1911 | | 138 |
| Payne | Isabel Jeanette | | | 1911 | | 138 |
| Payne | Mary Elizabeth, Dame | | 1801 | 1855 | 54 | 136 |
| Payne | Mary Elizabeth, Dame | | 1801 | 1855 | 54 | C17 |
| Pearman | Edward | | 1877 | 1953 | 76 | 155 |
| Pearman | George | | 1911 | 1992 | 81 | 288 |
| Pearman | Rosa Mary | | 1878 | 1934 | 56 | 155 |
| Pedder | Frederick | Agricultural Labourer | 1858 | 1944 | 86 | 180 |
| Penrice | Anna Maria | | | | | C42 |
| Penrice | Anna Maria | | | | | C16 |
| Penrice | Elizabeth | | | 1726 | | C42 |
| Penrice | Elizabeth, Dame | | 1678 | 1726 | 48 | C28 |
| Penrice | Henry, Sir | | | | | C42 |
| Penrice | Henry, Sir, | Judge at Admiralty | 1677 | 1752 | 75 | C16 |
| Penrice | Henry, Sir, L.L.D. | Admiralty Judge | 1677 | 1752 | 75 | C28 |
| Penrice | Spencer | | 1718 | 1739 | 21 | C32 |
| Penrice | Spencer | | | | | C42 |
| Penrice | Spencer | Esquire | 1719 | 1739 | 20 | C16 |
| Pestell | Jessie | | 1919 | 1985 | 66 | 254 |
| Pestell | Sidney William | | 1911 | 1990 | 79 | 254 |
| Phillips | Gertrude Maria Grace | | | | | 283 |
| Phillips | Philip Henry | Tutor | | | | 283 |
| Pigott | Alice | | | 1713 | | C42 |
| Pigott | Granado | | | | | C42 |
| Pigram | Ronald James | Historian | 1927 | 1986 | 59 | 266 |
| Pilkington | C.L. | Airman | | 1942 | | 001 |
| Pilkington | Charles Leslie | | | | | C15 |
| Pilkington | Charles Leslie | Airman | 1922 | 1942 | | 239 |
| Pilkington | H.C. | Landowner | | 1942 | | 001 |
| Pilkington | Hubert Carlisle | Landowner | 1879 | 1942 | | 239 |
| Pilkington | M.L. | Soldier | | 1942 | | 001 |
| Pilkington | Mark Leslie | | | | | C15 |
| Pilkington | Mark Leslie | Soldier | 1914 | 1942 | | 239 |
| Pilkington | R.H. | | | | | 001 |
| Pilkington | Ruth Honor | | 1891 | 1975 | | 239 |
| Prutton | Florence Maud | | 1904 | 1989 | 85 | 236 |
| Prutton | Ronald | | 1910 | 1975 | 65 | 236 |
| Pursell | Mary | | 1770 | 1832 | 62 | 098 |
| Pursell | William | Shop-Keeper | 1782 | 1835 | 53 | 098 |
| Radcliffe | Ralph, Sir | | | | | C06 |
| Read | Ethel | | 1888 | 1946 | 58 | 129 |
| Read | Thirza | Grocer | 1852 | 1929 | 77 | 129 |
| Reakes | Cecil | | 1882 | 1924 | 42 | 285 |
| Reeve | Olive | | 1913 | 1989 | 76 | 128 |
| Robinson | Annie | | 1905 | 1967 | 62 | 221 |
| Robinson | Annie E. | Bird Watcher | 1872 | 1935 | 63 | 154 |
| Rose | Frederick Charles | | | | | C15 |
| Salusbury | Anna Maria | | | | | C16 |
| Salusbury | Anna Maria, Dame | | 1718 | 1759 | 41 | C30 |
| Salusbury | Anne | | 1804 | 1831 | 27 | C19 |
| Salusbury | Elizabeth Anne | | 1812 | 1882 | | 135 |
| Salusbury | Elizabeth Mary | | | 1867 | | C18 |
| Salusbury | Elizabeth Mary | Landowner | | | | 134 |
| Salusbury | Elizabeth Mary, Dame | Landowner | | 1867 | | 003 |

| Salusbury | | Robert, Sir, | Baronet & M.P. | 1756 | 1817 | 61 | C21 |
|---|---|---|---|---|---|---|---|
| Salusbury | | Sarah, Dame | | | | | C13 |
| Salusbury | | Sarah, Dame | | | | | C14 |
| Salusbury | | Sarah, Dame | Landowner | | | | C45 |
| Salusbury | | Sarah, Dame | Landowner | | | | 122 |
| Salusbury | | Sarah, Hon. Dame | Landowner | | | | C27 |
| Salusbury | | Sarah, Hon. Dame | Landowner | 1722 | 1804 | 82 | C22 |
| Salusbury | | Sarah, Hon. Dame | Landowner | 1722 | 1804 | 82 | C26 |
| Salusbury | | Thelwall J.T. Rev.Clerk Holy Orders | | 1801 | 1880 | | 135 |
| Salusbury | | Thelwall, Rev, Clerk Holy Orders | | | | | C17 |
| Salusbury | | Thelwall, Rev, Clerk Holy Orders | | 1766 | 1813 | 47 | C19 |
| Salusbury | | Thomas Robert, Sir, | Baronet | | 1835 | | C18 |
| Salusbury | | Thomas, Sir L.L.D. Admiralty Judge | | 1707 | 1773 | 66 | C25 |
| Salusbury | | Thomas, Sir, Judge at Admiralty | | | | | C16 |
| Salusbury | | Thomas, Sir, Judge at Admiralty | | | | | C13 |
| Salusbury | | Thomas, Sir,L.L.D. Admiralty Judge | | 1707 | 1773 | 66 | C22 |
| Salusbury | Hughes | Dorothy Ivy | Mrs | 1906 | 1971 | | 012 |
| Salusbury | Hughes | Guy | Landowner | 1882 | 1955 | | 012 |
| Salusbury | Hughes | H.G. | Landowner | 1853 | 1926 | | 012 |
| Salusbury | Hughes | Henrietta Louisa | | 1856 | 1914 | | 012 |
| Samwell | | Elizabeth | | | | | C11 |
| Samwell | | Joane | | | | | C11 |
| Samwell | | John | | | 1539 | | C11 |
| Saunders | | Harry Edward | | 1899 | 1979 | 80 | 287 |
| Saunders | | Kathleen Helen | | 1900 | 1992 | 92 | 287 |
| Saville | | Ernest | | | | | C15 |
| Sawyer | | Henry Charles | Landed Proprietor | 1802 | 1857 | 55 | C02 |
| Sawyer | | John Gooch | | 1798 | 1849 | 51 | 051 |
| Sawyer | | Mary Hill | Landowner | 1809 | 1839 | 30 | C01 |
| Schubert | | Ernest | | 1878 | 1963 | 85 | 210 |
| Schubert | | Sophia Gertrude | | 1884 | 1973 | 89 | 210 |
| Seaton | | Paul Henry | | 1946 | 1990 | 44 | 270 |
| Sheppard | | Eileen Mary | Independent means | 1883 | 1955 | | 100 |
| Sheppard | | Elizabeth | | 1782 | 1828 | 46 | C01 |
| Sheppard | | Jane | | 1715 | 1767 | 52 | C03 |
| Sheppard | | Mary | | 1752 | 1826 | 74 | C02 |
| Sheppard | | Richard | Gentleman | 1782 | 1837 | 55 | C01 |
| Sheppard | | Richard | Gentleman | 1744 | 1803 | 59 | C02 |
| Sheppard | | Richard Thomas | | 1803 | 1837 | 34 | C01 |
| Sheppard | | Thomas | Gentleman | 1714 | 1793 | 79 | C03 |
| Sheppard | | William | Gentleman | 1742 | 1785 | 43 | C05 |
| Sheppard | | William | Gentleman | 1711 | 1778 | 67 | C04 |
| Simkins | | Gwendoline Elizabeth | | 1888 | 1964 | 76 | 195 |
| Simkins | | Reginald James | Soldier | 1890 | 1947 | 57 | 195 |
| Sinfield | | Gladys | | 1907 | 1983 | 76 | 217 |
| Sinfield | | Percy John | Publican | 1908 | 1958 | 50 | 217 |
| Smith | | Agnes | | 1863 | 1936 | 73 | 148 |
| Smith | | Alfred James | | | | | C15 |
| Smith | | Alice Dorothy | | | | | 159 |
| Smith | | Bert | | 1883 | 1939 | 56 | 159 |
| Smith | | Charles | Gardener | 1865 | 1938 | 73 | 148 |
| Smith | | Elizabeth | Strawplaiter | 1845 | 1923 | 78 | 096 |
| Smith | | Florence Ethel | | 1886 | 1930 | 44 | 085 |
| Smith | | Frank | | 1904 | 1985 | 81 | 218 |
| Smith | | George Edward | | 1901 | 1969 | 68 | 218 |

| | | | | | | |
|---|---|---|---|---|---|---|
| Smith | Henry Richard | Drover | 1889 | 1955 | 66 | 085 |
| Smith | James | Agricultural Labourer | 1844 | 1919 | 75 | 096 |
| Smith | Lucy Emily | | 1871 | 1959 | 88 | 096 |
| Smith | Samuel | Coachman | 1831 | 1908 | 77 | 146 |
| Smith | Sarah | | 1839 | 1897 | 58 | 146 |
| Smoothy | Agnes | | | | | 035 |
| Smoothy | Albert | | | | | 035 |
| Smoothy | Albert Adams | | 1872 | 1947 | 75 | 093 |
| Smoothy | Albert T.B. | Farmer | 1840 | 1891 | 51 | 067 |
| Smoothy | Edgar | | 1843 | 1857 | 14 | 028 |
| Smoothy | Elizabeth Ann | Farmer's Wife | 1816 | 1845 | 29 | 028 |
| Smoothy | Frederick Charles | | 1878 | 1881 | 3 | 035 |
| Smoothy | Rebecca | Farmer's Daughter | 1841 | 1849 | 8 | 028 |
| Smoothy | Thomas | Farmer | | | | 028 |
| Smoothy | Thomas | Farmer | 1816 | 1866 | 50 | 067 |
| Spencer | Brocket, Sir | | | 1668 | | C41 |
| Spencer | Brockett, Sir | | | | | C06 |
| Spencer | Brockett, Sir | | | | | C34 |
| Spencer | Brockett, Sir | Baronet | | | | C33 |
| Spencer | Brockett, Sir, | Baronet | 1605 | 1668 | 63 | C35 |
| Spencer | Hellen | | | | | C41 |
| Spencer | Hellen, Dame | | | | | C06 |
| Spencer | Hellen, Dame | | | 1614 | | C37 |
| Spencer | John, Sir | | | 1633 | | C41 |
| Spencer | John, Sir | | | 1712 | | C42 |
| Spencer | John, Sir | | | 1699 | | C42 |
| Spencer | John, Sir | | 1678 | 1699 | 21 | C31 |
| Spencer | John, Sir | Baronet | | | | C06 |
| Spencer | John, Sir | Baronet | 1678 | 1699 | 21 | C06 |
| Spencer | John, Sir, | Baronet | 1645 | 1712 | 67 | C24 |
| Spencer | Mary | | | | | C34 |
| Spencer | Mary | | | | | C41 |
| Spencer | Mary, Dame | | | | | C06 |
| Spencer | Richard, Sir | | | | | C41 |
| Spencer | Richard, Sir | Baronet | | 1624 | | C37 |
| Spencer | Richard, Sir | Baronet | 1647 | 1687 | 40 | C34 |
| Spencer | Richard, Sir | Knight | | | | C06 |
| Spencer | Richard. Sir | Baronet | | | | C06 |
| Spencer | Susanna | | 1640 | 1712 | 72 | C33 |
| Spencer | Susannah, Dame | | 1620 | 1692 | 72 | C35 |
| Spencer | Thomas, Sir | | | | | C41 |
| Spencer | William, Sir | | | | | C41 |
| Spring | Henry | | 1770 | 1854 | 84 | 010 |
| Spring | Sarah | | 1767 | 1842 | 75 | 010 |
| Steward | Anne | | 1804 | 1831 | 27 | C19 |
| Steward | Samuel | | | 1876 | | C48 |
| Steward | Samuel | Esquire | | | | C19 |
| Stokes | Cyril James | | 1890 | 1901 | | 131 |
| Stokes | Emmie | Dressmaker | 1870 | 1932 | 62 | 130 |
| Stokes | George | Gardener | 1852 | 1939 | 87 | 131 |
| Stokes | Mary | Dressmaker | 1858 | 1930 | 72 | 131 |
| Stokes | Ruth | Strawplaiter | 1866 | 1939 | 73 | 130 |
| Stokes | Walter | Soldier | 1894 | 1917 | 23 | 131 |
| Swain | George | Blacksmith | 1858 | 1918 | 60 | 075 |
| Swain | Mary Ann | | 1855 | 1945 | 90 | 075 |
| Taylor | Emma Mary Ann | | 1889 | 1977 | 88 | 174 |

| | | | | | | |
|---|---|---|---|---|---|---|
| Taylor | Walter | | 1888 | 1947 | 59 | 174 |
| Thew | Terence Gordon | | 1934 | 1959 | 25 | 214 |
| Thew | William Brown | | 1903 | 1966 | 63 | 214 |
| Thirlwall | Daphne Patricia Wynn | | 1926 | 1975 | 49 | 117 |
| Thompson | Alan | | 1929 | 1955 | 26 | 184 |
| Thompson | Nora Ellen | | 1899 | 1975 | 76 | 184 |
| Thompson | Sidney | | 1887 | 1972 | 85 | 184 |
| Thorne | May | | 1891 | 1974 | 83 | 110 |
| Thorne | Sidney J. | Farm Bailiff Churchwarden | 1886 | 1969 | 83 | 110 |
| Thrussell | Ann | Housekeeper | 1805 | 1865 | 60 | 024 |
| Titmuss | Emma Alexina | | 1843 | 1929 | 86 | 088 |
| Tompkins | Albert Joseph | | | | | C15 |
| Townend | Algernon Cyril A.F.C. | | 1890 | 1957 | | 197 |
| Tufton | John, Sir | | | | | C41 |
| Tufton | Mary | | | | | C41 |
| Walker | Albert | | 1883 | 1967 | 84 | 190 |
| Walker | Charles | Carter & Road Sweeper | 1881 | 1967 | 86 | 225 |
| Walker | Frances Cordelia | | 1912 | 1967 | 55 | 216 |
| Walker | Joe | | | | | C15 |
| Walker | John | | | | | 013 |
| Walker | Mary Alice | | 1883 | 1965 | 82 | 225 |
| Walker | Winifred | | 1881 | 1953 | 72 | 190 |
| Ward | Charles | Huntsman | 1819 | 1887 | 68 | 079 |
| Ward | Sarah | Independent means | 1817 | 1896 | 79 | 280 |
| Watts | Ronald | | | | | C15 |
| Waugh | Florence M. | | | 1991 | | 108 |
| Waugh | Robert | Chauffeur & Publican | | 1970 | | 108 |
| Webb | Annie G. | | 1900 | 1979 | 79 | 111 |
| Webb | Lewis William | | | | | C15 |
| White | Arthur | Painter & Decorator | 1895 | 1944 | 49 | 169 |
| White | Dorothy Esme | | 1901 | 1962 | 61 | 186 |
| White | Harry James | | 1865 | 1912 | 47 | 102 |
| White | James Thomas | | 1897 | 1955 | 58 | 186 |
| White | Mary | Tenant Farmer | 1869 | 1936 | 67 | 102 |
| White | Ruby | | 1895 | 1984 | | 102 |
| White | Violet | Housekeeper | 1895 | 1991 | 96 | 169 |
| Whittamore | John William | Stablehelper | 1851 | 1925 | 74 | 090 |
| Whittenbury | Benjamin | Gardener | 1889 | 1945 | 56 | 176 |
| Whittenbury | Mary | | 1878 | 1952 | 74 | 176 |
| Whittenbury | Sarah Ann | | 1852 | 1923 | 71 | 276 |
| Whittenbury | Thomas | Gamekeeper | 1850 | 1928 | 78 | 276 |
| Wild | Henry Frank | | 1892 | 1981 | 89 | 224 |
| Wild | Lily Rose | | 1895 | 1965 | 70 | 224 |
| Wilkinson | C.A., Rev | | | | | 005 |
| Wilkinson | Mary Eleanor | Independent means | 1819 | 1911 | | 005 |
| Wilmot | Bessie | Shopkeeper & Post Office | | 1940 | | 140 |
| Wilmot | Cecil Bernard | | | | | C15 |
| Wilmot | Cyril Bernard | Soldier | 1898 | 1917 | 19 | 140 |
| Wilmot | Dorothy Maybel | Kept Post Office | | 1971 | | 198 |
| Wilmot | Edwin Joshua | | 1862 | 1906 | 44 | 140 |
| Wilmot | Harold Joshua | Bookseller | | 1962 | | 198 |
| Wilmot | Kathleen Mary | Sunday School Teacher | | 1957 | | 198 |
| Winch | Harold George | | | | | C15 |
| Woodfield | Alfred | | 1878 | 1955 | 77 | 128 |
| Woodfield | Gertie | Cook | 1894 | 1983 | 89 | 258 |
| Woodfield | Gwendolyn May | | 1907 | 1982 | 75 | 084 |

| Woodfield | Harold Edward | | 1907 | 1986 | 79 | 084 |
| --- | --- | --- | --- | --- | --- | --- |
| Woodfield | Hubert George | Chauffeur | 1900 | 1966 | 66 | 227 |
| Woodfield | Sarah | | 1882 | 1972 | 90 | 128 |
| Woodfield | William | | 1889 | 1943 | 54 | 170 |
| Woodfield | Alice Louisa | Parlour-maid | 1902 | 1964 | 62 | 227 |
| Woodman | George A. | | 1911 | 1992 | 81 | 290 |
| Woollatt | Emily | | 1852 | 1929 | 77 | 091 |
| Woollatt | Henry | | 1851 | 1931 | 80 | 091 |
| Wright | Beauchamp Vaughan | | 1889 | 1955 | 66 | 201 |
| Wright | Dorothy Mabel | | 1897 | 1983 | 86 | 201 |
| Wright | Edward Vaughan | Bell-ringer | 1930 | 1975 | 45 | 200 |

# APPENDIX "B"

## SUPPLEMENTARY INFORMATION ON THE WAR MEMORIAL NAMES

## THE VILLAGE WAR MEMORIAL

Positioned on the King's Walden Road opposite the church lych gate, the memorial consists of a slender Crucifix on three octagonal bases. It is constructed of Portland Stone and is approximately four metres high. The figure of Christ was taken from a carving in Worcester Cathedral. The cost was £215 and it was designed and built by Messrs Farmer & Brindley of London. The Memorial was unveiled on 7th March 1920 by Viscount Hampden the Lord Lieutenant of Hertfordshire and dedicated by the Rev. E.P. Gatty, the Vicar of the Parish.

Upper Octagon 1914/19

IN MEMORY OF THE MEN OF OFFLEY WHO GAVE THEIR LIVES IN THE GREAT WAR 1914-1919 SUCH A DEATH IS IMMORTALITY

1915  FREDERICK DYER   FREDERICK HARPER
      EDWARD REGINALD GRAHAM-HUGHES   JOE WALKER

1916  SIDNEY THOMAS FLECKNEY   BERTIE GEORGE MARLOW
      WILLIAM HARRY MOODY

1917  HAROLD WALTER CAIN         CHARLES DAVIS
      CHARLES GOSLING            JOHN MONK
      HENRY ERNEST PEARCE        CECIL BERNARD WILMOT

1918  GEORGE FREDERICK FLECKNEY   GEORGE HERBERT NEGUS
      ALBERT CHARLES MARLOW   ALBERT JOSEPH TOMPKINS

1919  ROBERT STANLEY BIRD

Middle Octagon 1939/46

AND IN THE WORLD WAR 1939-1946

DERRICK O'FLAHERTY
LEWIS HILL
FREDERICK ROSE
WILLIAM CLARK

CHARLES PILKINGTON
MARK PILKINGTON
WILLIAM HUMPHREY

EDWARD GEORGE EWINGTON
ERNEST SAVILLE
HAROLD WINCH
KENDRICK SALUSBURY HUGHES

LEWIS WILLIAM WEBB
HUBERT SAMUEL BUNKER
RONALD WATTS

First World War Supplementary Information.

"Soldiers died in the Great War 1914-1919" by H.M.S.O.
"Officers died in the Great War 1914-1919" by H.M.S.O.
"Officers who died in the service of British, Indian and East African
        Regiments & Corps 1914-1919" by S.D. & D.B. Jarvis.
"National Register of the Great War" (Luton volume) 1920.
Hertfordshire Express  - 27th April 1918.
                       - 30th April 1918.
                       - 18th May 1918.
                       - 28th September 1918.
Information from the Commonwealth War Graves Commission.
Offley Parish Magazines.
Army List 1902.
Other Sources indicated in brackets ( ).

## Those who died.

CAIN H.W. Pte 1st Herts. Volunteered Sep 1914. Western Front 1915. Killed in action at Ypres 1917. Buried British Cemetery South of Ypres. Entitled to 1914/15 Star, British War and Victory Medals. Address Angel Cottage, Offley. According to the Parish Magazine he was accidentally killed. He may also have been in the Buffs. According to "Soldiers died" he was born Offley, enlisted Hatfield (Offley), 265748, died on 16th November 1917.

DAVIS CHARLES. Born Offley, Enlisted Luton, 48231, Pte Killed in action France & Flanders on 31.7.1917, Royal Fusiliers.

DYER F. Cpl 1st Northamptons. Already serving at commencement of war he had served in India for three years. In Retreat from Mons. Presumed killed in action on 9.5.1915. He had been missing for some time. Entitled to Mons Star, British War and Victory Medals. Address Garden Fields, Offley. He left a wife, Mrs S. Dyer, and three children. This is the same person as DYER EDWARD recorded on the Church War Memorial according to Mr Aubrey Dyer. See Churchyard Memorial 192 for his brother and his parents. He was 32 years of age and the first soldier from Offley to be killed. He had been in several engagements and on one occasion had part of his cap badge shot away.

FLECKNEY GEORGE FREDERICK. Royal West Surreys. Pte.

FLECKNEY SIDNEY THOMAS. Born Kings Walden, Enlisted Luton, 13164, Pte Killed in action France & Flanders on 4.6.1916, 1st Bedfords. He was reported missing after an engagement on the 4th June 1916. The Parish Magazine states 2nd Bedfords whereas elsewhere he is shown as 1st Bedfords.

GOSLING CHARLES. Brigadier General C.M.G. Born Offley 1868, the son of Francis Gosling (Churchyard Memorial 004) and educated at Eton. Commissioned in King's Royal Rifles as a 2nd Lieut on 22 August 1888. Promoted to Lieutenant on 25th February 1891 and to Captain on 5th February 1897. In Mounted Infantry during South African War. In Natal 1899 and action at Rietfontein and the defence of Ladysmith. Served also in Cape Colony and Orange River Colony. He was a Captain when he was appointed Adjutant of the 5th Battalion on the 26th June 1901. D.A.G. until May 1904. In the Great War he was a Brigade Commander in 1915 with the temporary rank of Brig. General. He was wounded in February 1915, again in May 1915 and in 1916. He was killed in action 12th April 1917. He was married. His memorial is at Mindel Trench British Cemetery, St Lawrent-Blagy, France. He was without doubt a "fighting" officer rather than a "chateau" officer.

HARPER FRED. Born Kings Walden, Enlisted Hitchin (Offley), 13942, Pte Killed in action France & Flanders on 4.9.1916, 1st Bedfords. He was the first Offley recruit according to the Parish Magazine.

HUGHES EDWARD REGINALD GRAHAM. Church Memorial 8 records "In loving memory of Edward Reginald Graham Hughes Second Lieutenant in the 52nd (Oxfordshire & Buckinghamshire) Light Infantry killed in action, in France on the 25th September 1915 - aged 19. Buried at Givenchy - near Bethune. Quit you like men, be strong" and consists of a brass plaque set in a wooden frame and situated on the south wall towards the east end of the south aisle. He was almost certainly in the 2nd Battalion, consisting of mainly regular soldiers, which was part of the 5th Brigade of the 2nd Division of the First Army. His death occurred on the first day of the Battle of Loos. He was leading his men in an attack. The day was a classic example of the ineptitude of the British Generals and on this occasion of Sir John French which was ultimately to cost him his job, but also the lives of hundreds of thousands of men.  2/Lt Hughes is buried at the Guards Cemetery, Windy Corner, Cuinchy, France.

MARLOW ALBERT CHARLES. Hampshires, Pte. He died on the 31st August 1918 two days after being wounded in France. He had recently been transferred from Salonika where he had been for three years.

MARLOW BERTIE GEORGE. 1st Herts, Pte. He was killed instantly in 1916 when a shell landed in a trench.

MONK JOHN. Born Offley, Enlisted Hitchin (Offley), 14127, Pte Died of wounds France & Flanders on 15.10.1917, 2nd Bedfords. He volunteered in Sep 1914 and was sent to the Western Front in 1915. Fought at Arras, Ypres and was killed in the Ypres Sector. Entitled to 1914/15 Star, British War and Victory Medals. Address Garden Fields, Offley.

MOODY WILLIAM HARRY. Born Peckham Surrey, Enlisted Hitchin (Buntingford), 14167, Pte Killed in action France & Flanders on 27.7.1916, 1st Bedfords.

NEGUS GEORGE HERBERT. Born Offley, Enlisted Hitchin (Offley), 4/7349, Cpl Died of wounds France & Flanders on 27.1.1918, 8th Bedfords. He married Constance Mary Read on the 8th December 1907 at Offley. He died in hospital in France after being severely wounded four times according to the Parish Magazine.

PEARCE HENRY ERNEST. According to "Soldiers died" he enlisted Hitchin (Offley), 60187, Pte Killed in action France & Flanders on 14.4.1917, 32 Btn Royal Fusiliers but formerly 6453 in the Bedfords. According to the "National Register - Luton" he volunteered April 1915 and sent to Western Front 1915. Engaged at Ypres and killed on the Somme on 14.4.1916. Entitled to 1914/15 Star, British War and Victory Medals. Address Angel Cottage, Offley. His death in 1916 is more likely. It is probable that his family kept the "Red Lion" Public House (S.83).

SMITH ALFRED JAMES. Not mentioned on the Village War Memorial as he died after the memorial had been erected in 1920. He died at the Military Hospital Colchester and was buried at Offley on 8th August 1922 aged 20 years. He does not have a Commonwealth War Graves Commission Memorial but he is recorded on the Offfley Church War Memorial.

TOMPKINS ALBERT JOSEPH. Probably from a farming family at Wandon End. Born Offley, Enlisted New Court Middlesex (Luton), 203540, 2/4th Bn Oxford & Bucks Light Infantry, formerly 2779 Royal Bucks Huzzars. Long missing he was reported killed on the 21st March 1918 according to the Parish Magazine.

WALKER JOSEPH. Born Pirton, Enlisted Hitchin (Offley), 16092, Pte Died at sea on 17.11.1915, 8th Bedfords. He had been wounded and his death occurred when the hospital ship "Anglia" was mined in the Channel and 85 people were lost.

WILMOT CYRIL BERNARD. Born Hitchin, Enlisted Hitchin, 31770, Pte Killed in action France & Flanders on 2.1.1917, 11th Bn Northumberland Fusiliers. He is also mentioned on his parents gravestone in Offley Churchyard Memorial 140.

Those who survived.

| | |
|---|---|
| Royal Engineers | Wm. Stoten, Cpl |
| | Geo. Harley, Cpl |
| | Walter Claridge, Cpl |
| | Ed. King, Lce Cpl |
| | Ed. Taylor, Dvr |
| | Hugh Marlow, Dvr |
| | Chas. Claridge, Dvr |
| | Ernest Simkins, Sapper |
| | Albert Gutteridge, Driver |
| | Leon Lake, Pte |
| A.V.C. | Frank Marlow, Pte |
| | A.H. Leary, Lce Cpl |
| A.S.C. | Guy Hughes, Lieut |
| | Art. Monk, Pte |
| | Chas. Dyer, Pte |
| | Frank Monk, Pte |
| | Art. Whittenbury, Pte |

|  |  |
|---|---|
|  | Reg. Simkins, Pte |
| King's Royal Rifles | Herbert Gosling, Major |
|  | Fred Morley, Pte |
| Oxford & Bucks L.I. | R. Hughes, Colonel |
|  | Geo. Claridge, Sergt |
| Bedfords | Frank Drewitt, Lce Cpl |
|  | Cushi Brown, 2nd Lieut |
|  | Alfred Woodfield, Cpl |
|  | Albert Walker, Pte |
|  | John Day, Pte |
|  | Frank Woodfield, Pte |
|  | Alfred Martin, Pte |
|  | Claud Cannon, Pte |
|  | Charles Robinson, Pte |
|  | Sidney Eddy, Pte |
|  | Frank Folds, Trooper |
|  | Jack Fleckney, Pte |
|  | Hy. Brown, Pte |
|  | Harry Simkins, Pte |
|  | Geo. Simkins, Cpl |
|  | Percy Claridge, Pte |
|  | Ellis Willmott, Pte |
|  | Geo. Gutteridge, Pte |
|  | Wm. Cushing, Pte |
| R.A.M.C. | Geo. Hawkes, Pte |
|  | Geo. Cannon, Pte |
|  | John McDonald, Pte |
|  | Wm. Craw, Pte |
|  | Walter Hall, Pte |
| Machine Gun Corps | Reg. Davis, Pte |
|  | Walter Taylor, Lce Cpl |
|  | Alfred McDonald, Pte |
|  | Geo. Coles, Pte |

|  |  |
|---|---|
|  | H.J. King, Pte |
|  | Walter Flecknoe, Pte |
| Inns of Court O.T.C. | Geo. Hall, Lce Cpl |
|  | John Hall, Pte |
| Queen's | Frank Harper, Pte |
|  | Fred Harper, Pte |
| Royal Sussex | Wm. Harper, Pte |
|  | Harry Fleckney, Pte |
| Royal West Surreys | Jas. Dyke, Pte |
|  | Harry Winch, Pte |
| Grenadier Guards | J. Hughes, Major |
| London Rifle Brigade | C.E. Johnston, Colonel |
| Northamptons | Herbert Woodfield, Pte |
| 71st Leinsters | Geo. Davis, Lce Cpl |
| Hertfords | Fredk. Taylor, Pte |
| London Regt | Percy Cooke, Pte |
| Shropshire Yeomanry | F. Perkins, Lieut |
| Cheshires | John Marriott, Pte |
| Wiltshires | Hubert Horwood, Pte |
| Royal Fusiliers | Art. Hill, Pte |
| 59th Divn Band | S. Bunker, Lce Cpl |
| R.M.L.I. | John Wilcox, Pte |

|  |  |
|---|---|
|  | George Waller, Engineer |
| Royal Navy | Eric White, Cadet |
| Middlesex | Chas. Dyke, Cpl |
| R.A.F. | J. White, Lieut<br>Walter Lake, 2nd Lieut<br>Harold Monk, Cpl<br>Alan Calder, Pte<br>Horace Ayres, Engr.<br>Maurice Lake, Cadet |
| R.G.A. | Geo. Monk, Gunner<br>Geo. Dyer, R.S.S., Pte<br>Fred Ayres, Gunner<br>Chas. Harper, Gunner<br>Walter Harper, Gunner<br>Ed. Burgess. |
| R.F.A. | Art. Marriott, Driver<br>Ernest Marriott, Gunner<br>Murray Woodfield, Driver |
| Essex | Chas. Hawkes, Staff Sergt<br>Frank Ayres, Pte |
| Princess Patricia's L.I. | Wm. Lake, Sergt |
| Royal Defence Corps | Chas. Dyke |
| Coldstream Guards | Fred. W. Cole, Pte |
| Labour Company | Alfred Monk, Pte<br>Horace MacDonald, Pte<br>Lewis Ayres, Pte<br>Geo. Day, Pte<br>Art. Hares, Pte |

Geo. Clark, Pte
Charles Chapman, Pte
Jack Bird, Pte
Fred Davis, Pte
Chas. Marlow, Pte
Victor Horwood, Pte
Henry Smith, Pte
Robert Bird, Pte (Died 1919)
Wm. Groom, Pte
Bert Holton, Pte

## Second World War Supplementary Information.

Offley Parish Magazines.
The War Diary of Mr Doug Hodgson.
Discussion with Eugenie & Stanley Baker.
Discussion with Reg Coxall.
Discussion with Brian Limbrick.
Discussions with Mrs Daisy Ruffet.
Information from the Commonwealth War Graves Commission.
Offley Burial Registers.
"Long Range Desert Group" by W.B. Kennedy Shaw O.B.E.
Other Sources indicated in brackets ( ).

## Those who died.

BUNKER HUBERT SAMUEL. Private in the Queen's Royal Regiment. He died of wounds on the 14th October 1944 aged 38 years. Hubert had been brought up at Cockernhoe and attended Cockernhoe school. He was a keen footballer for Cockernhoe Club before the war. He was called up in December 1940 and served through the North African actions from Alamein to Tunisia until the German Afrika Corps and the Italians surrendered. He later took part in the landings at Salerno in Italy and advanced to the north east coast of Italy. Whilst at Ancona operating mortar bombs, an explosion killed a partner and gave Hubert fatal wounds. He was buried in the

Ancona Military Cemetery. He left a widow and one child. His daughter visited his grave in 1992 in company with her husband and Hubert's brother Stan aged 85 years. (Daughter Tricia).

CLARK WILLIAM. Leading Seaman in the Royal Navy. He was killed on the 27th March 1943 aged 20 years. His home was at Elmtree Avenue, Cockernhoe and he volunteered for the Navy when he was 17. He saw service on the battleship H.M.S "Warspite" and made a visit to Pearl Harbour. In 1942 he was included in a crew sent from Britain to America to man the old American aircraft carrier U.S.S. "Rio de Janeiro" which was being loaned to the Royal Navy for the protection of the Arctic convoys to Russia. Later, the ship renamed H.M.S. "Dasher" was returning from Arctic waters and, whilst off the Isle of Arran in Scotland and approaching the refit port of Greenock, was refuelling its aircraft. A high octane explosion erupted and sank the ship in four minutes, watched by eyewitnesses on the Arran shore. Of the ship's complement of 500 only 120 survived and William was one of those reported missing and later presumed dead. Relatives of the dead and missing were refused information from the War Office at the time. His parents were Mr & Mrs H. Clark. On the 50th Anniversary of the disaster, 27th March 1993, survivors attended a memorial service at the location of the incident. William's brother John was able to attend. (Sister Mary and brother John).

EWINGTON EDWARD GEORGE. Sergeant Rear Gunner in the R.A.F. He was killed on the 4th April 1944 aged 19 years. Ted was born at Tea Green, one of three brothers and he attended Cockernhoe and Offley schools. He worked for Commer Cars Luton at the time of his call-up in 1941 and this was followed by training in Lancashire and drafting to a Lancaster bomber base at Doncaster. He took part in many operations over Germany, France and the Netherlands.
On the 4th April 1944 during a heavy storm whilst on operations over Belgium, the Lancaster was struck by lightning and crashed. The crew of seven all perished, though initially Ted was posted as missing. He was buried in a military cemetery in Belgium. He was a married man. (Brother William).

ELSIE HANDLEY. Her name does not appear on the village war memorial but is on the church war memorial. Private in the A.T.S. She was killed on the 18th July 1944 aged 24 years. Elsie's home was at West End Farm, Offley where she lived with her family. After call-up into the A.T.S. as No. 830083, she was stationed at Colchester and assisted with aircraft location plotting. Early in the morning of the 18th July 1944 Elsie was at home on leave, when an R.A.F. aircraft struck the farmhouse and Elsie, her mother and her sister were all killed. The next day the incident was reported as follows:- "The ruins of a burned-out farmhouse at Offley Hertfordshire were still being searched last night for the bodies of the farmer's wife, Mrs George Handley, and their daughters Elsie aged 24 and Mary aged 36, who were killed when an R.A.F. plane crashed on the house in the morning. Mr Handley and two sons were milking cows in a shed, but they could not get near the house for the flames. It is feared that six airmen were killed. The plane, with one engine in flames, circled over Offley village before crashing. It hit some trees, then a field and ricocheted on to the farmhouse". (Brother George and an extract from the Daily Mail 19th July 1944).

HILL LEWIS ALBERT. Sergeant Pilot in the R.A.F.V.R. He was killed on the 18th October 1941 aged 22 years. He was born at Cockernhoe in 1919 and attended both Cockernhoe and Offley schools. After leaving school he was employed at Farr's Engineering and at Vauxhall Motors, Luton. He was a great cycling enthusiast prior to the war and covered hundreds of miles in the Southern Counties and North Wales with his two special mates Percy Ensbury and Doug Hodgson. In March 1939, in company with his cousin Derrick O'Flaherty, he volunteered for the R.A.F.V.R. at the Luton Flying Club. He was involved in the large scale bombing of Hitler's huge fleet of invasion barges moored at French ports in 1940, also the pinpoint bombing of the submarine bases at Brest. There were also several missions to Berlin and the cities of the Ruhr. He specialised in flying Wellington bombers and was at several air bases including R.A.F. Harwell in Berkshire and No.15 Squadron at Feltwell in Norfolk. At the time of his death he was in a rest period having completed 34 bombing operations. He was training a new pilot at the Lichfield Operational Training Unit and the accident occurred when the trainee attempted to land in gusty weather conditions. He is buried at St Thomas's Church, Stopsley. His operational log is held by his sister Vera. He left a widow and one child, Derrick. (Sister Vera and brother Norman).

HUGHES KENDRICK SALUSBURY. The son of Guy Salusbury Hughes (See Churchyard Memorial 12). He served in the R.A.F.V.R. as No.705597 and was awarded the D.F.C. in December 1942. He was a Squadron Leader with 23 Squadron flying Boston IIIs and later Mosquitoes. He was engaged in numerous sorties when based in the U.K. including to Antwerp and Caen and was transferred to Malta on the 8th June 1943. After several sorties over Sicily and Italy, he and his navigator, Sgt Clark, failed to return from intruder duty in the Rome area, having left Luqa in Malta at 2355 hrs on the 20th July 1943 in Mosquito X.HJ727. A week earlier he had flown to Tripoli and obtained German radio and signalling equipment which he later had fitted to his plane with the intention of confusing the enemy. It is possible that this may have contributed to his death. He has no known grave and is commemorated on the Memorial at Malta on Panel 6, Column 1. The Memorial is at Floriana, King's Gate, the main entrance to Valletta. He was the husband of Mrs A.G.L. Salusbury Hughes of Warsash, Hants and their children were David and Celia. He was aged 33 at the time of his death.

HUMPHRIES WILLIAM DAVID. Sapper in the Royal Engineers. He was killed on the 23rd August 1943 aged 22 years. He had volunteered for the Queen's Royal Regiment before transferring to the Royal Engineers. He had been stationed at Tea Green and was billeted with Mr & Mrs Brangwyn at the Blacksmith's house and before embarkation had married Cockernhoe girl Dorothy Brown. He served in North Africa until the surrender of the German Afrika Corps and the Italians in Tunisia in 1943. He then took part in the invasion of Sicily and was engaged in bomb disposal operations when a booby trap explosion fatally wounded him. He died the same day. His partner escaped with wounds. The Padre wrote to his widow saying that he had been buried on the side of Mount Etna but later his body was moved to the War Cemetery at Catania. (Sister-in-law Barbara).

O'FLAHERTY DERRICK EDWARD. Sergeant Pilot in the R.A.F.V.R. He was killed on the 25th October 1940 aged 21 years. His home was at Luton Road, Cockernhoe and he attended both Cockernhoe and Offley schools and later joined the Luton Boys Club for whom he played football. He was an ardent fan of Luton Town Football Club. He also took up boxing with the Luton Boys Club and was quite a good club boxer for his weight. He was employed at Farr's Engineering of Luton. He had volunteered at the Luton Flying Club in March 1939 at the same time as his cousin Lewis Hill. His training took place at Padgate and other bases in the North West of England. He was attached to Fighter Command and specialised as a day fighter bomber pilot. At the end of the "Battle of Britain" in September 1940 when the Germans switched from mass day raids to night raids, R.A.F. fighter Squadrons were quickly converted to night fighters and the Blenheim proved the best available aircraft for the new role. It was during this conversion that Derrick lost his life. Whilst landing a Blenheim fighter bomber during night flying training exercises at the Stroud Gloucestershire R.A.F. Operational Training Unit, the undercarriage of his aircraft clipped the dry stone wall which surrounded the air base and he was killed. He was buried at St Hugh's Church, Cockernhoe. (Brother Kenneth).

PILKINGTON CHARLES LESLIE. Flying Officer, R.A.F.V.R. 149 Squadron born 11th February 1922 died 11th March 1942. He was piloting a bomber which crashed on landing after a mission to Essen in Germany. His home was at Little Offley and he died at Holywell Row, Mildenhall. He was buried at Offley on the 14th March 1942 (Churchyard Memorial 239). His Squadron, 149, stationed at Mildenhall, was featured in the famous Ministry of Information film "Target for Tonight" showing Wellington bomber "F for Freddy". Most of the crews there had lost their lives by the end of the war.

PILKINGTON MARK LESLIE M.C. Captain, the Lifeguards No.76537 born 12th January 1914 died 18th November 1942. He served in Palestine, Abyssinia, Transjordan and with the Long Range Desert Groups in North Africa where he was killed (Churchyard Memorial 239) whilst using a lewis or bren gun trying to repel machine-gun fire from an Italian CR 42 fighter in Wadi Tamet 50 miles from the coast near El Ageila and Marble Arch in Tripolitania, when the Group was on its way from Kufra to Birtala, a one thousand mile journey behind enemy lines. He had been attached to the Long Range Desert Group from the Arab Legion for only one month at the time of his death. If they had not stood up to the strafing, all the patrol would have been lost. He is buried in Plot 10, Row H, Grave 3 in Tripoli War Cemetery, Libya. His wife was Susan Violet Pilkington.

ROSE FREDERICK CHARLES. Trooper in the 5th Royal Tank Regiment. He was killed on the 26th November 1941 aged 21 years. He attended Offley school and was keen on football. After leaving school he worked at a garage in Hitchin. His army number was 7932235 and he was posted to North Africa. On the 18th November 1941 General Auchinleck launched an attack codenamed "Crusader" against General Rommel for the relief of Tobruk. The battle was confused and ranged over hundreds of miles of desert and it was during this battle that Fred was killed. He has no known grave and his name appears on Column 24 of the Alamein Memorial. (Jack Claridge and Vic Mace).

SAVILLE ERNEST. Gunner in the Bedfordshire Yeomanry. He died of disease on the 7th July 1943 aged 24 years. He was born at Tea Green and attended both Cockernhoe and Offley schools. Prior to the war he worked as a gardener at Putteridge Bury. He volunteered for the Territorial Army early in 1939 together with Dick Guy another Tea Green man and with Jim Fraser. Ernie was a popular cheerful character with his Territorial mates who called him "Colonel". Their Regiment was the Bedfordshire Yeomanry No 512 Battery (T.A.) of the 148th Field Regiment Royal Artillery equipped with 25 pounders. He married shortly before sailing with the 18th Division. This Division was intended for the build up in North Africa but was diverted to Singapore when the Japanese entered the war on the 9th December 1941. They landed at Singapore on the 29th January 1942 and the surrender to the Japanese took place a fortnight later on the 15th February 1942. The whole of the 18th Division became prisoners of war and were later put to work on building the notorious Thailand-Burma railway, often known as the Railway of Death. The prisoners suffered all manner of deprivation, malnutrition, lack of medicines and medical equipment, hard labour in steaming jungles and savage treatment by their captors. He died of disease and was buried at the Tamarkan prisoner of war camp in Thailand. (Brother Horace and his service mate Jim Fraser).

WATTS RONALD. Leading Aircraftsman in the R.A.F.V.R. He died of disease on the 29th July 1945 aged 27 years. He was brought up at Offley where his father was the village blacksmith and he attended the village school. After leaving school he worked for Gibbs & Dandy of Luton who made tile surrounds for fireplaces. He was especially interested in motor cycles and cars. He volunteered for the R.A.F.V.R. shortly after the war commenced and became Leading Aircraftsman No. 1251128 and was engaged in aircraft maintenance at several bases, including one near Blackpool. He was sent to Kuala Lumpur in Malaya and was then moved to Java and, on the 19th January 1942, became a prisoner of the Japanese in Borneo. From time to time Japanese P.O.W. postcards were received from him stating that he was well and had received letters from home, although at least one card was not in his hand-writing. The record of the Japanese as captors is an indescribable catalogue of starvation, overwork in steaming jungles and ill-treatment towards their prisoners. His Certificate of Death states that he died of malaria on the 29th July 1945 at Sandakan in Borneo. This was just a fortnight before the Japanese surrendered as a result of the atomic bombs being dropped. Australian amphibious forces had been attacking Borneo from May to July 1945 and had been gradually forcing the Japanese out, but the area in which Ron was a prisoner was one of the last to be freed. He has no known grave and his name is remembered at Column 454 of the War Memorial at Singapore. He was unmarried. (Sister Joyce).

WEBB LEWIS WILLIAM. Private in the Queen's Royal Regiment. He was killed on the 26th September 1944 aged 22 years. He lived at Cockernhoe and before the war had worked for Halfords Cycles, Dunstable Road, Luton and later at Bailey's Cycles, Luton. He had been called up in 1942 to the Hertfordshire Regiment but transferred to the Queen's Royal Regiment later. In the army, he was a weapons specialist as an Assistant Armourer and was well-liked in his unit. His unit landed in Normandy on "D-Day" (6th June 1944) and fought through France, Belgium and Holland. During the Arnhem offensive, when ground troops of the 50th Division in 30 Corps were attempting to relieve the stranded Airborne units near Arnhem, he had bivouaced for the night and his cousin Ronald Fleckney was in an adjoining bivouac location. A German mortar blast killed several men including Lewis. His cousin was not hurt. Lewis is buried at the Uden Military Cemetery. Ronald took Lewis's brother Fred to Uden in 1946 and the family made a visit there in 1993. (Sisters Rita and Edna and from his cousin Ronald Fleckney).

WINCH GEORGE HAROLD. Private in the Royal Berkshire Regiment. He was killed on the 7th June 1944 aged 19 years. Harold was born at Cockernhoe, lived at Luton Road and attended both Cockernhoe and Offley schools. Before joining up he had worked for the builders, Whites of Round Green. Harold had been a member of the Cockernhoe Home Guard until he was called up, at which time he joined the Royal Berkshires. During the "D-Day" attack known as "Overlord" on the Normandy beaches on the 7th June 1944 Harold was in a landing craft when, only yards from the beach, it struck a mine causing serious casualties among the packed troops. Harold and another man were later found dead on the deck of the landing craft. His special mate, Ken Ayres, had landed earlier on a craft which was undamaged and had waited hoping that Harold would join him. After his death, his body was brought to Portsmouth and rests in the Copner Bridge Cemetery. His family make regular visits to his grave. (Brother Brian and from his service mate Ken Ayres).

Those who survived.

It has not been possible to include a reasonably accurate schedule.

Offley Village War Memorial
1993

# THE CHURCH WAR MEMORIALS

On the north side of the chancel wall are two green Westmorland slates with gold Roman lettering. Each slate is 137 cms high and 76 cms wide and they are positioned in the recess previously occupied by the organ. They were unveiled by the Lord Lieutenant of Hertfordshire, Major General Burns, on the 21st November 1969 and dedicated on the same occasion by the Vicar of St Peters, St Albans. The cost of the plaques was approximately £200 most of which was borne by David, Lord Lloyd though the Offley Branch of the British Legion contributed.

The names differ from those on the Village War Memorial in that these plaques do not mention Frederick Dyer or Henry Ernest Pearce but do mention Edward Dyer, Alfred James Smith and Elsie Handley. It seems that Frederick and Edward Dyer were one and the same person, Alfred James Smith died after the Village War Memorial had been erected and Elsie Handley (Churchyard Memorial 165) was killed in her home at West End Farm when a British bomber crashed on it. She was, however, at the time in the A.T.S. No.830083. The reason for the exclusion of Henry Ernest Pearce is not known. Other available details concerning individuals are shown earlier in this Appendix.

This information has been obtained from the following :-

Offley Parish Magazines.
Offley Parochial Church Council Minutes.
Offley Burial Registers.
Discussions with Mrs Daisy Ruffet.
Discussion with Mr Aubrey Dyer.

1st Panel

IN MEMORY OF THE
PARISHIONERS OF
OFFLEY WHO GAVE
THEIR LIVES WHILST
SERVING WITH THE
ARMED FORCES
1914-1918.
ROBERT STANLEY BIRD
HAROLD WALTER CAIN
CHARLES DAVIS
EDWARD DYER
GEORGE FREDERICK FLECKNEY
SIDNEY THOMAS FLECKNEY
CHARLES GOSLING
FREDERICK HARPER
EDWARD REGINALD
  GRAHAM HUGHES
ALBERT CHARLES MARLOW
BERTIE GEORGE MARLOW
JOHN MONK
WILLIAM HENRY MOODY
GEORGE HERBERT NEGUS
ALFRED JAMES SMITH
ALBERT JOSEPH TOMPKINS
JOE WALKER
CECIL BERNARD WILMOT

2nd Panel

IN MEMORY OF THE
PARISHIONERS OF
OFFLEY WHO GAVE
THEIR LIVES WHILST
SERVING WITH THE
ARMED FORCES
1939-1945.
HUBERT SAMUEL BUNKER
WILLIAM CLARK
EDWARD GEORGE EWINGTON
ELSIE HANDLEY
LEWIS ALBERT HILL
KENDRICK SALUSBURY HUGHES
DERRICK O'FLAHERTY
CHARLES LESLIE PILKINGTON
MARK LESLIE PILKINGTON
FREDERICK CHARLES ROSE
ERNEST SAVILLE
RONALD WATTS
LEWIS WILLIAM WEBB
HAROLD GEORGE WINCH
WILLIAM DAVID HUMPHRIES

APPENDIX "C"
OWNERS AND OCCUPANTS OF OFFLEY PLACE

(1) indicates succession at Offley Place
(1714) indicates year of marriage

**Sir JOHN SPENCER (1)** 3rd Earl
Purchased Manors of Offley St Leger & Cockernhoe in 1554 & settled on his son Richard in 1577.
d. 1586

- Sir John Spencer, 4th Earl & 1st Lord Spencer (1603) Althorpe Northants
  - Descendants in separate lines were Sir Winston Spencer Churchill & Princess Diana nee Spencer.
- Sir Thomas Spencer, Warwickshire
- Sir William Spencer, Oxfordshire
- **Sir RICHARD SPENCER (2)** Built Offley Place in 1600
  d. 1624 = Helen heir of Sir John Brocket d. 1614
  - **Sir BROCKET SPENCER (4)**
    b. 1605 = SUSANNA
    d. 1668  Daughter of Sir Nicholas Carew
             b. 1620
             d. 1692
    - **Dame Elizabeth Spencer (1677)**
      b. 1638 = Sir Humphrey
      d. 1709   Gore
      - **ELIZABETH GORE (8)**
        b. 1678 = Sir HENRY PENRICE (1714)(9) Col. Thomas Salusbury
        d. 1726  b. 1677
                 d. 1752
        Thomas Salusbury = Lucy d.1745
        d. 1714
        - **ANNA MARIA PENRICE (1751)(10)**
          b. 1718 = 1. Sir THOMAS SALUSBURY (11)
          d. 1759   b. 1707
                    d. 1773
          SARAH KING (1763)(12) = 2.
          nee BURROUGHS
          b. 1722
          d. 1804
    - **Sir RICHARD SPENCER (5)**
      b. 1647 = MARY MUSTERS
      d. 1687   2. = Sir Ralph Radcliffe
                    b. 1633
                    d. 1720
      - **Sir JOHN SPENCER (6)**
        b. 1678
        d. 1699
      - **Sir JOHN SPENCER (7)**
        b. 1645
        d. 1712
        - Spencer Penrice
          b. 1718
          d. 1739
      - Five other Sons
      - Morley Family = Samuel Burroughs
                        b. 1695
                        d. 1761
  - Another Son
  - Elizabeth Spencer
  - Alice Spencer
  - Ann Spencer
  - **Sir JOHN SPENCER (3)**
    d. 1633 = MARY ANDERSON
    - Alice Spencer = Sir James Altham
      - Mary Altham = Sir John Tufton
    - Susanna Spencer
      b.1640 = Abraham Nelson
      d.1712
    - Anne Spencer
      d.1714 = Roger Meredith
               b. 1637
               d. 1700
      - 1. Ann Percival
        2. (Welsh Wench!)
        John Salusbury
        d.1762 = Hester Maria Cotton (1739)
                 b.1706 d.1773
        - Hester Lynch Salusbury
          b. 1741 = 1. Thrale (1763) d.1781
          d. 1821   2. Piozzi d.1809
    - Alice Spencer
      d.1713 = Granado Pigott
               d. 1723
    - Norfolk Salusbury
      d.1736 = Elizabeth Williams
      - Henry Salusbury
      - Rev. Thelwall Salusbury
        b. 1803 = Ann Cecil
        Vicar of Offley
        Rector of Graveley
      - Elizabeth Salusbury = Thomas Hughes
    - Sir Robert Salusbury
      d. 1776 = Gwendoline Davis

186

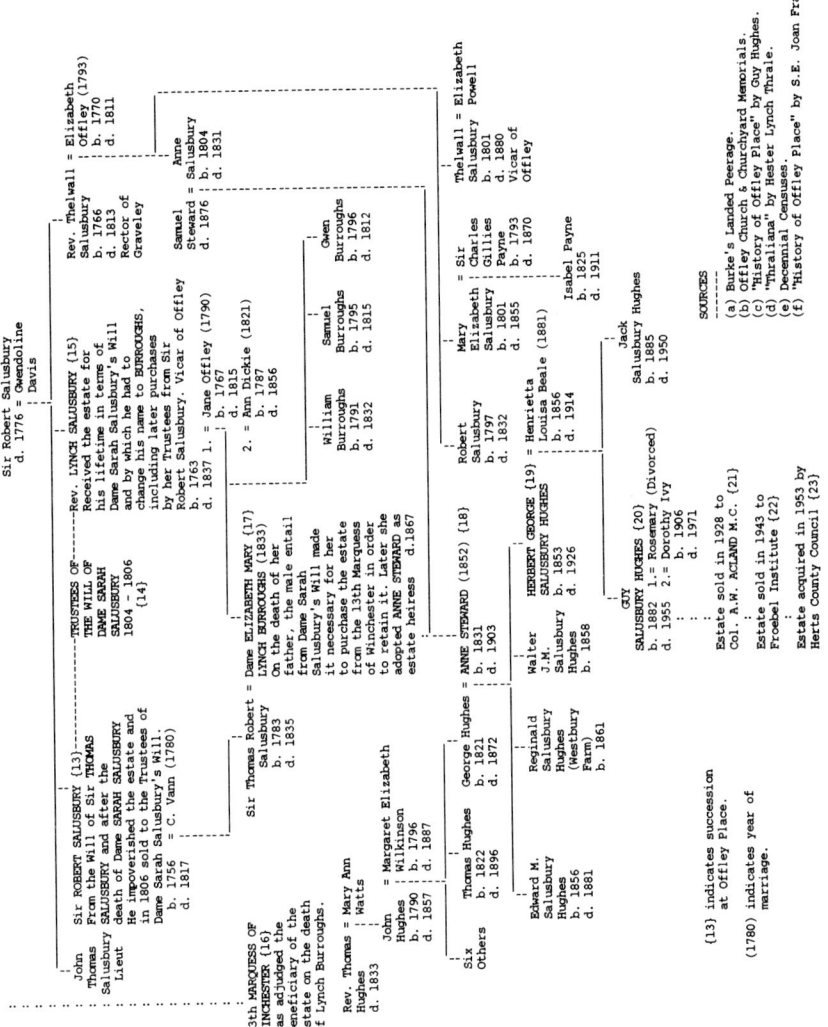

# INDEX

This Index is not exhaustive as a full version would be nearly as long as the rest of the book.

A.
Abdy, J.C.  37
Acland, Col.  79
Angels Farm  81
Allotments  77,78
Arundel, R.  25
Ashton, A.R.  32
Aspin, T.  27
Ault, G.  29
B
Badlesmere, H de  25
Baker, J.  28
Banham, P.G.  38
Bardin, J.  74
Bates, Mary  23,73
Bates, Thomas  18,70,84,121
Beale, Henrietta  51
Bells, Church  13,14
Bible, Breeches  23
Bier, Funeral  22
Birkitt Hill  66,67
Boer War  130
Bradenstoke Priory  12
Brasses, Church  13
Bull, The  73,74
Bullen family  40
Burgess, P.  101
Butcher's Shop  75
Byde, Thomas  70
C
Calleward, T.  26
Carpenters Arms  74
Chalice, small  37
Chalgrave Chauntry  12
Chamber, Eliza  15
Chancel  16,17,22,46
Chancel Gates  19
Chapel  76
Chauntrele, W.  27
Church, J  93,107
Churchyard  17
Civil War  14,15,27,28,130
Clare, F.  74
Claridge, A.W.  107,110
Clarke, C.  74
Claypits  88
Clock, Church  22
Clouds Hill  63,64,65
Clough, Dr & Mrs  78

Clubs  117,118
Clutterbuck, T.R.  62
Cock, The  73
Cockernhoe  11,22,64
Corn Rents  48
Coulton, curate  31
Cow Yard  77,93
Council Houses  69
Courtenay, J.M.  35
Cox, W.  86
Crawley, T.  86
Crawley, W.  120
Crawley's Alley  77
Curley, Mrs  99
D
Dane, T.  28,92
Dany, R.  25
Davis family  70,72,115
Day, Annie  23
Day family  107
De Hoo family  40
De la Mare, Amicia  12
De la Mare, Thomas  11
Dearman, T.  120
Delaweld, J.  26
Derman, Richard  13
Dickie, Ann  49
Dissenters  62
Dove, T.  28
E
Eagles Nest  67
Eccleshall, R. de  26
Ecu, William of  10,119
Edward I, King  39
Electricity  22,129
Eycote, R. de  26
F
Farmer, Richard  40
Fire Engine  77,97
Fires  75
Flints  88,89
Font  12
Forbes, Patrick  38
Fraser, A.  72
Friday, John  13
G
Gallery, Singing  18
Garage  87
Garden Fields  77,78

G (cont)
Gate, J. atte  26
Gate, T. atte  26
Gatty, P.E.  25,32,64,65,88
Glebe Farm  88,89
Gloucester Arms  74
Gloucester, Earl of  11,39
Gosling Ave,  79
Gosling family  58,59,118,130
Gravel, Henry de  25
Graveley  29
Great Offley House  82,83
Green Man, The  73
Grundewell, J de  25
H
Hale, C.  78
Hall family  72,75,86,125
Halliwell, T.  99
Handley family  66
Hardy, C.R.W.  31
Harley, Gertrude  98
Harold, King  7
Harrison family  51,67,72,79,82
   83,85,97,98
Hawkes, Elizabeth  46
Hawkes family  107
Heating the Church  20
Helder family  15,61
Henley, R.  27
Henry, Rev  65,32,81
Hepher, C.G.  37
Hodge, D.E.J.  36
Hoo  5
How, C.G.  35
Hudson, W.  26
Hughes, Anne  50,51
Hughes, Dorothy  23
Hughes, Edward  51
Hughes, George Edward  17,22,50,67
Hughes, Guy Salusbury  17,52,78,79
Hughes, Herbert George  51,82,128
Hughes, Reginald  51
Hughes, Thomas  50
Hughes, W.J.M.  72
Hull, W.  88
Hunters Moon  68
I
Icknield Way  4
Inclosure Acts  45,113
J
Johnston, C.E.  62
Jones, Alice  18
Jones, Gervas  30
Jordan, curate  32

K
Kidman family  18,86,88
Kings Walden  39
Knight, J.  26
L
Lake, J.  115
Lane family  18,88
Lawns, The  46,78
Lawrence family  96
Lay Subsidy Rolls  39,70
Lilley  36,39,120
Little Offley  51,61,62
Lloyd, David, Lord  23
Lloyd, George, Lord  65
Lobster Tail, The  73
Lodge  87
Lorchyn, R.  26
Loring, Sir Nigel  12
Lynham, W. de  26
Lyster, J.  26
M
Male Entail  47,49
Malolacu, H. de  25
Malpas, R.  26
Marsh family  62,82,84
Martin, K.  38
Maude, Mrs  46
Mears, C.W.  96
Mercia  5,6
Mill  88,89
Miller, Claude  22
Miller, Henry  85
Morley family  49,70
Morley, Julia  108
N
Nash, Nurse  117
Nicklin, I.  38
Nicks, J.  26
Northey, A.E.  31
Norton, J.  27
Norwico, J. de  26
Nurses  117
O
Oakley, R.  78,84,122
Offa, King  5,6
Offley family  47,48
Offley Grange  86
Offley Hoo Farm  84
Offley, W. de  26
Ogard, A. de  25
Old Post Office  76
Organ, Church  18,19,20,22,24
Orientation, Church  12
Osbaldeston, P.  28

O (cont)
Osborn, T. 29
P
Paine, A.S. 95,96
Paris, Matthew 4
Parish Council 128,129
Park family 87,99
Parochial Church Council 22
Patrons, Church 15
Penrice, Anna Maria 16,42,43,44
Penrice, Sir Henry 15,42.43
Perkyns, O. 27
Pews, Church 19
Pigott, Alice 42,91,92
Pilkington, Mrs R.H. 23,24,62,68
Plate, Church 15,16
Pond House 75,76
Prince Henry, The 74
Puttridge 70
R
Radcliffes of Hitchin 29,43,63
Read, T. 27,95,96
Recreation Club 79
Red Lion, The 74
Registers, Parish 15
Richards, A.G.G. 37
Ringer, T. 29
Riots 120,121
Road change 48
Roberts, F. 27
Ruffet, Mrs D. 52
Rufus, King 10
S
St Leger, Geoffrey de 11,39
St Leger, William 12
St Legers, Manor of 40
Salusbury, Elizabeth, Dame 49
Salusbury, Hester 16,44,45,113
Salusbury J.T. 31
Salusbury Lane 79
Salusbury, Lynch 30,46,47,48, 92,121
Salusbury, Sarah, Dame 6,17,45, 46,47,78,92
Salusbury, T.J.T. 29
Salusbury, Thomas, Sir 16,43,45
Samwell, John 13
Sawyer, J.W. 31
School 69
Senar, H. 36
Sewerage 129
Sharp, E. 95
Sheppard, Eileen 68,83
Sheppard family 62,82

Sherlock, W. 27
Shryvenham, J. de 26
Simpson's Cottages 74
Smoothey family 115
Sowdell Field 79
Spencer family 16,40,41
Stanewyk, L. de 25
Staple, The 40
Steward, Anne 50
Stigand, Archbishop 7
Stoke, J. de 25
Stratton, J. de 26
Sturgeon, A.W. 72,79
Sudyngton, T. 25
Sutton family 79
Swain, G. 73
Swift, R. 28
Sworder, J. 84
Symons family 78
T
Taylor, A.E.M. 83
Thrale, Hester 45,46
Thirnston, J. 26
Thomas, W. 28
Tower, Church 18
Transportations 121,122
Trylle, T. 26
Turner, J. 27
Tylecote Mr 67,98
V
Vestry 22
Vicarage 63,64,80,81
Village Hall 88
Vine Cottage 76
W
Walda, J. de 26
Walda, W. de 26
Walls, W. 26
Warren, E. 28
Water 128,129
Watts, H. 73
Waugh, R. 74
Well, L. de 26,48,57,58, 59,61
Wellbury 45,47,48,57,58
Wells 59,128 66
West End Farm 66
Westbury 45,70,71,72
Weston 29
Whicker, J.B. 93,94
White family 86
Whottan, T. 27
Whyte, R. 26
Wilkinson, Mary 67

W (cont)
William I, King  7
Willowes, R.  28,120
Windmill  89
Wool, buried in  15

Workhouses  48,49,68,69,88
 93,114,115,116
World War I  131,132
Wright, B.V.  87
Wulborough, J.  26

Y

Youth Club  35

# OLD REDDITCH PUBS

BY

ALAN W. FOXALL

First Published by Token Books February 2002

© Token Books. All rights reserved

ISBN 0 9542046 0 3

The author's moral right has been asserted

British Library Cataloguing-in-Publication Data. A catalogue record for this book is available from the British Library.

Whilst every effort has been made to trace ownership of illustrated material, in some cases this has not been possible. Please refer to the publisher in the event of any claims. (01527 543369)

No part of this book may be reproduced, stored in a retrieval system, or transmitted in any form or by any means, electronic, mechanical, photocopying, recording or otherwise, without prior permission of the publishers.

---

Sponsored by R.J.Saunders
**R & S Antiques**
120 Plymouth Rd. Southcrest,
Redditch, Worcs. B97 4PA
01527 544658
Established 25 years : 1977 - 2002

---

Made and printed in Great Britain by Warwick Printing Co. Ltd.
Theatre Street, Warwick CV34 4DR

# CONTENTS

Introduction. ... ... ... ... ... ... 1

Map of the Redditch District as it was before 1940. ... ... ... 2

Pubs that existed in the area from about 1830 to 1940 in alphabetical order. ... 3

Register of licensees in 1875. ... ... ... ... ... 7

Local pub signs. ... ... ... ... ... ... 9

"From Points to Pint Pots." By Ian Hayes. ... ... ... ... 10

Local Notes and Queries No. 88 - Extinct Public Houses. ... ... ... 12

Local Notes and Queries No. 34 - Crabbs Cross names. ... ... ... 13

Poetic memories of Redditch in 1840. ... ... ... ... 14

Location map of Evesham Street pubs. ... ... ... ... 15

Redditch area pubs in alphabetical order, together with their licensees, adverts, information, photographs, tokens, etc and "Pubs in the News." ... ... 16

Pub licensees names in alphabetical order. ... ... ... ... 224

Beer retailers names in alphabetical order. ... ... ... ... 244

1830 Beer Act, etc. ... ... ... ... ... ... 248

Brown's Shakespeare Brewery. ... ... ... ... ... 251

Smith and Spencer. ... ... ... ... ... ... 261

Analysis of Redditch pub and other related tokens. ... ... ... 263

Quote from the Redditch Indicator in **1894**....

"Redditch is notably a drunken, immoral town."
- according to the Temperance League.
"There are 84 public houses in our midst and we spend £42,000 per annum on intoxicating drink. That gives an average income of £500 to each licence holder."

# INTRODUCTION

The information within these pages came originally from the 'Redditch Needle District Almanack and Directory' (NDA) from 1873 to 1936. This was published every year by the Redditch Indicator Co. Ltd.

Kelly's Directories covered the years from 1850 to 1940 but were only printed every four years. The earlier date of 1835 came from Piggott's Directory, 1841 came from Bentley's Directory and 1855 from Billing's Directory.

Other sources include the 1850 Warwickshire Directory, Littlebury's Directory of Worcestershire for 1873 and the 1875 Register of Redditch Licensees.

Using more than one source of information creates its own problems such as different spelling of the same name i.e. Davis – Davies, Pinfield – Binfield, etc. Two licensees names sometimes occur for the same pub in the same year, this could be the result of different directory's publication dates or of a change of tenant. Where I have found conflicting information from two different sources i.e. Kelly's Directory and the Needle District Almanack (NDA) and have not been able to ascertain which is correct, I have included both. Errors in this book may be mine but could also be those of Victorian/Edwardian directory compilers. Other problems occur when boundaries are changed, parts of Headless Cross were once Webheath and Ipsley, parts of Webheath came under Feckenham. Before 1875 the Nevill Arms, for example, was called the 'New Inn' and was listed under Inkberrow.

During Victorian times the practice of house numbering was begun, which can be very helpful but numbers were also subject to change, the Golden Lion for example is recorded at various times as being at No. 22, 24 and 25 Red Lion St. If you combine all the above with the fact that there were four 'Bell' inns, four 'Crowns', four 'Red Lions' and many of the other pub names in the Redditch district were duplicated, you can see it was not an easy task. Even the 'Redditch Needle District Almanack' (NDA) sometimes confused the 'Woodland Cottage' in Mount Pleasant with the 'Woodbine Cottage' at Headless Cross.

The pubs are listed in alphabetical order together with their licensees, information, adverts and any available photographs. If a licensee issued 'pub tokens' these are illustrated wherever possible.

I would like to thank the Redditch Advertiser/Indicator for their permission to use the many newspaper cuttings both old and new.

I am indebted to several people for information and photographs and my thanks go especially to Ian Hayes for his article on 'Pointers' and records from Census returns, pub sales, photographs, etc. Contributions also came from Melvyn Amos, Miss Chambers, Mrs Chatwin, Maurice Clarke, Brian Collett, Phillip Coventry, Andrew Cunningham, Christine Humphreys, Chris Jackson, Philip Jarvis, Pat Lee, Peter Middleton, Miss Diana Oscroft, Ray Saunders, John Whitmore, Dave and Wendy Williams and Mike Wojczynski. Thanks also go to the Staff of Redditch Library for their help. I must also mention the great kindness and co-operation shown to me by the descendants of some of the old pub landlords.

I apologize to anyone that I have failed to mention – my only excuse is that the material in this book has been collected over a period of 20 years and I cannot now recall the source of some of it.

**Alan W Foxall**
Headless Cross 2001

# THE REDDITCH DISTRICT BEFORE 1940

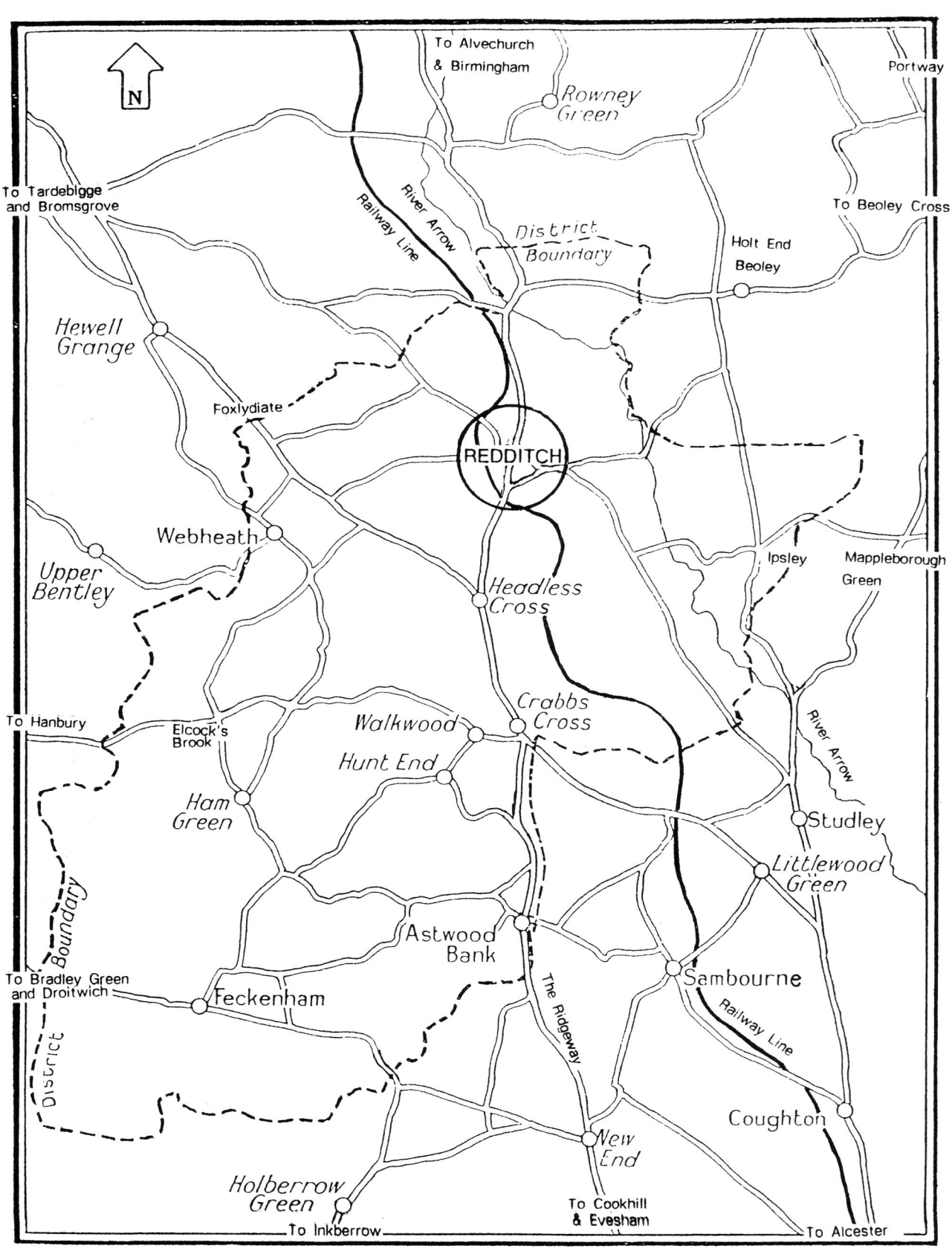

# A LIST OF PUBS IN EXISTENCE IN REDDITCH AND DISTRICT AT SOME TIME BETWEEN THE 1830's AND THE 1940's

| | |
|---|---|
| ACORN. Evesham Road, Crabbs Cross. | Redditch |
| ADAM AND EVE. Prospect Hill. | Redditch |
| ALMA TAVERN. 71/73 Ipsley Street. | Redditch |
| APPLE TREE. (Cherry Tree)? Headless Cross. | Redditch |
| | |
| BAKER'S ARMS. (Later "Oddfellow's Arms"), Foregate Street. | Astwood Bank |
| BEEHIVE. Alcester Street. | Redditch |
| BELL INN. 11 Britten Street. | Redditch |
| BELL INN. Pudding Bag Lane, (Parsons Road)? | Redditch |
| BELL INN. 163 Evesham Road, Headless Cross. | Redditch |
| BELL INN. Evesham Road. | Astwood Bank |
| BEOLEY CROSS INN. (See "Cross and Bowling Green"). | Beoley |
| BIRD IN HAND. Walford Street. | Redditch |
| BIRD IN HAND. (Later "Volunteer's Arms"), 8 George Street. | Redditch |
| BLACK BOY. Droitwich Road, Saltway. | Feckenham |
| BLACK HORSE. 6/9 Mount Pleasant. | Redditch |
| BOAT INN 9 Birchfield Road. | Redditch |
| BOWLING GREEN INN. (See "Cross and Bowling Green"). | Beoley |
| BREWER'S ARMS. 9 Bates Hill. | Redditch |
| BRISTOL INN. 16 Birchfield Road, Headless Cross. | Redditch |
| BRITANNIA INN. 35 Walford Street. | Redditch |
| BRITISH WORKMAN. Crabbs Cross. | Redditch |
| BROOK INN. Elcock's Brook, Callow Hill. | Feckenham |
| BULL'S HEAD. 77 Evesham Street. | Redditch |
| BULL'S HEAD. Wapping. | Redditch |
| | |
| CASE IS ALTERED. (Later "The Gate Hangs Well"), Headless Cross. | Redditch |
| CHERRY TREE. Steven's Row, Headless Cross. | Redditch |
| CRICKETER'S ARMS. 107/109 Beoley Road. | Redditch |
| CRICKETER'S ARMS. 87/89 Evesham Road, Headless Cross. | Redditch |
| CROSS AND BOWLING GREEN. Beoley Cross. | Beoley |
| CROSS AND CRAB TREE. Crabbs Cross. | Redditch |
| CROWN HOTEL. 18/21 Prospect Hill. | Redditch |
| CROWN INN. Crabbs Cross. | Redditch |
| CROWN INN. Feckenham Road. | Astwood Bank |
| CROWN INN. (NOT the Rose & Crown). | Feckenham |
| | |
| DOG INN. Ipsley Street. | Redditch |
| DOG AND PHEASANT. 164 Evesham Road, Headless Cross. | Redditch |
| DUKE OF YORK. (Later "Plough & Harrow"), Evesham Street. | Redditch |

| | |
|---|---:|
| EAGLE INN. 335 Evesham Road, Crabbs Cross. | Redditch |
| EIGHT BELLS. High Street. | Feckenham |
| ELBOWS (THE). Hewell Lane. | Tardebigge |
| | |
| FLEECE INN. (Earlier "Turf Tavern"), 59/61 Evesham Street. | Redditch |
| FLEECE INN. 524 Evesham Road, Crabbs Cross. | Redditch |
| FOLLY INN. Evesham Road, Headless Cross. | Redditch |
| FORESTER'S ARMS. 123/125 Evesham Road, Headless Cross. | Redditch |
| FOUNTAIN INN. 75/91 Evesham Street. | Redditch |
| FOUNTAIN INN. Ipsley Street. (Became Milward's "Washford Mills"). | Redditch |
| FOX INN. 79 Edward Street. | Redditch |
| FOX AND GOOSE. (Later "Royal Hotel"), 8 Market Place. | Redditch |
| FOX AND GOOSE. Foxlydiate. | Redditch |
| FOXLYDIATE HOTEL. Foxlydiate. | Redditch |
| | |
| GATE HANGS WELL. 154 Evesham Road, Headless Cross. | Redditch |
| GOLDEN CROSS. (See "Railway Inn"), 28/56 Unicorn Hill. | Redditch |
| GOLDEN LION. 22/24/25 Red Lion Street. | Redditch |
| GOLDEN SALMON. 133 Evesham Street. | Redditch |
| GRAPES (THE). Marsden Road. | Redditch |
| GREYHOUND INN. 1 Prospect Hill, (Church Green West). | Redditch |
| | |
| HARE AND HOUNDS. Evesham Road, Headless Cross. | Redditch |
| HART INN. George Street. | Redditch |
| HOLLYBUSH. Gorcott Hill. | Beoley |
| HORSE AND JOCKEY. 20 Evesham Street. | Redditch |
| HORSE AND JOCKEY (OLD). Ipsley Street. | Redditch |
| HUNGRY MAN. 91 Evesham Street. | Redditch |
| | |
| JUBILEE INN. 15 Edward Street. | Redditch |
| JUBILEE OAK INN. 135 Ipsley Street. | Redditch |
| | |
| KING'S ARMS. 1a Beoley Road. | Redditch |
| | |
| LAMB AND FLAG. 31/35 Unicorn Hill. | Redditch |
| LAMP TAVERN. 4 Walford Street. | Redditch |
| LORD NELSON. Church Green. | Redditch |
| LYGON ARMS. Droitwich Road, Saltway. | Feckenham |
| | |
| MAGPIE (THE). Churchyard. | Tardebigge |
| MALT SHOVEL. Corner of Evesham Street and Market Place. | Redditch |
| | |
| NAG'S HEAD. 23a/25 Alcester Street. | Redditch |
| NAVIGATION INN. Old Wharf. | Tardebigge |
| NEEDLE POINTER'S ARMS. ("Pointer's Arms"), 29/35 Evesham Street. | Redditch |
| NEVILL ARMS. New End. | Astwood Bank |
| NEW INN. (Later "Nevill Arms"), New End. | Astwood Bank |
| NEW INN. Mount Pleasant. | Redditch |

| | |
|---|---|
| ODDFELLOW'S ARMS. 8/10 Windsor Street. | Redditch |
| ODDFELLOW'S ARMS. (Previously "Baker's Arms"), Foregate Street. | Astwood Bank |
| OLD BRITON. 115 Evesham Street. | Redditch |
| OLD ROSE AND CROWN. ("Rose & Crown"), High Street. | Feckenham |

| | |
|---|---|
| PARK INN. 1 Evesham Road, Headless Cross. | Redditch |
| PLOUGH & HARROW. (Earlier "Duke of York"),161 Evesham Street. | Redditch |
| PLUMBER'S ARMS. 53 Walford Street. | Redditch |
| PLYMOUTH ARMS. Alcester Road. | Tardebigge |
| POINTER'S ARMS. (Later "Royal George"), 35 Evesham Street. | Redditch |
| PRINTER'S ARMS. 6 Evesham Street. | Redditch |

| | |
|---|---|
| QUEEN'S HEAD. 9/11 Queen Street. | Redditch |
| QUEEN'S HEAD. 148 Bromsgrove Road. | Redditch |
| QUEEN'S HEAD. Alcester Street. | Redditch |

| | |
|---|---|
| RAILWAY INN. (See "Golden Cross"), 28/56 Unicorn Hill. | Redditch |
| RAILWAY TAVERN. 45/46 Hewell Road. | Redditch |
| RED COW. Red Cow Yard,(Later Vine Street/Worcester Road). | Redditch |
| RED LION. 12/13 Red Lion Street. | Redditch |
| RED LION. Feckenham Road, Hunt End. | Redditch |
| RED LION. Church Road. | Astwood Bank |
| RED LION. Bradley Green. | Feckenham |
| RIFLEMAN INN. 35 Park Road. | Redditch |
| RISING SUN. 29 Alcester Street. | Redditch |
| ROSE AND CROWN. Heathfield Road, Webheath. | Redditch |
| ROSE AND CROWN (OLD). High Street. | Feckenham |
| ROYAL GEORGE. (Earlier "Pointer's Arms"), 35 Evesham Street. | Redditch |
| ROYAL HOTEL. (Earlier "Fox & Goose"), 8 Market Place. | Redditch |
| ROYAL OAK. Corner of Prospect Hill and Albert Street. | Redditch |
| ROYAL OAK. 533 Evesham Road, Crabbs Cross. | Redditch |

| | |
|---|---|
| SCALE AND COMPASS. 133 Birchfield Road, Headless Cross. | Redditch |
| SCOURER'S ARMS. 28 Prospect Hill. | Redditch |
| SEVEN STARS. 75 Birchfield Road, Headless Cross. | Redditch |
| SHAKESPEARE TAVERN. 34 Walford Street. | Redditch |
| SHIP (THE). (See "Royal George"), 35 Evesham Street. | Redditch |
| SPORTSMAN'S ARMS. 2 Peakman Street. | Redditch |
| STAR AND GARTER. 1 The Slough, Crabbs Cross. | Redditch |

| | |
|---|---|
| TALBOT HOTEL. (Previously "Vine Inn"), 30 Evesham Street. | Redditch |
| TARDEBIGGE (THE). | Tardebigge |
| TURF TAVERN. (See "Fleece Inn"), 59/61 Evesham Street. | Redditch |

| | |
|---|---|
| UNICORN HOTEL. 8 Unicorn Hill. | Redditch |
| UNICORN TAP. Unicorn Hill. | Redditch |

| | |
|---|---|
| VILLAGE INN. Holt End. | Beoley |
| VINE INN. (Later "Talbot Hotel"), 30 Evesham Street. | Redditch |
| VOLUNTEER'S ARMS. (Earlier "Bird in Hand"), 8 George Street. | Redditch |
| | |
| WAGGON (or WAGON) & HORSES. 14 Beoley Road. | Redditch |
| WARWICK ARMS HOTEL. Ipsley Street. | Redditch |
| WHITE HART HOTEL. 157 Evesham Road, Headless Cross. | Redditch |
| WHITE LION. 8 Red Lion Street. | Redditch |
| WHITE LION. Evesham Road. | Astwood Bank |
| WHITE SWAN. 32 Evesham Street. | Redditch |
| WHY NOT. Ridgeway. | Astwood Bank |
| WOODBINE COTTAGE. 92 Evesham Road, Headless Cross. | Redditch |
| WOODLAND COTTAGE. 42 Mount Pleasant. | Redditch |
| WOODMAN INN. Webheath. | Redditch |
| WOODMAN INN. Evesham Road. | Astwood Bank |
| | |
| YEW TREE INN. Droitwich Road, Saltway. | Feckenham |

## REGISTER OF LICENCES GRANTED IN THE DIVISION OF REDDITCH.
### SEPTEMBER 8TH, 1875

| LICENCE | NAME OF PROPERTY | NAME AND ADDRESS OF OWNER | NAME OF HOLDER OF LICENCE. |
|---|---|---|---|
| EXISE: BEER AND SPIRITS | REDLION INN, ALVECHURCH. | ESTHER HOLLIDAY, ALVECHURCH. | JOHN.ARCH.HENDERSON. |
| | SWAN INN, ALVECHURCH | REV.E.SPENCER, TAVISTOCK | HANNAH NEWBOLD |
| | HOPWOOD WHARF INN, ALVEC. | RICHARD PARKES, HOPWOOD | WM.PETTIFER. |
| | BOWLING GREEN INN. BEOLEY. | ROBERT MOLE ESQ. | JAMES READER |
| | VILLAGE INN, BEOLEY | REV.E.SPENCER, TAVISTOCK | JOHN WHITMORE |
| | LYGON ARMS INN, FECKENHAM | ELIZABETH BELLWING | GEORGE |
| | ROSE AND CROWN, FECKENHAM | CHARLES JAMES, FECKENHAM | MARTHA JAMES |
| | RED LION INN, HUNT END | REV.E.SPENCER, TAVISTOCK | JOSEPH CHAMBERS |
| | RED LION INN, ASTWOOD BANK | GEO.HOLLINGTON. ATW.BK. | WM.GOODYEAR. |
| | WHITE LION INN, " | HENRY HEMMING, " | CHARLES DAVIS |
| | NEVILLE ARMS, RIDGEWAY. | EWEL ABERGAVENNY | ROWLAND GREEN. |
| | ROSE AND CROWN, WEBHEATH | REV.E.SPENCER, TAVISTOCK | WILLIAM ANDREWS |
| | FOX AND GOOSE, FOXLYDAITE | RICHARD HEMMING, BENTLEY MANOR | JOHN SHINTON |
| | LAMB AND FLAG, REDDITCH | RICHARD DAVIS | EDITH DUNN |
| | PLOUGH AND HARROW, REDDITCH | TRUSTEES OF WHADCOAT | WILLIAM EDWARDS |
| | BELL INN, BRITTON STREET. " | MRS SARSONS, TARDEBIGGE. | EDWIN FRANCIS |
| | QUEENS HEAD, BROMSGROVE RD," | REV.E.SPENCER, TAVISTOCK | RICHARD FIELD |
| | CROWN INN, PROSPECT HILL, " | LEACROFT FREER, KINGSWINFORD | WILLIAM HOLYOAK |
| | FLEECE INN, EVESHAM ST. " | RICHARD WYERS | JOHN PINFIELD |
| | FOX AND GOOSE, CHURCH GREEN SOU. | BEN LATCHFIELD, LONDON | HUGH ROWTREE |
| | SPORTSMAN'S INN.REDDITCH | REV.E.SPENCER, TAVISTOCK | THOMAS RICKARDS |
| | GOLDEN CROSS INN, REDDITCH | FREDERICH ROBERTS | HERBERT SAMUEL |
| | UNICORN HOTEL, REDDITCH | REV.E.SPENCER, TAVISTOCK | ALFRED STINTON |
| | VINE INN, REDDITCH | MRS.T.M.BARTLEET | ANN SMITH |
| | RED LION HOTEL, REDDITCH | HERBERT SMITH | JAMES WEBB |
| | FOUNTAIN INN, REDDITCH | EMMA WHELE | JESSIE WHELE |
| | GREYHOUND INN, REDDITCH | REV.E.SPENCER, TAVISTOCK | ROBERT CROXALL |
| | HOLLY BUSH, GORCOTT HILL, BEOLEY | WM.GANDERTON, BEOLEY | WALTER JEFFERIES |
| | YEW TREE INN, FECKENHAM | JOHN ENGLISH | WM.BAKER |
| | ELCOCKS BROOK, FECKENHAM. | BEN HOPCROFT | BEN HOPCROFT |
| | FLEECE INN, CRABBS CROSS | FRED CHAMBERS | FRED CHAMBERS |
| | CROWN INN, CRABBS CROSS | THOMAS & JAMES MORRIS | RICHARD CANNADINE |
| | SEVEN STARS, HEADLESS CROSS | JOHN DUGGINS, HEADLESS CROSS | JOSEPH RALPH |
| | DOG & PHEASANT DO | ALFRED TOWNSEND, FINSTALL | FELIS CLARKE |
| | GATE HANGS WELL | MASONS ORPHANAGE, B'HAM | CHARLES EMMS |
| | SCALE & COMPASS, HEADLESS CROSS | REV.E.SPENCER, TAVISTOCK | WALTER JOHNSON |
| | RED LION, INKBERROW | JAMES ANDERSON | JAMES ANDERSON |
| | STOCKWOOD, INKBERROW | THOMAS SAVAGE | THOMAS SAVAGE |
| | BRISTOL INN, HEADLESS CROSS | JAMES THOMAS, REDDITCH | GEORGE McCLAND |
| | WOODBINE COTTAGE, DO | SAM THOMAS, REDDITCH | MARY LEYSTER |
| | WHITE LION INN, RED LION ST. | THOMAS ANDREWS | THOMAS ANDREWS |
| | HART INN, GEORGE ST. REDDITCH | MRS GIBBS, PARK ROAD | JOHN BEARD |
| | ODDFELLOWS ARMS, WINDSOR ST. | JAMES THOMAS, CLIVE ROAD | Wm.BARKER |
| | PRINTERS ARMS, EVESHAM ST. | MOSES CRANMORE | THOMAS UPTON CROW |
| | BIRD IN HAND, GEORGE STREET. | BEN CLARKE | BEN CLARKE |
| | WOODLAND COTTAGE, MOUNT PLEASANT. | TRUSTEES OF LORD WINDSOR. | SUSANNAH COOKE |
| | BREWERS ARMS, WINDSOR STREET. | HENRY IZOD | Wm.CROW |
| | WHITE SWAN, VINE STREET | ELIZ WHITE, FOXLYDAITE | ANN DUGGINS |
| | CRICKETORS ARMS, BEOLEY RD. | JAMES WEBB | THOMAS FOURT |
| | BEEHIVE INN, ALCESTER STREET | EDMUND FREE | EDMUND FREE |
| | RAILWAY TAVERN, HEWELL RD. | RICHARD HARVINSON, THE CEDAS | Wm.HOLLINGTON |
| | KINGS ARMS, BREEDON | JOHN FIELD, ALVECHURCH | JOSEPH HOLLINGTON. |
| | OLD BRITTON, EVESHAM STREET | GEO.WHITEHOUSE, BIRMINGHAM. | DAVID HOUGHTON |
| | THE ALMA, IPSLEY STREET. | JOSEPH SKINNER | Wm.HODGETTS |
| | BRITTANIA INN, WALFORD STREET | CHARLES FIELD, LITTLEWORTHS. | PETER HUNTLEY |
| | GOLDEN SALMON, EVESHAM STREET | Wm.WEBB | RUBEN MILLS |
| | SHAKESPERE TAVERN, WALFORD ST. | BEN BROWN | SAMUEL MILLWARD |
| | THE LAMP TAVERN, WALFORD ST. | MRS MILLS, ALCESTER ST. | GEO.RICKARDS |
| | RIFLEMAN INN, PARK ROAD. | ISAAC BROOKS. | JAMES RUDGE. |
| | ROYAL GEORGE, EVESHAM ST. | Wm.GIBBS | JOHN STEWARD |
| | HORSE AND JOCKEY. EVESHAM ST. | THOMAS WALFORD, BIRMINGHAM | HELEN SMITH |
| | NAGS HEAD, ALCESTER STREET. | Wm.BENNETT, ALCESTER STREET. | JANE WARDLE |
| | BIRD IN HAND, WALFORD STREET | CATHERINE BALLARD | JOHN WRIGHT. |

# REGISTER OF LICENCES GRANTED IN THE DIVISION OF REDDITCH – September 8th 1875

The surprising element of this list is the fact that the Reverend Edward Spencer of Tavistock, a town on the edge of Dartmoor, should be named as the owner of the following nine local pubs ......

| | | |
|---|---|---|
| Swan Inn, Alvechurch. | Village Inn, Beoley. | Red Lion, Hunt End. |
| Sportsman's Arms. | Greyhound Inn. | Rose & Crown, Webheath. |
| Unicorn Hotel. | Queen's Head, Bromsgrove Rd. | Scale & Compass. |

All becomes clear when it is revealed that he was related to the Mitchell's family. The firm of Henry Mitchell & Co. Ltd, Cape Hill Brewery, Birmingham later became Mitchells and Butlers Brewers of Birmingham.

Reproduced below is part of a page from the history of "Tavistock School : the First Thousand Years," by G Woodcock, 1978. The Reverend Edward Spencer MA died on December 12th. 1905 and is buried in Tavistock.

### 58    *Tavistock School: the First Thousand Years*

firm information. It was mainly on this ground that, in American terms, the "favorite son" was defeated, and Edward Spencer came from nowhere, walked right through the field, and got the job.

The Rev. Edward Spencer, who, in spite of ducal reservations about employing a parson, became the tenth master in succession to be in Orders, was thirty-six years old at the time of his appointment. Born in Middlesex, and schooled principally in France, he graduated from Paris in 1839 and from Cambridge in 1843. Four years as a Fellow of Sidney Sussex College, during which he was ordained, were followed by an Assistant Mastership at Fleetwood School and a chaplaincy to the Earl of Ellesmere. He took up the Tavistock appointment in January 1854; he was to hold it for thirty-five years. And in spite of a recurrent hypochondria, he was to live to the age of eighty-seven.

Spencer saw the key to the future development of the School in the curriculum. Soon after his arrival he introduced French, and by 1856 twenty-eight of the thirty-eight boys in the School were learning it. Some science and book-keeping were also introduced. When a prospectus was prepared in the 1860s, Spencer could write: "In addition to the usual English, Classical, and Mathematical Studies, the School Course includes French, Drawing, Drilling, and Lectures (Practical and Theoretical) on the Physical Sciences." The "drilling" had begun in 1860 when the Headmaster, deeply involved in the formation of the Tavistock branch of the Volunteer Movement which grew up at that time, employed a Corporal May of the 22nd Devon Volunteers, to teach drill.

# PUB SIGNS

The origin of pub signs dates back to Roman times when a leafy bush was hung outside the refreshment stops along Roman roads. If the hostelry had a room for gaming, then a checker-board would also be hung outside. This is the origin of the words 'Exchequer' and 'Cheque' ~ the word 'Inn' comes from the Saxon word for a public room. Since then pubs have had many uses in addition to providing rest and refreshment, such as courts, post offices, doctor's surgeries, theatres, etc. The 'Big Room' in the Red Lion, Red Lion St., Redditch, is a good example of this.

# FROM POINTS TO PINT POTS

> Extracts from an article by Ian Hayes concerning needle pointers who maybe, contrary to local legend, did not die young but became pub landlords instead. Originally published in the 'Worcestershire Industrial Archaeology Society' newsletter.

"There draws the grinder his labourious breath,
there, coughing at his deadly trade, he bends.
Born to die young, he fears no man, nor death.
Scorning the future, what he earns he spends."

The needlepointers of the Arrow Valley were, with some reason, prone to discontent. However, one dispute at least, the long strike of 1846 had a strong 'Luddite' theme, the operatives being anxious that there should be no easing of conditions in case this affected their income. In fact over the months when the machinery was idle, the proprietors were able to install extractor fans, and these were eventually accepted by the pointers. There was an immediate increase in life expectancy for the workers involved and this is illustrated by the fact that many were able to take up another occupation in later life.

An analysis of the 1851 census shows that, in the Redditch and Alvechurch area there were 57 people specifically described as pointers. It is likely that this is a fairly true total as most were proud of their status and would declare their trade as 'pointer' rather than 'needle maker.' Of the total only 10 were less than 20 years of age and by inference most of the remainder would have experienced conditions prior to the 1846 dispute. It is also significant that in a calling where the expectation of life was short, 27 of the total were over 30 years of age.

One census entry has particular relevance and interest, that of Samuel Brown, aged 29, who was not only a pointer but also sold beer on Chapel Green. By the nature of their dangerous occupation, pointers developed a huge thirst. A comparison between the names of the pointers and of Redditch pub landlords produces more examples of the 'points to pints' theme. For instance, William Cox of Headless Cross, pointer, who was landlord of the White Hart from 1850 to 64 when he died or retired at the age of 46.

It is, however, in the unravelling of the convoluted story of the Evesham Street pubs, where changes of owner, landlord, and even name took place frequently in the mid nineteenth century, that a look at some pointers, their families and their involvement in the licensed trade, helps to solve at least part of the puzzle.

## The Crow Family.

Thomas Crow, 43, needle pointer, his wife, Elizabeth, three sons including Thomas junior, also a pointer aged 17, two daughters, James Mills, a lodger, also a pointer and Ann Sanders, a servant, lived on the east side of Evesham Street, next to Benjamin Brown, maltster.

Thomas senior was listed in 1850, 1855 and 1860 as a 'beer seller,' the premises being dignified by the title 'Turf Tavern' in 1855. By 1861 the establishment, now called the 'Fleece Inn,' was occupied by James Oakley and the Crow family had moved elsewhere. However, Thomas junior (Thomas Upton Crow) reappeared in 1868 as landlord of the 'Printer's Arms' a licensed house leased by Moses Cranmore who had established a large store next door, on the corner of Evesham Street and Unicorn Hill. Thomas, who gave his age as 37 in 1871, remained as landlord until 1878 when he was suceeded by Mrs Rachel Crow, (presumably his wife).

Thomas senior and Thomas junior seem to have lived at least to the ages of 52 and 44 respectively, reasonably long life spans for pointers.

# George Mustin.

> "Right well I remember one day last December
> I called at George Mustin's bar for a drain ......"

The opening lines of a short poem commemorating the building of the Evesham Railway in 1866 immortalised George, who first appears in 1851 as a needle pointer, aged 33 with his wife Emma, 25 and two children in Albert Street. At this time a John Bryan, aged 49, was running a hair dressing business in Evesham Street, on the east side twelve doors north (towards Birmingham) of the Crow's 'Turf Tavern.' By 1855 he had decided to diversify and opened the uniquely named 'Needle Pointer's Arms' with facilities for both hairdressing and the sale of beer. (This sort of thing is not unknown in Redditch; the Rising Sun in Alcester Street rented a room to a hairdresser until the 1960's). John Bryan carried on until 1860 when the premises were occupied by George Mustin, who dispensed with the hairdressing side and then remained in business until he died in about 1869. His age at 51, would again have been a reasonable one for a pointer. By 1871 Emma Mustin (widow) aged 44 had taken over a property about 20 doors away, the other side of the Turf/Fleece which she developed into the more up market 'Fountain Inn.' The Pointer's Arms, meanwhile had become the 'Royal George,' the landlord was John Holbeche, son of a Rowney Green farmer and the pub remained a licensed house until about 1936. It survived as a tiny, single-fronted shop (Rainscourt's) until about 1970.

Emma Whele (nee Mustin) went from strength to strength, owning the Fountain and marrying the landlord, Jesse Whele, who had moved from Birmingham and was some 22 years younger than herself.

One final twist to the tale – Joseph Duggins, a needle pointer, took over the 'White Swan,' almost opposite the Royal George and held it as landlord from 1867 being succeeded by his widow Ann in 1873. Jesse Whele, on the decease of his wife, Emma, purchased various pubs in Redditch including the White Swan. This is only part of the Evesham Street story, for instance, John Holbeche moved to the Fleece Inn briefly, leaving his successor at the Royal George, John Steward to go into liquidation. John Holbeche then went on to occupy and in at least two cases own, pubs in Feckenham and Astwood Bank, before he died at the Rose and Crown, Portway in 1899, aged 58. However, he was not a pointer.

This brief examination shows, if nothing else, that if needle pointers could pull out of the trade before too late they still had some expectation from life. In the 1850's an automatic pointing machine was invented and tradition has it that the first one was purchased by the pointers and smashed on Chapel Green. However, by the 1870's the needle pointer was almost a thing of the past. A modified pointer's tram was retained for special orders involving high grade polishing and two of these, heavily protected, were certainly in use for finishing surgical needles at Showell's factory as late as 1984. Today the 'dry grinders' and indeed most of their pubs, are only a memory.

**Ian Hayes.**

# "LOCAL NOTES AND QUERIES" – No. 88.

> The series of articles entitled 'Local Notes and Queries' that appeared in the Redditch Indicator in the 1880's has been a mine of information on old pubs. Most of the articles had a local history theme and many were recollections of earlier times. No. 88 'Extinct Public Houses' is reproduced here in full – excerpts from it and others will appear where appropriate in the text.

### 88.—EXTINCT PUBLIC HOUSES.

It will be remembered by the readers of these columns that in Joseph Monks's account of the "state of the buildings in Redditch in 1776" only four inns were mentioned as being then in existence. These were the *Unicorn*, the *Horse and Jockey*, the *Fox and Goose*, and the *Crown*. Since that time many have sprung up, some of which have died a natural death, while others survive to the present day; and the non-existence of a number of those that are missing is owing to the transfer to the magistrates, in 1868, of an authority that had previously been in the hands of the excise.

Of the extinct public houses of Redditch I will first mention the *Royal Oak*. This was an old part-timbered house, standing at the corner of what is now Albert Street, but was formerly a fore-draught leading to a brickyard. The *Royal Oak* stood with its gable facing "Fish Hill," as that ascent into Redditch was then called, but was so much below the level of the ground that you had to descend two or three steps on entering, and the window sills in Albert Street were almost flush with the ground. Adjoining the inn was a blacksmith's shop, for William Gardner, the last landlord, carried on the calling of Tubal Cain as well as that of Gaius. He was not successful in either at Redditch; but after he left the town succeeded well as a worker in iron.

The earliest landlord of whom I have any account was "Tommy" Green—

A short squab man in an old drab suit,
Half of him waistcoat, and half top boot.

The house once did a flourishing trade amongst the old pointers from the Forge, but in later days the *Royal Oak* went to decay and was at last pulled down to make room for the enlargements which were constantly taking place at the British Needle Mills. I have heard the *Royal Oak* spoken of as a house where everything was very good, "the dominoes were solid brass." (F.K.)

The *Adam and Eve* was a name sometimes heard applied to a house kept by Benjamin Clark, but its sign bore no name save that of the landlord. It is now a private house, viz., the three storey one nearly opposite to the offices of Mr. Kerwood, solicitor.

The *Lord Nelson* was one of the houses condemned in 1868. It was next door to the house now inhabited by Mr. W. Jefferies, our ex-parish constable. The earliest landlord of whom I have as yet heard, was a Mr. Johns, from Morton Baggot. He was one of those who opposed the enclosure of the common about that village, and got into some trouble by taking unlawful steps to defend what he believed to be the rights of the poor.

It was a general belief at Morton Baggot that there were once in the church some stone tablets recording privileges granted to the villagers over the land called Morton Common, and that these stones were, by self-interested parties, taken down and used for paving the church. Accordingly Mr. Johns, being determined to leave no stone unturned to establish the rights of his neighbours over the common, got into the church and commenced taking up and examining the stones of the flooring. As he had not the authority of the churchwardens or the archdeacon, his work was arrested as well as himself, but whether any special penalty was inflicted upon him my informant could not tell. (H.R.) After the death of Mr. Johns his widow kept the house till it was closed under the "sweeping Licensing Act," of 1868, "because the landlady kept a dog that barked at the police" was the reason given to me.

The *Malt Shovel* stood where Mr. Mousley's chemist's shop now stands. The landlord was a Thomas Fowkes not the celebrated "Tommy," nor yet the stalwart Thomas Fowkes, the local preacher, who being challenged by Turpin Wright, fought a friendly "twirtle" with him on the Church Green and punished him severely, but a person who carried on the joint business of inn-keeping and nailing, hence the name of the inn.

The *Red Cow* stood in the Red Cow Yard, now the top of Worcester Road. It was kept by a Mr. Smallwood, and later on by his widow. From all accounts that have reached me this house was by no means a model one. In addition to ale and beer a strong concoction was sold there at one shilling a quart, called "Black Strap," and I meet with a person sometimes who tells me of strange orgies that were carried on there in early days. (F.K.)

The *Bull's Head*, now the Temperance Hotel, in Evesham Street, was formerly kept by James Avery, who combined the trades of inn-keeping and needle-making.

The *Duke of York* stood at the junction of the "Front" and the "Back Hills," and the site now occupied by the *Plough and Harrow* was the garden in front of it. On each side of the gate stood a yew tree, and thence a path led to the front door. It was formerly kept by a landlord of the name of Shrimpton, who cut his throat, but did not succeed in killing himself. Afterwards Mr. Richard Field kept the house.

The *Bell Inn*, kept by David Mole, was at the corner of a little "pudding bag" street and not far removed from being opposite to the *Woodland Cottage*. It has been described to me by one who as a youth knew the house well, as a place for unlimited drinking and gambling. On one occasion a company met together there and determined to literally "strip" one of their neighbours from "Boney's Island." So cleverly did they play their cards that this man was soon fleeced of all his money. They next, in order to carry out their resolution, proposed to him that he should stake his coat. This he agreed to, and of course soon lost it. The waistcoat was next staked and lost, and so on with the other garments, until at last the man was reduced to the outward condition of Adam before the fall. In order, however, to enable him to reach home they lent him his clothing for the occasion, and gratified at having succeeded in carrying out their intention, supplied him liberally with internal comforts as well as external necessaries. With David Mole the *Bell Inn* also died, and probably, not "deeply lamented" by the neighbours.

The *Cherry Tree*, kept by old Richard Pinfield ("Old Dick"), a fruiterer, took its name from the cherry tree growing in front. The house stood on the site now occupied by the two cottages erected by the late Mr. William Adams, at Headless Cross, and was virtually the last house in Stevens' Row. "Old Dick" wore a smock frock and bore the character of not being a very amiable man in his household. In the old days of the inns mentioned in this article gambling was a very ordinary amusement, and my informant tells me that he has known a man lose on a Saturday night, not only his money, but the grocery, etc., which he had been buying for the forthcoming week. The *Cherry Tree* was afterwards used as a Mormonite meeting house.

Of the old *White Hart* it will be sufficient to say that it stood back from the road where the stabling of the present *White Hart* stands, and was a favourite resort of the local boxers.

Further on towards Crabbs Cross was the *Hare and Hounds* kept by a Mr. Thomas Charman, and about a stone's throw from this was the *Folly*, a cottage inn, brick built, but roofed with thatch, and kept by James Millward, who also did a little needle selling, travelling with a small cart drawn by two dogs in the days when such means of conveyance was permitted. James Millward, as an innkeeper, was said to have been an eccentric man, usually seen in shirt-sleeves, and wearing one of the old square-made brown paper caps now rarely met with. C.C.C.

# LOCAL NOTES AND QUERIES

Giving the origins of some Crabbs Cross names these articles appeared in the Redditch Indicator in July 1886. They were part of a series.

### No. 30.—BONEY'S ISLAND.
#### Section I. ORIGIN OF THE NAME.

After asking many persons why the above term was applied to Crabbs Cross, I have found the general opinion to be that it was on account of this spot being a favourite locality for fights of every description some forty or fifty years ago.

In truth the selection of Crabbs Cross as the scene of "fistic" and other encounters was a judicious one, for being situated upon the borders of two counties, there was little probability that the sport would be stopped for long, a change of ground from the one county into the other placing the combatants out of the jurisdiction of the local magistrates of the one left by them. Redditch was not then a Petty Sessional Division, and there was no justice of the peace holding a commission for both counties.

The prize fights were for the most part between men of no very high position as pugilists, those names I have been able to collect being "Nobby Clark," "Tom Paddock," "Ben Terry," "Jimmy from Town," and such like. Some fights on Boney's Island, however, attracted crowds of spectators, and on the occasion when "Milky" was to fight some opponent whose name has not yet transpired, my informant tells me that he walked from the Island through a double row of vehicles extending as far as the Duke of York, or, as we should now say, the Plough and Harrow. On this occasion the sport was interrupted by Col. Clive for the one county, and Sir Francis Goodricke for the other, and the combatants had to make their way into distant parts.

Between local non-professional men there were fights without number, such as those between Stiler and the "Nutman," "Jimmy Skimpton" and "Bocker Duggins," et alii. Some fights were whimsical enough in their object ; a Charles James wanted an apprentice, and Harry Lewis* and Mobley met to try which was the better man to learn pointing. The battle-field for these friendly encounters was usually the old sand pit at the back of the cottages yet standing between the Alcester and Evesham highways.

Of the old bull-baiting days at Boney's Island, I have been able to learn little. Two of the Stevens family, however, are spoken of as taking a great interest in the sport, and George Wells, who lived in a loft forming part of Stiler's cottage, was the "berrard." One remarkable occurrence at a bull-baiting I have, however, heard related. A cripple had come on his crutches to enjoy the diversion, in the course of which the bull suddenly broke loose. The spectators fled panic stricken, and amongst them the cripple, who threw down his crutches and ran for his life. The fright cured him, and history furnishes us with many such instances of the effect of fear.

Cock fighting was another favourite pastime at Boney's Island, and there are many living who can point out the site of the cock-pit, and give the names of those who were its "main" supporters. Shooting at cocks at holiday times (Shrove Tuesday being the proper day) took place on the spot where Mr. Coleman's cottages stand now ; and this was also the favourite place for the game of pitch and hustle on Sunday mornings. From its proximity to the high road, and its commanding position, it was the spot chosen by "Nail" (Cornelius) Stiler and his companions from which to chaff and annoy old Ben Lilly and other Ranter preachers on their way to meeting in Morris's carpenter's shop. Keeping up the character of Boney's Island for fighting, the Ranter preachers took possession of the same spot for their camp, and retaliated by attacking the enemy in his stronghold.

From the foregoing remarks it will seem pretty clear that the nickname Boney's Island was derived from its inhabitants having the same propensities as the "Old Boney." Apart from this reason the name would have little meaning, for Bonaparte must have had a strong dislike to islands. Our country was the cause of his overthrow, Elba was the scene of his exile, and St. Helena that of his imprisonment and death.

J. M. WOODWARD.

* "Drowned upright" a few years ago in Mr. Coleman's fishpond.

(To be continued.)

### No. 34.—BONEY'S ISLAND.
[SECTION II.]

Having in the former section given the derivation of the nickname from the customs of the "islanders" I purpose now to mention some of the dwellings and the character of the inhabitants of them, beginning with the cottage of Nanny Sanders, the poultry dealer of the district. Her dwelling, an old thatched one, stood on the right hand side of the road, on the rise, as you go towards Astwood Bank, and here she used to sit at her door plucking fowl to sell to the needle "masters ;" the term "manufacturer" being then little used. By her cottage stood an old oak tree (lately cut down) in the branches of which her son used occasionally to "roost" when the cottage door was shut upon him. The cottage itself was burnt down some thirty years ago, as also was that of Mr. Knight on the opposite side of the road, and later on his wood yard also took fire and was destroyed. Some time before the latter calamity an adventurer, a saddler by trade, had taken up his abode in a cottage near to the Wesleyan Chapel. He had formed an acquaintance with Mr. Knight, and feeling acutely the great loss which had befallen his friend, drew up a statement of the circumstances and called upon persons in the neighbourhood for subscriptions. Amongst others the late Baroness Windsor gave a donation of £3 and a very fair sum of money was collected. The saddler did not pay this over to his friend as it came in, but duly informed him of the amounts, and said that he would hand it over in a lump. An invitation supper was prepared by Mr. Knight for this occasion, and at the close of the eating and drinking, the saddler said that he had not brought the sum with him but would step home and return with it in a few minutes. He left the room, and after that neither he nor the money was ever more seen in Crabbs Cross.

Returning to the right hand side of the road, the half-timbered cottage where James Hill lived comes next. This (now the dwelling of Mrs. Mogg) is one of better build than the preceding, being chiefly brick but partly of stone. Of this cottage, with the sandpit at the back, James Hill had the freehold, and he supplied sand for the building of the new castle at Studley, and thereby " hangs a tale."

Carpenter Morris had just then built the *Crown* on the triangular piece of waste at the fork of the Alcester and Evesham highways, the first house opened in the neighbourhood under the Beerhouses Act, and one which shows itself to be the work of a man who had gathered his materials together by degrees. In this house James Hill, thinking that he had a gold mine instead of a sandpit, would sit from morning to night drinking and making others drink. As each load of sand went off he called for more beer—

"Here, landlord, fill these pots again
And stick it to my score,
My cart will soon be here, and then
We'll drink to *one load more.*"

So day by day, and week by week,
As it went by the door,
As long as he had strength to speak,
He drank to *one load more!*

There is a saying "as dry as sand," and perhaps James Hill thought that it required "wetting." The result of this folly was, however, that in course of time he drank up his sandpit, cart, horses, barrows, etc., and the whole of his freehold !

There are several families of the name of Hill at Crabbs Cross at the present day, but the James Hill here spoken of was in no way connected with any of them, as I am assured by my informant.

And here, perhaps, a few words may be said of the public houses, past and present. Tradition names the old half-timbered cottage (formerly Stiler's, now the residence of Mr. T. Hunt) as having been a licensed house by the sign of the *Cross and Crab Tree*, and if this be true, it throws some light upon the derivation of the proper name of "Boney's Island"—Crabbs Cross, or as formerly written "Crab Crosse." The *Crown* (now extinct) has already been mentioned. The *Royal Oak* was formerly to be found on the opposite side of the road to where the sign is now, and when removed, another landlord re-opened the old beerhouse and called it the *Acorn,* facetiously remarking "that it had dropped from the *Oak.*" The *Royal Oak* sign, with a somewhat disproportionate King Charles (with his crown on!) partly seen through the foliage, is now in front of a half-timbered house, oftener spoken of as "the Old Workhouse," rather however from the number of families living in it then, than from any legitimate reason.

The *Eagle* is of too recent establishment to have any history pertaining to old Crabbs Cross, and so the *Star and Garter* alone remains to be spoken of. This house is the oldest licensed inn in the place, and is connected with many events in the history of the "island." Here the Princess Victoria halted horses on her way to Hewell Grange, and probably some of King Charles's troopers emptied black jacks before they were reviewed by His Majesty "near Crab Crosse," on their march to the siege of Hawkesley House.

J. M. WOODWARD.

# Redditch pubs in 1840 from a poem by 'an old Fish Hill boy.'

(Reproduced here, only in part, as it runs to 72 verses).

## A MEDLEY. FROM RECOLLECTIONS OF REDDITCH FIFTY YEARS AGO.

*July 5/90*

### BY AN OLD FISH HILL BOY.

Full fifty years are past and flown,
How short it seems, since I alone
Reluctant, went up Evesham Street,
Schoolmaster Tomlinson to meet.

I think I see his stately gait,
His swarthy face when I was late,
The desk, the cane, the rule of three,
Through all these years come back to me.

The town can boast of many men
Who once were under Henry's ken,
Some now who still among us roam,
Some gathered to their last long home.

'Twas then the chapel on the Green,
Not St. Stephen's modern mien,
Then Parson Clayton at its head,
Who us rough country bumpkins led.

Dissenters, too, they play'd their parts,
Breedon and Wapping their resorts,
From these sprang men of goodly fame,
Let's not forget J. Reading's name.

There then was Cooper Freeman's shop,
Who fired his barrels from the top,
Out in the street he toiled away,
From school to watch I'd often stay.

Draper Collier's corner shop,
Milkman Hathaway's white smock frock,
Ricketts's golden canister,
✱ The Unicorn steps and balusters.

On the Green liv'd Tailor Duggins,
Near Now road dwelt old John Buggins,
Next door to him was Henry Avery,
A spot that's now become so savoury.

A mighty man was Salter Allday,
The constable with powerful sway,
His name could soothe the savage breast,
His ash-plant "warm," I must confess.

Who can forget old Richard Hill,
Town crier, residing down Fish Hill,
His shrill small voice, when crying tripe
A caution was, on Saturday night.

Richard Humphries, the driver bold,
Took us by coach, Brum to behold,
He crack'd his whip for many years,
His coach is gone, let's shed no tears.

✱ Round and round went the Fountain horse,
A steady walk on a circular course,
I've gazed at him on many a day,
Poor brute, why did'nt he run away.

✱ The Malt Shovel kept by Billy Bray,
A jocund fellow in his day,
He said he hoped they'd lay him where
He still could hear the "fun of the fair."

Lawyer Gardner liv'd above the Hole,
Why he did so I've never been told,
Opposite was Dame Cutler's school,
I went there, so I'm no fool.

Boey Wilks had donkeys and cart,
Laden they'd up Fish Hill go smart,
One day from him a colt I bought
For two and-six, 'twas just worth nought.

What wicked men the pointers were,
To drink and curse and fight and swear,
A short and merry life they'd lead,
And of the future take no heed.

Hard times were those for folks who'd work
Twelve hours a day, one could'nt shirk,
The bell was rung and you must hear,
Or the "sack" you'd get first pay day near.

Saturdays brought them no enjoyment,
They stay'd till six at their employment,
Boys and girls of eight, nine, and ten,
Toed the mark with women and men.

Village stampers brought their packets,
Hung in wallets behind their jackets,
With ninety thousand on heel and toe,
'Twas a hardish walk from Crowder's Row.

✱ Printer Bromley close to the Crown,
A singer was of good renown,
Printer Heming, an agreeable man
The *Indicator* first began.

✱ Joseph Davis, host of the Crown,
As civil a man as any in town,
His chestnut mare the lightning struck it,
Over it fell, and "kicked the bucket."

Saddler Davis and Grocer Gibbs,
Tailor Palmer and Butcher Briggs,
With Widow Smith, who sold us sweets,
All were neighbours in Evesham Street.

A church going man was Joseph Hill,
Who lived for years at the old Forge Mill,
So was honest Currier White,
Who went on Sundays morn and night.

✱ George Smallwood kept the Old Red Cow,
Where hilly Worcester Road is now,
Just below, was Littleworth walk,
The Rack-hill fields were not far off.

Woodman Jarvis up Brock-hill Lane,
By Mrs. Twigg's—oh, twigg the name,
Beyond we fished in "Tarbic" cut,
Used pins for hooks, and cotton for gut.

Jolly's wagon was a jolly sight,
Jollily laden with a jolly freight,
Us boys used to think it jolly fun
When Jolly's horses began to run.

A funny fool once on the Green,
Ask'd what was the thinnest thing he'd seen,
He answer'd himself, and said no doubt
'Twas a "pennoth" of cheese from Tommy Fowkes.

Tommy was there, and heard it said,
He must have thought that clown ill bred,
Tommy, however, didn't seem teaz'd,
For the truth was told of that piece of cheese.

Mr. Osborne then seem'd to be "mayor,"
At every meeting he took the chair,
A business man, schoolmaster too,
Would square a matter 'twixt me and you.

Master Huins, both honest and good,
He often in the pulpit stood,
A patriarch of ancient days,
Warn'd us to shun all evil ways.

Old Mister Parr at the Paper Mill
Had many sons, and one's there still,
His men 'twas said they came from Kent,
And often on tramp for work they went.

Old Anthony Spragg, he swept the Green
On Saturday nights where the stalls had been,
Folks used to say that Anthony found
Among his sweepings many a pound.

✱ Barber Haden and Barber Bryan,
Which was best you'd got to try "em,"
They'd rig you up in a straight-back'd chair,
And charge a penny to cut your hair.

✱ The Red Lion Room was our Guildhall
For occasional parties, it held us all,
Dinners and dances were held therein,
A ticket we'd buy and then go in.

In harden aprons and paper caps
The scourers look'd such funny chaps,
Blue-pointers dress'd like other men,
For they were thought quite gentlemen.

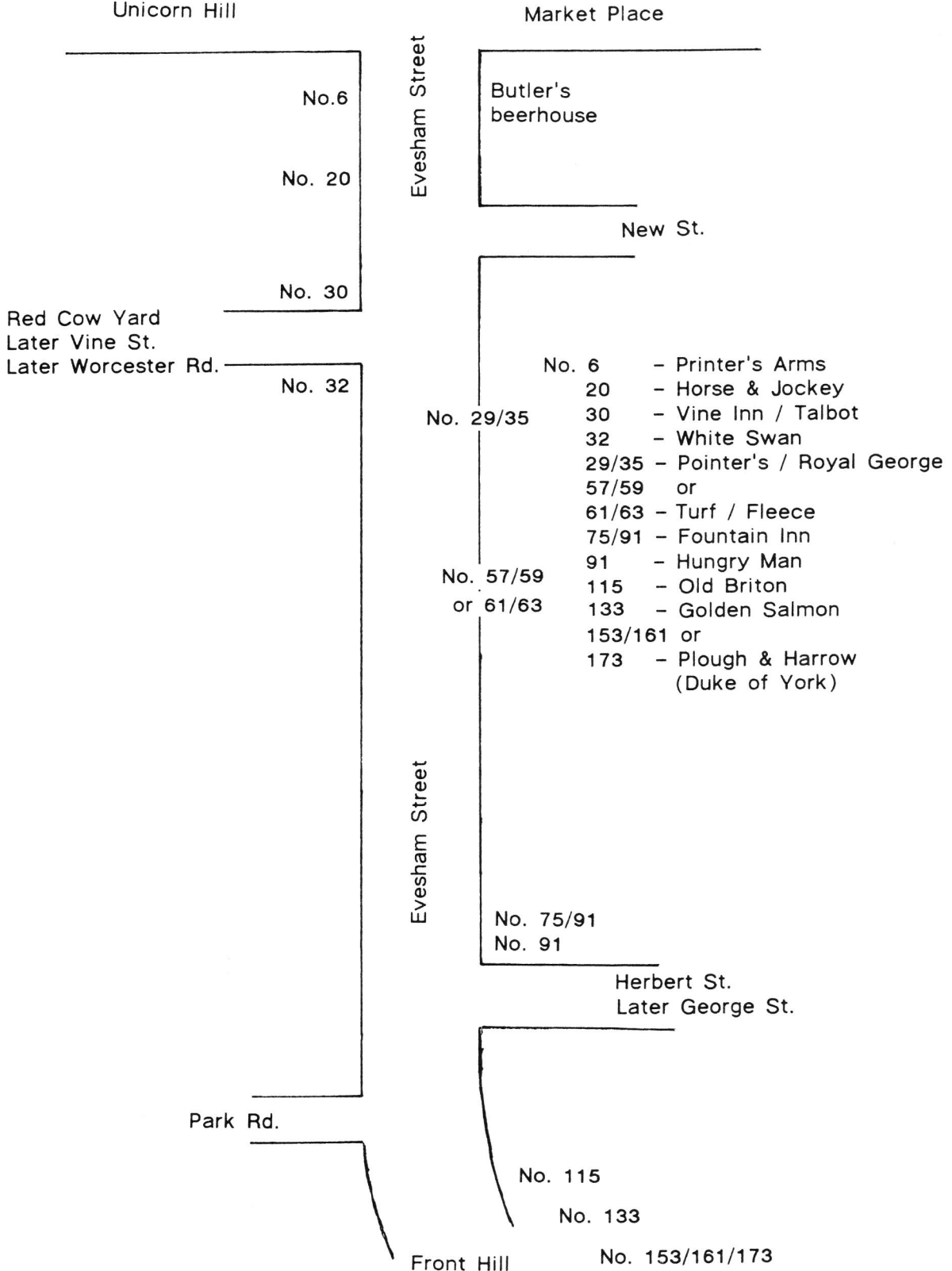

# REDDITCH AND DISTRICT INNS TAVERNS AND HOTELS

**THE ACORN.**　　　　　Evesham Road, Crabbs Cross.

The Royal Oak was originally on the opposite side of the road to its present position (now a private house) and when it had moved the old beerhouse was re-opened and called The Acorn "because it dropped off the Oak." See 'Local Notes and Queries' No. 34 (Boney's Island ).

Licensee – Thomas Morris (1850 Kelly's Directory).

---

**ADAM AND EVE.**　　　　Prospect Hill.

'Local Notes and Queries' No. 88. Licensee – Benjamin Clarke. 1860 – 64 (He was also a baker – Kelly's ).

> The *Adam and Eve* was a name sometimes heard applied to a house kept by Benjamin Clark, but its sign bore no name save that of the landlord. It is now a private house, viz., the three storey one nearly opposite to the offices of Mr. Kerwood, solicitor.

---

**THE ALMA TAVERN.**　　71/73 Ipsley Street.

During the Crimea War of 1853 to 56 major battles were fought along the river Alma. The pub closed in the 1950's and the licence was transferred to the 'Brockhill.' It was later used by the 'Sons of Rest' and demolished in the 1970's.

| | | | |
|---|---|---|---|
| William Wilks | 1864 | John B Hawthorn | 1884 – 87 |
| Mrs Mary Wilks | 1868 | Charles Crow | 1888 – 90 |
| James Matley | 1871 – 74 | William Kibler | 1891 – 1905 |
| William Hodgetts | 1875 – 78 | Thomas Skinner (Kelly's) | 1892 |
| Mrs Mary Hodgetts | 1879 – 80 | Thomas Francis Pye | 1906 – 31 |
| Charles Bennett | 1881 | Hector Charles Morris | 1932 |
| John Blundall | 1882 | F W Jeffs | 1934 |
| Charles Swann | 1883 | George Rowbotham | 1936 |
| Thomas Hayes | 1884 | Henry Northall | 1940 |

April 6th 1956.

The ceremony of "pulling the first pint" at The Brockhill, the new public house on the Batchley Estate, Redditch, was performed last week by Mrs. H. E. Houfton, J.P., chairman of Redditch Licensing Committee, seen here being instructed in the art by Mr. Robert H. Butler, chairman of the directors of the brewery company.

An article from the Indicator concerning the Brockhill pub taking over the licence from the Alma Tavern, Ipsley St.

## Pub. on piles

### FIRST NEW INN OPENED SINCE 1937

THE first public house to be opened in Redditch since 1937 rests on 27 foot piles sunk into the ground.

It is "The Brockhill," in Willow Way, Redditch, which was opened on Wednesday of last week after a civic and magisterial inspection the previous day. Normal foundations were out of the question because of the softness of the ground.

The name "The Brockhill" was chosen after a suggestion by local people who wished to perpetuate an early name for the surrounding district. The original choice —"The Pincushion"— was rejected by the Bench at the time as being unsuitable.

The owners, Mitchells and Butlers, Ltd., surrendered the licence of the old Alma Tavern, in Ipsley Street, to obtain the new one. Permission to hold the new licence was granted in 1950, but it was not found possible to start building until the end of 1954.

"The Brockhill" public rooms consist of a smoke room and a public bar, with an outdoor department between them, and there are facilities at the back for a garden service during the summer. Interior decoration has been carried out in the contemporary style.

The licensee, Mr. Wilfred Dunnicliffe, is a former member of Birmingham City Police Force.

The guests were welcomed by Mr Robert H. Butler, chairman of the directors of the brewery company, who also congratulated the architects and builders on having produced a house with a pleasant and friendly appearance, and the atmosphere of the traditional "local."

Mrs. Houfton, in reply, said the Licensing Committee were delighted with the house, which was well designed and well built, compact and easy to run and beautifully equipped.

The thanks and appreciation of the Council were expressed by Councillor Spencer.

A brass 3d token – actual size 24mm, for the Alma Sick and Dividend Society.

RIGHT: An extract from Local Notes and Queries No. 34 'Boney's Island' an old name for part of Crabbs Cross. It was written in July 1886 by J M Woodward of 'The Castle.'

> The *Royal Oak* was formerly to be found on the opposite side of the road to where the sign is now, and when removed, another landlord re-opened the old beerhouse and called it the *Acorn*," facetiously remarking "that it had dropped from the *Oak*." The *Royal Oak* sign, with a somewhat disproportionate King Charles (with his crown on!) partly seen through the foliage, is now in front of a half-timbered house, often spoken of as 'the "Old Workhouse," rather however from the number of families living in it then, than from any legitimate reason.

## APPLE TREE.         Headless Cross.

Billing's 1855 Directory gives Richard Binfield as licensee of the 'Apple Tree.' Local Notes and Queries No. 88, 'Extinct Public Houses' gives Richard Pinfield as licensee of the 'Cherry Tree.' No one wrote in querying the newspaper article so it can be assumed to be correct. Therefore the 'Apple Tree' in all probability, never existed.

---

## BAKER'S ARMS.        Foregate Street, Astwood Bank.

For details of licensees see under 'Oddfellow's Arms.' The name was changed in the late 1880's.

---

## BEEHIVE INN.         6 Alcester Street.

| | | | |
|---|---|---|---|
| James Lewis | 1850 – 55 | Miss Sarah Ann Free | 1887 – 90 |
| Mrs Ann Lewis | 1860 – 64 | John William Parkinson | 1891 – 1904 |
| Edmund Free | 1868 – 79 | F J Briggs | 1905 – 08 |
| Mrs Elizabeth Free | 1880 – 86 | | |

---

## BELL INN.         Britten Street. (Great Britain St. in early directories).

| | | | |
|---|---|---|---|
| W Bartleet | 1850 | Henry Young | 1896 – 1914 |
| William Fisher | 1855 – 60 | Miss Annie Young | 1915 – 21 |
| James Mills | 1860 – 64 | Miss Florence Young | 1923 |
| Edwin Francis | 1868 – 86 | Thomas Young | 1924 |
| Mrs Emma Francis | 1888 – 95 | Edgar Young | 1926 – 51 |

---

## BELL INN.         Pudding Bag Lane, (Parson's Road)? Redditch.

Kelly's 1868 Directory gives Thomas Lee as licensee of a beer house in Pudding Bag Lane. Local Notes and Queries No. 88 gives David Mole keeping the Bell Inn in a little "pudding bag street" opposite the Woodland Cottage in Mount Pleasant. This was probably an old term for what we would now call a cul-de-sac.

## FECKENHAM. 363

### HEADLESS CROSS.

Lacon Rev. F., Incumbent of St. Luke's
Avery William, and Son, needle and fish-hook makers
Binfield Richard, beer retailer, *Apple Tree*
Chambers Michael, blacksmith and Sub-Postmaster
Charman Thomas, needle maker
Clarke John, needle finisher, and Constable
Clarke William, needle maker
Cox William, victualler, *White Hart*
Crauer Henry, shopkeeper
Emms William, beer retailer, *The Case is Altered*
Francis James, needle and fish hook maker
Francis Letitia, ladies' seminary
Harris Sarah, dress maker
Hawkes Thomas, shoe maker
Haynes William, needle maker
Heynes William, farm bailiff
Hill Frederick, butcher
Johnson George F., land surveyor and beer retailer, *Square and Compasses*
Johnson James, carpenter
Johnson Richard, boot and shoe maker
Johnson William, needle maker
Jones Thomas, builder and shopkeeper
Leyster James, baker and shopkeeper
Middleton Jonathan, hosier and haberdasher
Mills James, beer retailer, *Bell*
Monnox Ingram, needle maker
Palmer Ann, farmer
Parker James, needle maker
Petford William, wheelwright
Robinson John, shopkeeper
Robinson William, carpenter
Shrimpton George, surgeon's and fancy needle maker
Spiers William, hair dresser and fish-hook maker
Townsend Alfred, needle stamper and beer retailer
Townsend Charles, needle maker
Wharrard Charles, needle finisher and shopkeeper
White Adam, carpenter
White Thomas, shopkeeper and leather seller
Williams John, carrier
Wilkinson Jonas, beer retailer
Wright Mark, butcher

Reproduced above is part of a page from Billing's 1855 Directory of the County of Worcester showing Headless Cross under Feckenham. The text mentions the 'Apple Tree' which was in all probability the 'Cherry Tree'. Also mentioned is 'The Case is Altered', later 'The Gate Hangs Well.'

ABOVE: A Baker's Arms 3d token.

RIGHT: Newspaper article from 1886 about the Baker's Arms and one of its customers

BELOW: Details of the Bell Inn opposite the Woodland Cottage.

### LOCAL NOTES AND QUERIES.
### No. 230.

#### PHILIP BEARCROFT BROOKE.

Some years ago, before the establishment of a Board School, there resided at Astwood Bank, a village schoolmaster of the old type, an old man named Philip Bearcroft Brooke. He came to Astwood from the village of Bishampton, near Evesham, Worcestershire, which was his native place, and was considerably advanced in years when he took up his abode with us. He was respectably connected, and was acquainted with some of the first families in the rural district from which he hailed. He used to tell us he was the only "gentleman" at Astwood, and he claimed to have a coat-of-arms, in which was a "Lion Rampant." The writer has heard him speak of his connection with some titled families, but whether he was distantly related to Lord Willoughby de Broke, I am unable to say. He had a small annual income, which, in addition to the amount derived from a private day school which he opened for boys of a tender age, sufficed to support him in an economical way. He usually spent his evenings in the smoke-room of the "Bakers' Arms" Inn (now the "Oddfellows Arms") kept at that time by the late Richard Rouse, senior, and subsequently by his widow, in whose small house (one room up and one down) opposite the pub., he lived and kept his school. In the smoke-room he always had his own seat; and when in company with his old friend Mr. Mander, at that time relieving officer for Feckenham parish, and another neighbour or two, he was in his glory, and would be very communicative. Though fond of his pipe and glass and social company, he was very moderate, and never drank to excess.

With reference to Mr. Brooke's private day-school, I may say that his scholars were usually much attached to him, and their parents were satisfied with the progress they made. The scholars, and the children generally in the neighbourhood, when speaking of their schoolmaster, familiarly called him "Old Daddy Brookes." In his last illness, which was not of long duration, I am told, the late widow Rouse, landlady of the "Bakers' Arms," attended him, and had some of the few household effects, books, &c., which belonged to him. He was interred in the graveyard at the Baptist Chapel. I was personally well acquainted with him part of the time he lived at Astwood, but not being in the neighbourhood at the time of his demise, I have no date of particulars of his death and burial.

This brief record is written out of respect for the memory of an old acquaintance, for "Why should auld acquaintance be forgot?"

EDWIN THORNTON.

Astwood Bank.

The *Bell Inn*, kept by David Mole, was at the corner of a little "pudding bag" street and not far removed from being opposite the *Woodland Cottage*. It has been described to me by one who as a youth knew the house well, as a place for unlimited drinking and gambling. On one occasion a company met together there and determined to literally "strip" one of their neighbours from "Boney's Island." So cleverly did they play their cards that this man was soon fleeced of all his money. They next, in order to carry out their resolution, proposed to him that he should stake his coat. This he agreed to, and of course soon lost it. The waistcoat was next staked and lost, and so on with the other garments, until at last the man was reduced to the *outward* condition of Adam before the fall. In order, however, to enable him to reach home they lent him his clothing for the occasion, and gratified at having succeeded in carrying out their intention, supplied him liberally with internal comforts as well as external necessaries. With David Mole the *Bell Inn* also died, and probably, not "deeply lamented" by the neighbours.

Edgar and Fanny Young outside the "Bell Inn," Britten Street, Circa 1930.

Henry Young's daughters Florence, (left) born 1874 and Annie, born 1863.

Henry Young, licensee of the Bell Inn, Britten St. 1896–1914.

The actual owner of the Bell Inn was Henry Young's sister Ada who was the wife of Thomas Peart a Brewer's Agent with premises in Church Green. Fred Young, for many years a butcher in Evesham Rd, Headless Cross, was from the same family. Information and photos courtesy of Henry Young's great grand-daughter Miss Diana Oscroft.

**BELL INN.**            163 Evesham Road, Headless Cross.

The present building was erected in 1898.

| | | | |
|---|---|---|---|
| James Mills | 1855 | Alfred George Dell | 1911 – 12 |
| Charles Henry Houghton | 1866 – 96 | ? Leason | 1913 – 14 |
| Mrs Ann Houghton | 1897 – 98 | George Cornwall | 1914 – 20 |
| J Francis | 1898 – 99 | Alfred James Wood | 1921 – 25 |
| Robert G Heynes | 1900 – 01 | Alfred Locke | 1925 – 27 |
| William Saunders | 1903 – 06 | Vernon James Ward | 1928 – 33 |
| Matthais Poole | 1907 – 08 | Samuel Henry Foster | 1934 – 36 |
| R Canadine | 1909 – 10 | Mrs May Foster | 1940 |

---

**BELL INN.**            Evesham Road, Astwood Bank.

| | | | |
|---|---|---|---|
| Mrs Sarah Wakeman | 1864 – 68 | Mrs Polly Croft | 1918 – 20 |
| Miss Susan Wakeman | 1872 – 82 | John F Croft | 1921 |
| John Walker | 1883 – 92 | John A Croft | 1923 – 28 |
| Mrs Susannah Walker | 1893 – 1913 | Mrs Polly Croft | 1929 – 40 |
| John F Croft | 1914 – 17 | | |

---

**BEOLEY CROSS INN.**   See under Cross and Bowling Green Inn.

---

**BIRD IN HAND.**   Walford Street.

The landlord from 1841 to 1868 was William Ledbury (recorded as Henry Ladbury in Kelly's 1850 Directory). He was also a shopkeeper and coal dealer. From 1868 the Bird in Hand name transferred to 8 George Street.

---

**BIRD IN HAND.**   8 George Street.

The name changed in 1882 – 83. See under 'Volunteer's Arms' for licensees.

The Bell Inn, Evesham Road, Headless Cross was rebuilt in 1898. Several pubs in Redditch were also rebuilt around this time: for example the Royal Hotel, the Fleece Inn, Crabbs Cross and the Park Inn.

# Valuation and Particulars of Trade Fixtures, Fittings, Furniture, Utensils, etc. at the Bell Inn, Headless Cross.

From Mr Alfred James Wood to Mr Alfred Lock(e) October 31st. 1925.

> \* Note. Each time a pub tenancy changed, a firm like Neasom & White, auctioneers and valuers were called in to make a valuation of the fixtures and fittings belonging to the property, i.e. the brewery. Some of these inventories have survived, as have a few auction catalogues, thanks to the foresight of a few local historians. From these records it is possible to build up a picture of the interior of pubs that have long been demolished. Photographic images of the interior of Redditch pubs are almost non existent.

**BAR.**
9ft. 6in. Painted and grained seat with back. 5 Cast iron spittoons.
Brass gas pendant with incandescent burner.
2 Electric drop lights with 1 opal and 1 enamel shade.
"Unique" cork drawer. Call bell fixed on counter.
Stained bar table on turned legs.
6ft. 6. X lft. 4. Stained drinking table on turned legs, covered in American cloth.
Cross-leg deal table. 10ft. deal form.
9ft. 6in. Stained, panelled front counter with door and flap.
3 Pull beer engine in mahogany case with piping to cellar and 3 barrel taps.
The shelving at back of bar forming bar fitting for jugs and glasses.
3 Sloopers. 2 Enamel drip basins. 2 Enamel funnels. Mallet. 3 Gimlets.
Corkscrew. 5 Brass barrel taps. 1 Wood tap.
5 Windsor chairs. Fender and ash pan.

**SMOKE ROOM.**
Gas pendant and bracket with incandescent burners.
2 Electric drop lights with 1 enamel and 1 opal shade.
Deal drinking table on turned legs, covered in American cloth.
Deal ditto with square legs. 2 Stained drinking tables on turned legs.
19 Round top bar stools. 16 Windsor chairs. 6 Other chairs.
Electric cable and lamp for target. Iron fender and ash curb. 2 Hearth rugs.

The inventory also lists 2 bedrooms and a box room. Hall and landing. Kitchen, scullery and cellar. Yard and garden with fence down both sides. The yard contained several tables chairs and forms. The garden had a poultry pen with front, top, 2 ends and a division forming two pens. At the far end of the garden was a wooden pig sty with felt covered roof and a brick floor.

The Bell Inn, Evesham Road, Headless Cross, with the White Hart in the background; about 1910.

The crudely made tokens reproduced below are almost certainly the product of a Redditch factory tool-room. The lettering is stamped (incuse) on a 32mm bronze flan. In normal pub tokens the lettering is raised as they were minted (in Birmingham) in the same way as a coin. It is not known whether the figure 3 was reversed by accident or design. An identical token was made ( with reversed 3 ) for the Shakespeare Tavern, Walford Street.

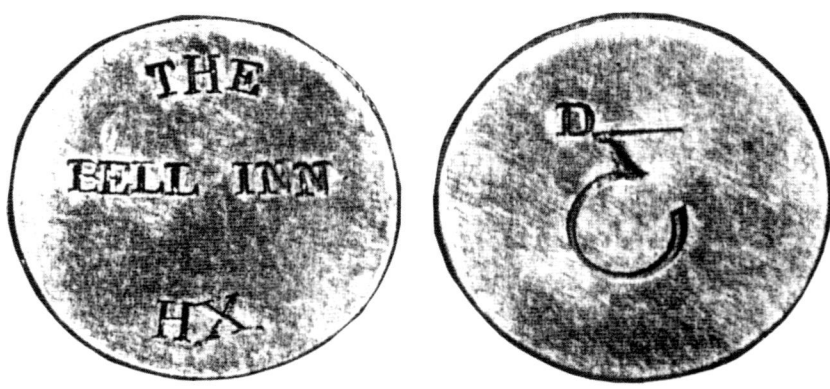

From the auction sale held by Charrington & Co. Ltd.
at the Grand Hotel, B'ham on Feb. 2nd & 3rd 1926.

LOT 56.

# THE "BELL" INN,

## Headless Cross, Redditch,

### WORCESTERSHIRE.

**FREEHOLD — ON BEER HOUSE — 7 DAYS.**

With frontage to main road and Bus route.

The Tenant is Mr. A. Locke; the net annual rental £25.

The main structure is two-storey, brick and slate built.

The accommodation includes:—

ON THE GROUND FLOOR: Entrance Passage, with wood floor; Bar; Smoke Room; Sitting Room; Kitchen; Cellar.

ON THE FIRST FLOOR: Four Bedrooms; and Clothes Closet.

OUTSIDE: Part-Paved Yard; Urinal; two w.c's; Coalhouse; also Garden.

Land Tax, 10/2.

REMARKS.—This Lot includes a narrow strip of Land on the North side of the Beer House, having a frontage of 9 feet only to the main road, and that strip of land is subject to restrictive covenants as to observing the building line, not allowing thereon any sale, manufacture or supply of intoxicating liquors or any club in which intoxicating liquors are supplied and maintaining a fence on the North side of that strip. These restrictions, however, do not apply to the Beer House itself or to the main portion of the Land held therewith.

*Sold, £2,000.*

The Bell Inn, Evesham Road, Astwood Bank with its near neighbour the Woodman, now demolished. The site is part of the Bell's beer garden and car park. The picture dates from about 1905.

## BLACK BOY.    Droitwich Road, (The Saltway) Feckenham.

The licence was held by the Gardner family for many years. The directories record Mrs Elizabeth Gardner 1841 – 54. William Styler 1872 – 73. There was also a Post Office on the premises.

---

## BLACK HORSE INN.    6/9 Mount Pleasant.

| | | | |
|---|---|---|---|
| John Wright | 1850 – 55 | William Frederick Masters | 1910 – 27 |
| William Masters | 1868 – 73 | Mrs Mary Jane Masters | 1928 – 31 |
| John Thomas Masters | 1874 – 1909 | John W Masters | 1932 – 40 |

---

## BOAT INN.    9 Birchfield Road, Headless Cross.

Information given by a local resident for the existence of a beer house. However, the name is not recorded in directories and no other evidence has been found.

---

## BOWLING GREEN INN.    See Cross and Bowling Green Inn.

---

## BREWER'S ARMS.    9 Bates Hill. ( Also occurs as Windsor Street ).
Later became the Windsor Club; Kelly's 1940 gives William Dobbins as secretary.

| | | | |
|---|---|---|---|
| George Mogg | 1854 – 75 | Edwin Arthur Pinfield-Wells | 1892 – 1901 |
| William Edward Crow | 1875 – 91 | Mrs Elizabeth Pinfield-Wells | 1901 – 18 |
| (He was also a coal dealer, he | | George Hill | 1920 – 23 |
| moved on to the Golden Cross) | | William C Hemming | 1923 – 28 |

---

## BRISTOL INN.    16 Birchfield Road, Headless Cross.

In later years the building was used by the Civil Defence and also the Boy Scouts. For a time it was the United Services Club. The site is now part of Headless Cross Green.

| | | | |
|---|---|---|---|
| William Hill (Butcher) | 1868 – 73 | Mrs Sarah Bunegar | 1908 – 13 |
| George McLand | 1874 – 76 | A James | 1914 |
| James Edward Houghton | 1882 – 94 | Edwin Henry Davis | 1916 – 20 |
| (He issued a 3d token ) | | Alfred Fowler | 1921 – 24 |
| Charles Henry Bunegar | 1895 – 1908 | | |

**BLACK BOY.**    Droitwich Road, (The Saltway), Feckenham.

The article reproduced below is from a 1950's Redditch Indicator.

# WHERE A KING SLEPT AND A MURDER WAS COMMITTED

PRACTICALLY all the ingredients needed for a first-class thriller are contained in the long and chequered history of an ancient building in the village of Feckenham.

It is the old Black Boy, which is said to date back to the time of Feckenham Forest, and during the centuries it has stood in Droitwich Road it has been the scene of adventure, romance, intrigue, and even murder.

It is one of the buildings which have been selected for preservation.

Although one of the oldest houses in the village, its history, gleaned mostly from its present owner, Mrs. G. Palmer, and from Mrs. Shakles, who takes a keen interest in the history of the village in which she has lived practically all her life, is believed to be one of the most authentic dealt with in this series.

Centuries ago, when the horse-drawn stage coaches were the only means of transport, the old Black Boy played an important part in the life of the village.

For at that time, and probably for many years afterwards, it served a three-fold purpose. It was hostelry, public house and post-office.

Here travellers could come to rest and refresh their horses and themselves.

To-day, the house and its outbuildings contain many reminders of those far-off days. In the old kitchen can be seen the old-fashioned wood racks for holding the beer mugs and plates for meals; the wide, open fireplace where logs burned merrily while weary travellers quenched their thirst and exchanged tales; the well-worn steps leading down to the cellar where the landlord of that time brewed his own beer—and which is now used by Mrs. Palmer for brewing her home-made wine, and the club room which has now been converted into a lounge by Mrs. Palmer.

## COACH HOUSE

Other reminders include the old coach house, with another wide, open fireplace, where they used to smoke the bacon and bake the bread; the old stables with their wide oak beams and tie-up for six horses; the old wooden structure for hanging the harness, and the

**The Black Boy, Feckenham.**

old granary where the crops were stored.

The interior of the house, too, is full of reminders of those early days. For instance, in some parts there is the old form of plastering, held together by horse-hair, the wide and open oak staircase, the doors with the Queen Anne handles; the half-timbered beams, double doors and doors with church-like shape, as well as numerous other features which all point to the antiquity of the place.

It is no wonder that Mrs. Palmer contends that the house has an atmosphere.

"At night I feel as if I am trying to walk through a crowd of people who have either lived here or visited the place during its long career," said Mrs. Palmer.

The same atmosphere exists in the stables, said Mrs. Palmer. But there the atmosphere is a hallowed one.

The house has had many distinguished visitors. King John himself is said to have slept there regularly during many of his hunting expeditions in Feckenham Forest.

### WHERE THE KING SLEPT

This is believed to be fact rather than village lore, and in order to support that belief Mrs. Palmer showed a reporter the bedroom where the King is said to have slept, and the room adjoining which he is said to have used as his dressing-room.

Even the name of the house has a story book flavour. It is said to have been named "The Black Boy"—and here again this is regarded as authentic—in appreciation of the Moors, of Spain, who came over to this country to help the various needle-making companies to improve the needle-making trade.

It is believed that the original trade mark was an apple and a serpent, but after the visit of the men from Spain it was changed to a Moor's head—hence the name "The Black Boy."

Its long history, however, was not always peaceful and jovial, for it is firmly believed that the house was once the scene of a murder, following a quarrel between two countrymen.

Until nearly 100 years ago, the building had been used as a public house. It is said that the licence was held by the Gardner family for close on 200 years.

One of the house's most prized possessions was a coat of arms in tapestry. On it was patterned the " horn of plenty," with a Latin inscription underneath, meaning, " I will rise again."

Unfortunately all trace of this valuable possession was lost when the house changed hands many years ago.

It is believed to have been first put there by someone of importance.

To-day all is quiet and peaceful, and probably the only revelry to be heard is when Mrs. Palmer invites her friends in at Christmas to sample the wine she makes in the centuries-old cellar.

## BLACK BOY.    Feckenham.

The book 'Notes & Queries of Worcestershire' by John Noake, London, 1856 under the title 'Ancient Inns' gives the following.

"The Black Boy at Feckenham is now (1856) closed as an inn. It had been in the family of the Gardeners about 139 years. The sign, which was of copper, stood the whole of that time until it was taken down in 1854".

The Black Horse, Mount Pleasant, in the 1960's.

Brewer's Arms 3d token. Later the pub became the Windsor Social Club.

From an auction catalogue of the sale by Bass Ltd.
held at the Grand Hotel, B'ham, Wed. 9th May 1928.

LOT 25.

# THE "BREWERS ARMS,"

## Windsor Street,

## REDDITCH

(Worcestershire)

FREEHOLD — ON-BEER HOUSE — 7 DAYS.

This House is let to Mr. Wm. C. Hemming, who has been in occupation for 5 years, and the previous tenant was also here for 5 years. The present NET ANNUAL RENTAL IS £51.

The main property is two-storey, brick and slate built and double fronted.

The accommodation includes:—

ON THE GROUND FLOOR: Entrance Passage and Outdoor Department; Smoke Room; Bar-Snug; and Kitchen.

ON THE FIRST FLOOR: Club Room and Two Bedrooms.

IN THE BASEMENT: Two Beer Cellars, brick paved and with brick Stillaging

OUTSIDE are Paved Yard; Urinal; W.C.; Washhouse; Private W.C.; and Coalplace.

Gas and Water services are laid on.

N.B.—There is an agreement as to a Right of Drainage under the adjoining property, and in respect of which 10/- a year is paid.

*REMARKS.— A well-situated Property in a good district.*

### ORIGIN OF THE NAME 'BRISTOL INN'

The name was meant to denote an establishment of the highest standards and quality. Frederick Hervey, Earl Bishop of Derry (1730 – 1803) on the death of his brother in 1779, succeeded to the Earldom of Bristol and a vast fortune. He was a great traveller and connoisseur of good living so that the hotels in which he stayed became known as 'Lord Bristol's Hotel' – an assurance of the highest possible standards. However, it is doubtful he ever came to Birchfield Road.

James Houghton's brass 3d token (23mm diameter) from about 1890.

The above photograph shows the corner of Evesham Road and Birchfield Road Headless Cross taken in the 1930's. The traffic island is now a mini island, all the buildings have gone to be replaced by Headless Cross Green. The lorry on the left of the picture is probably delivering to the Bristol Inn which was at number 16 Birchfield Road.

## BRITANNIA INN.    35/37 Walford Street.

The first Cunard ship, launched in 1840 was the 'Britannia'.

| | | | |
|---|---|---|---|
| James Pinfield | 1855 – 60 | Peter Huntley | 1875 – 76 |
| (He was also a needle finisher) | | Joseph Thornton | 1880 – 86 |
| James Hands | 1864 | William Thornton | 1887 – 94 |
| Henry Bint | 1868 – 72 | (He was also a 'Jobmaster') | |
| John Pinfield | 1873 – 74 | Mrs Christiana Thornton | 1895 – 1908 |

---

## BRITISH WORKMAN.    Crabbs Cross.

Not much is known about this establishment, it may have been a working mens club or even a temperance hotel. In 1874 it was run by William Downes and from 1875 to 77 by William Weaver who is described as a draper.

---

## BROOK INN.    Elcock's Brook, Callow Hill.
Often spelled Ellcott's or even Elcote or Alcoats.

| | | | |
|---|---|---|---|
| Richard Humphreys | 1841 | Richard Court | 1883 – 93 |
| Mrs Elizabeth Humphreys | 1854 – 68 | Mrs Mary Ann Court | 1894 – 1911 |
| William Humphreys | 1872 – 73 | Benjamin Hopcroft | 1912 – 32 |
| Ben Hopcroft | 1875 – 78 | Mrs Amy Belle Hopcroft | 1932 – 40 |
| Mrs Mary Hopcroft | 1879 – 82 | | |

Brook Inn

The Brook Inn, Ellcock's or Ellcott's or Elcote or Alcoat's Brook.

Below, a group gather to celebrate Coronation Day in 1911.

## BULL'S HEAD.   77 Evesham Street.

| James Avery | 1835 – 41 | George Fisher ? | 1855 ? |

(Also a needle maker)

By 1860 it had become the Temperance Hotel as mentioned in this extract from 'Local Notes & Queries No. 88.'

> The *Bull's Head*, now the Temperance Hotel, in Evesham Street, was formerly kept by James Avery, who combined his trades of inn-keeping and needle-making.

---

## BULL'S HEAD.   Wapping.
(The area behind the Red Lion – George/Herbert St).

George Fisher is recorded in the 1861 Census as being licensee of the Bull's Head, Wapping. The 1855 Kelly's Directory records George Fisher as a beer retailer in Evesham Street – the Bull's Head? From 1860 to 1868 Kelly's puts him in Walford Street and Herbert Street so he probably took the Bull's Head name with him.

---

## THE CASE IS ALTERED.   See 'The Gate Hangs Well' for details.

## ORIGIN OF THE NAME "CASE IS ALTERED"

Several theories are advanced for this name, one of which suggests it may be a legal term if, for example the landlord fell foul of the licensing laws. A more probable explanation is that it dates from the time of the Peninsular War and is a corruption of the Spanish words 'Casar de Salta' – a type of dance or more likely in this case 'Casa Alta' – High House as it is up hill all the way from Redditch.

### Extract from "Local Notes and Queries" No. 88.

The *Cherry Tree*, kept by old Richard Pinfield ("Old Dick"), a fruiterer, took its name from the cherry tree growing in front. The house stood on the site now occupied by the two cottages erected by the late Mr. William Adams, at Headless Cross, and was virtually the last house in Stevens' Row. "Old Dick" wore a smock frock and bore the character of not being a very amiable man in his household. In the old days of the inns mentioned in this article gambling was a very ordinary amusement, and my informant tells me that he has known a man lose on a Saturday night, not only his money, but the grocery, etc., which he had been buying for the forthcoming week. The *Cherry Tree* was afterwards used as a Mormonite meeting house.

### REDDITCH TRAGEDY.

#### HIGHLY ESTEEMED RESIDENT FOUND DEAD.

A painful sensation was caused on Monday night, at Redditch, when news transpired of the death, under tragic circumstances, of Mr. John Hemming Barker, of 86, Easemore Road, Redditch, whose body was found hanging in a workshop at Clarke's Yard, where he carried on business as a needle polisher to the trade. Mr. Barker, who was 68 years of age, was for some years engaged in the local trade—needlemaking. Subsequently he resided at Bromsgrove, where he was the genial host of the Bell Inn, High Street. He was highly esteemed and respected by a wide circle of friends, both at Redditch and Bromsgrove, and deep sympathy will be felt with the widow and his two sons, both of whom are grown up.

#### THE INQUEST: A PATHETIC LETTER.

The Coroner perused the letter—a lengthy one—and read a portion, which stated :—"My dear Will,—It is Monday again, and as usual nothing to do. Outlook as bad as possible. Not a bit of light in front. No hope, nothing to rest on. To me it has been most black, dreary, and dark all day. The very blackest of blinds has been down and obscured all that is bright and light. My mind is warped so that I cannot fix upon anything clearly. When I think what is the best thing to do under the circumstances my mind remains stationary. Then at another time thousands of thoughts come along and wedge, causing me in a way to pause, not knowing where to begin, so nothing is done again. I have not had a night's sleep for about 30 to 35 nights—tossing about in fits and starts, in and out of bed all night through. I am worn out with pain, sleeplessness, and worry, and feel that my head will certainly burst. I must not attempt another night at Easemore Road, or I should become a candidate for a lunatic asylum. My exit from the stage of life must be before the close of this day, or I shall become a great burden to someone, and that will not do at any price."

The Coroner added that deceased referred in affectionate terms to his wife, gave directions with regard to his business, and wound up :—"I am wanting you to have this to-night. If you do, and run down on your machine, you will find my body in the machine room, near the window facing the Fox and Goose field."

ABOVE: Francis Fourt's 3d token issued in the late 1880's.

RIGHT: Report in the Redditch Indicator for Saturday 24th September 1924 of the suicide of John Hemming Barker who was licensee of the Cricketer's Arms, Beoley Road from 1880 to 1887.

## CHERRY TREE.    Steven's Row, Headless Cross.

The licensee was a fruiterer and a cherry tree grew in front of the premises.

| | | | |
|---|---|---|---|
| William Pinfield | 1841 | Richard Pinfield | 1850 – 55 |

---

## CRICKETER'S ARMS.    107-109 Beoley Road

| | | | |
|---|---|---|---|
| Thomas B Fourt | 1872 – 78 | Edwin Henry Davis | 1897 – 99 |
| Mrs Emma Fourt | 1879 – 80 | Henry Fourt (Kelly's) | 1900 |
| John Hemming Barker | 1880 – 87 | Alfred Spencer (NDA) | 1900 |
| Francis Fourt | 1888 – 90 | Albert Parker Edwards | 1904 – 19 |
| (He issued a 3d token) | | Harvey Worth | 1920 – 21 |
| William E Goodall | 1891 – 93 | Henry Tomkins | 1924 – 28 |
| (His name is stamped on Fourt's token) | | John Hanson | 1932 – 40 |
| George Savage | 1894 – 96 | | |

---

## CRICKETER'S ARMS.    87-89 Evesham Road, Headless Cross.

Later Hemmings DIY shop, at present a tool hire firm.

| | | | |
|---|---|---|---|
| Benjamin Lea | 1872 – 73 | Frederick K Holmes | 1893 – 95 |
| Edward Green | 1888 | Mrs Emma Holmes | 1896 – 1916 |
| Mrs Mary Ann Edwards | 1892 | Harry Barker | 1921 |

---

## CROSS AND BOWLING GREEN.    Beoley Cross.

The name varies in directories – Bowling Green Inn up to 1890's then changes to the Beoley Cross Inn until about 1910.

| | | | |
|---|---|---|---|
| John Ganderton | 1841 | John Savage | 1898 – 1901 |
| William Ganderton | 1850 – 55 | William Wilson Yeomans | 1902 – 08 |
| Mrs Sarah Johnson | 1860 – 64 | Mrs Emma Caroline Yeomans | 1912 – 25 |
| James Reader | 1868 – 78 | Mrs Minnie Glover | 1926 – 33 |
| Joseph Edwards | 1879 – 82 | Walter Henry Carter | 1934 – 36 |
| Mrs Caroline Edwards | 1883 – 97 | Thomas White | 1940 |

---

## CROSS AND CRAB TREE.    Crabbs Cross. (Origin of the name)?

No record except Local Notes and Queries No. 34 'Boney's Island.'

A photohraph taken in 1910 of Cricketer's Arms landlord Mr Albert Parker Edwards. His family (left to right) is son Ralph, Ena, Mr Edwards, Bert (standing), Osmond, Mrs Edwards and Dolly.

Below is a picture of the pub taken about the same time. Note the Post Office next door.

This photograph shows Albert Parker Edwards and his wife behind the bar in 1904 shortly after taking over at the Cricketer's Arms.

The reverse side of the Francis Fourt Cricketer's Arms token illustrated below has the name GOODALL stamped on it. William E Goodall was Fourt's successor in 1891. The actual token is only 26mm. diameter.

> # THE ANNUAL PIGEON SHOOTING, at the BOWLING GREEN INN, BEOLEY, will take place on TUESDAY, DECEMBER 27.
> ## PRIZE—A FAT PIG.
> Shooting to commence at Twelve o'Clock.

Advert from the front page of the Redditch Indicator on Saturday December 24th 1859. (The paper's first year).

Beoley Garage and the Cross and Bowling Green.

## CROSS AND CRAB TREE.

Extract from "Local Notes & Queries" No. 34 'Boney's Island' (Crabbs Cross).

Written in July 1886.

> And here, perhaps, a few words may be said of the public houses, past and present. Tradition names the old half-timbered house (formerly Stiler's, now the residence of Mr. T. Hunt) as having been a licensed house by the sign of the *Cross and Crab Tree*, and if this be true, it throws some light upon the derivation of the proper name of "Boney's Island"—Crabbs Cross, or as formerly written "Crab Crosse."

## CROWN HOTEL.  18/21 Prospect Hill. (Fish Hill).

| | | | |
|---|---|---|---|
| Thomas Ireland | 1822 – 23 | Walter Hadgkiss | 1893 – 97 |
| Joseph Davis | 1835 – 41 | William Henry Biddle | 1900 – 01 |
| John Davis | 1850 – 74 | Edward Perks | 1902 – 08 |
| William Holyoake | 1875 – 80 | Dick Colley | 1909 – 10 |
| (He issued a 3d token) | | James Ambrose Mills | 1911 – 23 |
| Henry Davis | 1880 – 87 | (He issued a 2d token) | |
| (He issued a 3d token) | | John Henry Crossley | 1923 – 24 |
| George Melen | 1888 | Ralph Ernest Edwards | 1924 – 36 |
| Joseph Lander | 1888 – 92 | George William Davies | 1940 |

---

## CROWN INN.  Crabbs Cross.

Opened in the 1830's at the junction of the Slough and Evesham Road. See Local Notes and Queries No. 34. 'Boney's Island.'

| | | | |
|---|---|---|---|
| William Morris | 1841 – 55 | (Mrs Sarah Canadine recorded in 1868) | |
| (He was also a carpenter) | | Thomas Morris | 1880 |
| Richard Canadine | 1860 – 77 | | |

---

## CROWN INN.  Feckenham Road, Astwood Bank.

| | | | |
|---|---|---|---|
| Henry Hemming | 1841 – 54 | William Dolphin | 1880 |
| (He was a draper and grocer who | | (He was a baker and flour dealer) | |
| was also licensee of the White Lion) | | Michael Daniels | 1881 – 92 |
| Thomas Hawthorn | 1855 | (He was also a baker and farmer) | |
| (He was also a needle maker) | | John Holbeche | 1893 – 94 |
| Stephen Webb | 1860 – 64 | George E Walker | 1895 – 1930 |
| Benjamin Haynes | 1868 | Henry Walker | 1932 – 44 |
| Albert Perkins | 1872 – 80 | | |

---

## CROWN INN.  Feckenham.

Not to be confused with the 'Old' Rose and Crown.

| | | | |
|---|---|---|---|
| Sarah Sanders | 1841 | William Ford | 1855 |
| Oliver Sanders | 1850 – 54 | | |

---

ABOVE: The Crown, Prospect Hill, as it was in the early years of the 20th century.

BELOW: As it appeared for most of the 20th century before being "re-developed".

A photograph of the back of the Crown, Prospect Hill taken by Ian Hayes on the 15th of April 1987.

### CROWN HOTEL.
#### PROSPECT HILL. REDDITCH.

Headquarters of the Excelsior Football Club.

Wines, Spirits, and Cigars of the finest quality.
J. C. Holder's Celebrated Ales & Stout on draught.
Families supplied with Casks.
Bass's Ale and Guiness's Stout in Bottle.

Good Stabling.    Lock-up Coach-house.

Proprietor   -   W. H. BIDDLE.

LEFT: W. H. Biddle's 1900 advert which mentions J. C. Holder's Celebrated Ales. A large painted sign advertising Holder's Ales is visible in the earlier picture on previous page.

Two versus from the 72 verse poem "A Medley From Recollections of Redditch Fifty Years Ago." By an Old Fish Hill (Prospect Hill) Boy. Printed in the Redditch Indicator in July 1890.

> Printer Bromley close to the Crown,
> A singer was of good renown,
> Printer Heming, an agreeable man
> The *Indicator* first began.
> Joseph Davis, host of the Crown,
> As civil a man as any in town,
> His chestnut mare the lightning struck it,
> Over it fell, and "kicked the bucket."

Roof timbers from the oldest part of the Crown, Prospect Hill. These photographs were taken by Ian Hayes on the 31st August 1987.

James Ambrose Mills 2d admission token for the Crown Hotel, Prospect Hill. It may have been for access to the Bowling Green or Billiard Room or both as mentioned in the Walter J. Hadgkiss advert from the late 1890's which is reproduced below.

Henry Davis's Crown Inn token from the 1880's.

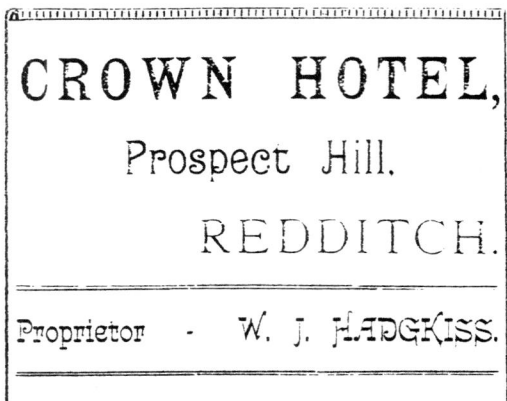

William Holyoake's token issued when he was licensee of the Crown Inn, Prospect Hill in the late 1870's

On the back is the name of the Birmingham manufacturer.

**Valuation & Inventory of Public House Fittings, Furniture, Stock in Trade & other effects at the Crown Hotel.**
Prospect Hill, Redditch in the County of Worcester. From Mitchell & Butler Ltd. to Ralph Ernest Edwards. Appraised by Frank Neasom on 11th. of June 1924.

**SMOKE ROOM.**
4ft. Cast iron fire curb. Pier glass with gilt frame 42in. X 42in.
4 Brass spittoons. 3 Polished birchwood stools.
4 – 2ft. Mahogany topped tables on cast iron frames.
Electric fan with stained bracket and stained sliding hatch.
2 Electric lights with shades. Coat hanger on door. Lino on floor.
Cast iron 6 hole umberella stand.

**COMMERCIAL ROOM.**
6ft. Axminster hearth rug. 2 Electric lights with shades.
2 Enamel cornice poles, rings & brackets. 2 Holland roller blinds & fittings.
2 Pairs casement curtains. Lino fitted to floor.

**BAR PARLOUR.**
Plate glass Chimney mirror in Rosewood frame. 4ft. Cast iron fire curb.
2 Brass curtain rods and fittings. 2 Pairs lace curtains.
Electric light bulb and shade. 2 Linen blinds and rollers.
3 Polished Birch arm smoking chairs. 3 Polished Birch circular seated chairs.
5 Polished Birch Windsor chairs. 3 – 2ft. Circular Mahogany topped tables.
Hearth rug – (Worn ). Lino laid to floor.

**TAP ROOM.**
2 Iron spittoons. 3 – 4ft. Stained framed deal top tables with rounded ends.
Coat hanger on door. 3ft. 3in. Cast iron fire curb. Lino fitted to floor.
Pier glass. 2 Short lace curtains and rods.

**BILLARD (sic) ROOM.**
Full size Billard (sic) table inlaid Burr Walnut frame and Mahogany lining by
Burrough & Watts Ltd. Full size Billard table by Hemming Bros. (in poor condition).
2 Billard table covers. 23 Billard cues. 8 Plain Ash Billard cues.
3 Long Billard cues. 2 Short rests. 2 Spider rests. Mahogany Snooker triangle.
Set 22 Ivory Snooker balls. Set 22 Bozaline Snooker balls.
3 Sets Bozaline Billard balls. Table brush. Table iron.
9 Polished Windsor chairs. Bentwood hat and coat stand and tray.
2 – 4ft. 9in. Wrought iron Club fenders with seat tops in green plush. (Worn).
6 Iron spittoons. Lino on floor. Oilcloth fitted under two Billard tables.
Mahogany 4 clip and hole cue rack. 2 Mahogany Billard marking boards. (Damaged).
Snooker marking board. Mahogany 24 hole cue rack. Stained 3 division cue rack.
16 Electric light bulbs, 4 opal shades and 12 Billard shades.
3 Enamel Cornice poles with brass ends and rings. 3 Prs. long green baize curtains.
3 Holland blinds, rollers and fittings. Coil spring to door to hall.

## CROWN HOTEL – Continued.

### BAR.
5 Pull beer engine in Mahogany case with lead lined trough, 5 taps and white porcelain handles with piping to cellar and 5 brass taps and unions.
5 Plated pint tankards. 4 Plated 1/2 pint tankards. 2 Pewter ale measures 1pt & 1/2pt.
Set of 4 Pewter Spirit measures. Large tin tundish. Small copper tundish.
12in. Pewter drainer. "National" Cash register No. 497804.
2 Glass wine decanters and stoppers. 2 Electric light bulbs and shades.
4ft. 6in. Mahogany Overmantle with heart shaped bevelled mirror and 3 brackets.
3ft. 6in. Cast iron fender curb. 4 Copper/brass spittoons. Rubber mat.
3ft. 10in. Circular Rosewood table on pillar and claw feet.
4 Polished birch stools. 2 Electric light bulbs and shades.
9 Oak smoking arm chairs with seats upholstered in leathercloth.
1 Polished birch arm smoking chair. Axminster hearth rug. Lino fitted to floor.

### UPSTAIRS CLUB ROOM.
2 Cast iron fire curbs. 6 – 7ft. 3in. Deal top tables. 9 Folding trestles for same.
Painted frame deal table. 15 – 7ft. Deal boxed forms. Electric light with shade.
5 Enamelled Cornice poles, rings and brackets. 5 Pairs of curtains.
Small deal table. 3 Damaged chairs.

This very comprehensive inventory continues, listing all the fixtures and fittings of 5 bedrooms, the kitchen, wine stores, cellar, bathroom, entrance hall and passage, the side entrance and yard, back landing and stairs, front landing and stairs, all of the Hotel's glassware and stocks of tobacco, beer (bottled and 226 gallons of draught ), wines and spirits and 1 1/2 tons of coal. Also listed is the ……

### BOWLING GREEN.
Garden hoe. Spade. Half moon trimmer. Pair garden shears. Pair border shears.
Garden roller by Ransom. Ransomes Lawn Mowers 15in. and 14in.
1 Painted garden table. 3 – 6ft. Painted garden seats with iron frames.
1 – 5ft. 9in. ditto. 4ft. Painted shelf on bracket supports. Painted notice board.
Painted bowls cupboard. 6ft. Cross legged garden table. 3 Collapsible iron tables.

# CROWN INN – Crabbs Cross

This is an extract from 'Local Notes & Queries' No. 34 – Boney's Island.

A series of articles that appeared in the Redditch Indicator in the 1880's.

The Crown Inn, Crabbs Cross must have been situated approximately where the large traffic island in now, by the Star & Garter.

Returning to the right hand side of the road, the half-timbered cottage where James Hill lived comes next. This (now the dwelling of Mrs. Mogg) is one of better build than the preceding, being chiefly brick but partly of stone. Of this cottage, with the sandpit at the back, James Hill had the freehold, and he supplied sand for the building of the new castle at Studley, and thereby "hangs a tale."

Carpenter Morris had just then built the *Crown* on the triangular piece of waste at the fork of the Alcester and Evesham highways, the first house opened in the neighbourhood under the Beerhouses Act, and one which shows itself to be the work of a man who had gathered his materials together by degrees. In this house James Hill, thinking that he had a gold mine instead of a sandpit, would sit from morning to night drinking and making others drink. As each load of sand went off he called for more beer—

"Here, landlord, fill these pots again
  And stick it to my score,
My cart will soon be here, and then
  We'll drink to *one load more*."

So day by day, and week by week,
  As it went by the door,
As long as he had strength to speak,
  He drank to *one load more!*

There is a saying "as dry as sand," and perhaps James Hill thought that it required "wetting." The result of this folly was, however, that in course of time he drank up his sandpit, cart, horses, barrows, etc., and the whole of his freehold!

There are several families of the name of Hill at Crabbs Cross at the present day, but the James Hill here spoken of was in no way connected with any of them, as I am assured by my informant.

**The Crown Inn**, Feckenham Road, Astwood Bank from the High Street in about 1910. The delivery cart in the foreground belongs to High Street greengrocers Turner & Son.

"D" COY. 9TH WORCS. BATTN.

ASTWOOD  BANK
HOTEL GUARD

# Dinner & Entertainment

ON

SATURDAY, DECEMBER 16th, 1944,

AT THE

CROWN HOTEL, ASTWOOD BANK,

By kind permission of Host: Mr. H. Walker.

Master of Ceremonies:
Lt. E. Ames

Grace - - - - - Cpl. H. Shakles

## Menu.

HAM AND TONGUE
ROLLS
SWEET
CHEESE AND BISCUITS

The Crown Inn, Astwood Bank, looking down Feckenham Road.

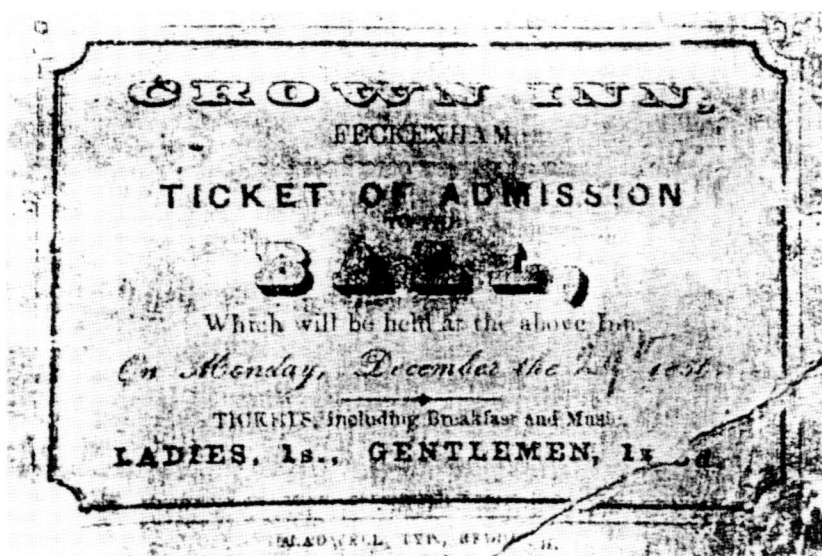
An admission ticket to a ball held at the Crown Inn, Feckenham on Monday December 29th, 1851. The price of 1/- included breakfast and music. This is a different inn to the present Rose and Crown.

# REDDITCH PUBS IN THE NEWS

### Redditch Indicator 1894.

REDDITCH is notably a drunken immoral town according to the Temperance League.

There are 84 public houses in our midst, and we spend £42,000 per annum on intoxicating drink. That gives an average income of £500 to each licence holder.

### Bristol 1892

A SMOKING concert, the fourth in a series of four at **Headless Cross Football Club**, took place at the Bristol Inn. Attendance was scarcely so large as at former occasions but as the evening wore on it increased.

Mr Bunegar officiated at the piano and Mr Johnson's exhibition of ventriloquism was greatly applauded.

Mr H Taylor's rendering of 'I'm selling up my happy home' and 'You should have heard her whistling' were both well received.

### Cricketer's Arms November 26 1898

PIGEON show. The third annual pigeon show, in connection with the Beoley Road Hospital, the nursing fund section, was held in the assembly room of the Cricketer's Arms Inn on Saturday.

A remarkably fine lot of birds was caged, especially in the homer class, most of the leading fanciers in the district contributing.

Mr V Woodfield, a well-known local pigeon breeder and fancier, acted as a judge, and the principal prize winners were: Messrs. J Heath, A Smith, G Greenhill, GW Blick, F Gregory, T Johnson, T Boswell.

Flying homers, W Young, G Chester, W Yates.

Any other variety, R Bennett, A Russell, W Oakley.

### Crown 1870

ON SATURDAY morning last between the hours of 4 and 5 o'clock a fire broke out on the premises Mr John Davis of the Crown Hotel.

Mrs Davis was first awakened by the smell of smoke and on going downstairs it was found that the chimney piece of the tap room was burned to the ground and a cupboard containing a valuable stock of cigars was in flames.

With the assistance of Mr T Owen of the fire brigade who resides next door and one or two commercial travellers who were staying at the hotel the fire was put out without any public alarm being given.

It is supposed that about 50 boxes of cigars were burnt and otherwise injured. The premises and stock are insured in the Lancashire office.

The house is very old and the fire is supposed to have originated from a beam which crosses the chimney having taken fire.

### Redditch April 8, 1899

Worcestershire Quarter Sessions – The Quarter Sessions were opened on Tuesday and the chairman, Mr J W Willis-Bund, drew attention to the returns of drunkenness in the county which have already been before the standing joint committee.

He suggested that if magistrates were really desirous of putting down drunkenness, they ought to deal more severely with the cases which come before them. It was remarked satisfactory to find that the amount of Sunday drinking was very small.

Mr R H Amphlett thought the returns were very unsatisfactory as showing an increase in drunkenness particularly in Northfield, Pershore and Redditch.

### Bristol Inn 1871

THE well known and widely dreaded Astwood Harry - refusing to leave a licensed House.

Henry Smith of Astwood Bank was charged with refusing to leave a licensed house on the 14th inst when requested to do so.

The defendant did not appear and PC John Fox proved service of summons.

William Hill deposed: I keep the Bristol Inn, Headless Cross. On Friday 14th inst the defendant Smith followed two gentlemen into my house and asked if they would give him a pint of ale. One of them did so.

He then commenced to abuse me. I requested him to leave he refused and threatened to dash my brains out against the grate.

In answer to the magistrates PC Haynes stated that he thought the defendant the worst character in Worcestershire. He had just come out of jail for a similar offence at Hunt End and had been convicted for felony and several other offences.

Fined £1 costs, 10s to be paid forthwith or one month's imprisonment.

### Baker's Arms 1866

The Needle District was horrified in the early part of this week by rumours of a deliberate murder said to have been committed at Astwood Bank, and there discovered after the the lapse of many days.

It became known that a widow named Elizabeth Mole was in custody; and on Monday an inquest was held at the Baker's Arms, Astwood before Mr Hughes, coroner and a Jury, of whom Mr William Welch of Hunt End was foreman.

After an enquiry, not very much protracted, the Jury bought in a verdict -Guilty of Wilful Murder.

### Bristol 1891

AN inquest was held at the Bristol Inn after William Bourne, aged 19, died two days after accidentally drinking liquid ammonia.

The inquest heard that the bricklayers labourer had not been in good spirits of late and appeared very 'funny' in his mind.

He had been complaining of headaches but had not talked about making away with himself and took glycerine each night to calm the pain.

But he bought some ammonia to clean clothes and in his dark room drank from the bottle instead of his medicine.

Neighbours said the intense pain sent him raving mad until he died two days later.

Dr Moreton, of Redditch, said the post mortem showed the interior of the stomach was very disorganised and in some parts was almost entirely burnt through.

The cause of death was shock but he said Mr Bourne would have died from his stomach wounds soon afterwards.

The coroner said there was no reason to suspect suicide but commented that he should have been more careful than to take medicine in the dark.

## DOG INN.   Ipsley Street.

Only mentioned by name in Billing's Directory of 1855.

John Price                  1854 – 55

---

## DOG AND PHEASANT.   164 Evesham Road, Headless Cross.

| | | | |
|---|---|---|---|
| Robert Heynes | 1872 – 74 | William Forester | 1900 – 01 |
| Felix Clarke | 1875 – 77 | (William Forester & Sons were plumbers and painters) | |
| Alfred C. Herman | 1880 – 85 | | |
| Mrs Caroline Herman | 1886 – 91 | J Dunn | 1902 – 06 |
| Joshua Nash | 1892 – 96 | Joseph Field | 1907 – 13 |
| Frederick Carson | 1896 – 99 | (Kelly's Directory gives Field as early as 1904) | |
| (He issued a 3d token on which the pub name is spelled Pheasent) | | Charles Field | 1914 – 40 |

---

## DUKE OF YORK.   Evesham Street. (Sometimes Mount Pleasant).

Later became the 'Plough and Harrow.'
Local Notes and Queries No. 88. (Right)
   ?   Shrimpton
Richard Field                1841
(Needle maker)

> The *Duke of York* stood at the junction of the "Front" and the "Back Hills," and the site now occupied by the *Plough and Harrow* was the garden in front of it. On each side of the gate stood a yew tree, and thence a path led to the front door. It was formerly kept by a landlord of the name of Shrimpton, who cut his throat, but did not succeed in killing himself. Afterwards Mr. Richard Field kept the house.

---

## EAGLE INN.   335 Evesham Road, Crabbs Cross.

| | | | |
|---|---|---|---|
| William Knight | 1860 – 64 | William Henry Johnson | 1892 – 96 |
| (Described as a shop-keeper) | | Albert Parker Edwards | 1897 – 1903 |
| Mrs Maria Knight | 1868 | (Moved on to Cricketer's, Beoley Road) | |
| Reuben Houghton | 1872 – 74 | John Frederick Hobday | 1904 – 14 |
| William Poole | 1875 – 87 | James Styler | 1916 – 27 |
| Mrs Mary Ann Poole | 1888 – 89 | James Sturges | 1928 – 40 |
| Charles Keyte | 1890 – 91 | | |

The Dog & Pheasant pictured above about 1930 together with Frederick Carson's 3d token from the late 1890's. Earlier, in 1893 – 94, Carson was manager of the Redditch Industrial Co-operative Society in Headless Cross who issued a token made of tin to the value of 2/-. Below is the Eagle, Crabbs Cross, in 1908.

## EIGHT BELLS.   High Street, Feckenham.

| | | | |
|---|---|---|---|
| John Deaken | 1841 – 73 | Mrs Ann Amelia Lewis | 1904 – 06 |
| (He was also a shoemaker) | | Edgar John Masters | 1907 – 20 |
| William Deaken | 1873 – 86 | L. Kings | 1921 |
| (Vestry clerk) | | Harry Anslow | 1921 – 29 |
| (The name is spelled Deaken in | | H. Stephens | 1930 – 32 |
| Kelly's and Deakin in Redditch | | W. Styler | 1933 – 36 |
| Needle District Almanack) | | Sam Whitehead | 1940 |
| Miss Ann Amelia Deaken | 1887 – 90 | A. F. Badger | 1950 – 54 |
| (She married ……) | | | |
| Alfred Lewis | 1891 – 1903 | | |

---

## THE ELBOWS.   Hewell Lane, Tardebigge.

The house name still exists.               Miss Elizabeth Billings   1841 – 68

---

## (THE FISH)   Prospect Hill (Fish Hill).

It was not a pub that gave its name to Fish Hill (as recorded in some local history books) but a shop owned by Bartleet's who were needle and fishing tackle manufacturers.

**LOCAL NOTES AND QUERIES.**
No. 31.—A correspondent referring to the query in the issue of July 3rd, states on the authority of a very old inhabitant, who died some fifteen years ago, that the name of "The Fish" as applied to Messrs. Bartleet's manufactory, originated from a small shop, kept by a Mrs. Bartleet, where Fish Hill House now stands, who amongst other articles sold fishing tackle, denoted by a little fish dangling at the end of a rod over the door. From this the establishment acquired the name "Bartleet's of the Fish," and the thoroughfare that of "Fish Hill." The name given to Messrs. Milward's works, the same informant stated, was derived from a public house, bearing the sign of the "Fountain," which formerly stood upon the site.

---

## FLEECE INN.   57/59, 61/63 Evesham Street.

The fleece was the source of Englands wealth from the Middle Ages. In the 1850's the pub was known as the 'Turf Tavern.'

| | | | |
|---|---|---|---|
| Thomas Crow | 1850 – 60 | John William Bennett | 1896 – 1903 |
| James Oakley | 1861 – 64 | ? Cheshire (NDA) | 1904 – 09 |
| Miss Catherine Mary Ballard | 1868 – 71 | Henry Davis (Kelly) | 1904 |
| Hugh Rountree | 1872 – 75 | (Also at the Red Lion and White Hart) | |
| John Pinfield | 1875 – 81 | John Green | 1908 – 09 |
| John Holbeche | 1881 | Mrs Maxwell | 1910 – 11 |
| John Wright | 1882 – 84 | William Richardson | 1912 – 21 |
| Mrs Catherine Wright | 1884 – 87 | David Skidmore | 1922 – 26 |
| Harry James Millward | 1888 – 90 | W. Martin | 1927 |
| W. E. Perks | 1891 | Thomas Kibler | 1928 |
| J. C. Baker | 1892 | George Hastings Emms | 1932 – 34 |
| Benjamin Johnson | 1892 – 94 | Horace Esme Grove | 1936 – 40 |
| G. Millward | 1895 | | |

### ORIGIN OF THE NAME "EIGHT BELLS."

Believed to have been an old coaching inn with stables at the rear. It got its name from the fact that William Deaken (or Deakin) was the foreman of the church bell-ringers for many years. Eight hand-bells were rung in the church on special occasions and the pub had replicas of these.

A postcard view of the "Eight Bells," High Street, Feckenham in the 1940/50's.

### "The Elbows" – An extract from the book by Margaret Dickins "A Thousand Years in Tardebigge." Published in 1931.

Opposite the chancel door is a stone to Elizabeth Billings, who was the last of the *'wise women,'* a Shakespearian name for women who professed some knowledge of herbs and surgery. She owned about fifteen acres and the public-house called The Elbows, the sign of which was two arms bent, an allusion to the saying 'Having a crooked elbow.' The lock-up, a possession of every parish under the old parish constable system, was an old cottage just north of the Elbows public-house, where its garden, of the same narrow shape, still remains. (i.e. in 1931) It kept its name of 'The Cage' till it was pulled down. One of its last tennants was an old man who had fought at Trafalgar.

The Fleece, Evesham St., photo taken about 1905 by Albert Green.

**FLEECE INN.**          524 Evesham Road, Crabbs Cross.

Rebuilt 1897.

| | | | |
|---|---|---|---|
| Job Harris | 1868 | Arthur Bakes | 1913 |
| James Ladds | 1870 | Joseph Maddocks | 1914 |
| Fred Chambers | 1872 – 1901 | John H. Smith | 1916 |
| (Butcher and shopkeeper) | | T. Downes | 1917 – 19 |
| Albert Edward Chambers | 1902 – 10 | James Edwin Windridge | 1921 |
| John E. Charman | 1911 – 12 | Charles Barnett Ballinger | 1924 – 40 |

---

**FOLLY INN.**          Evesham Road, Headless Cross.

A thatched cottage. See Local Notes and Queries No. 88.

| | | |
|---|---|---|
| James Millward (Needle seller) | Mrs Ann Millward | 1850 |

---

**FORESTER'S ARMS.**   123/125 Evesham Road, Headless Cross.

| | | | |
|---|---|---|---|
| David Pinfield | 1883 – 87 | David Jennings | 1912 – 27 |
| Samuel Jones | 1888 – 1900 | (He issued 1½d and 3d tokens) | |
| T. Gascoigne | 1900 – 06 | William Henry Jennings | 1928 – 36 |
| Joshua Davis | 1907 – 11 | William Griffin | 1936 |
| (He issued a 1½d token) | | | |

---

**FOUNTAIN INN.**       75/91 Evesham Street.

The Fountain and the Temperance Hotel were demolished in 1935 and replaced by the Hungry Man.
Tokens exist for the Fountain Inn Sick & Dividend Society. No licensee named.

| | | | |
|---|---|---|---|
| Emma Mustin | 1871 – 72 | George Ward | 1916 |
| Jesse Whele | 1873 – 1900 | Walter Sealey | 1921 – 24 |
| (Parcels agent) | | William E. D. Evans | 1928 |
| Walter J. Hadgkiss | 1901 – 06 | George Henry Glover | 1932 |
| Ernest James W. Bird | 1908 – 10 | Frank Richard Mansell | 1934 |
| James E. Harris | 1912 | | |

---

**FOUNTAIN INN.**       Breedon. (Bottom of Ipsley Street).

Purchased by Henry Milward in 1802 and incorporated into Washford Mills.

The original Fleece Inn, Crabbs Cross, began life as a row of cottages. The end one was a butchers shop run by Fred Chambers who in 1872 took over the pub next door. Eventually, Fred, who appears on the extreme right of the bottom picture, merged the two premises and concentrated on being a pub landlord.

> Advertisement.
>
> # FLEECE HOTEL,
>
> ## Crabbs Cross, Redditch.
>
> ### WINES, SPIRITS, AND CIGARS
> OF THE FINEST QUALITY.
>
> This House has long been noted for **DRAUGHT ALES & STOUT**, and the Proprietor wishes to point out that they are still UP TO THE EXCELLENT STANDARD.
>
> The FLEECE is one of the few free houses.
>
> ### Bass's Ales and Guinness's Stout in Bottles.
>
> Good Stabling.   Accommodation for Cyclists.   Lock-up Coach-house.
>
> PLEASURE GROUNDS, BOWLING GREEN, ETC.
>
> THE FLEECE HOTEL is in a fine, healthy situation, with splendid views in every direction, and the Proprietor now having every accommodation for catering, will give the most careful attention to getting up
>
> DINNERS, TEAS, &c.
>
> P.S.—CYCLE CLUBS AND PLEASURE PARTIES PLEASE NOTE ABOVE.
>
> Proprietor, ALBERT E. CHAMBERS.

The Fleece was rebuilt in 1897 while Fred Chambers (above) was licensee. He was succeeded by Albert Chambers (below). His 1902 advert in the Redditch Needle District Almanack shows the importance of passing trade, cycle clubs, etc.

(Family photographs courtesy of Miss Chambers of Edgiock Court).

The Fleece, Crabbs Cross circa 1930. The name on the board over the door is that of Charles Barnett Ballinger. Below is a Fleece Hotel hip flask.

The Folly Inn, Evesham Road, Headless Cross.

Extract from "Local Notes & Queries" No. 88. concerning "Extinct Public Houses," it was published in the Indicator in May 1887.

> Further on towards Crabbs Cross was the *Hare and Hounds* kept by a Mr. Thomas Charman, and about a stone's throw from this was the *Folly*, a cottage inn, brick built, but roofed with thatch, and kept by James Millward, who also did a little needle selling, travelling with a small cart drawn by two dogs in the days when such means of conveyance was permitted. James Millward, as an innkeeper, was said to have been an eccentric man, usually seen in shirt-sleeves, and wearing one of the old square-made brown paper caps now rarely met with.
> C.C.C.

The Forester's Arms, 123/125 Evesham Road, Headless Cross. The pub is left of the centre of the picture, marked by a large (gas?) lamp hanging out-side. The building is now occupied by a newsagent and was previously a chemist. Below are tokens issued by two of the licensees. J. Davis's name appears on a 1 1/2d token and there are 3d and 1 1/2d by David Jennings of similar design.

The Fountain Inn, 75 Evesham Street. Its neighbour at 77, the Temperance Hotel was in the 1850's a pub called the Bull's Head.

Below is the pubs 3d token, several specimens of which exist in local collections.

### Local Notes and Queries No. 31.

Giving the origin of the name of the Fountain Inn, Ipsley Street.

See next page for a more detailed explanation.

**LOCAL NOTES AND QUERIES.**

No. 31.—A correspondent referring to the query in the issue of July 3rd, states on the authority of a very old inhabitant, who died some fifteen years ago, that the name of "The Fish" as applied to Messrs. Bartleet's manufactory, originated from a small shop, kept by a Mrs. Bartleet, where Fish Hill House now stands, who amongst other articles sold fishing tackle, denoted by a little fish dangling at the end of a rod over the door. From this the establishment acquired the name "Bartleet's of the Fish," and the thoroughfare that of "Fish Hill." The name given to Messrs. Milward's works, the same informant stated, was derived from a public house, bearing the sign of the "Fountain," which formerly stood upon the site.

### The Fountain Inn,   Breedon.

(Breedon was the old name for the bottom of Ipsley St. and top of Beoley Rd). "*Fountain Works*" reproduced above from Milward's commemorative calender of 1980, marking 250 years of needle making. The print "shows the back of the old Fountain public house in Ipsley Street. The part with the archway still exists (since bricked in) and can be seen at the rear of the Lodge at our Redditch factory." (Later demolished and replaced by Halfords and Wickes ).

Henry Milward & Sons needle business started at the "Mills at Washford" on the river Arrow, now a pub. They later took over the premises of the old Fountain Inn, Ipsley Street and incorporated it into the new "Washford Mills" factory. The move to the Fountain meant the loss of water power to drive the machinery and it would appear from this verse from the poem about Redditch "by an Old Fish Hill Boy" that the power source in 1840 was a horse whim or mill as illustrated in this drawing by J M Woodward.

Round and round went the Fountain horse,
A steady walk on a circular course,
I've gazed at him on many a day,
Poor brute, why did'nt he run away.

## FOX INN.    79 Edward Street.

Reputed to have had the longest bar of any pub in Redditch.

| | | | |
|---|---|---|---|
| Josiah Green | 1868 – 91 | Mrs Myra Maries | 1916 – 21 |
| George Joseph Savery | 1892 – 97 | John Thomas Spiers | 1922 – 34 |
| Stephen George Millward | 1898 – 1903 | William Joseph Bruton | 1936 |
| George Frederick Maries | 1904 – 14 | George Frederick Carter | 1940 |

---

## FOX AND GOOSE.    8 Market Place.

The address in early directories is given as 'Chapel Green' and also 'Church Green South.' The Fox & Goose dates from 1807; it was rebuilt in February 1897 and re-named 'The Royal Hotel.'

| | | | |
|---|---|---|---|
| Thomas Fowkes | 1822 – 50 | Hugh Rountree | 1875 – 83 |
| James Walton | 1835 ? | John Fletcher | 1884 – 86 |
| William Francis | 1854 – 55 | William Reason | 1887 – 90 |
| (He was also a needle maker and he issued a 3d gaming token ) | | William Whiteway Alexander | 1891 – 96 |
| | | T ? Gathercole (or Frank) | 1896 |
| Henry Laugher | 1860 – 68 | (For 1897 on, see under entry for the 'Royal Hotel') | |
| Walter Harwood | 1872 – 75 | | |
| (He also worked as a castrator ) | | | |

---

## FOX AND GOOSE.    Foxlydiate.    Demolished 1947.

Appears in early directories under Webheath and also Feckenham. The Redditch Indicator for 1st May 1937 gives notice that the licence had transferred to the newly built 'Foxlydiate Hotel' across the road, on the site of the demolished Foxlydiate House.

| | | | |
|---|---|---|---|
| John George Hill | 1841 | Henry Aston | 1884 – 92 |
| William Yarnall | 1850 – 55 | Mrs Chesshire | 1893 – 95 |
| Thomas Powell | 1860 – 64 | Herbert Fred Chambers | 1896 – 1922 |
| Mrs Eliza Powell | 1868 | Mrs Chambers | 1923 |
| John Shinton | 1872 – 78 | Ernest Hubbard | 1923 – 25 |
| (Also at the 'Greyhound') | | Frank Juggins | 1926 – 28 |
| Mrs John Shinton | 1879 – 83 | William E D Evans | 1932 – 36 |

---

## FOXLYDIATE HOTEL.    Foxlydiate.

Built in 1938 and opened on February 8th 1939 on the site of Foxlydiate House.

| | | | |
|---|---|---|---|
| H C Newman | 1939 | Edward Kennedy | 1940 |

---

# FOX AND GOOSE HOTEL,
## REDDITCH,
# HENRY LAUGHER,
### PROPRIETOR.

#### H. L. HAVING PURCHASED A

# MARQUEE

Of large dimensions, would be happy to let it on hire, for Pic-Nic parties, or for other purposes, on moderate terms.

The Marquee is oblong, 60 feet by 33, and 14 feet high

The ends are adapted to form a circular Tent. It is therefore suitable for the accommodation, either of a large or a small assemblage of persons

The Marquee may be seen on the Cricketers ground on Tuesday.

H. L. takes this opportunity of sincerely thanking his friends and the public at large, for the extremely liberal support evinced towards him during his occupancy of the Fox and Goose Hotel.

**FOX AND GOOSE.**      Market Place, Redditch    (Later the Royal Hotel).

These two adverts from the Redditch Indicator appear to show licensee Henry Laugher as keen to expand trade both on the premises and also at outside functions. His marquee advert was published on Saturday 1st. September 1860 and the New Assembly Room which was to open on Monday December 10th was advertised in the paper on Saturday Nov. 24th. 1860.

## HOUSEWARMING.
# FOX & GOOSE COMMERCIAL INN,
## REDDITCH.
# HENRY LAUGHER,
### PROPRIETOR.

H. L. begs to announce that his HOUSEWARMING DINNER will take place in his New Assembly Room, on MONDAY, December 10th, and respectfully solicits the patronage and support of his friends and the public at large of Redditch and its vicinity.

**TICKETS, TWO SHILLINGS & SIXPENCE EACH.**

Dinner on the Table at Three o'clock.

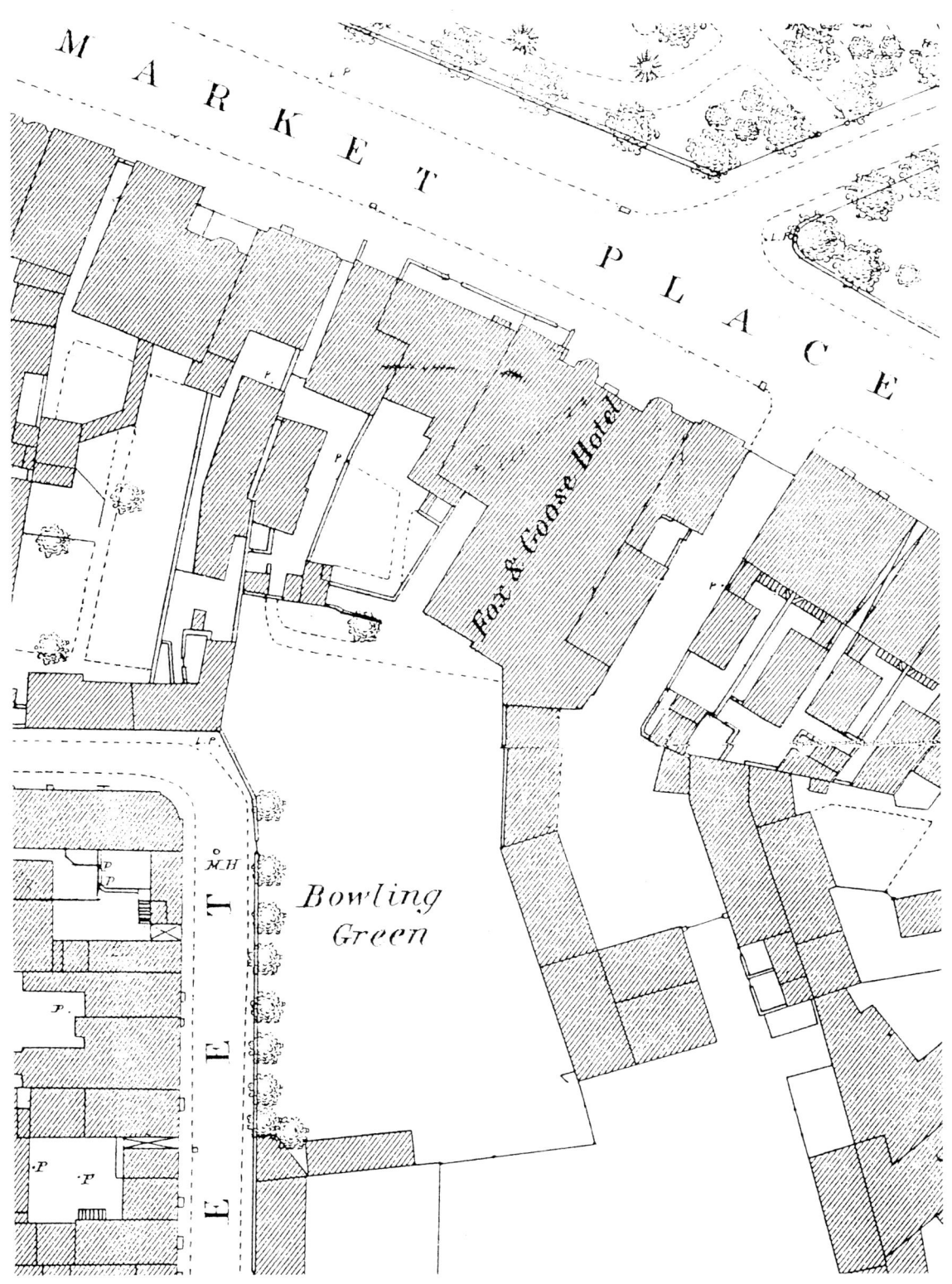

The Fox and Goose, Market Place, from a map of 1884.
Its large Bowling Green later became Royal Square and is now
part of the shopping centre.

14                  ADVERTISEMENT.

# FOX AND GOOSE HOTEL,

## REDDITCH.

## CYCLING TOURING CLUB QUARTERS,

*HEAD-QUARTERS OF THE*

### Redditch and District Cycling Club,

### REDDITCH TOWN FOOTBALL CLUB,

*Redditch Windsor Cricket Club, and the Redditch Athletic and Gymnasium Club.*

---

## STEDMAN & Co.,

WHOLESALE AND FAMILY

## Wine and Spirit Merchants.

*Good Accommodation for Commercials, Cyclists, and Tourists.*

THE HOTEL PORTER WILL MEET ALL TRAINS.

An Ordinary every day at 12 45.

Families supplied with high-class Wines, Spirits, Ales, Cigars, &c. Guinness's Stout, Bass's, Flower's, and Worthington's Ales, bottled by Kenway.

**PRICE LIST ON APPLICATION.**

Balls, Meetings, Clubs, Smoking Concerts, Theatrical Entertainments, Dinners, Pic-nic Parties, &c., catered for in the Large Room of the Hotel, which will accommodate upwards of 500 persons.

---

STEDMAN & Co., Proprietors.

**W. W. ALEXANDER, Manager,**
(Midland Counties' Handicapper.)

William Whiteway Alexander's 1892 advert.

MEMORANDUM.

From **W. W. ALEXANDER,** "FOX AND GOOSE HOTEL," REDDITCH.

To Messrs Flower & Sons
Stratford-on-Avon
Jan'y 31. 1893.

Dear Sirs,

Re Loan

Replying to your letter of yesterdays date, the terms stated therein will be quite satisfactory to me & I have handed Mr Dagge the first instalment of £10. as desired. I will consider the instalments due on the 1st day of each month.

I shall endeavour from time to time to reduce the principal in addition to these monthly payments.

Yours faithfully
W. W. Alexander

ABOVE: A note from William Alexander on Fox & Goose Hotel headed note paper, in acknowledgement of a loan from Stratford brewers Flowers & Sons – the repayment was £10 per month.

RIGHT: An anonymous 3d Fox & Goose brass token.

BELOW: Both sides of William Francis 3d token of the 1850's. Bronze and brass examples exist. The manufacturer of the token was John Mappin who, surprisingly, was also a surgical truss maker.

## FOX & GOOSE, MARKET PLACE, REDDITCH

The sale of the premises in November 1895 which resulted in its rebuilding. This was completed by February 1897 when it was renamed the Royal Hotel. W. W. Alexander ceased being its licensee in 1896 and the new hotel was run by Frank Gathercole.

BELOW: A newspaper cutting records the athletic prowess of W. W. Alexander and his part in founding the Birchfield Harriers. It also mentions his death in 1933.

---

SALE ON THURSDAY, NOVEMBER 14TH, 1895.

TO BREWERS, WINE AND SPIRIT MERCHANTS, AND PUBLICANS SEEKING A SOUND INVESTMENT.

VALUABLE LEASE, LICENSES, GOODWILL, POSSESSION, FIXTURES AND FURNITURE OF THE FOX AND GOOSE COMMERCIAL HOTEL, REDDITCH.

### NEASOM & WHITE,

BEG to announce that they have received instructions from Mr. W. W. Alexander, to Sell by Auction, at the GRAND HOTEL, BIRMINGHAM, on THURSDAY, the 14th day of NOVEMBER, 1895, at Four o'clock in the Afternoon, exact time, subject to conditions of sale to be then produced, the Valuable LEASE, LICENSES, GOODWILL, POSSESSION, FIXTURES, FURNITURE, and TRADE UTENSILS, of the Old Established Centrally-situated Commercial Family and Market Hotel, known as "The Fox and Goose" Hotel, situate in the Centre of the Thickly-populated and Thriving Manufacturing Town of Redditch.

The House contains on the Ground Floor Entrance Hall, Large Vaults, Billiard Room, for Two Tables, Bar Parlour, Sitting Room, Smoke Room, fitted with Bar, Large Committee Room, Kitchens, Larders, and Store Rooms.

In the Basement there are some excellent Commodious Cellars, which would be of great advantage to a Wine and Spirit Merchant.

The Second Floor (approached by Two Staircases), upon which there is a very large Assembly Room, known as the Oddfellows' Hall" (to which Two very large and influential Lodges are attached), fitted with Bar, and capable of seating 500 persons, Commercial Room, and Five Capital Chambers, Bath Room, W.C., Store Rooms, and Landings.

Upon the Third Floor are Four very good Chambers. At the rear of the House is a Capital walled-in Bowling Green, upon which are erections of Summer Houses and Refreshment Bars, with a private entrance to the Green. There is a large piece of Land, used for a monthly Stock Sale and for Travelling Theatres and Shows to a very great extent, a portion of which is let off to Tradesmen, who have erected Coach-houses thereon. At the rear of this land is a large productive Kitchen Garden.

The Stabling and Coach-houses, now let to Mr. Joseph Rountree Cab and Car Proprietor, are well and conveniently arranged, and comprises Stabling for upwards of 20 Horses, and Room for Twelve Carriages. There is a good approach to the main street, and a very good yard with carriage wash, to which the E.W. Water is laid on.

Adjoining the Hotel is a commodious Retail Shop, which is included in the lease, and now let to Mr. James Hawkeswood, butcher. The premises are held under a lease, of which 20 years are unexpired from November 25th, 1895, at the yearly rental of £269, from which can be deducted a very large amount for premises re-let to various tenants.

The House being so centrally situated, and the premises so convenient and commodious, commands a very large and lucrative business.

The Household Furniture, Fixtures, and Trade Effects are very good and substantial, and form a very large inventory.

The purchaser will be required to take to the Stock-in-trade at valuation.

Special attention is directed to the above important sale. The house being a very old-established one, well know and patronized by pleasure parties, commercial gentlemen, cyclists, residents in, and visitors to the town and neighbourhood, affords an opportunity to Brewers, Wine and Spirit Merchants, and the trade generally, seldom to be met with.

For further particulars, and copy of inventory, apply to Messrs. Slatter, Son, and Gibbs, Solicitors, Stratford-on-Avon; or Neasom and White, Auctioneers, Redditch; and to view the house and premises, to Mr. W. W. Alexander, the present proprietor.

---

### CRICKET REIGNED A CENTURY AGO

CRICKET was the pre-eminent game in Redditch a century ago, with games being played against teams from Stourbridge, Belbroughton, Kidderminster and other places, and many well-known local names appeared in the team lists.

Redditch possessed a football team about 90 years ago with a ground in Windsor Road, and the type of football played seems to have been a mixture of both codes. Again there were many well-known local names among the players.

Later on there were no fewer than three strong and useful Rugby teams in the town—the "Harriers," the "Alberts," and the "Alerts."

When the Rev. Wilson Lee came to Redditch the game was changed to soccer.

Perhaps one of the most widely known personalities in the athletic world who was a local man was the late Mr. W. W. Alexander: The landlord of the old Fox and Goose, now the Royal Hotel, he was a fine distance runner in his day, and was said to be one of the best judges of the prospective possibilities of the novice in the land.

But it was as the originator of international competitions, and as founder and honorary secretary of Birchfield Harriers, that he was best known. He died in 1933.

**MEMORANDUM.**

From: NEASOM & WHITE, Auctioneers & Valuers, Architects & Surveyors, REDDITCH.
Attendance at the New Inns, Bromsgrove Street, Birmingham, Every Thursday, 1 till 2-30.

Nov 15th 1895

To Messrs Slatter Son & Gibbs
Solicitors
Stratford on Avon

Fox & Goose

Dear Sirs,
I have seen Mr Wright — I have no doubt he will complete on the day named.

Yours truly
J Neasom

---

**MEMORANDUM.**

From: NEASOM & WHITE, Auctioneers and Valuers, REDDITCH.
Attendance at the New Inns, Bromsgrove Street, Birmingham, Every Thursday, 1 till 2-30.

Nov 13th 1895

To Messrs Slatter Son & Gibbs
Solicitors
Stratford on Avon

Dear Sirs,       Fox & Goose Hotel

Enclosed we beg to hand you the Inventory of the Fixtures, Trade Utensils and Furniture to be included in the Sale tomorrow.

Yours truly
Neasom & White

---

To Mr Harry Wright.

Re Fox & Goose Hotel, Redditch.

I authorize and request you to pay the purchase money of the Lease and effects of and about the above Hotel to Messrs Flower & Sons Limited.

W W Alexander

---

Documents relating to the 1895 sale of the Fox & Goose Hotel. The parties involved were local auctioneers Neasom & White, W. W. Alexander – hotel licensee, Messrs Slatter Son & Gibbs – solicitors for Flowers & Sons and Mr Harry Wright – the new owner.

## "FOX AND GOOSE"
## Family and Commercial Hotel,
### REDDITCH.

Every Accommodation for Cyclists, Tourists, Commercials, &c.

C.T.C. House, Headquarters of the Redditch and District Cycling Club, Windsor Cricket Club, Redditch Harriers, and the District Club House Birchfield Harriers (Midland Champions).

### Wholesale Wine and Spirit Merchant.

FAMILIES SUPPLIED WITH HIGH-CLASS WINES AND SPIRITS, AND SALT AND Co.'s CELEBRATED ALES AND STOUT IN CASK AND BOTTLES.

## BILLIARDS! BILLIARDS!

BILLIARD ROOM (TWO TABLES) OPEN ALL DAY.

The large Hall of the Hotel may be engaged for Balls, Smoking Concerts, Meetings, Clubs, &c.

LARGE DINING HALL WILL SEAT 350 PERSONS.

T. GATHERCOLE, Proprietor.

This advert from the Redditch Directory of 1896, the last year before rebuilding and change of name from 'Fox and Goose' – which was shared with the pub at Foxlydiate – to the much grander 'Royal Hotel.' A mystery surrounds the licensee Gathercole's initial – given as T, his name was Frank. (Unless of course, they were two different people or it was a printer's error).

Fox and Goose, Foxlydiate. Not to be confused with the Fox and Goose, Market Place, which was the pre 1897 name for the Royal Hotel. The Redditch Needle District Almanack of 1879 puts the pub in Webheath and in 1881 in Feckenham district.

ABOVE: A very rare postcard view of a Redditch pub interior. This photograph of the bar in the Fox and Goose, Foxlydiate was taken by Walker, of Stratford on Avon.

BELOW: A very early postcard photograph refers to the pub as the "Foxlydiate Inn".

The Fox and Goose was demolished in 1947. All that remains today are some of the steps once used by patrons of the pub when they dismounted from their horses, pony and traps, carriages, etc. It is best illustrated in this watercolour painting by J. M. Woodward.

The Redditch Indicator announced on the first of May 1937 that the licence of the Fox and Goose, Foxlydiate was to be transferred to the new premises on the opposite side of the road on the site of the old Foxlydiate House.

The scaffolding rises in 1938 on the site of the Foxlydiate Hotel.

The picture below shows workmen on ladders putting the finishing touches to the new building which opened for business on Wed. February 8th 1939.

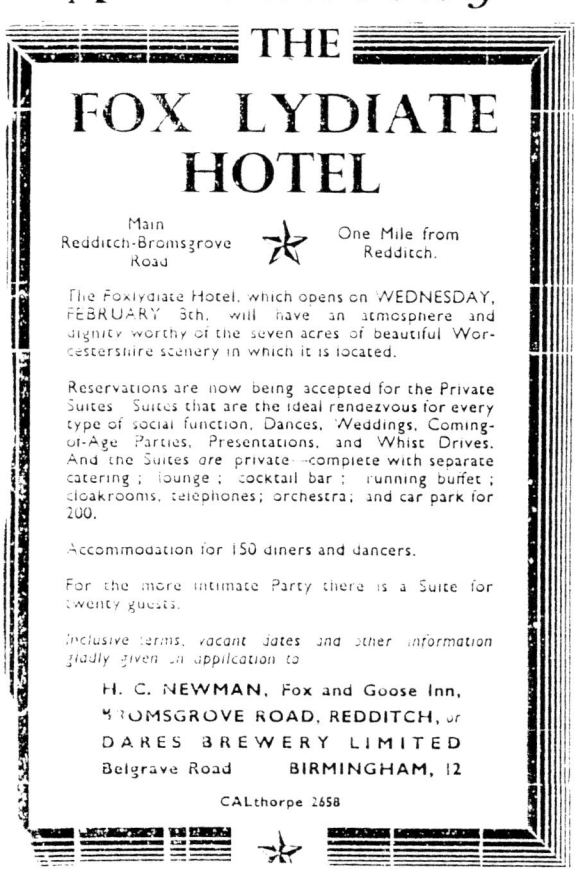

LEFT:
The advert announcing the opening on Wednesday February 8th 1939 of the new Fox Lydiate (sic) Hotel. Enquiries are directed to the new landlord H. C. Newman who apparently was living at the Fox and Goose.

BELOW:
Some of the crested cutlery originally provided by Dares Brewery.

# REDDITCH PUBS IN THE NEWS

## Eight Bells

**February 11, 1899.**

NEW sick and dividend society: On Saturday a public meeting was held at the Eight Bells Inn to consider the advisability of starting a new sick and dividend society. Mr E Cund was voted to the chair.

It was resolved that a society be formed to be called the Eight Bells Sick and Dividend Society.

A very successful start was made with upwards of 30 members joining. It was decided to hold monthly meetings and that it should be open for any person between the ages of 17 and 40 to join.

A vote of thanks was accorded to the secretary for the trouble he had taken in forming the society and to the chairman for presiding.

## Fleece and Red Lion

**December 8, 1900**

ON Tuesday morning Mr C Fenwick was riding a bicycleto the Enfield Works at Hunt End, closely followed through Crabbs Cross by Mr G Hollingworth, who was driving a horse and trap.

When near the Fleece Hotel, Mr Fenwick turned to go down Littlewoods, but the greasy condition of the road caused the machine to skid and dismounted the rider.

He managed to jump out of the way just as the wheel of the trap dashed into the machine, damaging it to such an extent as to make it unrideable.

Mr Hollingworth took compassion on the cyclist and conveyed him and his damaged machine to the Enfield Works.

But shortly afterwards when proceeding towards the Red Lion Inn, the horse was startled by the noise from the gas engines and bolted at a terrific speed to the Red Lion corner.

And in swerving round to mount Weavers Hill, the trap was overturned and Mr Hollingworth fell underneath.

Other than a few bruises the rider had a fortunate and marvellous escape. The horse escaped injury but the trap was wrecked.

## Fleece 1870

JOSEPH Phillips was charged with being on the premises of James Ladds, beerhouse keeper of Crabbs Cross, during prohibited hours.

Defendant pleaded guilty to being on the premises, but not to buying any ale.

P C John Wheeler, desposed: On Sunday morning, the 20th March, I was on duty in Crabbs Cross; at about a quarter to twelve I got to the premises of the Fleece beerhouse, kept by James Ladds, and saw Phillips with a pint jug in his hand.

He deposed "I went to the front door which was locked; Mr Ladds unlocked it and I went to the bowling alley where Joseph Phillips was in the act of putting the jug on a rail.".

But the jug contained fresh drawn beer; and P C Wheeler had seen him drink out of the mug. Phillips again said he had had no beer.

Defendant in defence, said that he did not buy any beer, neither was there any supplied to him; that he went to the Fleece, to take some water-cress to Mr Hill, a lodger who gave him some beer. The Chairman said he could have been fined 40s.

But, as it is a fact not generally known that persons being found on the premises of a licensed house during prohibited hours are liable with the landlord, he should inflict a small fine of 1s and 9s costs.

## Fox Inn 1872

REDDITCH Petty Sessions. Five minutes too long. Alfred Wilkes, dealer in vegetables, was charged with causing an obstruction in Edward Street, by leaving a horse and cart unattended on 6th inst.

PC White stated that at 8.35 on the evening in question he saw a horse and cart standing on the road outside the Fox Inn.

He watched the vehicle for 20 minutes and no-one came near it. The horse had a nosebag on and was partly across the road and there was no room for other vehicles to pass.

The defendant said he only had a half pint of cider and was not away more than five minutes. The chairman said: "It does not matter, you must not leave your horse and cart unattended. You were five minutes too long." Fined 2s6d and 8s costs.

## Fleece 1866

John Crook, painter, applied for a temporary transfer of the licence of the Fleece Inn, Redditch. Supt Jeffrey objected and called Insp Emms, who stated that when Mr Crook brought the form of application to the station he was the worse for drink. The bench refused the application.

## Fleece 1972

A MIDLANDS brewery was caught on the hop when they heard an elderly widow wanted to return to her birthplace - a Redditch pub - to celebrate a very special occasion.

When Nellie Curtain made arrangements to hold her 100th birthday at The Fleece the brewery thought there must be some mistake.

For displayed outside the pub is a plaque with the date 1897, making the pub only 75 years old.

But Nellie was adamant. "I was born at The Fleece in Crabbs Cross on February 24, 1872, and I can prove it."

And the proof came when Nellie's nephew, farmer Percy Chambers, unearthed a nineteenth century print of The Fleece, the original one that is.

For Nellie was born in the pub which was completely re-built in 1897.

And so brewery officials have had to admit that Nellie, who now lives in Coventry, was right.

Malcolm Powell the brewery's district manager said: "I heard the story with tongue in cheek. I doubted it up to a point particularly with the 1897 plaque outside but Nellie was right after all."

And John Bevan, director of the Astwood Bank firm which built the new Fleece, verified Nellie's claim.

He said: "Oh Nellie is certainly right. We did re-build The Fleece and I have been looking through our past records and found some more information about the old Fleece."

Licensee Al Sharpe said: "It is certainly a smack in the face for the brewery.

Nellie said: "It was my idea to hold a party at The Fleece.

"I had my 21st there and I was 15 years old when the pub was re-built."

## Gate Inn 1867

Messrs James and Lister Lea, of Birmingham, offered for sale by auction at the Unicorn Hotel, a freehold public house, the "Gate Inn" with a garden and two fields of freehold land situated at Headless Cross.

It was bought by Mr M Chambers of Headless Cross for a Mr Smith of Birmingham for £1,080.

## GATE HANGS WELL.   98/154 Evesham Road, Headless Cross.

At one time, the road to Evesham was a toll road and there was a toll-gate in Headless Cross. In the 1850's the pub was called 'The Case is Altered.'

| | | | |
|---|---|---|---|
| William Emms | 1850 – 55 | Robert Allen | 1908 – 14 |
| Thomas Emms | 1860 – 75 | (From 1904 in Kelly's directory) | |
| Charles Emms | 1875 – 87 | George Kendal | 1916 – 19 |
| Mrs Clara Emms | 1888 – 90 | Herbert Hall | 1921 – 34 |
| David Merry | 1891 – 1900 | George Frederick Carter | 1936 |
| Samuel Jones | 1900 – 02 | Fred Adams | 1940 |
| H Storey | 1903 – 06 | | |

---

## GOLDEN CROSS.   28/56 Unicorn Hill.

Renamed the 'Railway Inn' in 1896 – 'Little Railway' to locals. The railway came to Redditch in 1859 when the station was in Clive Road and the 'Railway Tavern' Hewell road was the nearest pub. The station was moved in 1868 to the bottom of Unicorn Hill. The name 'Golden Cross' was restored in the 1960's and the pub was rebuilt in the 1980's.

| | | | |
|---|---|---|---|
| Mrs Elizabeth Abbott | 1850 | James Garlick | 1890 – 91 |
| John Abbott | 1855 – 68 | William Edward Crow | 1892 – 96 |
| Frederick Roberts | 1870 – 75 | (See under 'Railway Inn' for further details) | |
| (Marine store dealer) | | | |
| Samuel Herbert | 1875 – 90 | | |
| (He issued a 3d token) | | | |

---

## GOLDEN LION.   22/24/25 Red Lion Street.

| | | | |
|---|---|---|---|
| Elizabeth Eaves | 1855 | C Price | 1892 |
| (And shopkeeper) | | Jesse Palmer | 1892 – 96 |
| James Eaves | 1860 – 68 | (Shoemaker) | |
| (And shopkeeper) | | Ann Bull | 1897 – 98 |
| Henry Parsonage | 1872 – 88 | Charles H Jakeman | 1900 – 02 |
| (Butcher) | | L Godson | 1903 – 07 |
| Mrs Henry Parsonage | 1889 – 91 | | |

The Gate Hangs Well, Evesham Road, Headless Cross in about 1914.

Young's butcher's shop on the left of the picture at No. 104 had moved by 1916 to the other side of the road at No. 139 where it remained until fairly recently. Perry and Sons 'Bon Marché' to the right of the pub was on the opposite corner of Birchfield Road and Evesham Road – now demolished and part of Headless Cross Green.

The Gate Hangs Well is a fairly common name for inns located on a toll or turnpike road. The inn sign often bears the legend: This Gate Hangs Well and hinders non. Refresh and pay and travel on.

The Woodward drawing below is believed to show the Park Inn on the left with the toll house opposite and Rectory Road forking right.

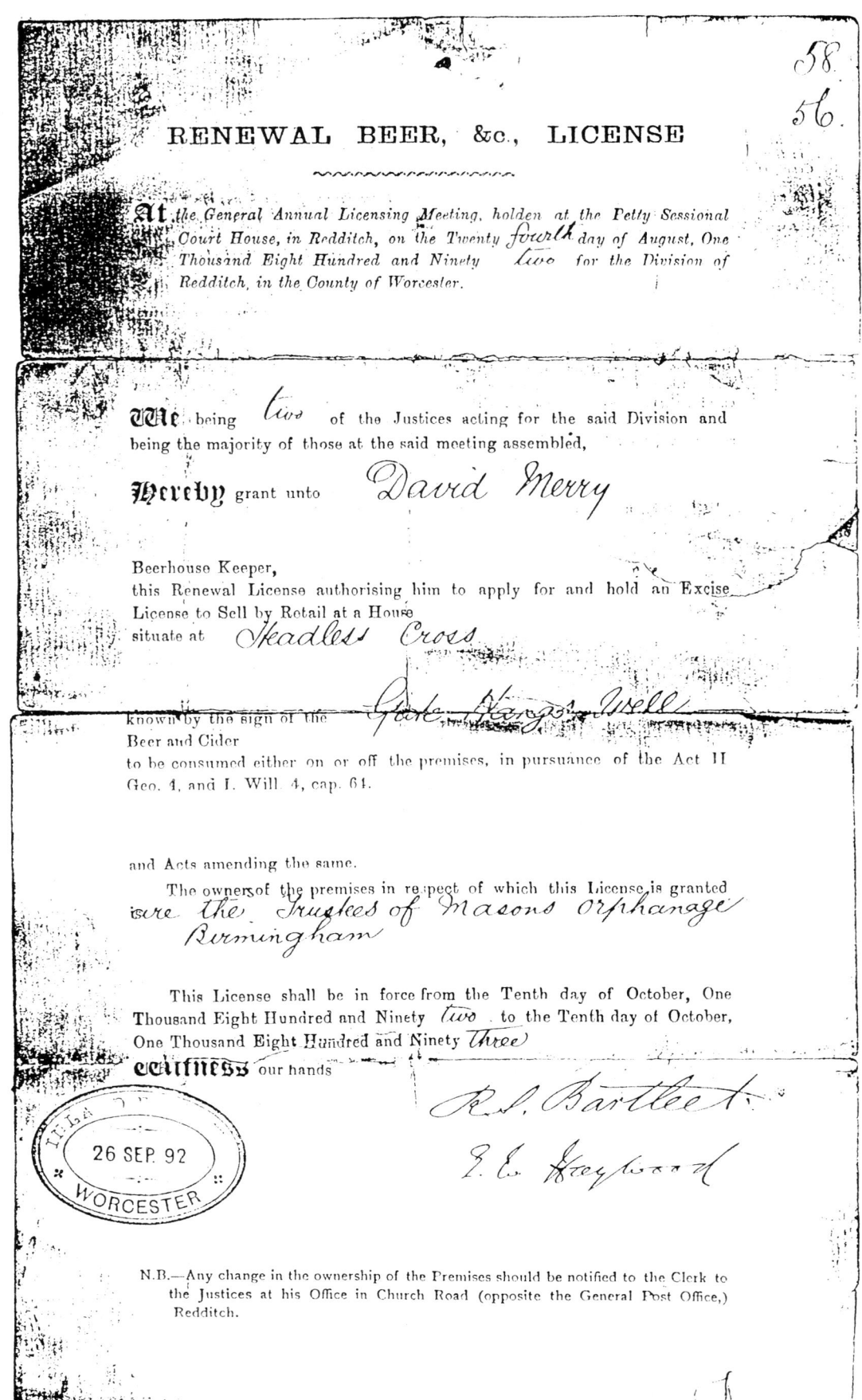

Beer licence renewal granted to David Merry of the Gate Hangs Well, Headless Cross in 1892. It is signed by R. S. Bartleet J.P., needlemaster and Deputy Lieutenant for the County and Edward Waldron Haywood J.P. who lived at the Sillins, Callow Hill.

Throughout its history the Golden Cross at the bottom of Unicorn Hill has had something of an identity complex. Golden Cross was its name up to 1896 when it was renamed the Railway Inn as by that time it was close to the railway station which had moved in 1868. However, there was already a Railway Tavern in Hewell Road near to the original Clive Road railway station. The locals solved this by refering to the Golden Cross/Railway Inn as the "Little Railway." The confusion was somewhat resolved in the 1960's when the name "Golden Cross" was restored. Fortunately it was retained when the pub was rebuilt in the 1980's. For more information see under the entry for Railway Inn.

Illustrated right is Samuel Herbert's 3d brass token from about 1880. It originally did not have a stated value but has been stamped with a figure 3.

# REDDITCH PUBS IN THE NEWS

## Golden Cross 1867

Bad manners and bad memory - James Heath and Charles James, fish hook makers, were being drunk and disorderly and refusing to quit a licensed house on Saturday evening last.

James pleaded "I know nothing about it;" and Heath represented himself as partly a flag-of-truce man and partly a sort of Red Cross Knight going on to the field of battle in the heart of the action to succour the sick and wounded.

The landlord of the Golden Cross, Mr Robertson, deposed that James knocked a man out of his chair and said he would fight anyone.

They left when the landlord sent for the police - getting away before they arrived.

James was fined £1 and expenses or one month with hard labour, and as they believed Heath was not as bad The Bench fined him 10 shillings

## Golden Cross April 1870

WILLIAM Griffin and Alfred Spencer were brought up in custody on a charge of stealing an iron frame and door, of the value of 5s, the property of Frederick Roberts, innkeeper and marine store dealer, Unicorn Hill, Redditch.

Alfred Lord, tinplate worker in the employ of John Hayward, whose premises adjoin those of prosecutor, said that on Wednesday last he saw Griffin dragging the iron frame and door down the entry from the road towards Mr Roberts' yard.

Spencer followed him and both placed it on the prosecutors scales; they then went towards the house; Mrs Roberts returned with Spencer and said the iron was her husband's and she would have nothing to do with it, and Spencer must go into the house until her husband came home.

Emma Roberts, wife of prosecutor, said that on the March 31, Spencer had asked her to go into the yard to see some iron; she knew it was her husbands, told him to go into the house and she would settle with him for it.

Spencer then went into the house; Mrs Roberts followed, shut the door and sent for the police.

Sergeant Hardman said he was sent for to the Golden Cross on Wednesday evening, when Mrs Roberts gave Spencer into custody; charged him with the offence.

Spencer was rather under the influence of drink at the time and said he would rather do a month than tell.

On the following morning Spencer said he did not intend to steal it, he and Griffin were down in the yard and got fooling.

Frederick Roberts identified the iron as his property, which he had purchased at a sale in Alvechurch; and the prisoners, Spencer and Griffin were committed to take their trial at the ensuing Worcester Quarter sessions.

## Golden Cross March 1870

Redditch Petty Sessions: A licence was granted to Frederick Roberts of the Golden Cross Inn, Redditch, the former occupier having fled the country.

## Golden Cross Sept. 1870

REFUSING to quit a public house - Walter Wilkes and George Thomas were each fined 5s and costs for refusing to quit the Golden Cross Inn, Unicorn Hill, on being requested to do so by the landlord and Wilkes was also fined 5s, for having been drunk and riotous.

## Golden Cross 1870

PRUDENCE Dears was charged with stealing a quart jug containing a pint of Jamaica rum, value 2s 6d, the property of Frederick Roberts, Golden Cross Hotel, Redditch, on the 4th of May.

Frederick Roberts: "I keep the Golden Cross Hotel, Redditch. This morning I had occasion to go into the backyard, about 12 o'clock or so, to set a man to do some work.

"I was about five or ten minutes. As I was returning into the house I met the prisoner in the passage, coming out of the house backwards.

"She had the jug and the contents now produced in her hands, and turned into the brewhouse with it and put it in the mash tub.

"She then turned round to me and said: 'Eh! I want 3d of port wine.'

"She asked me if it was the best, for the lad was very bad, and she began to cry. She then went backwards up the passage into the brewhouse.

"I followed her out, and saw her in a stooping position near the mash tub.

"She got up and went away. I went to the mash tub and found the jug containing the Jamaica rum.

"I saw her again and asked her what she meant by stealing my Jamaica rum.

"She said: 'Eh! I put the jug in the tub, but did not put the rum. Never drawn no rum from the taps.'

"So I sent for a policeman. When she looked at him she begged for forgiveness. She was sorry what she done then.

"There was no one in the house, except the servant, and he was upstairs at the time."

Prisoner pleaded guilty; and the magistrates told her she had made herself liable to three months imprisonment, but, in consideration of her son's poor health and pleas on her behalf, the sentence would only be 14 days in the House of Correction, but also with hard labour.

They hoped that this would be a warning to her.

## Golden Cross Aug. 1995

# Sewage fall in pub

A WOMAN caught short in a Redditch pub plunged down an open manhole into a pool of raw sewage.

The accident at the Golden Cross, Unicorn Hill, happened when work to mend blocked lavatory pipes in the ladies was being carried out.

A contractor working for Wolverhampton and Dudley Breweries, which owns the recently refurbished pub, had opened the toilet sewer to dislodge the blockage.

When he moved outside to work a drain was left uncovered.

A pub regular went to the loo unaware of the hole and fell through into the drain and was covered in sewage.

### Very sorry

Redditch Borough Council environmental health officers visited the pub to discover what happened on Saturday evening. A witness said the woman was furious and threatened legal action.

A spokesman for the brewery said: "We were very sorry to learn about this incident. We are conducting an investigation

"Obviously we will be speaking to the contractor who was on site at the time as well as the pub staff and other people who saw what happened."

But he added no apology had been given to the woman because he did not have full details.

## GOLDEN SALMON.   133 Evesham Street.

| | | | |
|---|---|---|---|
| Richard James | 1860 – 74 | John Pinfield | 1883 – 84 |
| Reuben Mills | 1875 – 78 | Samuel Richard Parker | 1885 – 90 |
| Reuben Thornton | 1879 | Harry James Millward | 1891 |
| Beniah Hobbis | 1880 – 81 | Albert Maries | 1892 |
| John Yates | 1882 | Augustus Bartleet | 1893 – 1927 |

(From 1928 the Golden Salmon name ceases but Bartleet remains at No. 133 Evesham Street until 1934).

---

## GRAPES (THE).   Marsden Road. (Later Ma's Den).

Although an "off-licence" it was known locally as the smallest pub in Redditch as the licence allowed for drinking on the premises "for 2 standing" only.

---

## GREYHOUND INN.   1 Prospect Hill, (Later Church Green West).

This pub name dates from the time of the Tudors who used it on their coat of arms. It also, of course, has sporting connections.
The pub existed long before Smallwood Hospital of which it became part when the hospital was extended in the 1920's.

| | | | |
|---|---|---|---|
| John Shinton | 1846 – 73 | William Henry Malins | 1879 – 1914 |
| (Also at the Fox & Goose, Foxlydiate; | | Ralph Ernest Edwards | 1916 – 24 |
| he was also a tripe dresser) | | (Moved to the 'Crown' by 1928) | |
| Robert Yoxall | 1874 – 78 | | |

---

## HARE AND HOUNDS.   Evesham Road, Headless Cross.

| | | |
|---|---|---|
| Thomas Charman | Date unknown. | 'Local Notes and Queries No. 88.' |

> Further on towards Crabbs Cross was the *Hare and Hounds* kept by a Mr. Thomas Charman, and about a stone's throw from this was the *Folly*, a cottage inn, brick built, but roofed with thatch, and kept by James Millward.

---

## HART INN.   18 George Street.

| | | | |
|---|---|---|---|
| John Willis | 1868 | John Beard | 1873 – 78 |
| Reuben Mills | 1872 | William Pinfield-Wells | 1904 |

Two views of the Greyhound Inn next to Smallwood Hospital of which it became part in the 1920's. In the picture below the licence board can be seen next to the upstairs window.

**IF you want a glass of HOME BREWED, or of BURTON ALE, in good condition, go to**

## SHINTON'S

*NOTED PORK-PIE AND TRIPE HOUSE,*

**FISH HILL, REDDITCH.**

The above advert from the front page of the Redditch Indicator of Saturday March 10th. 1860 gives the address of 'Shinton's' pork pie and tripe house as Fish Hill, (i.e. Prospect Hill) Redditch. Although beer was on sale, there is no mention of The Greyhound Inn. Things are further complicated by Kelly's Directory for 1860 where John Shinton is described as a beer retailer & tripe dresser with the address given as Church Green. His Indicator advert for Saturday December 22nd 1860 (below) is headed 'Greyhound Inn.' This may indicate that 1860 was the date when the pub acquired its name. The usual address given in directories is Chapel (later Church) Green West. Also recorded is No. 1 Prospect Hill.

## GREYHOUND INN, REDDITCH.

### JOHN SHINTON,

GRATEFUL for past favours, begs most respectfully to inform his Friends and the Public generally that, in addition to his

**HOME-BREWED AND BURTON ALES,**

Now in fine condition, he has

**WINES, SPIRITS, AND CIGARS**

Of the best Quality.

N.B.—TRIPE SUPPERS Three Nights a-week, Thursdays, Fridays, and Saturdays.

## HOLLYBUSH INN.    Gorcott Hill, Beoley.

| | | | |
|---|---|---|---|
| John Hutton | 1841 | William John Trevor | 1908 – 11 |
| Samuel Johns | 1855 | John R Roberts | 1912 – 16 |
| William Box | 1874 | Clifford Leworthy | 1917 |
| Walter Jefferies | 1875 – 89 | Alfred Munslow | 1918 |
| Mrs Jefferies | 1890 | Fred Dracey | 1918 – 22 |
| William Whitehouse | 1891 – 1903 | Harry Timson | 1923 – 31 |
| John Banner | 1904 – 07 | Leslie John Beard | 1932 – 40 |

---

## HORSE AND JOCKEY.    20 Evesham Street.

On March 2nd 1904 the license of the 'Horse & Jockey' was refused by Redditch Magistrates. On April 6th the appeal at Worcester Quarter Sessions against the decision to close the inn was dismissed.

| | | | |
|---|---|---|---|
| George Smith | 1860 – 68 | Stephen George Millward | 1895 – 96 |
| (He was also a shoemaker) | | C (Phillip)? Dolphin | 1897 – 99 |
| Mrs Helen Smith | 1871 – 79 | John Edwin Bassett | 1899 – 1903 |
| William H Young | 1880 – 92 | Thomas William Smith | 1904 |
| Albert Maries | 1893 – 94 | | |

---

## (OLD) HORSE AND JOCKEY.    Ipsley Street. (Near the 'Green').

| | | | |
|---|---|---|---|
| Henry Smith | 1860 | William Coldrick | 1884 – 90 |
| Joseph Court | 1864 – 80 | (He was a wheelwright) | |
| (Also a needle hardener) | | | |

---

## THE HUNGRY MAN.    91 Evesham Street. (Corner of George Street).

Replaced the demolished 'Fountain Inn' and Temperance Hotel in 1935.

| | | | |
|---|---|---|---|
| Malcolm Stuart Marson | 1936 | Lionel Preston Hewitt | 1940 |

---

## JUBILEE INN.    15 Edward Street.

| | | | |
|---|---|---|---|
| Henry Young | 1868 – 95 | William Crook | 1917 – 18 |
| (Plumber and glazier) | | Frederick Yates | 1918 – 24 |
| Charles Laight | 1896 | Frank H Millward | 1925 – 28 |
| Thomas Bullock | 1897 – 1916 | John Howard Ness | 1928 – 36 |

Holly Bush Inn, Gorcott Hill circa 1910.

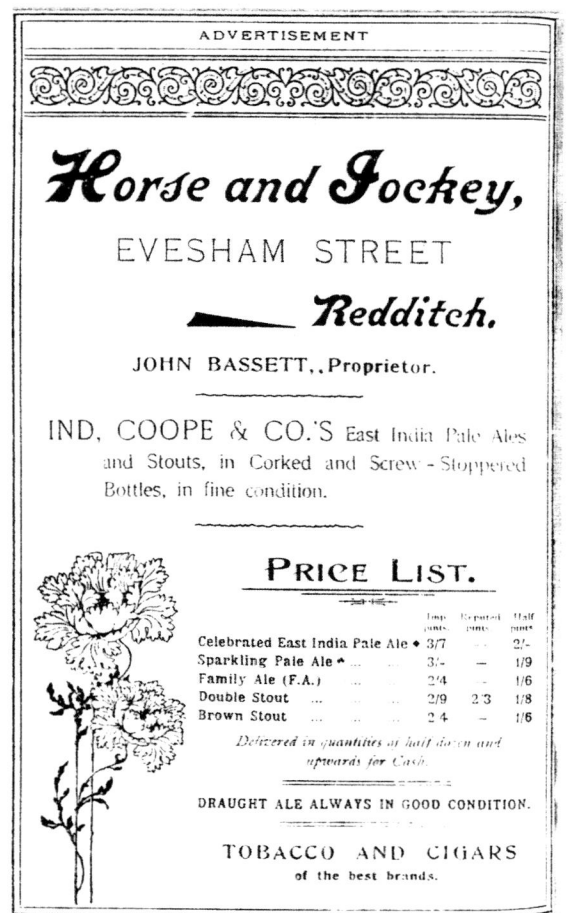

John Bassett's 1900 advert for the Horse and Jockey in Evesham Street.

The (Old) Horse and Jockey was "near the Green" in Ipsley Street.
Quote from the 1936 book about the Redditch needle industry by H. Guise.

"Of the hardeners, there were Joseph Court, whose shop was at the 'Horse and Jockey,' near where now stands the Warwick Arms Hotel; etc. etc.

# HORSE AND JOCKEY.

**JOHN BASSETT,**
Proprietor.

EVESHAM STREET,
REDDITCH.

IND, COOPE & CO.'S East India Pale Ales and Stouts, in Corked and Screw-Stoppered Bottles, in fine condition.

### PRICE LIST.

|  | Imp. Pints | Rep. Pints | Half-Pints |
|---|---|---|---|
| Celebrated East India Pale Ale | 3/7 | — | 2/- |
| Sparkling East India Pale Ale | 3/- | — | 1/9 |
| Family Ale (F.A) | 2/4 | — | 1/6 |
| Double Stout | 2/9 | 2/3 | 1/8 |
| Brown Stout | 2/4 | — | 1/6 |

*Delivered in Quantities of Half-Dozen and upwards for Cash only*

Draught Ale always in Good Condition.   Tobacco and Cigars of the Best Brands.

John Edwin Bassett's advert from the 1901 Redditch and District Directory. He was licensee of the Horse and Jockey from 1899 to 1903. The inn closed one year later.

**THE HUNGRY MAN.**  Corner of Evesham Street and George Street.

(Compare the above view of Evesham Street and the Hungry Man with the one of the Fountain Inn and Temperance Hotel which it replaced).

**Valuation and Inventory of Fixtures, Fittings, Trade Utensils, Etc. at the Jubilee Inn,** Edward Street, Redditch. From Mr Frank H Millward to Mr John H Ness on 5th December 1928.

**BAR**.
Frame of 6 painted jug and glass shelves. Small painted frame with glazed slide for out-door trade.
Small painted deal fitting of 2 shelves and 2 drawers.
Frame of 2 painted shelves in recess. Small shelf from door to same.
Small frame of 4 shelves. 2ft 6in. Shelf & supports. 2 Shelves & supports in recess.
Blind roller to door. Blind roller to window. Lino to floor. 2 hearth rugs.
4 Pull Beer engine in Mahogany case with brass taps, pewter lined trough,
4 lengths of piping to cellar, 3 lengths of piping to barrels and 4 brass union taps.
Small cash shelf. Oak framed overmantle with bevelled mirror.
Stuffed Fox in glazed case with supports. 6 Windsor chairs. 5 Oak top bar stools.
Three 24in. Circular Mahogany top bar tables on iron stands. 3 Iron Spittoons.
Electric lamp. Opal shade. Iron fender curb.
*Allowance on gas fire on Hire purchase from Redditch Gas Company.
3 Pewter Ale Measures, viz. quart, pint and $^1/_2$ pint. 52 Pint jugs.
46 – $^1/_2$ pint glass (stamped.) 6 Ale glasses. 10 Pressed $^1/_2$ pint glasses.
10 Lemonade glasses. Enamelled funnel. 2 Brass waiters ? 1 Black waiter ?

**SMOKE ROOM.**
Painted strip with iron hat & coat hooks. 12ft. Painted deal seating on 4 turned supports with painted and grained matchboard back and 2 shaped arms.
2 Painted and grained draught boards. (*To keep out draughts not play games on*).
8ft. Painted deal seating on floor turned supports with painted and grained match
-board back and 2 shaped arms. 11ft. 6in. Ditto.
Brass gas bracket with incandescent burner.
Two 4ft. X 1ft. Polished top bar tables on iron stands.
3ft. 3in. X 1ft. 6in. Painted deal table covered with American Cloth.
4ft. X 1ft. 9in. Ditto. 4 Oval top bar stools. 5 Round top bar stools.
Linoleum planned to floor. Gilt framed pier glass (damaged ).
Cast iron fender curb. 2 Electric lamps. 5 Enamel shades. Windsor chair.
7 Cast iron spittoons. 8 Day wall clock in inlaid case.

The inventory also lists 3 bedrooms with lino, electric lamps and shades.
The floor of the landing and stairs was covered in oilcloth with 10 brass stair rods. On the landing was a strip of 3 coat hooks, a hat and coat hook and a small shelf with supports. The lobby contained just a gas bracket, door to Smoke Room and 6 iron guard rods on the entrance door.
The kitchen had a painted framed pier glass. (*i.e. large mirror*). Lino and lamp.
In the scullery was a deal cupboard over the furnace, electric lamp, towel roller and painted deal table covered in American cloth.
The cellar contained two 3ft. 6in. shelves with supports, a 10 ft. shelf and supports (in 3 pieces). A 3ft. wooden barrel tram, 4 brass union taps, mallet, gimlet, 2 spanners, 2 enamelled bowls, enamelled bucket and a tin fining funnel.
It was gas heated with flexible pipe and galvanized guard and there were 2 gas brackets with ceiling protectors.
All that is listed outside at the front is a framed licence board and letting ?
In the yard was a deal table top and 2 wood trestles and an 8ft. and a 4ft. deal form. A shed is listed with a note 'Allowance for addition to shed.'

The stock list was quite small with less than 20 gallons of draught beer and a few dozen bottles of beer and mineral waters.

ABOVE: The Jubilee Inn, Edward Street. Just one of a terrace of houses.

BELOW: The Jubilee Oak Inn, on the corner of Ipsley Street and Red Lion Street. This picture shows it in later years reduced to the status of an "Off Licence."

The Jubilee Oak Inn on the corner of Ipsley Street and Red Lion Street in about 1905 when it had a garden on the frontage with Ipsley Street and plants climbing up the walls and around the front door.

Below is Francis Young's 1896 advert indicating that he also had premises in Peakman Street.

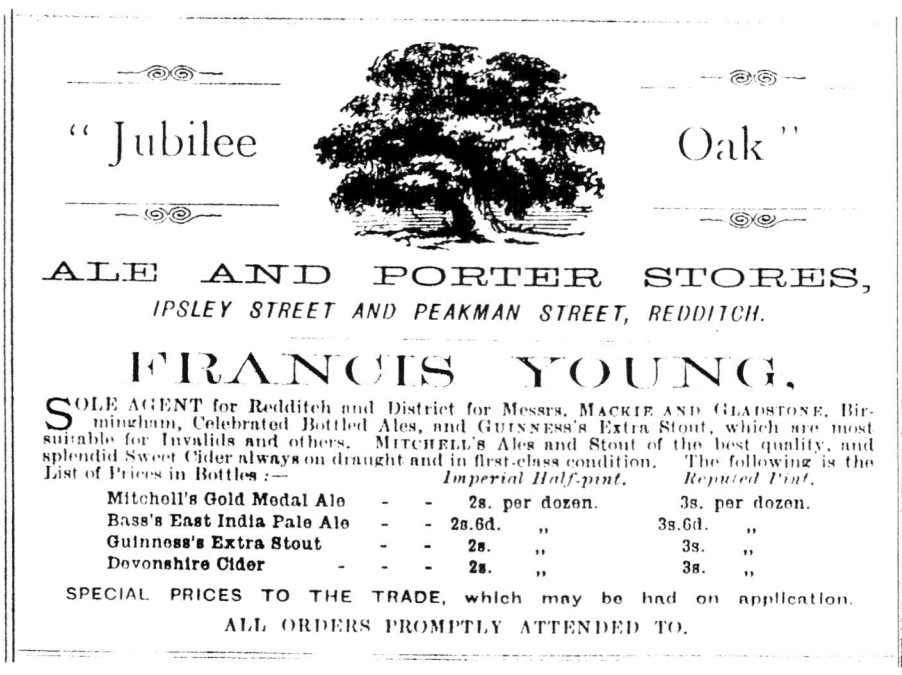

## JUBILEE OAK.      135 Ipsley Street, (corner of Red Lion Street).

The Jubilee Oak tree was planted on Ipsley Green to commemorate Queen Victoria's Jubilee of 1887. It was grown from an acorn gathered several years earlier from the 1,000 year old oak tree on Beoley Mount.

| | | | |
|---|---|---|---|
| Paul Higgs | 1868 | Albert Victor Mason | 1915 – 16 |
| (Shopkeeper) | | Mrs Beatrice Haden | 1921 – 32 |
| James Briggs | 1873 – 88 | Alfred Edwin Futrill | 1932 – 33 |
| (Butcher) | | Ernest Stokes | 1933 – 36 |
| J Barker | 1889 – 90 | Mrs Elizabeth M Stokes | 1940 |
| Francis Young | 1891 – 1915 | | |

## KING'S ARMS.      1 Beoley Road, (Breedon).

| | | | |
|---|---|---|---|
| William Tolley | 1855 – 64 | Frederick Arthur Lees | 1911 – 14 |
| (Farmer) | | Charles Bradnock | 1916 – 20 |
| Joseph Hollington | 1868 – 77 | William Marshall | 1921 – 24 |
| Mrs Sarah Hollington | 1878 – 87 | James Frederick Smith | 1928 |
| David Pinfield | 1888 – 1910 | Horace Alfred Lawford | 1936 |

## LAMB AND FLAG.      31/35 Unicorn Hill, (corner of Hill Street).

The Lamb and Flag is the Coat of Arms of the Templars and also the Merchant Tailors. The pub closed about 1938, during the war it was used by the Auxilliary Fire Service and later by the Sons of Rest.

| | | | |
|---|---|---|---|
| Henry Allen | 1841 | David H Maxwell | 1890 |
| (Butcher) | | George Savage | 1891 – 93 |
| Thomas Powell | 1850 – 55 | William Henry James Young | 1894 – 99 |
| Uriah Dunn | 1864 – 73 | Frederick S Summers | 1900 – 01 |
| (Butcher) | | John Jakeman | 1904 – 15 |
| Edith Dunn | 1874 – 77 | Richard Warner Jones | 1916 – 20 |
| Reuben Grey | 1878 – 82 | John Hanson | 1921 – 28 |
| James Slatter | 1883 | (Moved on to become a hairdresser) | |
| Thomas Ryland | 1884 – 88 | Reuben Edward Bannister | 1932 |
| William Oliver Gray | 1888 | Albert Edward Yates | 1936 |
| Mrs Wade | 1889 – 90 | | |

## LAMP TAVERN.      4 Walford Street.

| | | | |
|---|---|---|---|
| George Rickards | 1860 – 80 | Harry Shelton | 1902 – 03 |
| Mrs Keziah Rickards | 1881 – 99 | Mrs Emma Shelton | 1904 – 13 |
| John Frederick Hobday | 1899 – 1901 | Thomas Theay | 1913 – 36 |

The old King's Arms before its turn of the century reconstruction.

In the picture below standing outside is licensee David Pinfield who was there from 1888 to 1910. With him is his daughter Kate and sons Frederick and Alfred.

The King's Arms after its rebuilding circa 1900. Breweries seem to have been investing in Redditch pubs about this time as several others were also rebuilt, the Nevill Arms and the Park Inn, the Fleece, Crabbs Cross and the Fox and Goose/Royal Hotel – both in 1897 and the Warwick Arms and the Bell Inn, Headless Cross in 1898.

Lamb and Flag, Unicorn Hill. Shown above in 1936 when Albert Edward Yates was licensee. Both pictures illustrate the large, ornate lamps that were a feature of Redditch pubs in the early years of the 20th century. The bottom picture looking up Unicorn Hill dates from about 1905.

**Valuation and particulars of fixtures, fittings, furniture. stock in trade etc. at the Lamp Inn,** Walford Street. Redditch. Duly appraised by me this 21st day of February 1913. (Frank Neasom of the firm of Neasom & White, Auctioneers & Valuers, Redditch).

### BEDROOM.
Window blind, roller and fittings. Gas bracket.

### LANDING.
Deal table 5' 3" X 2' 6". Foxes head.

### STORE ROOM.
Deal tables 6' 9" X 2' 6" and 5' 6" X 2' 4".

### CLUB ROOM.
Gas pendant, 2 roller blinds, strip of 6 hat pegs.

### SMOKE ROOM.
8 Windsor chairs. 4 lath backed chairs.
Brass gas pendant with incandescent burner and shade.
Deal table with cover 4' X 2' 3". 2 deal tables with covers 3' 6" X 1' 9".
Painted seat with back and support 4' 6". Painted seat round room 10ft.
5 pull ale machine with piping and taps. Small counter with drawer.
6 Iron spittoons. 3 match stands. 6 framed pictures. 3 division cigar box.
3 pewter ale measures and tundish. 32 pint jugs. 3 quart jugs. 11 Jubilees.
6 lemonade glasses. 20 pressed ale glasses.
Cast iron fender and small ash pan. Painted chair rail round room 28ft.

### TAP ROOM.
Wood seating with back and 2 ends forming screen 10ft X 6ft.
Painted seating round room 17ft.
Gas pendant with incandescent burner and shade.
Deal table on turned legs 3' X 1' 9". Oak top table 4' 6" X 1' 9".
6 bars (iron) to window. American clock. 6 pictures. 5 iron spittoons.
Kitchen fender and cast iron dust preventer.

### PASSAGE.
Strip of 3 hat and coat hooks. Gas bracket and shade. Deal table 3' 6" X 2' 3".

### BACK PASSAGE.
2 shelves and supports 10ft.

### OUTSIDE. (FRONT)
Sign board. 24 letters on window.

### OUTSIDE. (BACK)
10ft deal form. Two 6ft forms. Two zinc buckets.

### CELLAR.
2 gas brackets.
11ft wood barrel tram. Two 6ft wood barrel trams. 7' 6" barrel tram.
4 wood sloopers. Mallet. Spanner. Gimlet. 2 shelves.

### STOCK IN TRADE.
5oz. Black Jack tobacco. $3^1/_2$oz. Anchor Roll Twist. 14 packets Woodbines.
15 – 1d Smokes. 12 – 2d Smokes. 7 – 3d Smokes.
21 bottles Allsops Stouts – $^1/_2$pt. 4 doz. and 2 minerals.
$3^1/_2$ doz. – 1/2 pt. Allsops IPA. 4 doz. – $^1/_2$pt. Cyder (Sic ).
$9^1/_2$ doz. Allsops Stout. $35^1/_2$ gal. X Ale. 20 gal. XXX Ale.
12 gal. LB Ale.

## LORD NELSON. Church Green.

See Local Notes and Queries No. 88. Closed in 1868 under new licensing laws.

| | | | |
|---|---|---|---|
| Thomas Johns | 1860 | Mrs Alice Johns | 1864 – 68 |
| (He came from Morton Baggot) | | | |

---

## LYGON ARMS. Droitwich Road, (Saltway), Feckenham.

The Lygon family were Lords of the Manor.

| | | | |
|---|---|---|---|
| Thomas Price | 1860 | George Mills | 1896 |
| (He was also a grocer) | | W Sprosen | 1897 |
| William Harrison | 1864 | Frederick Richard Sprosen | 1898 – 1936 |
| William Styler | 1868 | Mrs Sprosen | 1936 |
| William Bellamy | 1872 – 73 | James Shakels | 1940 |
| Mrs Bellamy | 1874 – 75 | A G Hawkes | 1950's |
| George Laight | 1876 – 95 | | |

---

## MAGPIE (THE). Tardebigge Churchyard.

The Hemming family were innkeepers here for many generations the last being Miss Sarah Hemming when the inn was converted into a school about 1815. The old building was demolished in 1843 and the new school built.

---

## MALT SHOVEL. Corner of Market Place and Evesham Street.

| | |
|---|---|
| Billy Bray | Before 1840 |
| Thomas Fowkes | 1841 – 54 |

(He was also a maltster. There was a different Thomas Fowkes at the 'Fox & Goose' at the same time).

---

## NAG'S HEAD. 23a/25 Alcester Street.

| | | | |
|---|---|---|---|
| George Wardle | 1860 – 68 | John Albert Halford | 1912 – 14 |
| Mrs Jane Wardle | 1872 – 78 | Alfred Smith | 1916 – 23 |
| (She was also a dairykeeper) | | (He was also at the 'Royal Hotel') | |
| Reuben Mills | 1879 – 98 | William Richardson | 1924 – 25 |
| Mrs Sarah Mills | 1899 – 1900 | William J Stevens | 1925 – 31 |
| Walter William Harbridge | 1900 – 04 | Howard Sealey | 1932 – 34 |
| Thomas Blackford | 1905 – 08 | Reuben Street | 1934 – 36 |
| Mrs Christiana Thornton | 1909 – 11 | Frederick Barclay | 1940 |
| George Edward Adderley | 1911 – 12 | | |

---

ABOVE:
Extract from "Local Notes and Queries" No. 88, giving details of the Lord Nelson pub.

RIGHT:
The Lygon Arms, Feckenham. Part of a postcard dated 1909. The name on the board over the door is Frederick R. Sprosen. The lady in the doorway is, presumably, Mrs Sprosen who took over the licence in 1936.

The smithy opposite the Lygon Arms.
The blacksmith, seen here in the white shirt, was Mr. Newman.

The postcard reproduced above is from the period just before the Second World War. The name on the licence board above the door is S. A. Sprosen. This may well refer to the wife of Frederick Richard Sprosen who followed him as licensee in 1936 – presumably on his demise. The Annual Ball below was advertised in the Redditch Indicator on Saturday December 24th, 1859, the paper's first year of publication.

FECKENHAM.
THE ANNUAL BALL will take place at the LYGON ARMS INN, on MONDAY, DECEMBER 26.

The Malt Shovel, top left, was at No. 2 Market Place until 1852 when William Mousley opened his chemists shop there. These postcard views are copies of watercolour pictures in the style of J. M. Woodward and were produced about 1905. The poem refers to the 1840's, the other quote is from the 1880's.

Greaves and Beck from Al'church wharf,
Brought the coals by horse and cart,
Dixon, too, of Stoney Lane,
From Tarbic wharf supplied the same.
The Malt Shovel kept by Billy Bray,
A jocund fellow in his day,
He said he hoped they'd lay him where
He still could hear the "fun of the fair."
Lawyer Gardner liv'd above the Hole,
Why he did so I've never been told,
Opposite was Dame Cutler's school,
I went there, so I'm no fool.

The *Malt Shovel* stood where Mr. Mousley's chemist's shop now stands. The landlord was a Thomas Fowkes not the celebrated "Tommy," nor yet the stalwart Thomas Fowkes, the local preacher, who being challenged by Turpin Wright, fought a friendly "twirtle" with him on the Church Green and punished him severely, but a person who carried on the joint business of inn-keeping and malting, hence the name of the inn.

The Nag's Head above in about 1905 when Thomas Blackford was licensee and below, just before it and its neighbour the Rising Sun were demolished.

One Redditch licensee who did not return from World War One.

NAG'S HEAD
Corporal John Albert Halford 3913.
Worcestershire Regiment. Aged 42.
Killed in action – 13th. Nov. 1915.

# Valuation and Particulars of Fixtures and Fittings, Trade Effects etc. at the Nag's Head Inn, Alcester St. Redditch.

From Mr William Richardson to Mr William J Stevens. 12th. of October 1925.

## SMOKE ROOM.
24ft. Mahogany framed seating with padded back, 4 shaped arms on turned supports and shaped draught board, upholstered in American leather. Cocoanut mat. Lino planned to floor. 6 Iron spittoons. 2 Oval bar stools. Electric drop light with opal shade, bulb, wiring and switch. Short crimson curtains to bay window. No. 3 Blount door spring. Four 23in. Round polished top bar tables on iron stands.

## BAR.
Two No.3 Blount door springs. 5 Electric drop lights with 4 opal & 1 enamel shade.
Switchboard with 8 switches and wiring.
6ft. 6in. Loose Mahogany framed seat with padded back, shaped arms in American leather.
4ft. Mahogany framed, fixed seat with padded back, shaped arms and
turned legs, upholstered in American leather.
4ft. - 5ft. 6in. - 10ft. and 14ft. 6in. Ditto as above.
3ft. 6in. Painted Bar table on turned legs covered with American cloth.
3ft. - 3ft. 3in. and three 5ft. Ditto as above.
3 Windsor chairs. Oval top stool.
4 Pull Beer Engine with piping and taps complete by Gaskell & Chambers.
Copper wash up with fluted drainer and waste pipe to cellar.
Water supply pipe and tap as fixed.
The Bar fitting with Mahogany front and bevelled glass back fixed at back of bar.
19ft. 6in. Painted and grained panelled front counter with circular ends fitted
with Cash Till. 20 Key National Cash Register No. 1516182/334.
2 Pier glasses in painted frames. 2 Iron Spittoons. Deal stool. Cork extractor.
Dwarf crimson curtains to bay.

## PASSAGE.
Half glazed door to Bar with sliding glazed panel forming Out-Door Department.
Electric drop light with opal shade, bulb and wiring. Ditto with enamel shade.
Blount door spring. Small coil spring on back door.

The inventory also lists stairs and landing with oilcloth and 11 brass stair rods. 4 Bedrooms with electric lights and paper roller blinds. A scullery with painted corner cupboard, gas bracket, 7ft 6in. shelf next to furnace, various other shelves in sizes from 2ft. 9in. to 6ft. 6in. A pantry with 2 shelves. The private kitchen with just an electric light and lino. The cellar had 4 shelves at Cellar head, 3 brass union taps, spanner, gimlet, mallet and a wood slooper. There was an electric light fitting with 2 switches, a shelf on iron brackets and a wooden tap. Out side the back the yard was illuminated by a lamp with iron piping from the scullery. There was a lean-to shed with felt covered roof built on to the fence. Also fixed to the fence was part of a lath seat. A cross legged ale table 7ft. 10in. X 2ft. 6in. with a zinc covered top was accompanied by a 9ft. seat with back on iron supports. Listed also are 2 saw dust tubs.

From the auction sale held by Charrington & Co. Ltd.
at the Grand Hotel, B'ham on Feb. 2nd & 3rd 1926.

LOT 60.

# THE "NAG'S HEAD,"

### Alcester Street, Redditch,

## WORCESTERSHIRE.

### FREEHOLD — ON BEER HOUSE — 7 DAYS.

A well-known centrally-situated House.

The present Tenant is Mr. W. J. Stevens; the net rental agreed is £30 for the first year commencing 14th October, 1925, and £40 per annum subsequently.

The main structure is two-storey, brick and slate and brick and tile built, with stucco front.

The accommodation includes:—

ON THE GROUND FLOOR: Paved Entrance Passage; Smoke Room; Bar; Kitchen.

ON THE FIRST FLOOR: Four Bedrooms.

IN THE BASEMENT: Good Cellar.

OUTSIDE: Paved Yard, with cartway entrance from Smith Street; Scullery; Urinal and two w.c's; Coach-house; and Coalplace.

Electricity, Gas and Water Services are laid on.

REMARKS.—The back part of the Land comprised in this Lot is subject to the reservation of the rights reserved to the Lord of the Manor on enfranchisement by the Copyhold Act, 1852, Section 48.

*Page Seventy-two*

*Sold. £4,100.*

**NAVIGATION INN.**    Tardebigge Old Wharf.

From 'A Thousand Years in Tardebigge' :    John Hunt    Circa 1800.

---

**NEEDLE POINTER'S ARMS.**   See under 'Pointer's Arms.'

---

**NEVILL ARMS.**    New End, Astwood Bank.

Note that the name is spelt NEVILL without a 'E' as the landowner was the Marquis of Abergavenny whose family name was Nevill. Originally known as the 'New Inn' it is shown on a Post Office map in Kelly's Directory for 1850 but does not appear in the text in that year. Later editions list it in the parish of Inkberrow. It had been renamed by the 1870's and was rebuilt Circa 1900.

| | | | |
|---|---|---|---|
| Thomas Andrews | 1841 | Tom Green | 1900 |
| John Gee | 1855 | Joseph Mealing | 1904 – 08 |
| Benjamin Harris | 1860 – 65 | Frederick Hunt | 1908 – 20 |
| Rowland Green | 1873 – 75 | George Danks | 1920 – 28 |
| John Phillips | 1887 – 99 | Walter Thomas Hodgetts | 1932 – 40 |
| (He issued a 3d token) | | | |

---

**NEW INN.**    New End, Astwood Bank.

See above.

---

**NEW INN.**    Mount Pleasant.

The only know reference to the name of this inn is from Billing's Directory of Worcestershire for 1855 although James Francis appears in Kelly's 1854 as a beer retailer.

James Francis    1854 – 55    (He was also a needlemaker)

John Phillips brass 3d token and below his advert from the 1897 Redditch Needle District Almanack and Directory.

(*Note that on the token NEVILL is spelt correctly but incorrectly as NEVILLE in the advert).

### Neville Arms Inn. Ridgeway.

ALES, WINES, AND SPIRITS OF BEST QUALITY.  CIGARS, &c.

Good Accommodation for Cyclists.

JOHN PHILLIPS, Proprietor.

# NEW INN/NEVILL ARMS.

The earliest known landlord of the New Inn was John Tiler who, with his wife Mary, sold beer to passing travellers. They also kept pigs to make into bacon. When he died in the summer of 1750 he left an estate valued at £19. 17s. 3d. In 1803 Thomas Stanley was landlord and he owned 23 acres of land in the area. The Marquis of Abergavenny sold the property by auction at the Globe in Alcester in 1887. It was bought by John Phillips who was almost certainly the sitting tenant paying a rent of £80 per annum. The pub was demolished and rebuilt (as were several others in the area) at the end of the 19th or early 20th century.

THE ANNUAL
PIGEON SHOOTING
WILL BE HELD AT THE
NEW INN, RIDGWAY,
ON WEDNESDAY, DEC. 26.
DINNER ON THE TABLE AT FOUR O'CLOCK.

B Harris will be glad to see a good muster of his friends on this occasion.

Licensee Benjamin Harris's advert in the Redditch Indicator on Saturday December 15th, 1860.

Extract from 'Local Notes & Queries' Published in the Redditch Indicator in the 1880's.

The Nevilles are the present lords of Abergavenny; but in the old parish church of Abergavenny there are numerous monuments to a family named Herbert, who were lords of Abergavenny long before the Nevilles. There is one to "Lady Eva de Cantelupe, Baroness of Abergavenny," dated as far back as the 13th century. Some of the family were knights who served in the "Holy Wars."

The "New Inn" public-house belongs to the Abergavenny estate, hence its name the "Neville Arms." Some years ago, there was, I believe, a signboard over the doorway, bearing the arms of the Neville family.

Astwood Bank.     EDWIN THORNTON.

Francis Emma, straw bonnet maker, Mount Pleasant
Francis James, needle maker, and beer retailer, *New Inn*, Mount Pleasant
Francis William, needle maker, *Fox and Goose* commercial hotel, Chapel Green
Freeman James, cooper, Chapel Green West

Billing's 1855 Directory for the County of Worcester records the existence of the 'New Inn', Mount Pleasant, Redditch.

RIGHT
Grace Walters outside the Oddfellow's Arms, Windsor Street, circa 1940.

BELOW
The Oddfellow's Sick Club 3d token.

# Oddfellow's Arms,

WINDSOR STREET.

Proprietor - GEORGE MORTON

Bass' Special Ales.
Northampton Stout.

George Morton's advert from 1897.

## ODDFELLOW'S ARMS.   8/10 Windsor Street.

The Oddfellow's society still exists and bears some similarity to Freemasons.

| | | | |
|---|---|---|---|
| William Davis | 1854 – 73 | Alfred Partridge | 1911 – 36 |
| (Shoemaker) | | Mrs Grace Mary Walters | 1940 |
| William Barber | 1875 – 96 | (During Mrs Walter's tenancy the pub | |
| George Morton | 1897 – 1908 | was known simply as "Grace's"). | |
| Edward Alexander | 1908 – 10 | | |

*Note : George Morton (above) has his name spelled M<u>a</u>rton in a newspaper report of 1898. The Redditch Directory from 1897 to 1899 spells it Mor<u>e</u>ton but from 1900 on spells it Morton which is presumably correct.

---

## ODDFELLOW'S ARMS.   Foregate Street, Astwood Bank.

Known as the 'Baker's Arms' up to about 1890. It was a meeting place for the 'Farmer's Glory Lodge' of the Order of Oddfellow's, Manchester Unity. They issued a 25mm. brass token, value 3d.

| | | | |
|---|---|---|---|
| Richard Rouse | 1854 – 68 | Benjamin Haden | 1902 – 17 |
| (Shopkeeper – baker)? | | Mrs B Haden | 1918 |
| Mrs Jane Rouse | 1872 – 82 | William Crook | 1918 – 26 |
| William Henry Reading | 1883 – 90 | Albert Alfred Millward | 1927 |
| Harry James Millward | 1891 – 96 | Charles H Lewis | 1928 – 36 |
| George Millward | 1897 – 1901 | Rowland Goucher | 1940 |

---

## OLD BRITON.   115 Evesham Street.

Billing's 1855 Directory gives the address as Mount Pleasant.

| | | | |
|---|---|---|---|
| James Davis | 1854 – 55 | James Ambrose Mills | 1900 – 07 |
| (Boot and shoe maker) | | John Frederick Gibbs | 1908 |
| David Houghton | 1860 – 80 | A H Cooper | 1909 – 10 |
| George F Dobbins | 1880 – 83 | Edwin Corfield (or Garfield) | 1910 – 12 |
| Francis Harbon | 1884 | Thomas Harris | 1913 |
| Henry Gamson | 1884 – 90 | (Killed in action) | |
| E Wells | 1891 | Joseph Rigby | 1914 |
| John Frederick Smith | 1892 – 1900 | | |

---

## OLD ROSE AND CROWN.   Feckenham. (See under 'Rose and Crown').

**Valuation and Particulars of Fixtures, Fittings, Furniture, Trade Utensils and Effects at the Old Briton Inn,** Evesham Street, Redditch from Mr A H Cooper to Mr Edwin Corfield. 29th. November 1910.

### SMOKE ROOM.
Draught board. 5ft. & 6ft. Seats with backs. Deal seat with return end 11ft. Deal seat 17ft. Seat with back and arms 5ft. 12 stools. 12 Iron spittoons. 5 Stained tables with leather tops. Pier glass. 2 Screens near door. 4 Shelves and supports at Bar end 25ft. 5 Pull Beer engine with piping and 5 brass union taps. New tap for Beer engine. 32 yards of lino fitted to floor. Oak fender curb. 4 Roller blinds. 4 Short curtains. 5 Electric lamps. 3 Shades. Quoit board. Pitching boards rings. 2 Brass gas brackets. 2 Patent gas burners. 11 Key National Cash Register. Express cork drawer. Iron stove as fixed. Deal counter with return end. 3 Pewter Ale measures. Copper funnel. 2 Bowls. Jugs & Glasses – 4 wine glasses, 22 lemonade glasses, 6 large ale glasses, 56 pint jugs, 5 – $1/2$ pint cups, 6 Quart jugs, 11 Glass pints, 15 – $1/2$ pint Jubilees, 11 Ale glasses, 7 Ale glasses on stands.

### TAP ROOM.
Stained deal table with leather top. 2 Windsor chairs. Stool. Match boarded screen. Deal seating round room 14ft. 4 Iron bars to window. Blind roller. Fender. 2 Fire irons and ash pan. Grate on fire bars and drawer plate. Oak corner cupboard with 1 draw. Electric lamp and shade. Glazed door with spring. 3 Iron Spittoons. Gas bracket in lobby. Pier glass in black and gold frame. Brass gas bracket. Patent gas light. Deal table as fixed to wall.

### CELLAR.
5 Trams. 1 Electric lamp. 3 Shelves. Gas bracket. 12 Brass taps. 1 Wood tap. 4 lengths of rubber piping with connections. Mallet. Spanner. Tundish. Pewter measure. 4 Wood stoopers.

### BREWHOUSE.
Racks on floor. Washing trough. 2 Shelves.

Also listed Outside (Front) – Sign. In the yard a wood and iron coalhouse. In the (private ?) Living Room – Electric and gas lamps, painted corner cupboard, roller blind and lino. There were 3 Bedrooms with gas and electric light, roller blinds and a wardrobe with rail and 12 hooks.

The stock consisted of nearly 50 gallons of draught beer, 36 gallons of cider, 26 bottles of IPA, 9 bottles of minerals, 73 – 1d smokes, 310 – 2d cigars, pipes.

ADVERTISEMENT.

# The Old Briton Inn,

J. A. MILLS, Proprietor.

EVESHAM STREET,

# Redditch.

## WORTHINGTON'S ALES.

Northampton Stout on Draught.

WORTHINGTON'S BOTTLED ALES AND GUINNESS'S STOUT.

Prime Cigars and Tobacco.

James Ambrose Mills advert from the 1900 Needle District Almanack and Directory.

# REDDITCH PUBS IN THE NEWS

### Hart Inn 1871

IRISH row. James McDermott and James McGarry were charged with assaulting the police on Sunday last in George Street. Defendants pleaded guilty.

Pc John Kingdon stated that about 7pm he was called to the Hart Beer House. There were three Irishmen drunk and making a disturbance. The witness ordered them out, but they would not go. The witness took hold of one to take him to the station. McDermot tried to rescue him and McGarry struck the witness in the mouth. The first prisoner was lost in consequence of the the interference of the other two. James Andrew also bore testimony to the assault. They were sentenced to 21 days hard labour each.

### Nevill Arms
### March 17, 1900

A WELL-attended smoking concert took place at the Neville Arms on Monday evening in aid of the fund for the wives and families of reservists.

Mr Page presided and proposed "The Queen", which was warmly received.

"Success to our troops in South Africa" was also submitted by the chairman.

A capital programme of vocal and instrumental music was rendered during the evening by Messrs Parry, Perkins, Jones, Newberry, Styler, Clark, Smith, Carwardine, Cale, Savage and others.

The sum collected, 11s 6d, together with the proceeds of the concert, will be handed over to the fund.

The singing of the National Anthem closed the concert.

### Oddfellow's

### November 5 1898

George Marton landlord of the Oddfellows Arms, Redditch, was charged with permitting drunkenness on his premises on October 19. Mr F Holyoake (Droitwich) appeared for the police and Mr GW Hobson (Redditch and District Licensed Victuallers' Association). It appeared that Sergeant Holloway and Pc Owen went into the kitchen and found a man named Grummit sitting there drunk.

For the defence Mrs Marton said she supplied witness and another man with a pint of ale and they had another pint.

Grummit was sitting so quietly that she never noticed his condition but when she saw he was partially intoxicated she ordered him to leave. As he was about doing so the police came in. Mr Hobson urged that if a technical offence had been committed it was of a very trivial character. The defendant was fined £1 and costs.

### King's Arms
### July 26, 1889

EDWIN Gittus was charged with running a traction engine without a licence in Beoley Road, Redditch, and not consuming its smoke as much as was practible.

David Pinfield, landlord of the King's Arms Inn, said he saw the engine kick up a great smother, but Mr Gabbs, defending, said there was not a tittle of evidence to show that the level of smoke was too high.

PC Hill said he also saw the engine in the Market Place where by releasing steam, it frightened two horses.

After consideration it was decided the wrong parties had been summoned.

### New Inn 1865

Benjamin Harris of the New Inn, Ridgeway, was fined £5 in costs for permitting drunkenness in his house on June 7.

The defendant pleaded it was club night and a few members had stayed late to enjoy the evening. They left immediately when the police officer arrived to remind them of the law.

Harris was charged in full and the penalty was paid.

Samuel Powell of the White Lion, Astwood Bank, was fined £1 4d and costs for selling alcohol on a Sunday.

He pleaded that a few friends were over from Birmingham and he looked on them in the light of travellers and unwittingly allowed them to have some refreshments.

### Lamb & Flag
### November 5, 1949.

THE Sons of Rest premises in Unicorn Hill are to be reopened next Wednesday after extensive improvements and redecoration.

The committee's aim has been to convert the old Lamb and Flag Inn into a comfortable homely centre in which the old age pensioners can spend their leisure hours.

They have installed fluorescent lighting, a new fireplace and provided extra games equipment and other amenities.

This has been done entirely from voluntary donations.

Originally an appeal was made for £100 but as the cost of improvements is going to be at least £175, the appeal is going to be continued.

About £250 will be required to carry out all the improvements.

### Lamb and Flag

### April 16, 1949

PLANS for redecorating and improving the premises in Unicorn Hill, the meeting place of the 'Sons of Rest,' have been made by a new committee formed recently and an appeal for £100 is being made to enable the work to be carried out.

The premises, formerly the old Lamb and Flag Inn, are badly in need of repair and redecoration so that the elderly men of the town can spend a few leisure hours in comfortable and attractive surroundings. More recreational facilities are also needed.

Alderman Hughes will remain as president with Mr H D Spencer as chairman, Mr R G Mills as secretary and Mr L G Boyd as treasurer.

Old townsmen over 65 years of age will be welcomed as members of the movement.

### Oddfellow's June 1896

ROSE SHOW. The first of a series of weekly shows in aid of the Redditch Nursing Fund was held at the Oldfellows Arms, Windsor Street, on Saturday evening, when, in spite of the prevailing blight, some remarkably handsome blooms were exhibited.

Mr Hancocks, gardener to Mr S Allcock, officiated as judge. His awards begin as follows: J.Court 1st, G.Baylis 2nd, Jos Standley 3rd.

## PARK INN.  1 Evesham Road, Headless Cross.

Rebuilt in its present "mock Tudor" style about 1900. Three Park Inn pub tokens are known. One is single sided (uniface) 23mm. 3d with the legend – Park Inn. Headless Cross. Another is for the Park Inn Sick and Dividend Society, 3d, 26mm. The third has the letters I.M.B. on it and was issued by the Independant Mutual Bretheren Friendly Society. They were based at several Redditch pubs from 1880 to 1886. This is also a 3d token.

| | | | |
|---|---|---|---|
| Matthew Wilkinson | 1837 | George Farr | 1907 – 14 |
| Joseph (Jonas)? Wilkinson | 1850 | William Thomas Palmer | 1916 – 19 |
| Mrs Ann Wilkinson | 1864 – 89 | George Shepherd | 1921 – 24 |
| Jonas and John Wilkinson | 1890 – 98 | George Ernest Jones | 1928 – 36 |
| Frederick Shelton | 1899 – 1904 | William Day England | 1940 |

---

## PLOUGH AND HARROW.  153/161/173 Evesham Street.

The original pub on this site was called the 'Duke of York.' It became the Liberal Club in the 1970's.

| | | | |
|---|---|---|---|
| Seymour Greaves | 1850 | Mrs Mary Ann Edwards | 1887 – 91 |
| George Charman | 1854 | Henry Jones | 1892 |
| (Also a needle maker) | | Arthur Leonard Smith | 1893 – 1906 |
| Samuel Smith | 1860 – 64 | Thomas Henry Charman | 1906 – 21 |
| Joseph Morris | 1868 | Mrs Clara Charman | 1922 – 26 |
| Francis Cook | 1872 – 73 | Thomas Howard Charman | 1927 – 34 |
| John Johnston | 1873 – 74 | Frederick William Sallis | 1936 |
| William Edwards | 1875 – 86 | Joe Onions | 1940 |

---

## PLUMBER'S ARMS.  53 Walford Street.

| | | | |
|---|---|---|---|
| William Talbot | 1884 – 91 | Alexander Duffin | 1910 – 36 |
| William Henry Stalworth | 1892 – 1910 | Ralph Manning | 1936 – 40 |

---

## PLYMOUTH ARMS.  Alcester Road, Tardebigge.

Built about 1810 on land owned by the Windsor – Clive family of Hewell Grange who were the Earls of Plymouth. It was closed by them in 1879.

| | | | |
|---|---|---|---|
| John Barron | 1816 | Ambrose Moythan | 1869 – 79 |
| John Durham | 1820 – 54 | | |
| Samuel Taylor | 1854 – 69 | | |
| (Farmer) | | | |

The old Park Inn before it was rebuilt in about 1900. Outside stands John and Jonas Wilkinson, their wives and families.

Below, Jonas in later years when he played bowls for the White Hart.

The initials I M B on the token refer to the Independant Mutual Bretheren Friendly Society. This society existed in Redditch from 1880 to 1886 when the Park Inn was run by Mrs Ann Wilkinson.

PARK INN
BY
JONAS & JOHN WILKINSON
Licensed to brew & sell ale, beer, porter & cider for consumption on the premises. Dealer in tobacco.

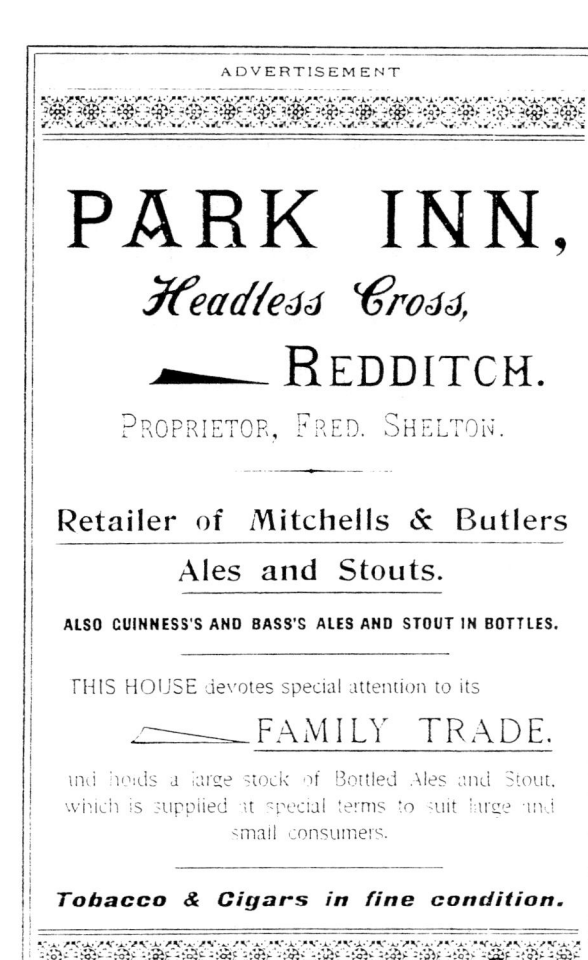

Two more Park Inn 3d tokens illustrated above. To the right is Fred Shelton's 1900 advert in the Redditch Trade Directory.

The Plough and Harrow in about 1910.

The above picture of Walford Street shows the Plumber's Arms – the white painted premises, right of centre – possibly during the 1911 Coronation celebrations. In the bottom picture, taken in the 1970's, most of the street has been demolished and the Plumber's Arms lasted only a little longer.

Plymouth House, now a nursing home was once the Plymouth Arms. Built to cater for the navvies constructing the canal and later the canal users as well as travellers from Bromsgrove to Redditch and beyond. In 1878/79 the inn was closed by Lord Robert Windsor – Clive who was prominent in the Temperance movement. The Plymouth Arms token reproduced below can be dated to the years 1851 – 55 which were the dates when the manufacturer Thomas Pope & Co. were in St Pauls Square, Birmingham. (Information from the book on Worcestershire Inn Tokens by John Whitmore). This would indicate that it was issued by Samuel Taylor.

# PLYMOUTH ARMS INN,
## TARDEBIGGE.

### VALUABLE
## Live & Dead Farming Stock,

Comprising—capital COW and CALF, three In-calf and other HEIFERS, four valuable HORSES and MARES, fifteen well-aired TEGS, three In-pig SOWS & GILTS, two pockets of prime Worcester HOPS, patent weighing Machine, Iron and other Ploughs, Gears, Harness and other Agricultural Implements, capital Cabin Boat, with a few articles of

## HOUSEHOLD FURNITURE,

COMPRISING—Mahogany Sofa, hair seating, Mahogany Chairs, Mahogany Pembroke and other Tables, Mahogany Sideboard, with cellaret and drawers, Time-piece over Stable (Crank) Ditto in Mahogany frame, Gold and Silver Watches, and other effects, will be

### SOLD BY AUCTION, BY
## MR. C. STEEDMAN,

On the above premises,

### ON MONDAY, APRIL the 1st., 1861,
### SALE TO COMMENCE AT TWELVE O'CLOCK.

Catalogues will be ready in a few days, and may be had at the principal Inns in the neighbourhood, the place of sale, and at the Office of the Auctioneer, High-street, Bromsgrove.

The Redditch Indicator advert above refers to the Plymouth Arms as an inn. This was published on Saturday March 23rd, 1861. Below it receives Hotel status on Saturday July 12th, 1862. Note also differing ways of spelling Tardebigge.

## FISHING AND BOATING.

## Plymouth Arms Hotel,
### TARDEBIGG,
## SAMUEL TAYLOR,
**PROPRIETOR,**

BEGS, most respectfully, to thank his numerous friends for their past kind patronage, and to inform them and the Public at large, that the Reservoir is now well stocked with Fish, and that he has for Anglers and Pleasure Parties, Boats upon the most improved principles. For terms, apply at the Hotel,

## POINTER'S ARMS.     29/35 Evesham Street.

In 1841 John Bryan had a Hairdresser's shop but it was not licensed premises. In 1855 Billing's Directory names it as the 'Needle Pointer's Arms.' By 1860 George Mustin had taken over and renamed it 'The Royal George.' For details of licensees see under 'Royal George.'

---

## PRINTER'S ARMS.     6 Evesham Street.

So named because James Maries, the first licensee was a printer. It is usually described in directories as a 'Refreshment House.'

| | | | |
|---|---|---|---|
| James Maries | 1841 – 50 | Mrs Rachel Crow | 1879 |
| (Printer) | | William Willis | 1880 – 82 |
| Mrs Mary Ann Abell | 1864 | (Refreshment rooms) | |
| Thomas Upton Crow | 1868 – 78 | (Willis then moved to the 'White Swan') | |

---

## QUEEN'S HEAD.     9/11 Queen Street.

Demolished and rebuilt in 1935.

| | | | |
|---|---|---|---|
| Simeon Shrimpton | 1860 – 64 | Simeon Shrimpton | 1888 – 1903 |
| (Needle manufacturer and grocer) | | Mrs Harriet Shrimpton | 1904 – 20 |
| Charles Smallwood | 1868 – 76 | George Henry Glover | 1921 – 28 |
| Josiah Storrs | 1876 – 82 | (Heavy weight boxer) | |
| (He issued a 3d token) | | Thomas Owen Grimes | 1932 |
| John Guise | 1883 – 87 | George Delahay | 1936 |
| (He was also a builder and the Globe Express parcel office agent) | | William Ronald Marsh | 1940 |

---

## QUEEN'S HEAD.     148 Bromsgrove Road. (Red Lane).

| | | | |
|---|---|---|---|
| William Yarnall | 1860 – 64 | Alfred Harden Lewis | 1892 |
| John Guest | 1868 | Thomas Harrison | 1893 – 96 |
| Richard Field | 1873 – 82 | (He issued a 3d token) | |
| Henry Blackford | 1883 – 85 | Edwin Pentycross | 1897 – 1905 |
| Jonah Warner | 1886 – 88 | Ralph Ernest Edwards | 1905 – 14 |
| George E Drew | 1889 – 90 | Bernard Webb | 1916 – 40 |
| F Bangham | 1891 | | |

> Browning Edward, Solicitor, Clerk to County Magistrates, and Clerk of County Court; agent to the European Life, and Equity and Law Life Offices, Fish Hill
> Bryan John, beer retailer, and hair dresser, *Needle Pointers' Arms*, Evesham st
> Buggins G., needle scourer, Adelaide st

> Old Anthony Spragg, he swept the Green
> On Saturday nights where the stalls had been,
> Folks used to say that Anthony found
> Among his sweepings many a pound.
> Barber Haden and Barber Bryan,
> Which was best you'd got to try "em,"
> They'd rig you up in a straight-back'd chair,
> And charge a penny to cut your hair.
> The Red Lion Room was our Guildhall
> For occasional parties, it held us all,
> Dinners and dances were held therein,
> A ticket we'd buy and then go in.

ABOVE: References to 'Barber Bryan' of the Pointer's Arms in Billing's 1855 Directory and the poem about Redditch in 1840 by 'an Old Fish Hill Boy.'

BELOW: Similar references to the Printer's Arms in Bentley's 1841 Directory and the Needle District Almanack of 1879.

120  BENTLEY'S

> Malins William, sawyer, Unicorn Hill [Cottages]
> Manders Wm., gardener, Hewell
> Maries James, beerseller and printer, Evesham-street
> Markham Isaac, gardener, Hewell Gardens [Cottages]

DIRECTORY.—REDDITCH.

> Cranmore, Moses, draper, Evesham street
> Cross, Charles & Son, engineers, Windsor street
> Crow, John, shopkeeper, Beoley road
> Crow, Rachael (Mrs.), *Printers' Arms*, Evesham street
> Crow, W., *Brewers' Arms*, Windsor street
> Dance, William Bray, butcher and game dealer, Market place

This 3d token issued by Josiah Storrs about 1880 has had the name A. BLICK stamped on it. Blick does not appear in any directory and may not have been a licensee.

The Queen's Head, Queen Street shown above before it was rebuilt in 1935. The 1920's picture below of the Queen's Head ladies outing was taken by local photographer Joe Harman. On the extreme left is licensee George Henry Glover. His son 'Darkie' is in the foreground, apparently wearing a table-cloth as an apron.

> **TAYLOR'S**
> **Extra Stout and Fine Ales**
> MAY be depended upon as genuine, if purchased from the Agent,
> **SIMEON SHRIMPTON,**
> PUBLICAN,
> **QUEEN STREET, REDDITCH.**

Adverts from the Redditch Indicator in the year 1860 both giving Simeon Shrimpton as sole agent for Taylor's Ales. The top one published on Sat. March 10th describes Shrimpton as a publican but neither mention the Queen's Head. The bottom advert is from 20th October 1860. Kelly's 1860 Directory has him as a needle manufacturer, grocer and beer retailer.

> **SIMEON SHRIMPTON,**
> QUEEN STREET, REDDITCH,
> SOLE AGENT FOR
> **TAYLOR'S SUPERIOR ALES,**
> AND EXTRA STOUT,
> BEGS respectfully to acknowledge the favours received during the past year, and to assure his numerous friends that he continues to supply prime ALES, &c., upon the shortest notice.
> N.B No rise in the price of these superior Ales, and Stout. One trial will suffice to prove the qualities; which is respectfully solicited.

The pub name 'Queen's Head,' Queen Street is absent from the 1860 adverts above, however, the 'Queen's Head' is recorded by name in Alcester Street in February 1861 with licensee Joseph Baines.

The Queen's Head about 1910 in a very leafy Bromsgrove Road. The pub is still there but, alas, the trees are long gone.

The reproduction below of the Thomas Harrison 3d token is rather indistinct as it is taken from one that was found buried in the ground. Its date of issue would have been about 1895.

**QUEEN'S HEAD.**     Alcester Street.

Known only from the advert in the Redditch Indicator for February 16th 1861.

Joseph Baines                 1860 - 61              (Cabinet maker and upholsterer)

---

**RAILWAY INN.**     56 Unicorn Hill. ("Little Railway" to locals).

See 'Golden Cross' for licensees before 1896. It became the 'Golden Cross' once more in the 1960's and was demolished and rebuilt in the 1980's.

| | | | |
|---|---|---|---|
| William Francis Haden | 1896 - 1904 | Richard Henry Maries | 1927 - 32 |
| (Also a coal merchant) | | (By 1934 he had a fish and chip shop | |
| Mrs Haden | 1905 | at 47 Unicorn Hill) | |
| Frederick Shelton | 1906 - 08 | William Harry Matts | 1932 |
| Mrs Florence Shelton | 1909 - 24 | William Tunks | 1936 |
| John Shelton | 1924 | Ernest Pollard | 1936 - 40 |
| Stephen Wright | 1925 - 27 | | |

---

**RAILWAY TAVERN.**     45/46 Hewell Road. (Brockhill Road 1855).

The railway arrived in Redditch in September 1859. This was the nearest pub to the original station in Clive Road. Before this date it was probably just an anonymous beer-house. It was rebuilt in 1938 by Mitchell & Butler's brewery.

| | | | |
|---|---|---|---|
| T Richards | 1850 | Mrs Elizabeth Dudley | 1908 |
| Joseph Albutt | 1855 | Thomas Blackford | 1909 - 10 |
| George Ames | 1860 - 64 | Charles Henry Stanley | 1911 - 17 |
| William Hollington | 1868 - 81 | Samuel Clarke | 1921 - 24 |
| (Hair pin maker) | | Harry Howard Clements | 1927 - 33 |
| Robert Yallop | 1882 - 86 | Horace Esme Grove | 1934 |
| Mrs Mary Yallop | 1887 - 89 | John James Holmes | 1936 |
| George Frederick Guest | 1890 - 96 | Leslie George Griffiths | 1940 |
| Mrs Elizabeth Guest | 1897 | | |
| Edwin Dudley | 1898 – 1907 | | |
| (He issued a 3d. token) | | | |

---

**RED COW.**     Red Cow Yard, later Vine Street, eventually Worcester Rd.

See 'Local Notes and Queries' No. 88.

George Smallwood          1835 - 61              Mrs Elizabeth Smallwood    1864 - 70

---

## TO PUBLICANS & OTHERS.

## DAILY AND CO'S.,
### SODA AND SELTZER WATERS, LEMONADE AND GINGER NECTAR, ETC.

## JOSEPH BAINES,

CABINET Maker, Upholsterer, &c., Queen's Head, Alcester Street, Redditch, has entered into arrangements with the above company to supply all these articles at a very low rate. All orders sent to Mr. J. Baines will be executed on the shortest notice.

A fine glass of Leamington, Burton, and home-brewed ales always on hand.

N.B. A Tripe supper on Friday and Saturday evenings.

The advertisement reproduced above, from the Redditch Indicator dated Saturday February 16th 1861, is the only evidence so far discovered for the existence of the Queen's Head, Alcester Street. Kelly's Directory for 1860 gives Joseph Baines – beer retailer and cabinet maker in Alcester Street but no pub name. It must have been a pub as an out-door would not have served "tripe suppers on Friday and Saturday evenings." Kelly's Directory of 1863 has Baines in Church Green as a cabinet maker only. By 1868 he had moved again to premises in Unicorn Hill, cabinet making only.

A Midland Red charabanc about to depart from the Railway Inn, Unicorn Hill with a party of regulars. Date about 1920.

William Francis Haden's advert from 1896 (and 1897) for stabling at his Railway Hotel Mews, Unicorn Hill. The picture above was taken in 1896 by J. H. Fox & Co. photographers also of Unicorn Hill. The notice on the wall reads …… NOTICE. Horses stabled at these stables are charged 6d per head. Feeds 6d and 8d. W. F. Haden *proprietor*.

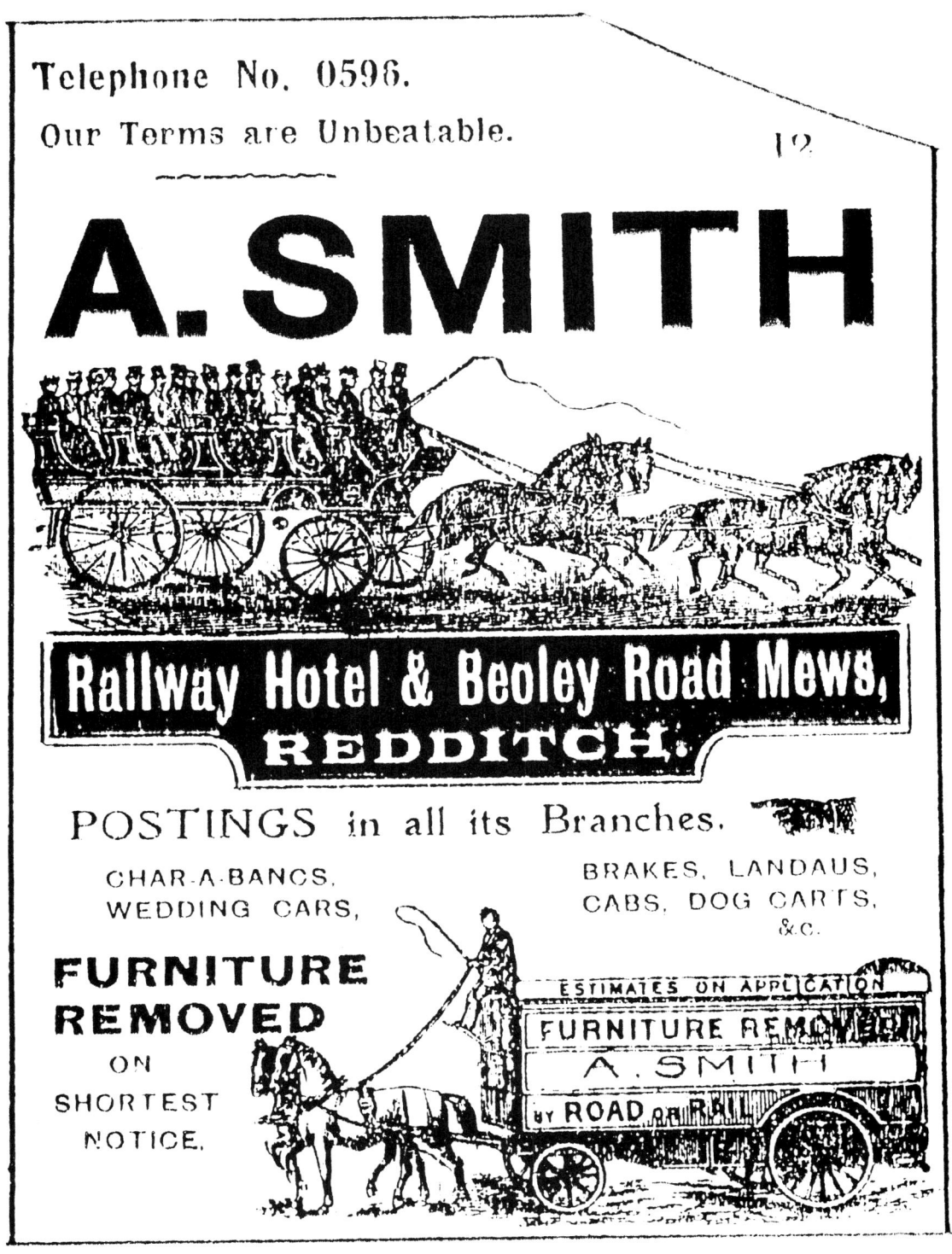

An advert from about 1905 for A. (Alfred) Smith's transport business using the Railway Hotel (Mews), Unicorn Hill. The advert also mentions Beoley Road Mews – these would have been at the Wagon & Horses pub where he was licensee.

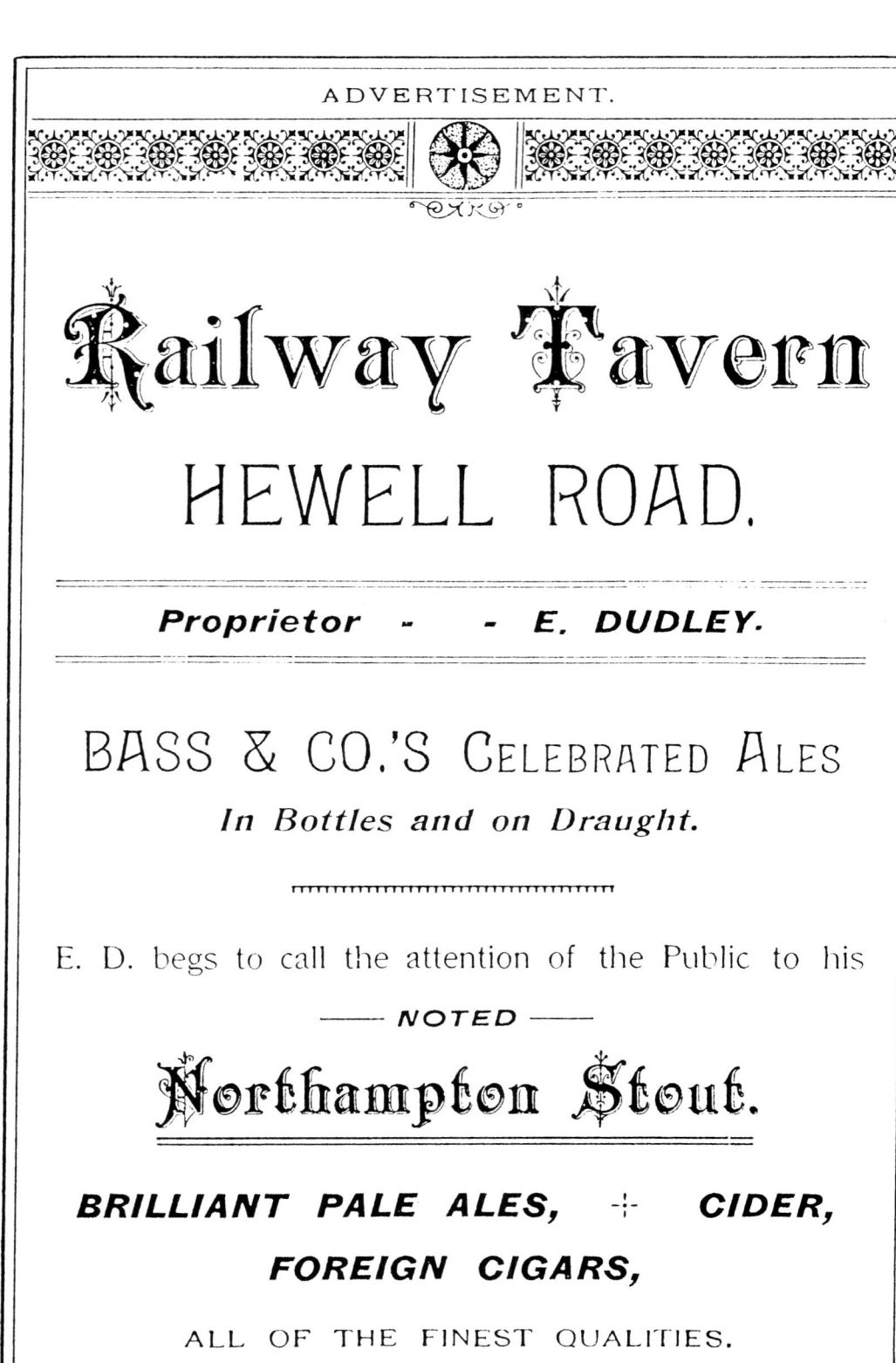

Edwin Dudley's advert from the 1900 Redditch and District Directory.
He issued a brass 3d pub token but no picture of this exists.

**Inventory and Valuation of Household Furniture and Trade Effects at the Railway Tavern, Hewell Road, Redditch.** Belonging to the estate of the late Mrs Mary Yallop duly appraised this 19th day of June 1889 for the purposes of Probate.

**FRONT ROOM.**
( This appears to be the only public room).
Fender. Dust preventer and 2 fire Irons. 8 day Clock. 7 Pictures. Small Timepiece.
Pair Small Pictures. Seating, Screen and Boarding round room. Two Deal Tables.
Windsor chair. 14 Spittoons. 2 Spill cans and 1 Match cup. 3 Sporting Pictures.
Wire blind (Lettered ). Venetian blind. Twolight gas bracket and 2 shades.
4 Pull Ale Machine, piping and taps. 3 Basins. 16 Pint jugs. 4 Quart jugs.
12 Ale glasses. 3 Measures. 2 Tundishes and tin pail. Stool. Cribbage board.
Oilcloth on floor.

**BREWHOUSE.**
Stoneware. Glass bottles. 2 Windsor chairs. Clothes horse. Maid. 2 Buckets.
2 Saucepans. Iron boiler. Pair paliasses. Zinc pan. Sundries.

**KITCHEN.**
Deal table. 5 Windsor chairs. Fender and dust preventer. An American clock.
Pair of brass candlesticks. Lamp. Picture. Gas bracket. 4 Spill cans.
Side of bacon. Tea and dinnerware.

**BACK KITCHEN.**
Deal table. Small Mahogany table. 2 Windsor Chairs. Fender, ashpan, fire irons,
tea kettle and bellows. 2 Flat irons. 3 Pictures. Bagatelle board.

The inventory also includes a Pantry with plate warmer, dinner warmer and baskets.
A Sitting Room with much furniture, china and family pictures. There are an unspecified
number of Chambers (Bedrooms) with iron bedsteads, paliasses, 2 feather beds, etc.
The only contents of the Cellar recorded are 18 bottles of Port wine. Other stock includes
four 36 gallon barrels of Ale, one 36 gallon barrel of Beer, one 18 gallon barrel of Stout
and 12 bottles of Ginger Beer. Outside are 2 water butts, bucket, watering can, 2 old seats
and 'Bumble Block Pins and Pitchers' ??

The Railway Inn/Tavern, Hewell Road in the early 1920's with the licensee Samuel Clarke standing outside.

THE RED COW was one of the oldest pubs in the town ; George Smallwood the licensee came to Redditch from Smethwick and his wife Elizabeth from Aspley Heath, just over the Birmingham to Alcester Road from Bransons Cross. She took over the running of the pub on George's death in the early 1860's until its closure about 1870, when, at the age of 67, she retired to an adjoining cottage. By 1871 the Red Cow premises were occupied by Edmund Fellows who was a baker.

The verse on the right is from the poem about Redditch in 1840 by 'an Old Fish Hill Boy.' The pub stood in Red Cow yard which became Vine Street and was a cul-de-sac until it became Worcester Road.

> A church going man was Joseph Hill,
> Who lived for years at the old Forge Mill,
> So was honest Currier White,
> Who went on Sundays morn and night.
> George Smallwood kept the Old Red Cow,
> Where hilly Worcester Road is now,
> Just below, was Littleworth walk,
> The Rack-hill fields were not far off.
> Woodman Jarvis up Brock-hill Lane,
> By Mrs. Twigg's—oh, twigg the name,
> Beyond we fished in " Turbie " cut,
> Used pins for hooks, and cotton for gut.

> The Red Cow stood in the Red Cow Yard, now the top of Worcester Road. It was kept by a Mr. Smallwood, and later on by his widow. From all accounts that have reached me this house was by no means a model one. In addition to ale and beer a strong concoction was sold there at one shilling a quart, called " Black Strap," and I meet with a person sometimes who tells me of strange orgies that were carried on there in early days. (F.K.)

The extract on the left is from 'Local Notes and Queries No. 88 – Extinct Public Houses.'

It has been suggested that, as the Temperance Hall, Worcester Road (Kingfisher Hall), was built virtually on the site of the Red Cow – if the pub had survived up to the 'Redevelopment,' the New Town Centre might have been called "The Red Cow Centre."

## RED LION.    12/13 Red Lion Street.

At the rear of this old pub stood, for many years, what must have been one of Redditch's major landmarks – The Malt House – built in the mid 1700's. Its outbuildings became the Rifle Volunteer's Drill Hall and eventually a theatre. The "New Theatre Assembly Room, Red Lion Inn," was flourishing in the 1830's. Known as the 'Lion Big Room,' it was used by visiting theatricals and local amateurs alike. The pub's licence was withdrawn on 1st May 1937.

| | | | |
|---|---|---|---|
| Herbert Willis | 1822 – 23 | Bernard Sealey | 1896 – 99 |
| Tobias Tay | 1835 | James Blackford | 1900 – 02 |
| John Brown | 1841 | Henry Davis | 1904 – 08 |
| Richard Williams | 1850 | (Also at the 'Fleece', Evesham Street) | |
| Thomas Page | 1854 | William Barnes | 1909 – 12 |
| (Also a saddler) | | Albert Dorrington | 1916 – 19 |
| George Rickards | 1855 | William James Clarke | 1921 |
| (He issued 2d. and 3d. tokens) | | Thomas Mason | 1924 – 27 |
| James Webb | 1860 – 86 | Frank Enoch Bridges | 1928 |
| (Coal dealer) | | Samuel James Field | 1932 |
| Mrs Mary Webb | 1887 – 90 | Samuel Atkins | 1934 |
| Henry Davis | 1891 – 96 | John Joseph Biggs | 1936 |

## RED LION.    Feckenham Road, Hunt End.

In 1901 the address is given as "The Common."

| | | | |
|---|---|---|---|
| George Townsend | 1850 – 54 | William Henry Chambers | 1898 – 1913 |
| Joseph Hobday | 1855 – 68 | Hubert Baldwin | 1914 – 29 |
| Joseph Chambers | 1868 – 97 | James Parry | 1930 – 40 |
| (Needle stamper) | | | |

## RED LION.    Church Road, Astwood Bank.

A 3d. token was issued by the 'Red Lion Sick & Dividend Society.'

| | | | |
|---|---|---|---|
| William Goodyear | 1872 – 95 | William Henry James | 1905 – 19 |
| Henry Smith | 1896 | Garnet Frederick Edwards | 1920 – 27 |
| Ernest Smith | 1897 – 98 | Albert Parker Edwards | 1928 – 32 |
| Daniel Dibble | 1899 – 1904 | Edward Joseph Perkins | 1932 – 40 |

## RED LION.    Bradley Green. (Under Inkberrow or Feckenham).

| | | | |
|---|---|---|---|
| Henry Harbert | 1841 – 50 | William Marshall | 1884 – 96 |
| W Court | 1854 – 64 | Harry Bent | 1900 |
| Mrs J Court | 1868 | Thomas Buttery | 1904 – 16 |
| John Bate | 1872 | Mrs S Buttery | 1921 |
| William Hicks | 1876 – 80 | Frederick Bridge | 1924 – 40 |

# THE MALT HOUSE – Red Lion Street.

Illustrated below in a contemporary water colour and an old photograph (right) – it is believed to have been built in the 1740's. The conical section was the drying cone and the adjacent malting floor was in a building that measured 80ft by 30ft. As it could seat 300 it was used for social functions, concerts and theatrical performances in what came to be known as the "Assembly Room" or the "Red Lion Big Room" from as early as the 1830's. In 1860 it became the 39th Rifle Volunteers Drill Hall.

Extract from a poem from 1840.

> The Red Lion Room was our Guildhall
> For occasional parties, it held us all,
> Dinners and dances were held therein,
> A ticket we'd buy and then go in.

A map of 1884 showing the Malthouse in the Red Lion yard. The Red Lion arch led through into Silver Street and the part of town known as 'Wapping.'

LOCAL NOTES AND QUERIES.

No. 216.

GRAND CONCERT.

The public are respectfully informed that
On Monday, August 17, 1835,
The Celebrated
FREDERICK HARTMAN FAMILY,
Whose Performances have been received with the most distinguished success in many of the fashionable and other Towns in England during a most extensive professional Tour and lastly at Oxford, Cheltenham, Worcester, and Birmingham, will give
AN EVENING
CONCERT,
AT THE
ASSEMBLY ROOM, RED LION INN,
REDDITCH,
Consisting of the most Favourite
SONGS, DUETS,
GLEES, OVERTURES,
PIANO-FORTE,
HARP, & VIOLIN
CONCERTOS
From the most distinguished Composers.

The Concert to Commence at Eight o'Clock.
Tickets—Front Seats, 2s.—Back Seats 1s. each, to be had at the Red Lion, and at the Printer's, where Programmes of the Performance may be seen.
Schools and Children Half-price.

*Bromley, Printer, Albion Office, Redditch.*

CORONATION.

A PUBLIC BALL
WILL BE HELD IN THE
ASSEMBLY ROOM, RED LION INN, REDDITCH,
On the 28th of June, 1838.

LADY PATRONESSES.

| MRS. CLAYTON | MRS. MILWARD |
| MRS. HEMMING | MRS. C. BARTLEET |

STEWARDS.

| MR. MILWARD | MR. ROYSTON |
| MR. WALTER HEMMING | MR. W. W. GOULD |
| MR. JAMES HOLYOAKE | MR. W. FIELD |
| MR. THOMAS HOLYOAKE | MR. BALDEN |

Tickets to be had of the respective Stewards; at the Bar; and of Mr. Osborne, Bookseller.

LADIES' - - Five Shillings
GENTLEMEN'S - Six Shillings.
THE LEAMINGTON BAND WILL ATTEND.

*Dancing to commence at 10 o'clock.*

OSBORNE, PRINTER AND BOOKSELLER.

ABOVE: The Red Lion in the 1930's.

LEFT: Notices of entertainments in the Red Lion Assembly Room in 1835 when William IV was king and in 1838 when a public ball was held to celebrate Queen Victoria's Coronation.

BELOW: Richard Humphries, who lived near the Red Lion, ran a coach from the pub to Birmingham from as early as 1824.

LOCAL NOTES AND QUERIES.

No. 151.—HUMPHRIES' COACH.
From the Needle District Almanack for the present year, I find that "Humphries' coach" commenced running from Redditch to Birmingham, September, 1824. Had the coach any particular name, and what was it? The writer has gone by it on several occasions, one of which was from Birmingham to Redditch, in the summer of 1839, immediately after the riot in the Bull Ring, when Bourne's shop and premises were burnt and gutted, and the metropolitan police were parading the streets. The proprietor, Richard Humphries, and family, lived in Red Lion Street, near to the Red Lion Inn, from which the coach started to Birmingham.

A photograph of the Red Lion, Red Lion Street, taken in 1934 when Samuel Atkins was licensee – He is the gentleman third from the right. (Enlarged below).

Also reproduced below is George Rickards token of the late 1850's. He issued 2d and 3d versions.

# Red Lion Hotel,

PROPRIETOR:—
JAMES BLACKFORD.

## RED LION STREET, REDDITCH.

**ALES, WINES, AND SPIRITS IN GRAND CONDITION.
CHOICE CIGARS.**

GOOD STABLING AND ACCOMMODATION FOR CYCLISTS.

## The Old Drill Hall

Is attached to this Hotel, and will be found replete with all accessories for **Entertainments, Bazaars, Balls, Meetings, &c.** The Hall has seating accommodation for **300** people, and may be engaged on most reasonable terms, with or without attendants.

*All communications will have the prompt personal attention of the Proprietor.*

James Blackford's advert from the Redditch and District Directory for the year 1900.

**BERNARD SEALEY,**

*RED LION HOTEL,*

Red Lion Street, Redditch.

*Mitchell's Ales and Stout*

On Draught and Bottle.

Spirits of the most noted Brands. Cigars, &c.

**FAMILIES SUPPLIED.**

---

ABOVE: Bernard Sealey's 1898 advert.

LEFT: James Webb's advert from the Redditch Indicator 21st April 1866.

BELOW LEFT: A page of the 1897 Needle District Almanack.

BELOW: An advert from the Indicator of April 1866 by Elijah Fourt who probably conducted his plumbing business from outbuildings in the Red Lion yard. By 1882 he was the licensee of the Warwick Arms.

---

**JAMES WEBB,
RED LION INN,
REDDITCH,
AGENT FOR
IND COOPE & CO'S
INDIA,
PALE, STRONG, & MILD ALES,**
Supplied in Casks of Eighteen Gallons, and upwards, delivered direct from the Brewery, BURTON-ON-TRENT

---

14    *The Needle District Almanack*

**C. PALMER,**

Baker, Corn Factor and Seedsman.

19, ALCESTER STREET, REDDITCH.

AGENT FOR GREEN'S CONDIMENT & CONDITION POWDERS
For Horses and Cattle, and Space for Poultry.

HYDE'S & CAPERN'S SEEDS, FOODS, & SHELL GRAVEL
For all kinds of Birds.

FOSTER'S PEARL-COATED ROUP PILLS FOR POULTRY & PIGEONS.

VICTORIA DOG BISCUITS.

---

**BERNARD SEALEY,**

Red ⁂ Lion ⁂ Hotel.

RED LION STREET, REDDITCH.

**MITCHELL'S ALES AND STOUT**

On Draught and Bottle.

Spirits of all the most Noted Brands. Cigars, &c.

**FAMILIES SUPPLIED.**

---

**ELIJAH FOURT,**
(LATE BARROW & FOURT),

*Plumber, Glazier, Paper Hanger, House, Sign, and Ornamental Painter,*

RED LION INN,
RED LION STREET, REDDITCH.

The partnership lately existing between Robert Barrow and Elijah Fourt, under the style of "BARROW & FOURT," having been dissolved by the Bankruptcy of R. Barrow, the said E. Fourt begs respectfully to inform the inhabitants of Redditch and the neighbourhood, that he will, in future, carry on the business; and trusts, by using the best materials—employing none but competent workmen—punctuality, and strict attention to all orders, combined with moderate charges, to merit and receive the same liberal patronage and support which was bestowed on the late firm.

*Beer Machines, Lead Pumps, Water Closets, &c., fitted and Repaired.*

Graining, Marbling, Enamelling, &c.
ESTIMATES GIVEN.

April 19, 1866.

Wanted a respectable Youth as an APPRENTICE.

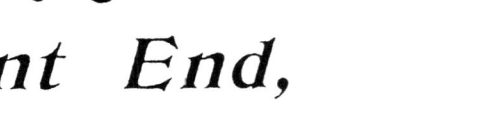

William Henry Chambers advert for the Red Lion, Hunt End, from the 1900 Redditch and District Directory. He was there until 1913.

The Red Lion, Hunt End, in about 1905. W. H. Chambers name appears on the licence board over the doorway. His advert below is from 1901.

### RED LION HOTEL, Hunt End, Redditch.

**W. H. CHAMBERS.** Proprietor.

Wines, Spirits.   Mitchell & Butler's Ales, etc.
OF THE FINEST QUALITY.
Excellent Accommodation for Dinner Parties, Cyclists, etc.

A brass 3d token issued by the Red Lion Sick and Dividend Society, Church Road, Astwood Bank.

## THE FECKENHAM COURT LEET

The Feckenham Court Leet and Court Baron met under the Jubilee Oak in the village at 11am on the third Thursday in November of each year, when the Manor Court Bailiff read out a proclamation. All those concerned then moved to the Rose and Crown where the Lord of the Manor's Steward took the chair and the eleven Jurymen appointed their Foreman, their Ale Taster, their Beadle, their Reeve and their Bread Weigher and the Chief Rents were paid. The Court then adjourned to the Red Lion at Bradley Green for dinner.

The Red Lion, Bradley Green.

## RIFLEMAN INN.  30/35/36 Park Road. (Occasionally Littleworth).

| | | | |
|---|---|---|---|
| James Rudge | 1868 – 80 | Frank Shakespeare Jennings | 1906 – 10 |
| Thomas Harvey | 1881 – 85 | Charles Alfred Hobbs | 1911 – 15 |
| Mrs Harvey | 1886 | Edwin Apperley | 1916 – 21 |
| Alfred Edwin Nokes | 1887 – 95 | William James Morris | 1922 – 28 |
| Enoch Edwards | 1896 – 1905 | Albert Edward Wood | 1928 |
| (Dog breeder) | | George Frederick Maries | 1932 – 40 |

---

## RISING SUN.  29 Alcester Street.

The 'Rising Sun' appears on the crest of the Distillers Company.

| | | | |
|---|---|---|---|
| John Guest | 1841 – 64 | John Gough Millward | 1893 – 1919 |
| (and a grocer) | | Mrs Emma Millward | 1920 – 27 |
| Mrs Maria Guest | 1866 – 84 | William Edwin Banks | 1928 |
| (also a grocer) | | Harry Stevens | 1932 |
| George Frederick Guest | 1887 | James William Edgington | 1934 – 36 |
| (also a grocer) | | Kenneth J Cull | 1940 |
| Henry James Webb | 1888 – 92 | | |

---

## ROSE AND CROWN.  Heathfield Road. (Webheath Lane in the 1900's).

The Rose and Crown emblem commemorates the marriage of Henry VII and Elizabeth of York which ended the conflict between the houses of York and Lancaster in the Wars of the Roses. The pub was demolished and rebuilt in the 1980's.

| | | | |
|---|---|---|---|
| Thomas Charman | 1841 | Mrs Jessie Hadgkiss | 1909 – 19 |
| John Andrews | 1850 | F Harvey | 1920 |
| William Andrews | 1854 – 84 | Ernest Hubbard | 1921 – 23 |
| Mrs Andrews | 1885 | Harry Vann | 1924 |
| William Carwardine | 1886 – 1905 | Mrs Emma Vann | 1925 – 40 |
| Walter J Hadgkiss | 1906 – 08 | | |

---

## ROSE AND CROWN.  High Street, Feckenham.

In most Victorian Directories it appears as the 'Old' Rose and Crown.

| | | | |
|---|---|---|---|
| James James | 1841 – 50 | William Halford | 1896 – 97 |
| Mrs Martha James | 1854 – 82 | George Laight | 1898 – 1901 |
| Harry James Millward | 1883 – 88 | Edward Alexander | 1902 – 07 |
| John Holbeche | 1889 – 92 | Joseph Cull | 1908 – 09 |
| Elizabeth Marshall | 1893 – 96 | William Henry Dyer | 1910 – 40 |

**Valuation and Particulars of Fixtures, Fittings, Trade Utensils, etc. at the Rifleman Inn, Park Rd. Redditch.** From Mr C A Hobbs to Messrs Ind Coope & Co Ltd. 25th. October 1915.

### BAR.
Enamel wash up bowl. Galvanized tray and drainer. Copper beer warmer. Automatic spring cash till with 8 divisions. The "Acme" patent cork drawer. Massive brass 2 light gas pendants. 2 Inverted incandescent burners. 2 Glass shades. 2 Enamel ceiling shades and hooks. Board and 3 preserved fish. 2 Preserved fish. 8 Day Clock in Mahogany case. Map of England and Wales. Pair of deer horns. 4 Pair of sheep's horns. 4 Round wood stools. Glass gas bracket with reflect mirror. Ditto with incandescent burner. 3 Framed Prints. Framed Photo. Framed Engraving. Copper funnel. Pewter measures, pint & quart. 1 Wood tap. 2 Door springs. Bell on door. Tobacco drawer as fixed under counter. Glass sign in Mahogany frame – "Foreign Wines." Moveable shelf under counter. 4 Pewter measures – $1/2$pt. – Gill – $1/2$ Gill accomadetion (Sic) ? Pewter tundish. Incandescent burner and glass. 3 Division Mahogany cigar case. 10 Metal rowers ? New fittings to Beer Engine viz new brass tap, 5 buckets and rods, 5 lengths of pipes to cellar, 3 new brass unions. 24in. Round marble top table on iron stand. Venetian ash pan. 2 Green serge window curtains and fittings. Lino on floor behind bar 4ft. X 8ft. 6in.

### SMOKE ROOM.
New lino on floor 15ft. X10ft. 6in. 5 Mahogany top drinking tables on iron stands 3ft. X lft. $3^1/2$in. 5 Round stained Stools. 4 Finger plates on doors. Two-light brass gas chandeliers with 2 incandescent burners and 2 glass shades. 2 Enamel bell shades and hooks. Brass gas bracket. Glass gas globe. Two 10ft. Mahogany framed seats upholstered in leather . 40ft. Painted & grained matchboarding round room. 2 Arm smoking chairs. Two 3ft.9in. X 1ft. 8in. mahogany lead light window screens. 4 Gilt framed paintings. Large framed print in oak frame "Sailor Boy." Pair coloured prints in Mahogany frames. Pair small oil paintings in gilt. Pair large oil paintings in gilt. 4 Framed prints. Framed print in Mahogany frame "The Duchess of Devonshire." Walnut framed Overmantle with 4 bevel glass plate. Stuffed Owl in glass case. 4 Ornaments. Ashpan. 4 Earthenware Spittoons.

### CLUB ROOM.
3 Mahogany framed chairs in leather. 7 Span back chairs. 1 Birch round back arm smoke chair. 1 Arm Windsor chair. 4 Chairs with perforated seats. 4 Bentwood stools. 9ft. Stained strip and 6 brass hooks. 3ft. ditto and 12 hooks. 5ft. ditto and 12 hooks. 4ft. ditto and 13 hooks. 4ft. ditto and 14 hooks. Brass gas bracket. Double bronze gas bracket. 2 Venetian blinds and fittings. 3 Framed pictures. 3ft. X 3ft. square deal table with draw, on turned legs. 10ft. Deal form. 5ft. Mantleboard and fringe.

### CELLAR.
3 Shelves over steps. 3 Iron stoopers. 3 Brass taps. 7 Brass union taps. 3 Wood taps. 36 Wood barrel scotches. Tin oil filler. Dipstick. 4 Gallon jar.

Also listed are 4 Bedrooms. Front and back stairs. A gas lit passage with seats, coat hooks and door mats. A gas lit kitchen with matchboard surround, deal table and 5 chairs and 2 framed prints. In the yard was a wooden stable with 2 doors, manger and rack and a brick floor. Outside, the front of the building was illuminated by a large gas lamp. There was a metal licence board and a framed sign board "Rifleman Inn" with iron brackets and stay.

Park Road, Redditch in 1953 (above) with a crowd outside the Rifleman Inn celebrating the Coronation. (Below) A photo by Ian Hayes taken in July 1970 shortly before it was demolished.

## TO LOVERS OF DOGS OF ANY BREED.

"MOUNT LEO,"
Prize Winner at Birmingham Dog Show.
This dog was a Perfect Wreck three months before using
EDWARDS' POWDERS.

I, ENOCH EDWARDS, after thirty years' experience of Breeding Dogs, and giving my powder and advice free to Lords, Members of Parliament, Ladies of Title, and Clergymen, have been asked by the public to place before them, for Sale, my DOG CONDITION POWDER, which is guaranteed to Prevent and Cure all kinds of Disease, giving them good Coats for Show purposes, and preventing all bad smells which Dogs are subject to. It is never known to fail.

These Powders had a Fair Test at the Birmingham Dog Show last year, five classes of Dogs being treated with it for the Show. An Honour was taken by a St. Bernard, "MOUNT LEO," in the Open Class, which three months before the Show was a perfect wreck; and three Honours were taken by a Red Setter, "CARRIE GREENHEART"; and other Honours were taken by a Mastiff, two Collies, and a Bulldog, thus showing that these Powders suit all classes of Dogs.

This Powder is strongly recommended in cases of Indolent Constipation, and where the natural Digestive Functions are prevented by Worms in the Stomach or Intestines, causing Emaciation, Indigestion, Stoppage of the Bowels, and symptoms of severe Abdominal Irritation. Also for the relief of the pain caused by Piles in old Dogs, and in affections of the Liver such as Jaundice, manifested by yellowness of the mouth and eyes and intense constipation; and for cases of Diarrhoea, which are often caused by Fermenting Foods in the Stomach and Intestines, or irritants in the shape of Bacteria in the secretions of these passages. This powder will at once prove efficacious by quickly expelling the cause of the complaint, thus rendering the system free from foreign irritants of any kind.

Dogs of different breeds may be seen at my address, 36, Park Road.

This Powder may be obtained from me in Boxes, Price 1s., by post 1s. 1½d. Label, giving full instructions with each box. Testimonials on application.

With orders for one box or more, stating the condition of the dog, advice will be sent free.

**DISTEMPER, DIARRHŒA, AND TONIC POWDERS,**
6d. Per Box, by Post 7d.

**MANGE OILS FOR DOGS AND CATS** (never known to fail),
6d. per Bottle, by Post, 8½d.

AT STUD.—Four grand rough-coated St. Bernard Dogs, all of the best blood obtainable: Plinlimmon, Lord Bute, Duke of Mablescroft, and St. Bedivere, by breeding or other arrangements. **ST. BERNARD PUPPIES ON SALE.**

**ENOCH EDWARDS,** 36, PARK ROAD, REDDITCH, WORCESTERSHIRE.
(Late of Pack Horse, Alcester Road, and Bournbrook, Bristol Road.)

Adverts from 1897 (above) and 1896 (below) by Enoch Edwards who was at the Rifleman from 1896 to 1905. He was previously licensee of the Pack Horse, Alcester Road and the Bournbrook, Bristol Road, Birmingham. Not only was he a pub landlord and dog breeder of some note but he was also something of a veterinarian, selling patent pet medicines to cure mange, distemper and diarrhoea. If you gave your dog 'Edwards' Powders' you could turn a "Perfect wreck" into a "prize winner" in three months.

### Rifleman Inn, Park Road
(CLOSE TO RAILWAY STATION).

PROPRIETOR - ENOCH EDWARDS.
(Late of "The Pack Horse," Alcester Road).

*Breeder of St. Bernard and other Dogs. Two Grand St. Bernards at Stud. Puppies usually on Sale.*

DOGS GOT UP FOR SHOWS. THIRTY YEARS' EXPERIENCE.

The Guest family ran the Rising Sun for at least 40 years. During this time it served hot meals, tea and coffee and was also a grocers shop. Maria Guest was the licensee for about 20 years. This Redditch Indicator advert appeared on the front page of the paper on the 4th August 1866.

## THE FAIR! THE FAIR!!

### Where are you going for Refreshments?

TO

## MARIA GUEST'S,

### RISING SUN, ALCESTER STREET,

### Grocer and Provision Dealer.

HER REFRESHMENTS ROOMS are open daily.—HOT JOINTS at ONE O'CLOCK.
*Teas and Coffees of first-rate quality, and low prices.*
**BRITISH AND FOREIGN WINES.**
A well-selected stock now ready for Sale.

Two 'Rose and Crowns' circa 1900. Above is the one in Webheath (now rebuilt) with licensee William Carwardine in the doorway. The one below in Feckenham has the name *Old* Rose & Crown on the wall. The building remains much the same today.

## ROYAL GEORGE.  29/35 Evesham Street.

Originally called the 'Pointer's Arms' in the 1850's when John Bryan was the licensee. The pub was named after the warship which sank at Portsmouth in 1782. (See panel). There was a picture of 'The Royal George' in the window which resulted in the locals referring to the pub as 'The Ship.' (Later Rainscourt's shop).

| | | | |
|---|---|---|---|
| John Bryan | 1850 – 55 | Lewis Glover | 1892 – 1900 |
| (Hairdresser) | | Charles Wharrad | 1901 – 04 |
| George Mustin | 1860 – 68 | T Smith | 1905 – 07 |
| John Holbeche | 1871 – 74 | Charles Frederick Salisbury | 1908 – 09 |
| John Steward | 1875 – 76 | C W Athersmith | 1910 |
| Alfred Field | 1876 – 80 | Charles Valentine Laight | 1912 – 14 |
| Benjamin Harman | 1880 – 87 | John H Smith | 1914 – 15 |
| James Henry Bott | 1888 – 91 | Frederick Barclay | 1915 – 36 |

## ROYAL HOTEL.  8 Market Place.

Rebuilt and renamed in February 1897. For licensees before this date see under 'Fox & Goose.'

| | | | |
|---|---|---|---|
| Frank Gathercole | 1897 – 98 | D Hopkins | 1905 – 08 |
| William Thomas Mortiboy Smith | | George H Field | 1908 – 12 |
| | 1900 – 02 | (Also Mrs M A Field) | |
| George Herbert Shepherd | 1903 – 04 | Alfred Smith | 1912 – 36 |
| | | Ernest Smith | 1940 |

## ROYAL OAK.  Prospect Hill / Albert Street.

Pulled down to make way for enlargements to British Mills. See 'Local Notes and Queries' No. 88.

| | | | |
|---|---|---|---|
| Thomas Green | | William Gardner | 1835 – 60 |
| (Unknown date) | | (Also a blacksmith) | |

## ROYAL OAK.  533 Evesham Road, Crabbs Cross.

So called because the inn was on Charles II escape route from Worcester to Boscobel in 1651. "In May 1643 Charles I reviewed 10,000 men at Crabbe Crosse."

| | | | |
|---|---|---|---|
| Joseph Mills | 1841 – 55 | Clarence Charles Mills | 1906 – 20 |
| Mrs Mary Mills | 1860 – 66 | Mrs Harriet Mills | 1921 – 23 |
| John Henry Mills | 1868 – 79 | William Henry Jennings | 1924 – 27 |
| (Needle maker) | | Samuel Henry Foster | 1928 – 33 |
| Thomas Styler | 1880 – 83 | S Blundell | 1934 – 35 |
| Reuben Canadine | 1884 – 88 | Leonard Pinchbeck | 1936 |
| Ernest Watton | 1889 – 92 | Charles Hall | 1940 |
| Matthew Mills | 1894 – 1905 | | |
| (He issued a 3d token) | | | |

**Valuation and Particulars of Fixtures, Fittings and Effects at the Royal George Inn, Evesham Street, Redditch.** From Mr John H Smith to Mr Frederick Barclay (when the inn has been modernised ). Made by me this 8th. day of December 1915. (Frank Neasom).

### BAR.
2 Mahogany top tables on iron stands. Standard deal table on turned legs covered with American cloth. Ditto with polished top. 2 Bentwood chairs. 4 Windsor chairs. Iron fender (damaged). Ash curb. Linoleum on floor. 5ft. painted seat with painted and grained matchboard back from fireplace to window. 6ft. Painted seat in window. 6ft.6in. X 2ft.9in. painted and grained window board. 11ft. Painted seat with painted and grained matchboard back. 2 Painted and grained draught (excluding) boards near side door. 4ft. Painted seat. 13ft. Painted and grained counter with zinc top and door fitted with shelves. Patent cash till.
6 Pull Beer Engine (4 pulls out of order) with coloured handles, 6 brass taps and pewter lined tray with 2 lengths of pipe. Nest of 4 painted glass shelves.
Round stained stool. Wood guard to cellar flap. E. P. Express cork drawer.
3 Electric drop lights and 2 shades. Brass gas pendant. Flexible gas pendant fitted with shade and incandescent burner. 2 Door springs fitted to door.
5 Iron Spittoons. Iron fender curb fixed to floor. Red blind, roller and fittings. Red curtain and rod. Set of 3 Pewter Ale measures – quart, pint and $1/2$ pint.
Tin funnel. B.S.A. Air gun and target.
5 Quart jugs. 22 Pint jugs. 32 – $1/2$ pint Jubilees. 13 Stout glasses. 16 Ale glasses. 5 – $1/2$ pint ale glasses. 23 Small pressed ale glasses. 6 Pint Jubilees. 2 Stone jars 1 Chester and 1 Baylis.
*(Note – J F Baylis of Ipsley Street, Redditch was a Ginger Beer manufacturer who was eventually taken over by P Spencer & Sons).*

### CLUB ROOM.
Venetian blind and fitting. 4 Electric drop lights and shades. Strip of 3 hat and coat hooks. 4 Painted and grained corner cupboards as fixed. Linoleum on floor. Painted seating round room with shaped ends. Air gun target in cupboard with electric fitting etc. as fixed.

The rest of the accommodation in the inventory is less detailed. It includes stairs leading to a back bedroom, back and front attics and box room. Downstairs was a pantry, kitchen, gas lit yard and a scullery with furnace. Outside the front of the building there was a large framed sign board. A flight of steps led down to a gas lit cellar.

*NOTE :  For more information on this pub see under its original name of 'The Pointer's Arms.'

# 'THE ROYAL GEORGE'

She was a 100 gun warship, comparable in size to Nelson's 'Victory'. She sank in seconds in a flat calm as she rode at anchor at Spithead, Portsmouth, at 9.20 on the morning of the 29th August 1782. The ship was heeled over for repairs but, due to negligence, too much water was allowed to enter her lower gun ports and she sank with the loss of over 800 lives, including 300 women and 60 children who were visiting the crew as they were not allowed shore leave as the ship was due to sail.

**ROYAL GEORGE**
Sergeant Charles Valentine Laight. 2994. Worcs. Regiment. Aged 57. Killed in action. 15th May, 1919.

Royal George licensee C.V. Laight joined the Worcester Regiment during WW1 although he was in his mid fifties.

The Royal Hotel, Market Place in the early 1930's

## "ROYAL HOTEL"

### Family and Commercial Hotel,

**Market Place, REDDITCH.**

Every Accommodation for Cyclists, Tourists, Commercials, &c.

C.T.C. House, Headquarters of the Redditch and District Cycling Club, Windsor Cricket Club, Redditch Harriers, and the District Club House Birchfield Harriers (Midland Champions)

o

### Wholesale Wine and Spirit Merchant.

FAMILIES SUPPLIED WITH HIGH-CLASS WINES AND SPIRITS, AND SALT AND Co.'s CELEBRATED ALES AND STOUT IN CASK AND BOTTLES.

---o---

## BILLIARDS! BILLIARDS!

**BILLIARD ROOM (TWO TABLES) OPEN ALL DAY.**

---o---

The Large Hall of the Hotel may be engaged for Balls, Smoking Concerts, Meetings, Clubs, &c.

**LARGE DINING HALL WILL SEAT 350 PERSONS.**

---o---

F. GATHERCOLE, Proprietor.

---

Frank Gathercole's advert from the Redditch Needle District Almanack and Directory of 1897 is identical to the one that appeared the previous year when the Hotel was called the Fox and Goose, except that his ? name is given as T Gathercole. His initial is also given as T in the 1896 index of advertisers but no one by the name of Gathercole appears in the 1896 Trades Directory alphabetical list.

From the auction catalogue of the sale by Bass Ltd.
held at the Grand Hotel, B'ham, Wed. 9th May 1928.

LOT 26.

# THE "ROYAL" HOTEL,

Market Place,

## REDDITCH

(Worcestershire).

FREEHOLD — FULLY-LICENSED — 7 DAYS.

occupying a fine central position;

together with

### THE ADJOINING RETAIL SHOP,

which forms part of the main block;

and also a

### BOWLING GREEN, YARD, STABLING and OUTBUILDINGS AT THE REAR.

THE LICENSED PREMISES, YARD AND OUTBUILDINGS are let to Mr. Alfred Smith, who has been in occupation for 14 years. The total NET ANNUAL RENTAL IS £100.

This is an imposing property, the main structure being three-storey brick and tile built and having an attractive front elevation.

The accommodation includes:—

ON THE GROUND FLOOR: Tiled Entrance Vestibule and Spacious Hall; large Commercial Room; Excellent Front Vaults with Outdoor Department from side passage; a large and comfortable Smoke Room; Shooting Room, with w.c., lavatory and urinal adjoining; Private Sitting Room; Kitchen, fitted with range; Scullery; Coalplace; and Store.

ON THE FIRST FLOOR are Spacious Landing; Large Assembly Room; A CAPITAL BILLIARD ROOM (at present accommodating six tables, which are the property of the tenant); W.C., Lavatory and Urinal; Sitting Room; Two Bedrooms; and Bathroom, fitted with bath, hot and cold supplies.

ON THE SECOND FLOOR are Landing; Seven Bedrooms; and w.c.; also Four Staff Rooms, with back staircase.

IN THE BASEMENT there is extensive paved Cellaring including Beer Cellar with brick Stillaging; Spirit Cellar; Bottled Beer Cellar; and Store Cellaring.

OUTSIDE, approached by a cartway from Market Place, there is a Yard with ranges of brick and tile Outbuildings including Garage, Stores, and Stabling for ten Horses with Loft over part, and a range of open Shedding. There is also a BOWLING GREEN with w.c. urinal and lavatory.

Electric Light, Gas, Water and Telephone services are installed.

THE LOCK-UP SHOP is let to Mr. Gardner, Fruiterer, at a NET RENTAL OF £30 6s. 8d. PER ANNUM.

10/6 per annum is receivable from P.O. for pole in yard.

*REMARKS.—This is an important central Property on a main business thoroughfare, and with ample Trading and other accommodation.*

Page Thirty-four.

> Extract from the 'Redditch Needle District Almanack and Directory' for the year 1898 giving details of events of the year 1897.
>
> February (9)—Annual Institute Conversazione. (10)—Annual Postmen's Dinner at the Royal Hotel, when 60 officials sat down. (11)—"Royal Hotel" the new name given to the re-built old "Fox and Goose Inn," dating from about the year 1807.—Urban District Council approve of offer of Mr. Coleman to erect suitable Municipal offices at Unicorn Hill. Also prepared a memorial to the Midland Railway Company, requesting a better train service to Birmingham. (16)—"A History of Alvechurch," a lecture

The extract above from the Needle District Almanack gives
February 11th 1897 as the opening of the 'Royal Hotel'

---

**ROYAL HOTEL MEWS.**

SPECIAL NOTICE TO HORSE BREEDERS AND OWNERS.

Horses carefully and thoroughly broken to harness and saddle, and made quiet with all traffic. Having good harness and vehicles, with twenty years' practical experience and knowledge of the management and treatment of young horses, I cannot fail to give satisfaction. Any letter or wire should be addressed—

**WALTER READ, 51, PROSPECT ROAD, REDDITCH.**

NO CONNECTION WHATEVER WITH ANYONE ELSE OF THE SAME NAME.

This is to certify that Mr. Walter Read has broken several of my colts to saddle and harness and has always given me entire satisfaction.—(Signed) Jno. Gold, M.R.C.V.S. May 11th, 1906.

---

Walter Read ran his horse breaking business from the Royal Hotel yard. He makes it plain that he is not connected with the horsebreaking firm of F. Read of Evesham Street. His 1910 advert also quotes the satisfaction of Gold's the local vet with his services.

Of the extinct public houses of Redditch I will first mention the *Royal Oak*. This was an old part-timbered house, standing at the corner of what is now Albert Street, but was formerly a fore-draught leading to a brickyard. The *Royal Oak* stood with its gable facing "Fish Hill," as that ascent into Redditch was then called, but was so much below the level of the ground that you had to descend two or three steps on entering, and the window sills in Albert Street were almost flush with the ground. Adjoining the inn was a blacksmith's shop, for William Gardner, the last landlord, carried on the calling of Tubal Cain as well as that of Gaius. He was not successful in either at Redditch; but after he left the town succeeded well as a worker in iron.

The earliest landlord of whom I have any account was "Tommy" Green—

    A short squab man in an old drab suit,
    Half of him waistcoat, and half top boot.

The house once did a flourishing trade amongst the old pointers from the Forge, but in later days the *Royal Oak* went to decay and was at last pulled down to make room for the enlargements which were constantly taking place at the British Needle Mills. I have heard the *Royal Oak* spoken of as a house where everything was very good, "the dominoes were solid brass." (F.K.)

Extract from 'Local Notes & Queries' No. 88 – Extinct Public Houses.

This Royal Oak was at the bottom of Prospect Hill.

RIGHT: Matthew Mills' 3d token from about 1900.

In 1762 John Mills, an early Crabbs Cross needle maker also kept a Token shop and gave exchange under the 'Truck' system. This was a system whereby wages were paid partly in company tokens, only of use in company controlled shops. The system was banned in 1848.

The Royal Oak (below) in about 1920. Now a private house.

This photograph taken in 1895 shows Matthew Mills and family outside the Royal Oak, Crabbs Cross. As well as running the pub he was also a needle maker. Many Victorian landlords had other occupations, Fred Chambers at the Fleece on the other side of Evesham Road, for example, was a butcher. When this photograph was taken the pub had two bay windows – the right hand one is not shown. By the 1920's the window on the right of the door had been altered to make all three of the front windows into bays.

## SCALE AND COMPASS    111/133 Birchfield Rd, (Nailpasser Gn) Headless Cross.

The 1855 directory gives 'Square and Compasses' – either version is a Masonic symbol. The token issued by W H James gives the address as Web heath (Sic).

| | | | |
|---|---|---|---|
| Joseph Johnson | 1854 | Enoch Styler | 1907 – 08 |
| George Farmer Johnson | 1855 – 64 | Mrs Styler | 1909 – 10 |
| (He was also a Land Surveyor) | | John Howard    (NDA) | 1911 – 13 |
| Thomas Johnson | 1866 | (From 1908 in Kelly's Directory) | |
| Frederick Johnson | 1868 | Ronald B Martin | 1916 – 19 |
| Walter Johnson | 1872 – 86 | Edward Hopkins (Kelly's) | 1920 – 27 |
| Mrs Mary Johnson | 1887 – 89 | (James Hopkins in the NDA) | |
| William Henry James | 1890 – 1904 | Harry Carwardine | 1927 – 40 |
| (He issued a 3d. token) | | | |

---

## SCOURER'S ARMS.    28 Prospect Hill.

| | | | |
|---|---|---|---|
| Charles Davis Snr. | 1855 – 73 | William Russell | 1909 – 12 |
| Mrs Matilda Davis | 1874 – 76 | H Eames | 1913 – 14 |
| Charles Albert Davis Jnr. | 1880 – 90 | Frank Davis | 1916 – 24 |
| Edward Such | 1891 – 1900 | Albert Henry Stanley | 1926 – 28 |
| Mrs Elizabeth Such | 1901 – 04 | | |

---

## SEVEN STARS.    75 Birchfield Road, Headless Cross.

'Seven stars' has religious and Masonic symbolism.

| | | | |
|---|---|---|---|
| David Allcock | 1868 – 75 | William Alfred Allcock | 1898 – 1909 |
| Joseph Ralph | 1875 | Henry Owen (Kelly's) | 1909 – 19 |
| Levi Ralph | 1876 – 84 | (J Owen in the NDA) | |
| Francis Waring | 1888 – 96 | Edwin Henry Davis | 1920 – 40 |
| William Wright | 1897 – 98 | | |

---

## SHAKESPEARE TAVERN.    34 Walford Street.

There was also a Shakespeare Brewery in Walford Street. The Shakespeare Tavern Sick & Dividend Society issued a 3d token.

| | | | |
|---|---|---|---|
| George Ames | 1855 | William J Rowberry | 1898 – 1900 |
| Samuel Millward | 1860 – 84 | Charles Francis Field | 1900 – 09 |
| George William Chantler | 1884 – 85 | Mrs Emma Field | 1910 – 14 |
| John Thompson | 1888 – 89 | William E Godson | 1916 – 30 |
| Samuel Richard Parker | 1891 – 93 | William Griffin | 1932 |
| Robert G Heynes (NDA) | 1893 – 96 | | |
| (Herbert Robert in Kelly's) | | | |

The Scale and Compass, Birchfield Road, circa 1930 with licensee Harry Carwardine, wife and pet dog. (Enlarged below).

The Scale and Compass was demolished in the late 1950's. The Archers is now occupying the same site.

ABOVE: A pewter cup, presented at the 1944 Scale & Compass Flower Show by H. T. Guise.

BELOW: W. H. James' 3d brass token. He was licensee 1890 – 1904.
Note the address given as Web Heath. (Sic).

*Estate of the late Mrs. ALICE BARTLEET.*

*Plans and Particulars*

# FREEHOLD PROPERTIES,
## AT REDDITCH.

## EDWARDS, SON & BIGWOOD

Are instructed by the Trustees to SELL BY AUCTION.

AT THE UNICORN HOTEL, REDDITCH.

### On Wednesday, May 29th, 1907,

AT SIX p.m. TO THE MINUTE, THE FOLLOWING DESIRABLE FREEHOLD PROPERTIES:—

**Lot 3.—The Valuable Freehold BEERHOUSE, "The SCOURER'S ARMS,"** and **TWO FREEHOLD DWELLING HOUSES,** Nos. 28, 26, and 24 PROSPECT HILL. The **Beerhouse** is let to Messrs Brown and Co. at £23 per annum, subject to a deduction of £3 per annum for compensation charge (tenant paying rates and doing inside repairs), on a lease having four years unexpired at Midsummer, 1907, the lessee having the option of renewal for a further two years; it contains large Smoke Room, Bar, two Kitchens, Pantry, Cellar, Coal Place, with Room over, four Bedrooms, and a Workshop. No. 26 is double-fronted, and contains two Sitting Rooms, Kitchen, Scullery, and three Bedrooms; it is let on an annual tenancy at £14 per annum, the tenant paying all rates, except water rent. No. 24 contains four Rooms, Cellar, and Brewhouse, and is let on a monthly tenancy at £13 per annum, the tenant paying Poor Rate only. Total Annual Income, **£50** per annum.

**Area of Land, 883 Square Yards or thereabouts.**

The Scourer's Arms, Prospect Hill in the process of demolition.

Below, the pub Air Rifle team who were runners up in the Redditch and District league in 1924 – 25.

**Valuation and Particulars of Fixtures, Fittings, Trade Utensils, etc. at the Scourer's Arms, Prospect Hill, Redditch.** From Messrs. Ind Coope & Co. to Albert Henry Stanley. 14th. September 1926.

**SMOKE ROOM.**
3ft.2in. X 2ft.11in. Cross leg Ale table, covered in American cloth.
4ft. X 2ft.9in. Painted deal table on turned legs with 2 drawers, covered in American cloth.
3ft.5in. X 2ft. Painted deal table on square legs, covered in American Cloth.
3ft.2in. X 2ft. Painted deal table on turned legs with one draw, covered in American Cloth.
Piano in Walnut case by Joseph Riley. 2 Windsor chairs, one damaged.
2 Gas brackets with inverted incandescent burners and glass shades.
6 Iron Spittoons. Air gun target with bracket and gas burner.
2 Hat and coat hooks on door. Deal framed seating round room upholstered in American leather with 3 arms and 2 draught boards. Matchboard Dado on back wall.

**BAR.**
5 Pull Ale Engine with piping to 2 pulls (3 pulls out of order). 20 Pint jugs.
49 – $^{1}/_{2}$ Pint jugs. Brass gas bracket with inverted incandescent burner.
Painted nest of 6 glass Cubs ? 2 Deal shelves with return ends over beer engine.
Pewter pint and $^{1}/_{2}$ pint measures. Fixed table with lead covered top and cash till.
2 Deal shelves over door.

**PASSAGE.**
Gas bracket. Matchboard Dado. Wicket gate to Cellar.

**CELLAR.**
Small shelf at cellar head. 7ft. Deal barrel frame. 9ft. Deal barrel frame.
Gas bracket with ceiling shade and hook.

**STOCK IN TRADE.**
10 Gallons of XXX Ale. 2 Barrels of XXX Ale. 1 Firkin of AKK. $4^{1}/_{2}$ dozen pints of Guiness. $2^{1}/_{4}$ dozen $^{1}/_{2}$ pints of Guiness. $2^{3}/_{4}$ dozen pints of L B ale. $^{1}/_{4}$ dozen $^{1}/_{2}$ pints Double Diamond Ale. 40 Packets of Woodbines. 2 dozen and 9 boxes of Matches. 11 Large bottles Lemonade. 16 Packets of Gold Flake Cigarettes.

**STORE ROOM.**
Table top with 2 iron legs (taken from Back Kitchen ). 2 Pair Stags horns.
Arm Windsor chair (broken). Painted deal cupboard. B.S.A. airgun.
Also listed in the inventory a gas lit sitting room and kitchen, a coal house and two bedrooms.
Outside at the front was the pub licence board which was illuminated by a gas lamp (damaged ).

Shakespeare Tavern, Walford Street. The tower of the Shakespeare Brewery can be seen in the background.

Shakespeare Tavern/Inn tokens. The one on the left is brass and the one below – both sides are illustrated – is bronze.

This token was made locally. A similar one occurs for the Bell Inn, Headless Cross (with the 3 also reversed).

**SPORTSMAN'S ARMS.**  2 Peakman Street.

| | | | |
|---|---|---|---|
| Thomas Rickards | 1854 – 98 | Albert Alfred Millward | 1922 – 27 |
| (Also a dairy farmer) | | Alfred Holman Measures | 1928 |
| Albert Wilkes | 1899 – 1918 | Harry Howard Clements | 1934 – 40 |
| William James Evans | 1921 | | |

---

**STAR AND GARTER.**  1 The Slough / Evesham Road, Crabbs Cross.

In earlier times a venue for prize fighting, cock fights and bull baiting. The 'Star & Garter Hotel' issued a 1½d. token for admission to the bowling green.

| | | | |
|---|---|---|---|
| John Gibbs | 1850 | Henry Shrimpton | 1885 – 86 |
| Thomas Avery | 1854 – 55 | Henry Shrimpton Jnr. | 1887 – 1908 |
| Mrs Hannah Clarke | 1860 | John Swallow | 1909 – 14 |
| (Farmer) | | William Crook | 1916 – 20 |
| Solomon Eades | 1864 – 77 | Mrs Sarah Crook | 1921 – 27 |
| (Farmer and shopkeeper) | | Garnet Frederick Edwards | 1928 – 35 |
| Richard Canadine | 1878 – 84 | Frederick Henry Moss | 1936 – 40 |

---

**TALBOT HOTEL.**  30 Evesham Street.

'Talbot' is an old term for a breed of hunting dog that was white with black spots. In 1925 the old Vine Inn was knocked down and rebuilt on the same site.

For licensees before 1925 see under 'Vine Inn.'

| | | | |
|---|---|---|---|
| F Crouch | 1925 – 28 | Robert Charles Walter Starkey | 1940 |
| Harry Evans | 1928 – 32 | Albert Edward Yates | 1946 |
| Reginald Snelgar | 1932 – 36 | | |

---

**TARDEBIGGE (THE).**  Hewell / Tardebigge.

Built in 1911 as a village hall, it was used during and after WW1 as a recovery hospital. In recent years it has been a Country Club and is now a pub and restaurant.

---

**TURF TAVERN.**  59/61 Evesham Street. (Later 'Fleece Inn').

The licensee was Thomas Crow from 1850 – 60 for later licensees see under Fleece Inn.

ADVERTISEMENT.

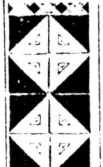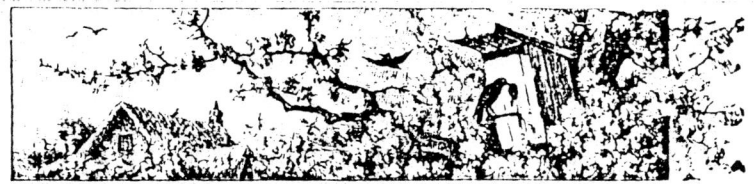

# Sportsman's Arms,

## PEAKMAN ST.,

## REDDITCH.

ALBERT WILKES, PROPRIETOR.

### Mitchells & Butlers Ales and Stout.

BASS'S AND GUINNESS'S STOUT IN BOTTLE.

### Wines & Spirits of the finest quality only.

IMPORTER OF FOREIGN CIGARS

OF THE CHOICEST BRANDS.

*A trial solicited for proof of excellence.*

1900

The Sportsman's Arms in the 1920's or 30's. Note the huge light over the doorway, they were a feature of many of Redditch's pubs for much of the early 1900's,

The Star and Garter, No. 1 The Slough about 1920. In earlier times it was a venue for prize fighting, bull baiting and cock fights.

Below are examples of more peaceful pursuits, the token being for admission to the Bowling Green and the advert from the Redditch Indicator of Saturday August 25th 1860 is for a Pic-nic.

## STAR AND GARTER INN,
### CRABB'S CROSS.
UNDER THE PATRONAGE OF THE HAND & HEART
LODGE, STUDLEY, & THE LOYAL BRUNSWICK
AND EARL OF PLYMOUTH LODGES, REDDITCH.

## A PIC-NIC
WILL TAKE PLACE AT THE ABOVE INN,
### On Monday, September the 3rd.
*Parr's Quadrille Band is Engaged.*
### TICKETS, 1s. 6d. each.

The Talbot Hotel shortly after it was built in 1925. It replaced the Vine Inn.

On the right the Talbot in about 1960 looking down Worcester Road.

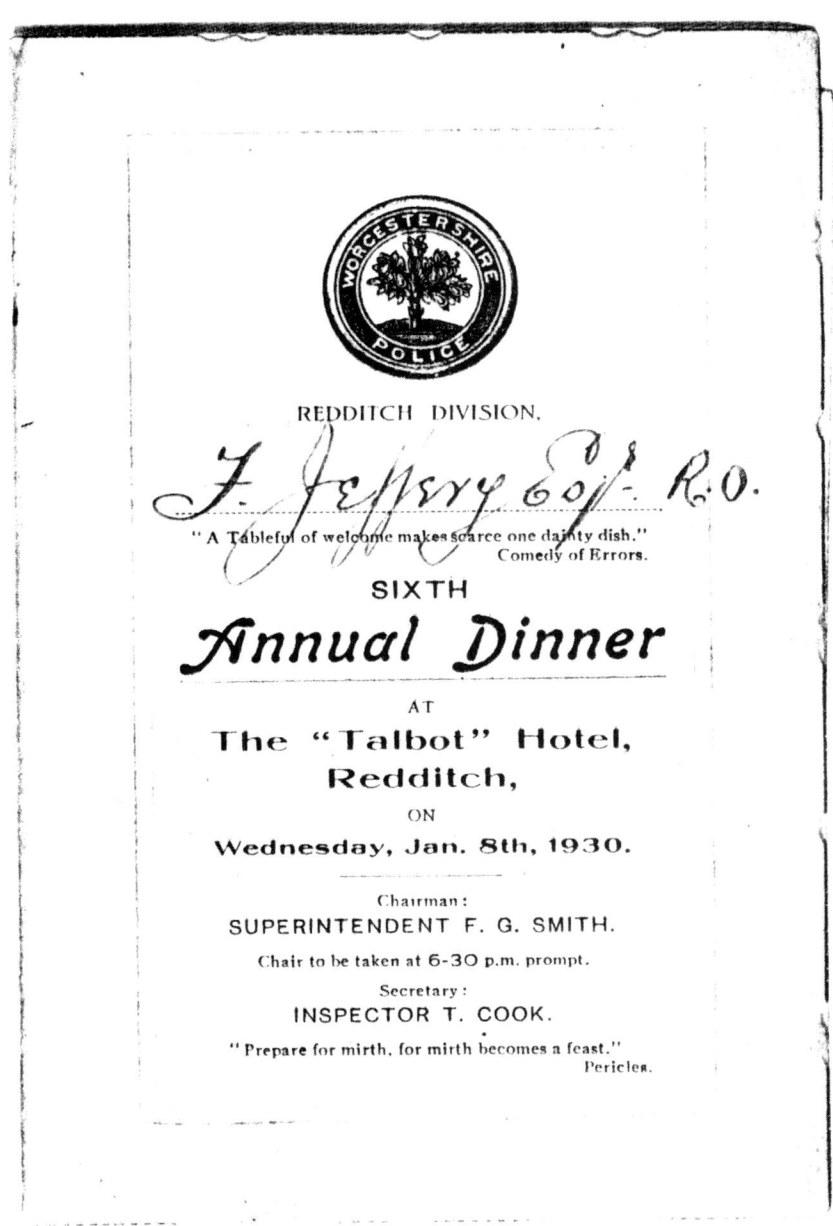

The Talbot Hotel with its town centre location was a popular venue for functions in peace and war. The 'C' Company Home Guard dinner was in 1944.

The Tardebigge was built in 1911 as a village hall. It was used as a recovery hospital in WW1 and has, in recent years, been a Country Club, pub and restaurant.

Bott John, shopkeeper, Windsor st
Bott Joseph, fish-hook and fishing tackle swivel maker, Evesham st
Boulton Jesse, needle and fish-hook maker, Mount Pleasant
Boulton William, and Son, needle and fish-hook makers, Chapel Green
Bradshaw William, and Sons, needle makers, Edward st
Briggs James, farmer, Tan House Farm
Briggs James, butcher, Evesham st
Briggs Thomas, butcher and dealer, Evesham st
Clarke W., and Sons, needle and fish-hook makers, Mount Pleasant
Connell Edward, professor of music, Brockhill Road
Cook George, needle maker, Littleworth
Cox Stephen, and Son, needle and fish-hook makers, Mount Pleasant
Crow James, needle and fish-hook maker, Edward st
Crow Thomas, beer retailer, *Turf Tavern*, Evesham st
Danks John, fish-hook maker, New End
Davis Charles, beer retailer, Fish Hill

An extract from Billing's Directory and Gazetteer for the County of Worcester 1855 recording that Thomas Crow was at the Turf Tavern in Evesham Street.

## UNICORN HOTEL.    8 Unicorn Hill.

One of the town's oldest inns, it was rebuilt in the late Victorian era and again in the 1950's. In earlier days it was a coaching inn. It was demolished in 1998.

At one end was Rickett's shop, they were there from the 1820's to the 1880's and were grocers and tea dealers. This fact combined with the shape of the building gave it its local name of 'The Cannister' as illustrated in these verses from a poem about Redditch and its inhabitants written in about 1840.

> Draper Collier's corner shop,
> Milkman Hathaway's white smock frock,
> Rickett's's golden canister,
> The Unicorn steps and balusters.
> On the Green liv'd Tailor Duggins,
> Near Now road dwelt old John Buggins,
> Next door to him was Henry Avery,
> A spot that's now become so savoury.

| | | | |
|---|---|---|---|
| John Mence | 1822 – 23 | R N Mayne | 1919 |
| George Dakin | 1835 – 41 | Nellie Isabelle Hobson | 1919 – 21 |
| Jesse Castree | 1850 – 55 | Philip Alan Simpson | 1924 – 25 |
| John Castree | 1860 – 64 | R R Gearing | 1926 – 27 |
| Alfred Stinton | 1864 – 90 | Adrian Richard Wheildon | 1928 – 30 |
| (He issued two different 3d. tokens.) | | Walter Fallows | 1932 – 33 |
| Thomas Hyde | 1891 – 1917 | Kenneth Reginald H Fowler | 1934 – 36 |
| (He issued a 3d. token.) | | Ralph Edgar Goostry | 1940 |
| Benjamin Brown | 1917 – 18 | | |

---

## UNICORN TAP.    Just below the Unicorn Hotel.

A small building separated from the hotel by an enclosed yard; it had its own licence up to about 1900.

| | | | |
|---|---|---|---|
| Rowland Stubbs | 1860 – 82 | William Francis Haden | 1890 – 96 |
| Reuben Fullwell | 1884 – 88 | (Coal merchant and car proprietor) | |
| Rowland Stubbs | 1888 – 89 | Thomas Hyde | 1900 |

ABOVE: The Unicorn Hotel as it appeared during the Victorian era. The tea dealer's shop at the front and the general shape of the building gave it its local name of the 'Cannister'.

BELOW: A similar view but taken in the 1930's. The shop and pub were rebuilt in late Victorian times.

# Redditch August Fair!

## UNICORN HOTEL
### Bowling Green & Pleasure Gardens.

The above will be open to the Public, as usual, during the three days of the Fair.

The Worcestershire YEOMANRY BAND
Is engaged to be in attendance.

## ADMISSION FREE.

Public patronage is respectfully solicited.

---

## UNICORN COMMERCIAL, FAMILY, AND RAILWAY HOTEL,
### AND GENERAL
## POSTING ESTABLISHMENT, REDDITCH,

## JOHN CASTREE,
*(Trustee to the Estate of the late Jesse Castree.)*
PROPRIETOR.

WINES, SPIRITS, and CIGARS of the best quality.
Dublin Porter, and Burton Bitter and Pale Ales.

### AN ORDINARY EACH DAY.

CARS, HEARSES, MOURNING COACHES, and POSTING at Reduced prices.

A PLEASURE VAN for hire, moderate charges.

### THE BOWLING GREEN, AND PLEASURE GARDENS,

Open to the public on *Tuesdays, Thursdays, Saturdays,* and *Sundays.*

Public patronage is respectfully solicited.

Front page of the Redditch Indicator Saturday, August 2nd 1862.

ABOVE: The Unicorn Hotel and Tap about 1910.

BELOW: In this view looking up Unicorn Hill the large painted sign on the wall of the hotel is advertising billiards.

# ALFRED STINTON,

OF THE

# UNICORN HOTEL, REDDITCH,

## WINE, SPIRIT,
### ALE AND PORTER MERCHANT.

*Sole Agent for Thompson & Son's BURTON ALES, and Mander's DUBLIN STOUT.*

---

| | |
|---|---|
| London Gin, 12s., 13s., and 14s. | per gallon. |
| Old Jamaica Rum, from 16s. to 20s. | ,, |
| Fine Old Codia, 22s. 6d. | ,, |
| Old Cognac Brandy, 28s., 30s., 32s. | ,, |
| Old Irish Whiskey, 16s. to 22s. | ,, |
| Old Scotch Whiskey, 16s. to 21s. | ,, |
| Old Crusted Port, from 48s. to 80s. | ,, |
| Pale Sherry, from 30s. to 42s. | ,, |
| Fine Old Dry Amontilado, 42s. | ,, |
| Champagne, 48s., 60s. 80s. | ,, |
| Martel's Fine Old Case Brandies, 62s. per case. | |

---

*Wholesale Bottler of Bass, and Thompson & Son's*
### EAST INDIA PALE ALES;
AND
*Mander's and Guinness's STOUT.*

---

**SAMPLES AND PRICES SENT ON APPLICATION.**

Alfred Stinton's advert from the Redditch Indicator of 15th December 1866. A very merry Christmas could be had with Scotch Whiskey at 16/- for a gallon. He was licensee of the Unicorn Hotel from 1864 to 1890.

H INDICATOR July 21/90

### DEATH OF MR. ALFRED STINTON.

We regret to have to record the death of Mr. Alfred Stinton, of the Unicorn Hotel, which took place on Friday (yesterday) morning. The deceased gentleman had been in indifferent health for some time past, and about a week ago he was stricken with paralysis, although on the day previous to his decease he appeared to be somewhat better than usual. About twenty-six years ago Mr. Stinton took possession of the Unicorn Hotel, which at that time, as many of our readers will remember, presented somewhat the appearance of an old-fashioned country inn of the better sort. Some years after the hotel was partially rebuilt, thereby adding greatly to its appearance as well as improving the accommodation. Mr. Stinton was, with the exception of a brief interval, a member of the Local Board for something like twenty years, and remained connected with it up to the time of his death. For many years he filled the office of chairman, and with the exception of a short interregnum, remained in that position until 1889, when in consequence of failing health he resigned the responsibilities and cares of office. He was chairman of the Board during the memorable struggle between the advocates of the two rival schemes of drainage which from twelve to fourteen years ago agitated the town, and by his practical knowledge, and firmness, tempered with courtesy, he piloted the Local Board through a critical period in its history. Mr. Stinton was also president of the Redditch Licensed Victuallers' Association. In private life he was liberal in his charity and a firm friend. He was beloved by his family, and respected by all who knew him, and his loss will be deeply mourned by a large circle of relatives and personal friends.

Alfred Stinton's 3d tokens are both for admission, one to the bowling green at the rear of the premises, the other could be the same or for the billiard room. This one, the one below, was copied exactly except for the name by the next licensee of the Unicorn, Thomas Hyde.

Glazed earthenware flagons and glass hip flask from the Unicorn Hotel. The top one bearing the name of Jesse Castree dates from the 1850's. Thomas Hyde was there from 1891 to 1917.

# UNICORN HOTEL, REDDITCH.

### Old-established and Family Hotel.

## WINES & SPIRITS
#### OF THE FINEST QUALITY.

*The conveniences of the Hotel are BILLIARD ROOM, BOWLING GREEN, COFFEE ROOM, COMMERCIAL ROOM, DINING ROOM, and PRIVATE SITTING ROOM.*

## Commercial Dinner Daily at 1 o'clock.

### EXCELLENT CHAMBER ACCOMMODATION & BATHROOM.

The above Hotel has recently been renovated throughout, and fitted with Electric Light.

## THE YARD, LIVERY, AND BAIT STABLES

Having recently been taken to by the Proprietor, are supplied with entirely new Vehicles on the latest Modern Principles, and an

### EXCELLENT STUD OF HORSES AND COBS.
#### Turn-outs for all purposes.

Terms strictly moderate.  Other Vehicles to order.

*A Cab and Porter meets all trains,*

T. HYDE, Proprietor.

1897

The doorway of the Unicorn Hotel with Thomas Hyde's name on the licence board above it. His 3d token was for admission to the bowling green or the billiard hall.

*Advertisement.*

Telephone 0585.　　　　Telegrams—"Unicorn Hotel, Redditch."

# T. HYDE,
## UNICORN HOTEL, REDDITCH

POSTING IN ALL BRANCHES.

SADDLE & HARNESS HORSES, & CARRIAGES FOR HIRE BY THE DAY OR WEEK.

---

## WEDDING CARRIAGES,

BROUGHAMS & LANDAUS for Evening Parties.

Also PRIVATE 'BUS to carry Ten.

CHAR-A-BANCS AND BRAKES for Pleasure Parties.

Estimates given for any number.

---

## Complete Funeral Undertaker and Furnisher

ALL WORK GUARANTEED.

Orders for Country Funerals will have prompt attention.

T. HYDE will attend at any Country Address on receipt of Postcard, free of extra expense.

---

T. Hyde, Unicorn Hotel, Redditch.

This 1911 advert shows that Thomas Hyde was not only landlord of the Unicorn Hotel but also ran an extensive carriage hire business catering for day trips, weddings and funerals.

ABOVE: The gates of the Unicorn yard with the 'Unicorn Tap' the white building on the right.

BELOW: The inaugural meeting of Redditch and District Motorcycle Club in the yard of the Unicorn Hotel about 1920.

Looking up Unicorn Hill to the 'Unicorn Tap'.

William Francis Hayden (below) was at 'The Tap' from 1890 to 96.

WILLIAM F. HADEN,
CAB AND CAR PROPRIETOR
AND
COAL MERCHANT.
UNICORN HOTEL MEWS & MIDLAND RAILWAY WHARF.

W.F.H. begs to inform the Public that he has
Broughams, Landaus, Hansoms, Dog Carts, & Carriages
OF EVERY DESCRIPTION.

A Speciality in Weddings. The only pair of Greys in the District.
CHARGES STRICTLY MODERATE.
ORDERS BY POST RECEIVE PROMPT ATTENTION.

**Inventory and Valuation of Household Furniture, Trade Effects and Fixtures at the Unicorn Tap, Unicorn Hill, Redditch.** From Mr Alfred Stinton (licensee of the Unicorn Hotel) to Mr Rowland Stubbs. Appraised by me this 18th. day of February 1888. Signed by Thomas Neasom.

*(Note – The Unicorn Tap was a smaller building below the Unicorn Hotel and separated from it by a yard).*

| | Value £ | s | d |
|---|---|---|---|
| **SMOKE ROOM.** | | | |
| Table. | 1 | 0 | 0 |
| 6 Chairs. | | 12 | 0 |
| 2 Gas brackets. | | 4 | 0 |
| 4 Spittoons. | | 1 | 0 |
| 2 Blinds and rollers. | | 4 | 0 |
| **BAR.** | | | |
| Table. | | 10 | 0 |
| Gas bracket and globe. | | 2 | 6 |
| 2 Seats. | | 5 | 0 |
| Cupboard and nest of shelves. | | 15 | 0 |
| Partition and door. | | 10 | 0 |
| 8 Measures. | | 8 | 0 |
| 3 Quart jugs. | | 2 | 6 |
| 9 Pint jugs. | | 3 | 0 |
| 13 Glasses. | | 2 | 0 |
| 3 Crushers ? | | | 6 |
| 4 Pull Beer Machine, piping and taps. | 5 | 0 | 0 |
| 2 Shelves. | | 2 | 0 |
| Stove and piping. | | 4 | 0 |
| 6 Droppers ? | | 2 | 6 |
| Wash pipe. | | 2 | 0 |
| **KITCHEN.** | | | |
| Blind and roller. Shelf. Form with back. 2 Seats. Gas bracket. Pull and ring. Pipe rack. | £1 | 6s | 0d |
| **PANTRY.** | | | |
| 4 Shelves. | | 4 | 0 |
| **CELLAR.** | | | |
| Mallet, spanner and gimlet. | | 1 | 6 |
| Gas bracket. | | 2 | 0 |
| Odd trams. | | 2 | 0 |
| **PASSAGE.** | | | |
| Drop latch. | | | 8d |
| 2 Shelves. | | 5 | 0 |
| 3 Benches. (In yard). | | 15 | 0 |
| **CHAMBERS.** | | | |
| 2 Blinds and rollers. | | 4 | 0 |
| Gas bracket. | | 2 | 0 |

The modern Unicorn as rebuilt in the late 1950's and below during demolition in 1998.

# REDDITCH PUBS IN THE NEWS

### Red Lion 1870

FROM the coroner, a tale of a visitation by God in Redditch. On Saturday afternoon last an inquest was held at the Red Lion Inn, Redditch, before Ralph Docker Esq, coroner, on the body of William Handy.

He was a travelling umbrella maker, who died suddenly at Prescott's lodging house on Wednesday.

Susan Handy deposed: "The deceased was my husband, about 50 years of age. He had no fixed residence. We came to Redditch about a month ago on Monday and lodged at Mrs Prescott's in Ipsley Street.

"My husband has followed his occupation during that time. We were out all day on Wednesday. We had our tea, which he did eat very heartily.

"We did not go out again and and my husband put two umbrellas together before going to bed at half past eleven. My husband had no beer nor cakes nor supper. He sang several times and seemed normal."

Mrs Handy went on: "We had been in bed about half an hour when he was took with something resembling snoring. I tried to rouse him but could not. He did not speak and was insensible. I went downstairs to get some water. When I came back he was dead. I was not away more than a minute.

"He had not struggled and the was no discolouration. I lit candles and went for a doctor."

The jury returned a verdict that the deceased died from natural causes through the visitation of God.

### Seven Stars  Aug. 1871

PROHIBITED hours. Charles James and Henry Johnson, of Ipsley, were charged by P.C. John Kingdon, with being found on the premises of David Allcock, beerhouse keeper, of Headless Cross, during prohibited hours on Sunday July 16th.

Both defendants pleaded guilty to being on the premises but said they had not had anything to drink.

P.C. Kingdon deposed that on Sunday the 16th of July, he visited the house of David Allcock and found four men in the cellar, one of whom got through the cellar window, and the two defendants on the cellar steps.

He also saw two pint jugs partly full of beer on a table in the back room.

In answer to enquiries as to character, Kingdon said James had been convicted several times for drunkenness, but he knew nothing against Johnson. Fined 1s., and costs 6s.6d. each, or 7 days hard labour.

### Unicorn 1894

Thomas Hyde, Unicorn Hotel, was summonsed under a bye-law of the Redditch Urban Council, with keeping pigs within 38 feet of a dwelling house on October 1.

### Rose & Crown
#### August 11, 1900

THE annual dinner in connection with the Loyal Webheath League of Druids took place at the Rose and Crown Hotel on Tuesday.

After dinner, dancing was indulged in on the beautiful lawn, to the melodious strains of Willis' String Band, after which the gentlemen adjourned to the assembly room for a musical evening.

Mr TW Baylis presided, and the toasts of the "Queen" and "Army and Navy" having been drunk with a musical honour, the chairman also proposed the "medical profession" coupled with the name of Dr John Littlejohn, who responded suitably to the proposed toast.

### Rose & Crown June 1895

THE short tale of an expensive drink from Redditch petty sessions. Jack Wisty Senior, farmer, Upper Berrow, pleaded guilty to being drunk at the Rose and Crown, Feckenham, om May 30th. Defendant pleaded guilty.

Pc Wargeant stated that defendant was so drunk he cocked an oddity and had to be taken home in a wheelbarrow by three men. Fined 5s and 16s 6d costs - Mr Hobson prosecuted.

### Unicorn Hotel
#### April 30 1898

REDDITCH Bowling Club. The club, which has has its habitation at the Unicorn Hotel for 50 or 60 years, has been compelled to look out for a new green.

At an influential meeting held on Monday arrangements were made for securing the bowling. The bulk of the members and several new ones have already subscribed, and a most successful season is anticipated.

Applications for admission to membership can be made to the hon secretary or to a member of the committee.

### Talbot Hotel
#### April 9, 1949

Mr RG Salter of Bournville was the speaker at a meeting of the Redditch branch of the NFU held at the Talbot Hotel last Friday. His subject was "The landowner's responsibilities and difficulties."

He spoke of the increasing power the state had on ownership of land and of the great cost of improving and building farms and buildings.

Mr FJ Coney thanked Mr Salter for his talk. It was decided to nominate six members to learn hedging and ditching.

Mr ASD Partridge gave a report of the work of the County Executive Committee which met at Worcester on March 26.

An appeal was made by the County Crops Committee that the maximum acreage of spring wheat be sown. After some discussion it was decided that the summer outing should be Cheddar on Thursday, June 2.

# VILLAGE INN.  Holt End, Beoley.

John Whitmore appears in directories as a shopkeeper from 1850 but not as a beer retailer until 1872.

Mention must be made here of the unusual octagonal brass 3d token issued by one of the Whitmores. Only one specimen is known and is owned by the present day John Whitmore.

| | | | |
|---|---|---|---|
| John Whitmore | 1872 – 81 | Francis Goode | 1908 |
| Mrs Maria Whitmore | 1882 – 88 | John Frank Brown | 1909 – 12 |
| Alfred Whitmore | 1889 – 90 | Alfred Bennett | 1913 – 18 |
| Edwin Millington | 1891 – 96 | John Randall | 1919 – 25 |
| Alfred Hicken | 1897 – 1906 | John Thomas Wilson | 1926 – 36 |
| G Towers | 1907 | Edward Manson | 1940 |

The Village Inn, Beoley, about 1905. It was well known to cyclists as it provided teas and accommodation. The unusual pub token below was issued by one of the Whitmore family who were there from 1872 to 1890.

From the auction catalogue of the sale by Bass Ltd.
held at the Grand Hotel, B'ham. Wed. 9th May 1928.

LOT 23.

# THE "VILLAGE" INN,

## BEOLEY,

### Near REDDITCH

(Worcestershire).

FREEHOLD — FULLY-LICENSED — 7 DAYS.

3 miles from Redditch, 8 from Bromsgrove and 12 from Birmingham;

together with

## LARGE GARDEN AND PLEASURE GROUNDS, YARD AND OUTBUILDINGS.

The whole let to Mr. J. T. Wilson at a NET ANNUAL RENTAL OF £48. Mr. Wilson has occupied these premises for three years, and the previous tenant was in occupation for 8 years.

The main structure is two-storey brick and slate built.

The accommodation includes:—

ON THE GROUND FLOOR: Central Entrance Passage; Smoke Room; Front Bar; Tea Room; Sitting Room; Pantry; Kitchen, with range, boiler and sink; lean-to glazed Verandah-Greenhouse; also a Large Assembly Room, with front and back entrances.

ON THE FIRST FLOOR: Landing and Five Bedrooms.

IN THE BASEMENT: Brick paved Beer Cellar.

OUTSIDE: Large Open Yard, with gateway from road; Urinal and two W.C's; also large Garden and Pleasure Grounds.

The area, according to the Deeds, is 5,050 square yards or thereabouts.

Land Tax, £1 13s. 0d.

*REMARKS. This is an attractive Property, very pleasantly situated in a picturesque Village, and comparatively free from competition. It is well known as a Catering House.*

## VINE INN.          30 Evesham Street.

George Abell was a wine dealer which may be the origin of the pub's name. Demolished and rebuilt on the same site in 1925 and renamed 'The Talbot,' it was the venue for the first recorded RAOB (Buffs) Lodge in Redditch. John Welsbourne, licensee from 1854 to 61 is worthy of note as he and his family served the town as butchers for many years. His shop was in Alcester Street up to 1876 then moved to 18 Market Place until 1900 and 13 Market Place until 1923.

| | | | |
|---|---|---|---|
| William Francis | 1850 | Mrs A Field | 1894 |
| George Abell | 1851 | Frank Field | 1895 – 98 |
| John Welsbourne | 1854 – 61 | Walter Hadgkiss | 1900 |
| (A butcher, he issued a 3d. token) | | Edwin Henry Davis | 1901 – 11 |
| Thomas Jackson | 1864 | (Painter, plumber, paperhanger, etc) | |
| William Neale | 1868 | Oswald E Connolly | 1912 – 16 |
| Joseph Smith | 1871 – 75 | (He issued a 3d. token) | |
| Mrs Ann Smith | 1875 – 80 | Thomas G Hastings Thompson | |
| Alfred Field | 1880 – 93 | (He issued a 3d. token) | 1921 – 25 |
| (He issued a 3d. token) | | (See under 'Talbot' for later licensees) | |

---

## VOLUNTEER'S ARMS.    8 George Street.

In the late 1860's Benjamin Clarke moved here from the 'Adam and Eve' in Fish Hill (now Prospect Hill). At first the pub was called 'The Bird in Hand' but changed to the 'Volunteer's Arms' when Edwin Pinfield-Wells took over in 1883.

| | | | |
|---|---|---|---|
| Benjamin Clarke | 1868 – 81 | John Jakeman | 1891 – 1903 |
| Mrs Clarke | 1882 | (He moved on to the Lamb & Flag) | |
| Edwin Arthur Pinfield-Wells | 1883 – 90 | L Pinfield-Wells | 1904 – 08 |

---

## WAGON AND HORSES.    14/16 Beoley Road.

The inn probably got its name by being on one of the early carriers routes to Birmingham. This entailed fording the brook at the bottom of Beoley Road, when in flood, cargoes and lives could be lost.

| | | | |
|---|---|---|---|
| William Unitt | 1854 – 68 | Alfred Smith | 1901 – 12 |
| Lewis Unitt | 1872 – 78 | (He issued 1½d. and 3d. tokens) | |
| William Unitt | 1879 – 1900 | William F Russell | 1912 – 40 |
| (In 1904 William Unitt was a pork butcher at 17 Market Place). | | | |

In earlier times pub landlords often had other occupations. There were needle makers, grocers, printers, hairdressers, etc. John Wellesbourne whose 3d token is illustrated above was also a butcher. He was licensee of the Vine Inn from 1854 to 1861. He then left to open a butchers shop. Edwin Henry Davis was a plumber, painter and decorator.

### J. WELSBOURNE,

PURVEYOR OF

**BEST ENGLISH MEAT,**

13, Market Place, Redditch.

Estab. over 60 Years.    FAMILIES WAITED UPON FOR ORDERS.

### EDWIN H. DAVIS,

House, Sign, and

Decorative Painter,

PLUMBER, GLAZIER & PAPERHANGER,

Evesham Street,

REDDITCH.

Edwin Henry Davis was licensee from 1901 to 1911.

Below, the Vine Inn in about 1905 with him ? in a straw hat and his horse and dray at the kerbside.

Alfred Field was licensee from 1880 to 1893.

Oswald E. Connolly was licensee from 1912 to 1916.

Thomas G. Hastings Thompson was the last licensee of the
Vine Inn before demolition. He was there from 1921 to 1925.
This is an extremely late date for a pub token.

Waggon and Horses, Beoley Road. (Modern usage of the word wagon is with only one 'G'). Alfred Smith issued two values of his token – below – 3d and 1½d presumably the value of a pint of beer and a half pint.

## W. UNITT,

### WHOLESALE BOTTLER,

**BEOLEY ROAD & UNICORN HILL,**

*REDDITCH.*

Guinness's Extra Dublin Stout.
Bass's Burton Ales.
Worthington's Burton Ales.
Allsopp's Burton Ales.
Devonshire Cider. London Stout.
London Ale.
Unitt's "Tens" Extra Strong Ale.

Sole agent for Coombe & Co., Brewers, London.

Ales & Stout supplied in Casks.

*The above Ales are well stocked & in first-class condition.*

### "SYDRINA,"
**SPARKLING NON-ALCOHOLIC FRUIT DRINKS.**
*Made with Ripe Fruits.*

In addition to being the landlord of the Waggon & Horses, William Unitt was also a wholesale bottler as this 1897 advert shows. He later became a grocer and pork butcher at 17 Market Place. Waggoners travelling down Beoley Road *en route* for Birmingham could lose more than their load if the road was flooded (below). By the time Beoley Brook (river Arrow) was bridged several lives had been lost.

# WILLIAM UNITT,

## ALE AND PORTER MERCHANT,

"WAGGON AND HORSES," BEOLEY ROAD,

AND UNICORN HILL, REDDITCH.

---

Dealer in Burton Ales and Northampton Stout,

AND THE FOLLOWING BOTTLED ALES, STOUT, AND CIDER:—

*BASS'S ALES, GUINNESS' DUBLIN STOUT,*

AND DEVONSHIRE CIDER.

## AGENT FOR COMBE AND CO.'S LONDON STOUT

AND LIGHT BITTER ALES IN BOTTLES.

FAMILIES SUPPLIED.

---

### ADVERTISEMENTS.

## BEOLEY ROAD ALE AND PORTER STORES, REDDITCH.

# WILLIAM UNITT,

Dealer in Burton Ales and Northampton Stout,

Also the following Bottled Ales, Stout, and Cider:—

BASS'S AND WORTHINGTON'S ALES, GUINNESS'S DUBLIN EXTRA STOUT, AND DEVONSHIRE CIDER.

**LARGE STOCK OF CIGARS.**    **TRY A GLASS FROM THE WOOD.**

William Unitt adverts from the 1890's.

From the auction sale held by Charrington & Co. Ltd.
at the Grand Hotel, B'ham on Feb. 2nd & 3rd 1926.

LOT 59.

# THE "WAGGON AND HORSES,"

### Beoley Road, Redditch,

## WORCESTERSHIRE.

### FREEHOLD — ON BEER HOUSE — 7 DAYS.

The Tenant is Mr. W. E. Russell, who has been in occupation for thirteen years. The net annual rental is £40.

The main structure is two-storey, brick and slate built with cemented front.

The accommodation includes:—

ON THE GROUND FLOOR: Two Entrances and Passages; Outdoor Department; Bar, with w.c. adjoining; Smoke Room; Sitting Room; Kitchen; Scullery; Larder.

ON THE FIRST FLOOR: Club Room; Three Bedrooms; Bath Room, with lavatory basin but no fitted bath; and Clothes Closet.

IN THE BASEMENT: Cellar.

OUTSIDE: Small Paved Yard; Urinal; two w.c's; Coal-house.

Electricity, Gas and Water Services are laid on.

Land Tax, 14/7.

*Sold £2,000.*

## WARWICK ARMS.    Ipsley Street.

A most unusual, oval 3d. token was issued by the 'Warwick Arms Hotel' its purpose is unknown and no licensee is named but it is thought to date from about 1900.
J F Baylis, another token issuer, left the Warwick Arms and in 1882 started a soft drinks firm, still in Ipsley Street but a little higher up. He was eventually taken over by Spencers who later merged to become Smith and Spencers.
(NOTE : The NDA for the years from 1902 to 1907 states that Bernard Garfield lived at the "Old Warwick Arms." Where this was located is not known).

| | | | |
|---|---|---|---|
| Sarah Adams | 1841 | James Frederick Baylis | 1876 – 81 |
| (Maltster) | | (He issued a 3d. token dated 1876) | |
| Charles Adams | 1841 – 50 | Elijah Fourt | 1882 – 90 |
| Joseph Rickards | 1854 – 55 | Francis Fourt | 1891 – 98 |
| Thomas Cheesman | 1860 – 64 | Charles Joseph Wilshaw | 1900 – 26 |
| (Plumber, painter and paperhanger) | | P F Shakles | 1927 – 34 |
| Charles Plant | 1868 | William Henry Jennings | 1936 |
| Joseph Rickards | 1872 – 76 | Ernest Pollett | 1940 |

---

## WHITE HART.    157 Evesham Road, Headless Cross.

The White Hart was the badge of the popular King Richard II. The old White Hart was where the stabling of the present White Hart now stands. (Local Notes and Queries No. 88). Several licensees issued tokens but one exists with only the pub name. Frank Gathercole, however, issued a token with no pub name – he was also at the Fox & Goose, Market Place. There exists at least two examples of Briscoe's token with tulip or heart shaped holes in the centre. Information from locals suggest that they had to be slid over a similarly shaped rod to gain access to one of the Clubs or Societies that met at the pub.

| | | | |
|---|---|---|---|
| H Hunt | 1822 – 23 | George Mills | 1884 – 90 |
| William Cox | 1850 – 64 | John Dakin | 1891 – 94 |
| Thomas Briscoe | 1865 – 67 | James Edward Houghton | 1895 – 96 |
| (He issued a 3d. token) | | Mrs Elizabeth Houghton | 1897 |
| George Walker | 1867 – 68 | Frank Gathercole | 1900 – 01 |
| (He issued a 3d bowling green token) | | (He issued a 3d. admission token) | |
| George Morgan | 1873 – 74 | F Soobroy | 1902 |
| (Chemist. He issued a 3d. token) | | W Hirst (NDA) | 1903 – 07 |
| Francis Day | 1875 – 84 | Henry Davis (Kelly's) | 1904 |
| (He did not issue tokens but he | | John Edward Hirst | 1908 – 34 |
| stamped F D on earlier issues) | | Reuben Edward Bannister | 1936 – 40 |

The Warwick Arms taken in 1980. The ornate stone inn sign is still to be seen over the front door. It is thought that the Warwick, along with several other pubs in the area was rebuilt about 1900. References occur to the "Old Warwick Arms" but it is not well documented.

> *And Trades Directory.* 49
>
> LOYAL BRUNSWICK LODGE, I.O.O.F., M.U., 1522.
> Established 1838.
> Lodge House—Warwick Arms Hotel. Number of members, 230.
> Trustees—N. Cund, D. Sealey, E. Watkins  Treasurer—J. Field.  Secretary—R. King, 90, Beoley Road.  Bankers—Capital and Counties Bank.
>
> LOYAL PRINCE OF WALES LODGE, I.O.O.F., M.U., 5945.
> Established 1872.
> Lodge House—Crown Hotel.  Number of members, 150.
> Trustees—W. Smith, W. H. Hallam, W. Blore.  Secretary—W. Bladon, 39, Mount Pleasant.
> Bankers—Metropolitan Bank, Limited.
>
> LODGE OF PAST GRANDS, I.O.O.F., M.U.
> Established 1889.
> Lodge House—Warwick Arms Hotel.  Number of members, 30.
> Trustees—W. H. Smith and W. H. Hallam.  Secretary—W. Bladon, 39, Mount Pleasant.

Extracts from the 1898 Redditch Needle District Almanack and Trades Directory. Two of the Lodges of Independant Order of Oddfellows, Manchester Unity give their Lodge Houses as the Warwick Arms Hotel.

Reproduced below is the same list from the 1899 Directory. The same Lodges now both give their Lodge Houses as the <u>New</u> Warwick Arms Hotel. This would suggest that the rebuilding of the hotel took place in 1898/99.

> **FRIENDLY SOCIETIES.**
> LOYAL BRUNSWICK LODGE. I.O.O.F., M.U., 1522.—Lodge House, New Warwick Arms Hotel. Trustees, N. Cund, D. Sealey, E. Watkins. Treasurer, J. Field. Secretary, R. King, 68, St. George's Road. Bankers, Capital and Counties Bank.
> LOYAL PRINCE OF WALES LODGE, I.O.O.F., M.U., No. 5945.—Lodge House, Crown Hotel. Trustees, W. Smith, W. H. Hallam, W. Blore. Secretary, W. Bladon, 39, Mount Pleasant. Bankers, Metropolitan Bank, Limited.
> LODGE OF PAST GRANDS, I.O.O.F. M.U.—Lodge House, New Warwick Arms Hotel. Trustees, W. H. Smith and W. H. Hallam. Secretary, W. Bladon, 39, Mount Pleasant.
> JUVENILE LODGE OF ODDFELLOWS.—National Schools. President, P.G. J. F. Hughes. Hon. Treasurer, P.P.G.M., N. Cund. Trustees. P.G. W. T. Treadgold and P.P.G.M. W. Bladon. Secretary, P.G. A. Holtham, Birmingham Road. Meetings, every fourth Tuesday, at 7.30 p.m.

The Directory for the years from 1902 to 1907 record that Bernard Garfield lived at 'The Old Warwick Arms.' Where this was located is not known. The 1903 extract from the Directory is reproduced below.

> Gardner, Misses, registry office, Mount
> Gardner, H, 7 Albert street  [pleasant
> Gardner, Samuel, Oakly road
> Garfield, Bernard, old Warwick Arms
> Garfield, — box maker, Ipsley street
> Garfield Brothers, boot dealers, Market
> Garfield, Thomas, 15 Grove street  [place
> Garner, Miss Ann, 177 Beoley road

This unusual and stylish token probably dates from the period when the hotel was rebuilt circa 1900.

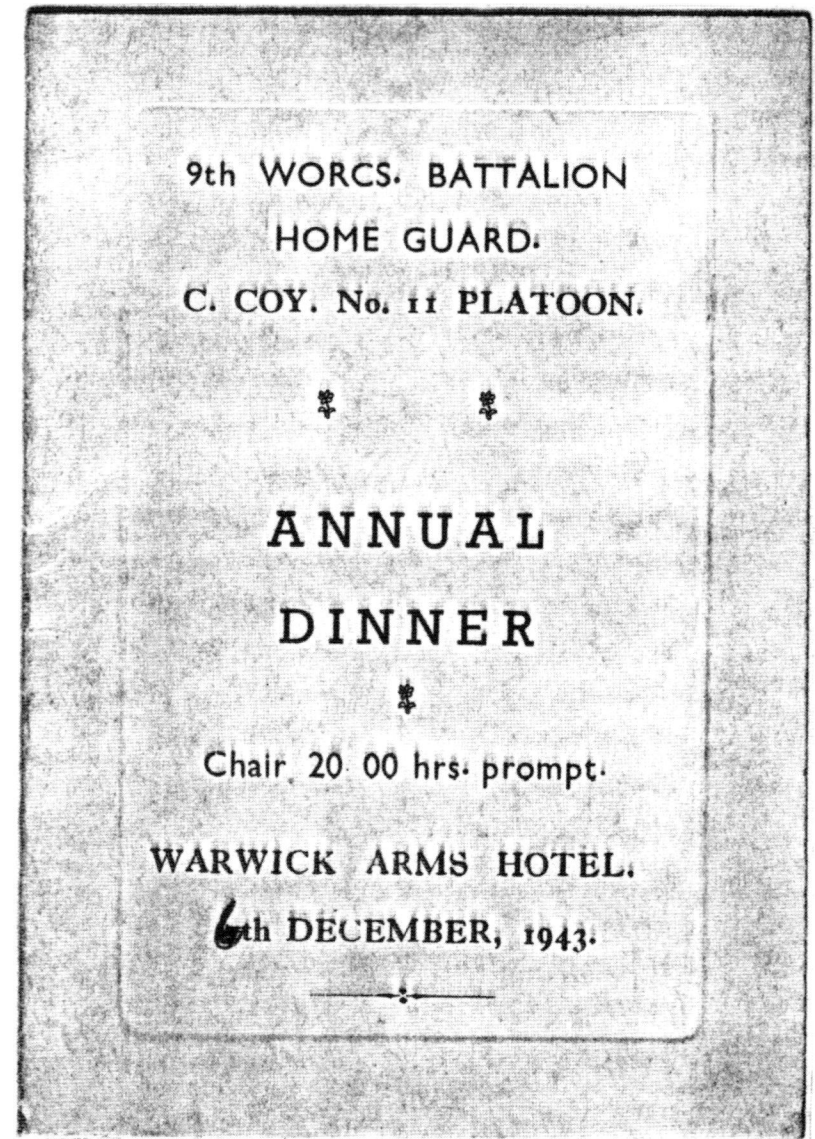

The menu for this wartime dinner at the Warwick Arms included soup, joint, seasonal vegetables, sweet or cheese and celery followed by coffee. All served by British Restaurant.

This coin-like token issued by James Frederick Baylis bears the date 1876 under the 'Young Head' of Queen Victoria. This may not be an accurate date of issue. Tokens in this style were often used as gaming counters. Baylis later started a soft drinks business in Ipsley St. and was then taken over by Spencers as shown by the advert below. ("Late J. F. Baylis & Co." in small lettering).

---

64  *The Needle District Almanack*

### STEAM SODA WATER WORKS.

# P. SPENCER & SONS,
LATE J. F. BAYLIS & CO.,

### Ærated and Mineral Water Manufacturers.

Specialities.  Soda Water, Lemonade, Ginger Ale, Hop Bitters, Orange Champagne, Ginger Beer, Stone Beer, &c.

Soda Water in Syphons for Invalids and family use.

**SOLE AGENTS FOR BASSARA**—the Non-alcoholic Drink. A light Table Beer. Awarded Gold and Bronze Medals.

Note the addresses, and send for Samples and Testimonials.

**IPSLEY AND OSWALD STREETS, REDDITCH.**

---

**WARWICK ARMS HOTEL,** IPSLEY ST., REDDITCH.

F. FOURT, Proprietor.

**Wines, Spirits, Burton Ales, Cigars, &c.,**
OF THE FINEST QUALITY.

EXCELLENT ACCOMMODATION FOR DINNER PARTIES, CYCLISTS, &c.  Free House.

Francis Fourt was licensee from 1891 to 1898.

J. F. Baylis & Co.'s stoneware Ginger Beer bottle. He was at the Warwick Arms from 1876 to 1881. He left to start up his soft drinks firm in Ipsley Street. He was then taken over by Spencers – their two glass bottles above have the words "Late Baylis & Co" embossed on them.

The advert below was in the Redditch Indicator on Saturday December 24th. 1859.

## TEA ENTERTAINMENT,
### AT THE WARWICK ARMS INN,
On Tuesday, December 27, 1859.

At Five o'Clock. Parr's Quadrille Band will be in attendance. Tickets, One Shilling and Sixpence each to be obtained of G. Hemming, Jun., William Street.

A rather faded photograph of the White Hart in about 1905, showing the shop next door which vanished long ago to make way for the car park. It appears to have leather aprons hanging outside. What seem to be cracks on the upper right of the photo are branches of a tree. The advert below appeared in the Redditch Indicator in 1859 – its first year of issue.

## TEA ENTERTAINMENT,
### AT THE WHITE HART INN, HEADLESS CROSS,
ON MONDAY, DEC. 26, 1859.

Tickets, One Shilling and Sixpence each.

# WHITE HART HOTEL,
## HEADLESS CROSS.

### FRANCIS DAY, PROPRIETOR.

### BREWING:
The facilities for Brewing Ales enable the Proprietor to produce them in fine condition, both Mild and Pale bodies.

## PICTURESQUE GROUNDS
### FOR PRIVATE AND SUMMER PARTIES.
### GRAND PAVILION.
For weather contingencies and Winter uses; and the Hotel resources in general for the several requirements of such an establishment. In all, the Public will find combined

### EVERY ARTICLE OF THE BEST QUALITY, AT MODERATE CHARGES.

The White Hart had a "Grand Pavilion" in "Picturesque Grounds" according to Francis Day's advert in the 1879 Needle District Almanack and Trades Directory. He did not issue a pub token bearing his name but he stamped F D on previous issues by Thomas Briscoe (1865–67) and George Morgan (1873–74). Several specimens exist of the Briscoe token with a 'tulip' shaped hole; it is believed to have admitted the bearer to a Society or Club room at the White Hart.

## WHITE HART INN, HEADLESS CROSS.

### THE ANNUAL
### TEA AND DANCING PARTY
WILL TAKE PLACE ON
### WEDNESDAY, DECEMBER 26.

Redditch Indicator Saturday December 15th 1860.

## HEADLESS CROSS
## CHERRY WAKE.

### NEXT MONDAY, JULY 14,
### A SHEEP WILL BE ROASTED
AT THE WHITE HART INN.

*Quadrille Dancing, and other Amusements on the Green.*

Redditch Indicator Saturday July 12th 1862

### CHERRY WAKE,
HEADLESS CROSS,
MONDAY NEXT, JULY 15th, 1867.

### MR. GEORGE WALKER,
WHITE HART INN,

BEGS respectfully to inform his friends and the public that he will have a SHEEP ROASTED upon the above occasion.

N.B.—*A Quadrille Band is engaged for Dancing.*

Redditch Indicator Saturday 13th July 1867.

> Extract from 'Extinct Public Houses'
> Local Notes & Queries No. 88.
>
> Of the old *White Hart* it will be sufficient to say that it stood back from the road where the stabling of the present *White Hart* stands, and was a favourite resort of the local boxers.

# A TALE OF THE TIMES OF THE HAND POINTERS.

*By J. M. Woodward and F. Scarlett Potter.*

### THE OLD "WHITE HART."

The old "White Hart" at Headless Cross is of some antiquity as a house of public entertainment, and it has a history. Late in last century it came into the possession of a certain William Causer, an old soldier, who inherited it under the will of an uncle. When the worse for liquor, he sold the whole property to a Mr. Field, of Bromsgrove, for £80 1s., and it is reported this hardy veteran was not again seen sober till all the buildings of the "White Hart," with its four acres of land, had passed down his throat.

From that period to the opening of the present narrative the old house changed hands some half-dozen times, the owner and occupier with whom we have to do being one Richard Rayer, to whom also it had come from an uncle. The name of "Rayer" is, it should at once be acknowledged, a fictitious one, though the man is not; for the real name of this landlord, who plays by no means a creditable part in the story, is at the present day borne by highly respectable families in the district, who are neither descended from nor akin to him.

As for the old inn, it stood back from the highway some fifteen or twenty yards; it was not equal in size to the large coaching-houses on the London and Kidderminster road, nor was it a regular stopping-place for the "Kiddy" Coach. Still it was of some importance as being the nearest point to the growing little town of Redditch, and that where "needle-masters" and others bound to that place chose to be set down.

The old "White Hart" was a two-storey building, with an entrance hall in the middle and four rooms on the ground floor. The room on the right hand of the entrance had a projecting window, and was generally occupied by those who took "something better" than ale; while on the left was a larger room generally well filled with a noisy company among whom the old hand-pointers figured conspicuously.

Besides the rooms ordinarily met with in inns, the old "White Hart" had a club-room built over the stabling, and reached by a flight of stone steps in front. This no doubt was a comparatively recent addition to the inn, but it must be remembered that clubs akin to the friendly societies of to-day were in existence at least a quarter of a century before the date of our narrative. This room Richard Rayer found very useful at the great gatherings which took place at the "White Hart" on the occasions of a cock fight or a prize-fight, when the ordinary rooms of the inn were quite inadequate for the accommodation of the visitors from the adjacent towns and villages. On such occasions the road from Redditch way for nearly a quarter of a mile was, say old people, "thronged like the thick of a fair."

Doubtless it was owing to the old "White Hart" and district lying close to the borders of two counties, and thus affording opportunities of quickly changing from the jurisdiction of the magistrates of either, that the inn became a favourable rendezvous for prize-fighters. The taste for pugilistic encounters spread to the inhabitants of the neighbourhood. Villages challenged each other. Jack Chelly and Tom Watton came from Feckenham and held the ring against all comers. Tom Wall was the champion of Studley. Later on "Bloxham Joe" fought Bill Bourne of Redditch; and even the ladies took an interest in this elegant pastime, for Arthur Lewis's mother held his clothes while he fought his man on Causer's Hill. In short the "White Hart" was the battle-ground of the locality.

As being fairly central and affording frequent excitement the old "White Hart" became a favourite meeting-place for the hand-pointers. They came from all the neighbouring mills and some from as far off as Stoke and Alcester, and their dissipation was not for a day or so, but for several. Often did they refuse to begin a "packet" until a sovereign had been advanced as an inducement, and this was generally spent before it was earned. For it must be remembered that the hand-pointer was a man who knew that from the day he took to his calling an early death was inevitably awaiting him, and the "pointer's cough" was only the prelude to the coffin. He was a doomed man; he got his money easily, and spent it recklessly. This only engendered vicious habits, and when he was living a fast life he was in reality dying a slow death. Life and money were equally squandered.

But to return to the old "White Hart." It will be sufficient to say that it was provided with all the usual out-buildings of a good inn and like many of its class with the means of carrying on farming on a small scale. Richard Rayer specially prided himself upon his fat pigs and his game fowls.

On the north side of the inn was a foredraught leading to Causer's hill, the only name which now keeps that of the old proprietors of the "White Hart" in remembrance. On one side of this was the skittle-alley, and on the other was the forge and house of Michael Chambers, the blacksmith. He was considered to be the best forger of hardeners' shears in the whole neighbourhood.

Near to the old "White Hart" was the turnpike gate, the former existence of which is indicated by the name of a public-house, the "Gate" inn, and somewhat to the rear of this was a cock-pit. A little further on nearer to Crabbs Cross, close to a stagnant pool were the Ipsley stocks. John Gibbs at the time of the narrative being parish constable; while at no great distance stood the mud cottage of old Rodney, the "white-witch," and that of Dan Jewell, the carpenter.

Extract from a Redditch Indicator article from the 1880's giving an insight into the "goings on" at the Old White Hart, Headless Cross.

The White Hart, Headless Cross about 1905, before it acquired a car park.

The Thomas Briscoe token below (bottom) dates from 1865–67. The other 3d White Hart token does not name the licensee, therefore the date is uncertain.

Landlord John Dakin with staff and others outside the White Hart in the early 1890's. Below the White Hart Bowls Club in 1889 and right George Walker's Bowling Green 3d admission token from 1867–68.

**WHITE LION.**         8/10 Red Lion Street.

According to the Redditch Indicator the pub's licence was withdrawn on the 1st of May 1937. The White Lion issued a 3d. token but no licensee is named.

| | | | |
|---|---|---|---|
| John Moore | 1835 – 41 | William Edwin Apperley | 1890 – 92 |
| (Needle manufacturer) | | Mrs Mary Ann Edwards | 1893 – 97 |
| Mrs Moore | 1845 | (Car proprietor) | |
| Stephen Moore | 1850 | Thomas Cund | 1898 – 1901 |
| Thomas Andrews | 1854 – 85 | Edwin Pinfield-Wells | 1902 – 28 |
| Charles Emms | 1886 | Mrs Pinfield-Wells | 1929 – 32 |
| Richard Herbert Bennett | 1887 | Frederick Henry Moss | 1933 – 34 |
| George Frederick Guest | 1888 – 90 | Kenneth J Cull | 1936 |

---

**WHITE LION.**         Evesham Road, Astwood Bank.

| | | | |
|---|---|---|---|
| Thomas Richards | 1830 | Sidney Macey | 1895 |
| Ann Richards | 1841 | Miss Laurie Gorton | 1896 |
| Henry Hemming | 1850 – 62 | James Gathercole | 1897 – 1900 |
| (Draper and grocer, also at the | | Joseph Alexander Perkins | 1900 – 05 |
| 'Crown' from 1841 – 54) | | (Sanitary Inspector) | |
| Samuel Powell | 1864 – 74 | Daniel Dibble | 1905 – 16 |
| Charles Davies | 1875 – 80 | Herbert James | 1917 – 28 |
| (Charles Davis in Kelly's) | | William H Whitehouse | 1932 – 36 |
| Mrs Sarah Ann Perkins | 1880 – 81 | Mrs Frances Clara Maude Dobbins | |
| Felix Webb | 1882 – 85 | | 1940 |
| Mrs Ann Webb | 1886 – 87 | | |
| Joseph Alexander Perkins | 1888 – 94 | | |

---

**WHITE SWAN.**         32 Evesham Street. (Corner of Worcester Road).

Earlier directories give the address as Vine Street which was the top end of Worcester Road.

| | | | |
|---|---|---|---|
| Thomas Davis | 1841 – 51 | J Bunegar | 1902 |
| George Moore | 1854 – 64 | David Hemming | 1903 – 10 |
| Joseph Duggins | 1867 – 73 | Reuben Canadine Jnr. | 1911 – 12 |
| Mrs Ann Duggins | 1873 – 82 | John Edward Charman | 1916 |
| William Willis | 1883 – 88 | John Millward | 1921 |
| Alfred Smith | 1889 – 1900 | William Robert Croxall | 1924 |

The illustration above (by or after Woodward) shows the 'Old Lock-up' on the corner of Red Lion and Alcester Streets. To the right of this building is the White Lion Inn. The building on the extreme right of the picture is thought to be the Beehive Inn.

### LOCAL NOTES AND QUERIES.
#### No. 87.

In Note No. 79, of March 5th, reference is made to "John Smith, the White Witch of Redditch." I became personally acquainted with this person hile residing at Redditch, about the year 1845. At that time he was living at the White Lion Inn, kept by Mrs. Moore, a widow. I was credibly informed that when a young man he worked at the finishing, in the employ of Messrs. Hemming & Son, by whom he was much respected; that he was a person of very studious habits; and that he could have had a more responsible position under his employers, but that he preferred the finishing because it left his mind free to *think* on the subjects which he studied. One of these was the ancient science of astrology, in connection with which he studied the medicinal properties of plants, and became a useful herbalist. At the time I knew him he was quite an elderly man; he had for some years given up work at the needles, and employed most of his time in spring, summer, and autumn in gathering herbs for the treatment of various diseases. He knew the day and hour to gather them so as to obtain the full benefit of their medicinal properties. He was frequently applied to by persons far and near, both as an astrologer and a herbalist, his whole time being occupied in his "profession." He was, unfortunately, too fond of tippling, and when short of money and in want of beer he would pawn his astrological books at the public-houses he frequented, so that the last few years of his life he had no books, and when applied to for astrological purposes he was obliged to visit his acquaintances who studied the science, to make the necessary "figure" for him before he could answer the queries of those who applied to him. He once took me to a small beerhouse on the Back Hill, and while there asked for one of his books for me to look at. It was a large volume of Barrett's Magus, a costly work on magic; a work I have seen advertised for sale in two or three volumes at the price of as many guineas. The volume shown to me was doubtless in pawn for drink, as it was handed back when I had looked over it.

In personal appearance, John Smith (Old Jack Smith he was commonly called) was remarkable; once seen he would not be easily forgotten. In stature he was about five feet two or three inches, strongly made, very broad shoulders, short neck, his head seemed to be placed almost between his shoulders, piercing dark hazel eyes that when he looked up seemed to penetrate one, and a very thick lower lip, but no beard. He was always dressed in well-worn black coat, waistcoat, and trousers, with strong low shoes, and a tall black hat. The tails of his coat reached nearly to his heels, and the brim of his hat seemed to rest upon his shoulders. He was a man of very few words, exceedingly reticent even to his associates, though possessed of considerable information, chiefly of an occult nature. A more eccentric character, in personal appearance, manners, and habits it would be difficult to conceive.

Local Notes & Queries No. 87 refers to one of the strange characters that lived and drank in the pub in the 1840's.

With no licensee named on the White Lion 3d brass token illustrated below it is not possible to date accurately but it is almost certainly late Victorian.

Both the White Lion and the Red Lion had their licences withdrawn on 1st May 1937. They were later demolished and the site was used for a Fire Station and Bus Station.

From the auction catalogue of the sale by Bass Ltd.
held at the Grand Hotel, B'ham Wed. 9th May 1828.

LOT 24.

# THE "WHITE LION" INN,

10, Red Lion Street,

## REDDITCH

(Worcestershire).

FREEHOLD — ON-BEER AND WINE — 7 DAYS.

together with

YARD AND OUTBUILDINGS.

The premises have been in the occupation of Mr. E. P. Wells for 26 years, and the CURRENT NET ANNUAL RENTAL IS £51.

The main structure is two-storey, brick and slate built, with cemented front.

The accommodation includes:—

**ON THE GROUND FLOOR:** Central Entrance Passage and Outdoor Department; Smoke Room; Bar; Snug; and Kitchen.

**ON THE FIRST FLOOR:** Landing; Sitting Room; Two Bedrooms; and Store Room.

**IN THE BASEMENT:** Brick paved Beer Cellar, with fall from Lobby.

**OUTSIDE:** Part paved Yard, with double gates to road; Flush W.C.; Urinal; Open Coalplace; and wood and asbestos sheeted Stable, with loft over.

Electricity, Gas and Water services are laid on.

Land Tax, £1 1s. 3d.

N.B.—This Property was formerly Copyhold, and the Mines and Minerals and other Rights under the Copyhold Act, 1894, are excepted. (See Special Conditions of Sale).

*REMARKS. This is a well known and central property.*

Page Thirty-two.

The White Lion, Evesham Road, Astwood Bank about 1910. Daniel Dibble's name appears on the sign painted on the pub wall. He was licensee from 1905 to 1916 and is the gentleman on the left of the group enlarged below.

ADVERTISEMENT.

# White Lion Hotel,

## ASTWOOD BANK.

*(Situate on Ridgway, main road from Birmingham to Evesham.)*

Good Accommodation for Cyclists.

STABLING, &c.

LARGE ASSEMBLY ROOM capable of holding 300 persons.

## BILLIARDS, BOWLING GREEN, &c.

Cigars, Wines, & Spirits of the Choicest Brands.

**Flower & Sons' Celebrated Ales.**

PROPRIETOR, JOSEPH A. PERKINS.

Joseph Alexander Perkins' advert from the Redditch and District Directory for the year 1900. Perkins was also the local Sanitary Inspector.

MOTOR BUS TERMINUS, ASTWOOD BANK.

The White Lion, Astwood Bank was the terminus for the first Birmingham to Redditch bus service. Due to commence on Saturday March 21st 1914 the first bus actually arrived on 4th April. (Information from Ian Hayes).

The Birmingham and Midland Motor Omnibus Company, Limited.

## BIRMINGHAM, REDDITCH and ASTWOOD BANK
### MOTOR OMNIBUS SERVICE.

Commencing SATURDAY NEXT, March 21st, 1914, and until further notice, the above Service will run daily as under (Sundays included) via Bristol Rd., Selly Oak and Northfield.

Leave BIRMINGHAM (Bull Ring), for Redditch and Astwood Bank at *8-15, 10-15 and 11-45 a.m. 1-45, 3-15, 5-15, and 6-45 p.m.

Leave REDDITCH for Astwood Bank, at *9-30 and 11-30 a.m., 1-0, 3-0, 4-30, 6-30 and 8 p.m.

Leave ASTWOOD BANK for Redditch and Birmingham at *10-0, 12-0, 1-30, 3-30, 5-0, 7-0 and 8-30 p.m.

Leave REDDITCH for Birmingham at *10-15, 12-15, 1-45, 3-45, 5-15, 7-15 and 8-45 p.m.

*Sundays excepted.

### FARES.

*To or from*

| | | |
|---|---|---|
| Birmingham (Bull Ring) and Hopwood | ... | 7d. |
| ,, and Alvechurch | ... | 9d. |
| ,, and Redditch | ... | 1/-. |
| ,, and Astwood Bank | ... | 1/3. |

Omnibus Offices, 65, Tennant Street, Birmingham.

O. C. POWER, Traffic Manager.

Tel. No.: 2371 and 72 Midland.

The White Swan, Evesham Street. (Corner of Vine Street, later Worcester Rd). David Hemming's name appears on this postcard view dated June 3rd 1906. He was licensee there 1903–10.

Below – the Why Not, Astwood Bank in the great snow of 1916

**WHY NOT.**            Ridgeway, Astwood Bank.

Named after the 1895 Grand National winner. It was run by the Savage family for many years.(They originated in the Stourbridge area). New End, Cookhill and the Ridgeway areas appear in Kelly's directories under Inkberrow and, due to change of boundaries, may also come under Alcester.

| | | |
|---|---|---|
| Thomas Savage | 1868 – 98 | (In 1864 a T. Savage was in Halesowen |
| (Parents of Alan Savage) | 1900 – 24? | Street, Oldbury) |
| Alan (& Fanny) Savage | 1925 – 40? | |

---

**WOODBINE COTTAGE.** 92/96 Evesham Road, Headless Cross.

"Woodbine" is another name for Honeysuckle.

| | | | |
|---|---|---|---|
| George Chambers | 1868 – 73 | George Wall | 1891 – 92 |
| Mrs Mary Leysters | 1873 – 82 | Oliver Moore | 1893 – 94 |
| (Shopkeeper) | | Levi Ralph | 1895 – 1903 |
| George Spiers | 1884 – 88 | (Boot and shoe dealer) | |
| A G Perry | 1890 | Henry Morton | 1904 – 08 |

---

**WOODLAND COTTAGE.**    42/102/112 Mount Pleasant.

The Needle District Almanack (NDA) occasionally confuses the Woodland and the Woodbine Cottages as in 1899 – "Woodbine Cottage, Mt. Pleasant" and in 1906 and 1910 – "Woodbine Inn, Mt. Pleasant." The dramatically named "Woodland Cottage Death and Dividend Society" issued a 3d. token, date unknown.

| | | | |
|---|---|---|---|
| George Parsons | 1841 – 73 | Mrs Emma Holbeche | 1899 – 1905 |
| Thomas Parsons | 1874 – 75 | William Frederick Shelton | 1905 – 10 |
| Mrs Susannah Cooke | 1875 – 78 | Mrs Elizabeth Shelton | 1911 – 14 |
| Thomas Cund | 1880 – 97 | Frank Warner | 1916 – 20 |
| R J Mogg | 1898 – 99 | Thomas Stevens | 1921 – 40 |

---

**WOODMAN INN.**    Webheath.

The location of this inn is not known but it seems to have been a "One man Band," which lived and died with its only licensee.

| | | |
|---|---|---|
| John Sealey | 1855 – 83 | (Hay dealer and coal merchant) |

The name on the licence board above the door of the Woodland Cottage, Mount Pleasant is William Frederick Shelton. He was the licensee from 1905 to 1910 when his wife Elizabeth took over, presumably on his demise. Did she pay his funeral expenses with some of the "Woodland Cottage Death & Dividend Club" 3d brass tokens illustrated below?

In 1899 Mr. R. J. Mogg of the Woodland Cottage, Mount Pleasant, transferred to the Rose and Crown, Portway on the death of it's licensee John Holbeche. The licence of the Woodland Cottage was in return taken over by John's widow Emma. John Holbeche had been something of a drifter as a pub landlord in the Redditch area. He was at the Royal George from 1871-74, then he appears at the Fleece in Evesham Street in 1881. By 1889 he is in Feckenham at the Rose and Crown followed by a spell at the Crown Inn, Astwood Bank. Then he took over the Rose and Crown, Portway where he died.

From the auction sale held by Charrington & Co. Ltd.
at the Grand Hotel, B'ham on Feb. 2nd & 3rd 1926.

LOT 57.

# THE "WOODLAND COTTAGE,"

## Mount Pleasant, Redditch,

### WORCESTERSHIRE.

#### FREEHOLD — ON BEER HOUSE — 7 DAYS.

A popular House on the main road to Astwood Bank, which is a bus route. It is worthy of the consideration of all interested in this type of Licensed House.

The Premises are let to Mr. T. Stevens, who has been in occupation for six years at a net annual rental of £30.

The main structure is two-storey, brick and tile built.

The accommodation includes:—

ON THE GROUND FLOOR: Smoke Room with servery; Snug; Tap Room; Sitting Room (Licensed); Kitchen; Scullery; Ladies' Lavatory adjoining; and Cellar.

ON THE FIRST FLOOR: Sitting Room and two Bedrooms.

OUTSIDE: Small Yard; Urinal; w.c.; and Garden.

Electricity, Gas and Water Services are laid on.

Land Tax, 12/6.

*Sold £3,000*

The Woodland Cottage, Mount Pleasant in the days when it had a fence and a garden (as mentioned in the 1926 sale catalogue, when it changed hands for £3,000) but no car park.

**WOODMAN INN.**      Evesham Road, Astwood Bank. (Adjacent to 'The Bell').

Thomas Windle issued a 3d. token for "Windle's Sick and Dividend Society." It is unusual for a Society to be named after the licensee rather than the pub.

| | | | |
|---|---|---|---|
| Henry Sutor | 1872 – 81 | William Thomas Mortiboy Smith | |
| Thomas Windle | 1882 – 87 | | 1892 – 94 |
| (He issued a 3d. token) | | Thomas Newberry | 1895 |
| John Bird | 1888 | William M Newberry | 1896 – 1901 |
| Mrs Emma Sutor (Kelly's) | 1888 – 90 | Henry Walker | 1903 – 21 |
| Archibald Norcott | 1889 – 91 | Francis Theodore Summers | 1922 – 40 |
| (Butcher and cab proprietor) | | | |

---

**YEWTREE INN.**      Droitwich Road, (Saltway) Feckenham.

The building still exists as a private house, hiding behind its yew tree.

| | | | |
|---|---|---|---|
| William Baker | 1855 – 1913 | Percy Briney | 1916 – 36 |
| (A shoemaker from Astwood Bank) | | (Haycutter) | |
| Mrs Baker | 1914 – 15 | | |

---

Thomas Windle's Sick and Dividend Society 3d brass token issued
at the Woodman Inn in the 1880's

The Woodman Inn, Evesham Road, Astwood Bank in 1905. Demolished in the early 1960's the site now forms part of the Bell Inn beer garden and car park. Extending out from the right of the pub, the small, dark building still exists.

## DOMESTIC TRAGEDY AT ASTWOOD BANK.

### ATTEMPTED MURDER AND SUICIDE.

Quite a gloom was cast over the village of Astwood Bank on Thursday morning when it became known that Mr. William M. Newberry, landlord of the Woodman Inn, and a much respected inhabitant of the village, had made a determined attempt to murder his wife, and also to take his own life. It was rumoured at first that both the assailant and his victim were dead, but this happily was untrue. From what can be learnt, it appeared that Mr. Newberry rose between six and seven o'clock on Thursday morning as usual. He afterwards returned to the bedroom, and attacked Mrs. Newberry, who was in bed, with a penknife, inflicting four wounds in her neck and throat, none of them, fortunately, being of a serious nature. He then made a terrible gash in his own throat, and following his wife downstairs sank exhausted through loss of blood in the bar. Medical aid was at once summoned, and pending the arrival of Drs. Littlejohn and Rutter, Mr. J. K. Andrews, chemist, attended to the injuries Newberry was subsequently conveyed in a precarious condition to the Smallwood Hospital, Redditch. No reason can be assigned for the committal of the rash act, except that through suffering from severe pains in the head caused by the fall from a vehicle some time ago his mind became suddenly unhinged. To all appearance the couple lived very happily together, and the affair caused quite a painful sensation in the village.

A report received from another correspondent says:—Careful enquiries have revealed no reason for the deed, although there was some suggestion that lately it has been noticed that Mr. Newberry has not been quite as usual in his manner. Some two years ago he met with a serious accident, which at one time was expected to prove fatal. Clearly there had not been the slightest quarrel between Mr. Newberry and his wife, who have been married for some years, and who have always lived very happily together. He has occupied the position of landlord of the Woodman Inn for some 10 or 12 years past. The first intimation that anything unusual was taking place was the screaming of Mrs. Newberry, which brought a neighbour to the inn to find Mrs. Newberry in her night-dress with blood running from her throat. Upstairs a shocking spectacle presented itself. Mr. Newberry was standing in the room with his throat badly cut, and on seeing the neighbour at the door he quickly and deliberately drew the knife across his throat again. It is stated that Mr. Newberry got up and dressed in the morning as usual, and also came down stairs and opened the door to admit a man named Arthur Smith, who is sometimes employed at the inn. The inn was closed on Thursday.

Some mystery hangs around this very painful case, and much reluctance is shown by people connected with it in giving information. Application was made to Inspector Hayes for policemen to watch the injured man lying in the hospital, and who was raving and very violent. Inspector Hayes could hardly accede to this, as no charge had been made against Newberry. The medical attendant then said Newberry had made a deliberate attempt to murder his wife. Since then the injured man has been under police surveillance at the hospital. If he recovers he will be charged with the crime, unless circumstances necessitate his removal to an asylum. On inquiry at the Hospital this (Friday) afternoon, we were informed that the injured man was progressing as well as could be expected.

William M. Newberry's advert from the Redditch Directory for 1900 and reports of his attempted murder of his wife and his suicide, in the Redditch Indicator on Saturday 2nd. and 9th. November 1901.

## THE ASTWOOD BANK TRAGEDY

### DEATH OF NEWBERRY.

William M. Newberry, late landlord of the Woodman Inn, Astwood Bank, who attempted to murder his wife on Thursday in last week, afterwards cutting his own throat in a shocking manner, died in the Smallwood Hospital, Redditch, on Thursday evening. Newberry has had most assiduous attention from the medical staff and nurses, but little hope was ever entertained of his recovery. At times, since his admission to the hospital, he has been very violent, and two constables have constantly been in attendance upon him. The deceased man, we are informed, was making as satisfactory progress as could be expected until about the middle of the week, when pneumonia set in, and owing to his weak condition he was unable to resist the disease, to which he succumbed on Thursday, as already stated.

From the auction sale held by Charrington & Co. Ltd.
at the Grand Hotel, B'ham on Feb. 2nd & 3rd 1926.

LOT 58.

# THE "WOODMAN" INN,

### Astwood Bank, near Redditch,

## WORCESTERSHIRE.

### FREEHOLD — FULLY-LICENSED — 7 DAYS.

With frontage to main Redditch-Evesham Road.

together with

## THE TWO COTTAGES ADJOINING.

The whole let to Mr. F. T. Summers at a net annual rental of £57.

The main structure is two-storey, brick and slate built.

The accommodation of the Licensed Premises includes:—

ON THE GROUND FLOOR: Paved Entrance Passage; Bar; Servery; Tap Room; Smoke Room; Sitting Room; Pantry.

ON THE FIRST FLOOR: Club Room, with exit to Yard; Sitting Room; Stock Room; and Two Bedrooms.

IN THE BASEMENT: Cellar.

OUTSIDE: Paved Yard, with covered cartway entrance; Scullery; Urinal and two w.c's; 2-stall Stable, with loft over; Coach-house and Coal-house.

Electricity, Gas and Water Supplies are laid on.

The accommodation of each Cottage includes: Living Room; Kitchen; Two Bedrooms; Wash-house; w.c.; Coal-house; Pigstye; and Garden.

*Sold, £3,400*

The Yewtree Inn, Droitwich Road, (The Saltway) Feckenham.

No longer licensed premises, it still exists as a private house, hiding behind the yew tree that gave the pub its name.

# REDDITCH PUBS IN THE NEWS

## Village Inn
### July 29, 1899.

ON Saturday, the employees of Messrs John Jewsbury and Co., brassfounders, Birmingham, to the number of eighty, had their annual picnic at the Village Inn, Beoley.

A capital spread was provided to which full justice was done. The church and other objects of interest in the neighbourhood having been visited, a very enjoyable day was brought to a close with an impromptu concert given by several members of the party.

The catering of Host Hicken was most satisfactory.

## Woodman Inn
### November 9, 1901.

WILLIAM M Newberry, late landlord of the Woodman Inn, Astwood Bank, who attempted to murder his wife on Thursday in last week, afterwards cutting his own throat in a shocking manner, died in the Smallwood Hospital, Redditch, on Thursday evening.

Newberry has had most assiduous attention from the medical staff and nurses but little hope was ever entertained of his recovery.

At times since his admission to the hospital he has been very violent and two constables have constantly been in attendance upon him.

The deceased man, we are informed, was making as satisfactory progress as could be expected until about the middle of the week when pneumonia set in and owing to his weak condition, he was unable to resist the disease to which he succumbed on Thursday, as already stated.

## Village Inn
### July 31 1897

A NIGHT Jar Shot. A remarkably fine specimen of what he believes to be a night jar has been shot by Alfred Hicken, landlord of the Village Inn, Beoley.

Mr Hicken, when shooting in Clifford Coppice at dusk the other evening, brought down the bird mistaking it in the darkness for a hawk.

## White Lion
### April 14, 1900.

ASTWOOD Bank -- At a meeting held at the White Lion Hotel on the 30th ult., it was decided to form Amateur Poultry, Pigeon and Cage-bird Society and those present were constituted a committee with power to add to their number.

The object in view is to encourage poultry keeping and to discuss the best methods to be adopted to ensure success and in order to make the movement as popular as possible.

It was decided to fix the entrance fee at 3d and a weekly subscription of 1d per member.

## Woodman Inn
### April 21, 1900

Astwood Bank -- Smoking concert.

A smoking concert in aid of the Reservists' Fund took place at the Woodman Inn on Saturday evening, Mr H F Yeomans presiding over a large attendance.

The toasts of the Queen and the Army and Navy were duly honoured.

A number of songs were rendered by local vocalists and selections on the gramophone were given by Mr J Cassell.

A collection was taken in aid of the fund.

## White Hart 1868

THE Old White Hart Club in Headless Cross - which has been in existence for a good many years - held its anniversary on Wednesday.

The rifle corps were hired for the occasion and in the evening villagers were invited to join members on the beautiful bowling green where a very pleasant time was spent.

The dinner was excellently prepared and served by host and hostess Mr and Mrs Walker and a toast was made for their hard work.

## Woodman (Webheath) 1866

● John Sealey, of the Woodman Inn, Webheath, was charged with selling cider at an illegal hour on the morning of Sunday, November 4. Pc Haynes proved the case.

He was fined one shilling and costs of 10 shillings.

## Woodman Inn
### December 24 1898

SERIOUS accident at a wedding. The marriage, which took place on Thursday morning, of Mr Clifford Hill (the well known Astwood Bank footballer and eldest son of Mr Compton Hill) and Miss Annie Huxley (eldest daughter of Mr George Huxley, builder) was preceded by a serious accident.

While waiting for the wedding party, Mr W Newberry (landlord of the Woodman Inn and Mews proprietor) who was in charge of one of the carriages, was seized with giddiness or some kind of fit and fell from the box seat to the ground.

He was conveyed into Mr Huxley's residence, and his condition being seen to be serious, medical aid was at once summoned.

The injuries sustained included a broken wrist, the rupture of a blood vessel in the head and probable concussion.

However the shock alone to the system must have been considerable.

Mr JK Andrews rendered first aid and Dr Wade of Redditch was promptly in attendance and a few hours later the unfortunate man was taken home. A curious feature of the accident is that Mr Newberry not only did not lose consciousness at first, but actually got up from the ground and finished placing the rug over the horse, the operation in which he was engaged when vertigo overtook him.

# PUB LICENSEES FOR REDDIITCH AND DISTRICT

ABBOTT Elizabeth (Mrs).    Golden Cross / Railway Inn.    1850
ABBOTT John.    Golden Cross / Railway Inn.    1855 – 68
ABELL George.    Vine Inn.    1851
ABELL Mary Ann (Mrs).    Printer's Arms.    1864
ADAMS Charles.    Warwick Arms.    1841 – 50
ADAMS Fred.    Gate Hangs Well.    1940
ADAMS Sarah.    Warwick Arms.    1841
ADDERLEY George Edward.    Nag's Head.    1911 – 12
ALBUTT Joseph.    Railway Tavern, Hewell Road.    1855
ALEXANDER Edward.    Rose and Crown, Feckenham.    1902 – 07
ALEXANDER Edward.    Oddfellow's Arms, Windsor Street.    1908 – 10
ALEXANDER William Whiteway.    Fox & Goose / Royal Hotel.    1891 – 96
ALLCOCK David.    Seven Stars.    1868 – 75
ALLCOCK William Alfred.    Seven Stars.    1898 – 1909
ALLEN Henry.    Lamb and Flag.    1841
ALLEN Robert.    Gate Hangs Well.    1908 – 14
AMES George.    Shakespeare Inn.    1855
AMES George.    Railway Tavern, Hewell Road.    1860 – 64
ANDREWS John.    Rose and Crown, Webheath.    1850
ANDREWS Thomas.    New Inn / Nevill Arms.    1841
ANDREWS Thomas.    White Lion, Red Lion Street.    1854 – 85
ANDREWS William.    Rose and Crown, Webheath.    1854 – 84
ANDREWS (Mrs).    Rose and Crown, Webheath.    1885
ANSLOW Harry.    Eight Bells.    1921 – 29
APPERLEY William Edwin.    White Lion, Red Lion Street.    1890 – 92
APPERLEY Edwin.    Rifleman Inn.    1916 – 21
ASTON Henry.    Fox & Goose, Foxlydiate.    1884 – 92
ATHERSMITH C. W.    Royal George.    1910
ATKINS Samuel.    Red Lion, Red Lion Street.    1934
AVERY James.    Bull's Head, Evesham Street.    1835 – 41
AVERY Thomas.    Star and Garter.    1854 – 55

BADGER A. F.    Eight Bells.    1950 – 54
BAINES Joseph.    Queen's Head, Alcester Street.    1860 – 61
BAKER J. C.    Fleece Inn, Evesham Street.    1892
BAKER William.    Yewtree Inn.    1855 – 1913
BAKER (Mrs).    Yewtree Inn.    1914 – 15
BAKES Arthur.    Fleece Inn, Crabbs Cross.    1913
BALDWIN Hubert.    Red Lion, Hunt End.    1914 – 29
BALLARD Catherine Mary (Mrs).    Fleece Inn, Evesham Street.    1868 – 71
BALLINGER Charles Barnett.    Fleece Inn, Crabbs Cross.    1924 – 40
BANGHAM F.    Queen's Head, Bromsgrove Road.    1891
BANKS William Edwin.    Rising Sun.    1928
BANNER John.    Hollybush Inn.    1904 – 07
BANNISTER Reuben Edward.    Lamb and Flag.    1932
BANNISTER Reuben Edward.    White Hart.    1936 – 40
BARBER William.    Oddfellow's Arms, Windsor Street.    1875 – 96
BARCLAY Frederick.    Royal George.    1915 – 36
BARCLAY Frederick.    Nag's Head.    1940
BARKER Harry.    Cricketer's Arms, Headless Cross.    1921

| | |
|---|---|
| BARKER J.   Jubilee Oak. | 1889 – 90 |
| BARKER John Hemming.   Cricketer's Arms, Beoley Road. | 1880 – 87 |
| BARNES William.   Red Lion, Red Lion Street. | 1909 – 12 |
| BARRON John.   Plymouth Arms. | 1816 |
| BARTLEET Augustus.   Golden Salmon. | 1893 – 1927 |
| BARTLEET W.   Bell Inn, Britten Street. | 1850 |
| BASSETT John Edwin.   Horse and Jockey, Evesham Street. | 1899 – 1903 |
| BATE John.   Red Lion, Bradley Green. | 1872 |
| BAYLIS James Frederick.   Warwick Arms. | 1876 – 81 |
| BEARD John.   Hart Inn. | 1873 – 78 |
| BEARD Leslie John.   Hollybush Inn. | 1932 – 40 |
| BELLAMY William.   Lygon Arms. | 1872 – 73 |
| BELLAMY (Mrs).   Lygon Arms. | 1874 – 75 |
| BENNETT Alfred.   Village Inn. | 1913 – 18 |
| BENNETT Charles.   Alma Tavern. | 1881 |
| BENNETT John William.   Fleece Inn, Evesham Street. | 1896 – 1903 |
| BENNETT Richard Herbert.   White Lion, Red Lion Street. | 1887 |
| BENT Harry.   Red Lion, Bradley Green. | 1900 |
| BIDDLE William Henry.   Crown Hotel, Prospect Hill. | 1900 – 01 |
| BIGGS John Joseph.   Red Lion, Red Lion Street. | 1936 |
| BILLINGS Elizabeth (Miss).   The Elbows. | 1841 – 68 |
| BINT Henry.   Britannia Inn. | 1868 – 72 |
| BIRD Ernest James W.   Fountain Inn. | 1908 – 10 |
| BIRD John.   Woodman Inn, Astwood Bank. | 1888 |
| BLACKFORD Henry.   Queen's Head, Bromsgrove Road. | 1883 – 85 |
| BLACKFORD James.   Red Lion, Red Lion Street. | 1900 – 02 |
| BLACKFORD Thomas.   Nag's Head. | 1905 – 08 |
| BLACKFORD Thomas.   Railway Tavern, Hewell Road. | 1909 – 10 |
| BLUNDALL John.   Alma Tavern. | 1882 |
| BLUNDELL S.   Royal Oak, Crabbs Cross. | 1934 – 35 |
| BOTT James Henry.   Royal George. | 1888 – 91 |
| BOX William.   Hollybush Inn. | 1874 |
| BRADNOCK Charles.   King's Arms. | 1916 – 20 |
| BRAY William (Billy).   Malt Shovel. | Before 1840 |
| BRIDGE Frederick.   Red Lion, Bradley Green. | 1924 – 40 |
| BRIDGES Frank Enoch.   Red Lion, Red Lion Street. | 1928 |
| BRIGGS F. J.   Beehive Inn. | 1905 – 08 |
| BRIGGS James.   Jubilee Oak. | 1873 – 88 |
| BRINEY Percy.   Yewtree Inn. | 1916 – 36 |
| BRISCOE Thomas.   White Hart. | 1865 – 67 |
| BROWN Benjamin.   Unicorn Hotel. | 1917 – 18 |
| BROWN John.   Red Lion, Red Lion Street. | 1841 |
| BROWN John Frank.   Village Inn. | 1909 – 12 |
| BRUTON William Joseph.   Fox Inn. | 1936 |
| BRYAN John.   Pointer's Arms. | 1850 – 55 |
| BULL Ann.   Golden Lion. | 1897 – 98 |
| BULLOCK Thomas.   Jubilee Inn. | 1897 – 1916 |
| BUNEGAR Charles Henry.   Bristol Inn. | 1895 – 1908 |
| BUNEGAR J.   White Swan. | 1902 |
| BUNEGAR Sarah (Mrs).   Bristol Inn. | 1908 – 13 |
| BUTTERY S. (Mrs).   Red Lion, Bradley Green. | 1921 |
| BUTTERY Thomas.   Red Lion, Bradley Green. | 1904 – 16 |

| | |
|---|---|
| CANADINE R.   Bell Inn, Headless Cross. | 1909 – 10 |
| CANADINE Reuben.   Royal Oak, Crabbs Cross. | 1884 – 88 |
| CANADINE Reuben (Jnr).   White Swan. | 1911 – 12 |
| CANADINE Richard.   Crown Inn, Crabbs Cross. | 1860 – 77 |
| CANADINE Richard.   Star and Garter. | 1878 – 84 |
| CANADINE Sarah (Mrs).   Crown Inn, Crabbs Cross. | 1868 |
| CARSON Frederick.   Dog and Pheasant. | 1896 – 99 |
| CARTER George Frederick.   Gate Hangs Well. | 1936 |
| CARTER George Frederick.   Fox Inn. | 1940 |
| CARTER Walter Henry.   Cross and Bowling Green. | 1934 – 36 |
| CARWARDINE Harry.   Scale and Compass. | 1927 – 40 |
| CARWARDINE William.   Rose and Crown, Webheath. | 1886 – 1905 |
| CASTREE Jesse.   Unicorn Hotel. | 1850 – 55 |
| CASTREE John.   Unicorn Hotel. | 1860 – 64 |
| CHAMBERS Albert Edward.   Fleece Inn, Crabbs Cross. | 1902 – 10 |
| CHAMBERS Fred.   Fleece Inn, Crabbs Cross. | 1872 – 1901 |
| CHAMBERS George.   Woodbine Cottage. | 1868 – 73 |
| CHAMBERS Herbert Fred.   Fox and Goose, Foxlydiate. | 1896 – 1922 |
| CHAMBERS Joseph.   Red Lion, Hunt End. | 1868 – 97 |
| CHAMBERS (Mrs).   Fox and Goose, Foxlydiate. | 1923 |
| CHAMBERS William Henry.   Red Lion, Hunt End. | 1898 – 1913 |
| CHANTLER George William.   Shakespeare Tavern. | 1884 – 85 |
| CHARMAN Clara (Mrs).   Plough and Harrow. | 1922 – 26 |
| CHARMAN John E.   Fleece Inn, Crabbs Cross. | 1911 – 12 |
| CHARMAN John Edward.   White Swan. | 1916 |
| CHARMAN George.   Plough and Harrow. | 1854 |
| CHARMAN Thomas.   Hare and Hounds. | ? |
| CHARMAN Thomas.   Rose and Crown, Webheath. | 1841 |
| CHARMAN Thomas Henry.   Plough and Harrow. | 1906 – 21 |
| CHARMAN Thomas Howard.   Plough and Harrow. | 1927 – 34 |
| CHEESMAN Thomas.   Warwick Arms. | 1860 – 64 |
| CHESHIRE ?   Fleece Inn, Evesham Street. | 1904 – 09 |
| CHESSHIRE (Mrs).   Fox and Goose, Foxlydiate. | 1893 – 95 |
| CLARKE Benjamin.   Adam and Eve, Prospect Hill. | 1860 – 64 |
| CLARKE Benjamin.   Bird in Hand, George Street. | 1868 – 81 |
| CLARKE (Mrs).   Bird in Hand, George Street. | 1882 |
| CLARKE Felix.   Dog and Pheasant. | 1875 – 77 |
| CLARKE Hannah (Mrs).   Star and Garter. | 1860 |
| CLARKE Samuel.   Railway Tavern, Hewell Road. | 1921 – 24 |
| CLARKE William James.   Red Lion, Red Lion Street. | 1921 |
| CLEMENTS Harry Howard.   Railway Tavern, Hewell Road. | 1927 – 33 |
| CLEMENTS Harry Howard.   Sportsman's Arms. | 1934 – 40 |
| COLDRICK William.   'Old' Horse and Jockey, Ipsley Street. | 1884 – 90 |
| COLLEY Richard (Dick).   Crown Hotel, Prospect Hill. | 1909 – 10 |
| CONNOLLY Oswald E.   Vine Inn. | 1912 – 16 |
| COOK Francis.   Plough and Harrow. | 1872 – 73 |
| COOKE Susannah (Mrs).   Woodland Cottage. | 1875 – 78 |
| COOPER A. H.   Old Briton. | 1909 – 10 |
| CORFIELD (or GARFIELD) Edwin.   Old Briton. | 1910 – 12 |
| CORNWALL George.   Bell Inn, Headless Cross. | 1914 – 20 |
| COURT J. (Mrs).   Red Lion, Bradley Green. | 1868 |
| COURT Joseph.   'Old' Horse and Jockey, Ipsley Street. | 1864 – 80 |

| | |
|---|---|
| COURT Mary Ann (Mrs).   Brook Inn. | 1894 – 1911 |
| COURT Richard.   Brook Inn. | 1883 – 93 |
| COURT W.   Red Lion, Bradley Green. | 1854 – 64 |
| COX William.   White Hart. | 1850 – 64 |
| CROFT John A.   Bell Inn, Astwood Bank. | 1923 – 28 |
| CROFT John F.   Bell Inn, Astwood Bank. | 1914 – 17 |
| CROFT John F.   Bell Inn, Astwood Bank. | 1921 |
| CROFT Polly (Mrs).   Bell Inn, Astwood Bank. | 1918 – 20 |
| CROFT Polly (Mrs).   Bell Inn, Astwood Bank. | 1929 – 40 |
| CROOK William.   Jubilee Inn. | 1917 – 18 |
| CROOK William.   Star and Garter. | 1916 – 20 |
| CROOK William.   Oddfellow's Arms, Astwood Bank. | 1918 – 26 |
| CROOK Sarah (Mrs).   Star and Garter. | 1921 – 27 |
| CROSSLEY John Henry.   Crown Hotel, Prospect Hill. | 1923 – 24 |
| CROUCH F.   Talbot Hotel. | 1925 – 28 |
| CROW Charles.   Alma Tavern. | 1888 – 90 |
| CROW Thomas.   Turf Tavern / Fleece Inn. | 1850 – 60 |
| CROW Thomas Upton.   Printer's Arms. | 1868 – 78 |
| CROW Rachel (Mrs).   Printer's Arms. | 1879 |
| CROW William Edward.   Brewer's Arms. | 1875 – 91 |
| CROW William Edward.   Golden Cross / Railway Inn. | 1892 – 96 |
| CROXALL Robert.   Greyhound Inn. | 1875 |
| CROXALL William Robert.   White Swan. | 1924 |
| CULL Joseph.   Rose and Crown, Feckenham. | 1908 – 09 |
| CULL Kenneth J.   White Lion, Red Lion Street. | 1936 |
| CULL Kenneth J.   Rising Sun. | 1940 |
| CUND Thomas.   Woodland Cottage. | 1880 – 97 |
| CUND Thomas.   White Lion, Red Lion Street. | 1898 – 1901 |

John Dakin, White Hart.

| | |
|---|---|
| DAKIN George.    Unicorn Hotel. | 1835 – 41 |
| DAKIN John.   White Hart. | 1891 – 94 |
| DANIELS Michael.    Crown Inn, Astwood Bank. | 1881 – 92 |
| DANKS George.    Nevill Arms. | 1920 – 28 |
| DAVIES Charles.    White Lion, Astwood Bank. | 1875 – 80 |
| DAVIES George William.    Crown Hotel, Prospect Hill. | 1940 |
| DAVIS Charles (Snr).    Scourer's Arms. | 1855 – 73 |
| DAVIS Charles Albert.    Scourer's Arms. | 1880 – 90 |
| DAVIS Edwin Henry.    Cricketer's Arms, Beoley Road. | 1897 – 99 |
| DAVIS Edwin Henry.    Vine Inn. | 1901 – 11 |
| DAVIS Edwin Henry.    Bristol Inn. | 1916 – 20 |
| DAVIS Edwin Henry.    Seven Stars. | 1920 – 40 |
| DAVIS Frank.    Scourer's Arms. | 1916 – 24 |
| DAVIS Henry.    Crown Hotel, Prospect Hill. | 1880 – 87 |
| DAVIS Henry.    Red Lion, Red Lion Street. | 1891 – 96 |
| DAVIS Henry.    Fleece Inn, Evesham Street. | 1904 |
| DAVIS Henry.    White Hart. | 1904 |
| DAVIS Henry.    Red Lion, Red Lion Street. | 1904 – 08 |
| DAVIS James.    Old Briton. | 1854 – 55 |
| DAVIS John.    Crown Hotel, Prospect Hill. | 1850 – 74 |
| DAVIS Joseph.    Crown Hotel, Prospect Hill. | 1835 – 41 |
| DAVIS Joshua.    Forester's Arms. | 1907 – 11 |
| DAVIS Matilda (Mrs).    Scourer's Arms. | 1874 – 76 |
| DAVIS Thomas.    White Swan. | 1841 – 51 |
| DAVIS William.    Oddfellow's Arms, Windsor Street. | 1854 – 73 |
| DAY Francis.    White Hart. | 1875 – 84 |
| DEAKEN John.    Eight Bells. | 1841 – 73 |
| DEAKEN William.    Eight Bells. | 1873 – 86 |
| DEAKEN Ann Amelia (Miss).    Eight Bells. | 1887 – 90 |
| DELAHAY George.    Queen's Head, Queen Street. | 1936 |
| DELL Alfred George.    Bell Inn, Headless Cross. | 1911 – 12 |
| DIBBLE Daniel.    Red Lion, Astwood Bank. | 1899 – 1904 |
| DIBBLE Daniel.    White Lion, Astwood Bank. | 1905 – 16 |
| DOBBINS Frances Clara Maude (Mrs).    White Lion, Astwood Bank. | 1940 |
| DOBBINS George F.    Old Briton. | 1880 – 83 |
| DOLPHIN C. (Phillip)?    Horse and Jockey, Evesham Street. | 1897 – 99 |
| DOLPHIN William.    Crown Inn, Astwood Bank. | 1880 |
| DORRINGTON Albert.    Red Lion, Red Lion Street. | 1916 – 19 |
| DOWNES T.    Fleece Inn, Crabbs Cross. | 1917 – 19 |
| DOWNES William.    British Workman. | 1874 |
| DRACEY Frederick.    Hollybush Inn. | 1918 – 22 |
| DREW George E.    Queen's Head, Bromsgrove Road. | 1889 – 90 |
| DUDLEY Edwin.    Railway Tavern, Hewell Road. | 1898 – 1907 |
| DUDLEY Elizabeth (Mrs).    Railway Tavern, Hewell Road. | 1908 |
| DUFFIN Alexander.    Plumber's Arms. | 1910 – 36 |
| DUGGINS Joseph.    White Swan. | 1867 – 73 |
| DUGGINS Ann (Mrs).    White Swan. | 1873 – 82 |
| DUNN J.    Dog and Pheasant. | 1902 – 06 |
| DUNN Uriah.    Lamb and Flag. | 1864 – 73 |
| DUNN Edith (Mrs).    Lamb and Flag. | 1874 – 77 |
| DURHAM John.    Plymouth Arms. | 1820 – 54 |
| DYER William Henry.    Rose and Crown, Feckenham. | 1910 – 40 |

| | |
|---|---|
| EADES Solomon.   Star and Garter. | 1864 – 77 |
| EAMES H.   Scourer's Arms. | 1913 – 14 |
| EAVES Elizabeth.   Golden Lion. | 1855 |
| EAVES James.   Golden Lion. | 1860 – 68 |
| EDGINGTON James William.   Rising Sun. | 1834 – 36 |
| EDWARDS Albert Parker.   Eagle Inn. | 1897 – 1903 |
| EDWARDS Albert Parker.   Cricketer's Arms, Beoley Road. | 1904 – 19 |
| EDWARDS Albert Parker.   Red Lion, Astwood Bank. | 1928 – 32 |
| EDWARDS Caroline (Mrs).   Cross and Bowling Green. | 1883 – 97 |
| EDWARDS Enoch.   Rifleman Inn. | 1896 – 1905 |
| EDWARDS Garnet Frederick.   Red Lion, Astwood Bank. | 1920 – 27 |
| EDWARDS Garnet Frederick.   Star and Garter. | 1928 – 35 |
| EDWARDS Joseph.   Cross and Bowling Green. | 1879 – 82 |
| EDWARDS Mary Ann (Mrs).   Plough and Harrow. | 1887 – 91 |
| EDWARDS Mary Ann (Mrs).   Cricketer's Arms, Headless Cross. | 1892 |
| EDWARDS Mary Ann (Mrs).   White Lion, Red Lion Street. | 1893 – 97 |
| EDWARDS Ralph Ernest.   Queen's Head, Bromsgrove Road. | 1905 – 14 |
| EDWARDS Ralph Ernest.   Greyhound Inn. | 1916 – 24 |
| EDWARDS Ralph Ernest.   Crown Hotel, Prospect Hill. | 1924 – 36 |
| EDWARDS William.   Plough and Harrow. | 1875 – 86 |
| EMMS Charles.   White Lion, Red Lion Street. | 1886 |
| EMMS Charles.   Gate Hangs Well. | 1875 – 87 |
| EMMS Clara (Mrs).   Gate Hangs Well. | 1888 – 90 |
| EMMS George Hastings.   Fleece Inn, Evesham Street. | 1932 – 34 |
| EMMS Thomas.   Gate Hangs Well. | 1860 – 75 |
| EMMS William.   Case is Altered / Gate Hangs Well. | 1850 – 55 |
| ENGLAND William Day.   Park Inn. | 1940 |
| EVANS Harry.   Talbot Hotel. | 1928 – 32 |
| EVANS William E. D.   Fountain Inn. | 1928 |
| EVANS William E. D.   Fox and Goose, Foxlydiate. | 1932 – 36 |
| EVANS William James.   Sportsman's Arms. | 1921 |

Albert Parker Edwards.

| | |
|---|---|
| FALLOWS Walter.   Unicorn Hotel. | 1932 – 33 |
| FARR George.   Park Inn. | 1907 – 14 |
| FIELD A.(Mrs).   Vine Inn. | 1894 |
| FIELD Alfred.   Royal George. | 1876 – 80 |
| FIELD Alfred.   Vine Inn. | 1880 – 93 |
| FIELD Charles.   Dog and Pheasant. | 1914 – 40 |
| FIELD Charles Francis.   Shakespeare Tavern. | 1900 – 09 |
| FIELD Emma (Mrs).   Shakespeare Tavern. | 1910 – 14 |
| FIELD Frank.   Vine Inn. | 1895 – 98 |
| FIELD Joseph.   Dog and Pheasant. | 1907 – 13 |
| FIELD George H. (Also Mrs. M A).   Royal Hotel. | 1908 – 12 |
| FIELD Richard.   Duke of York. | 1841 |
| FIELD Richard.   Queen's Head, Bromsgrove Road. | 1873 – 82 |
| FIELD Samuel James.   Red Lion Inn, Red Lion Street. | 1932 |
| FISHER George.   Bull's Head, Wapping. | 1861 |
| FISHER William.   Bell Inn, Britten Street. | 1855 – 60 |
| FLETCHER John.   Fox and Goose / Royal Hotel. | 1884 – 86 |
| FORESTER William.   Dog and Pheasant. | 1900 – 01 |
| FORD William.   Crown Inn, Feckenham. | 1855 |
| FOSTER May (Mrs).   Bell Inn, Headless Cross. | 1940 |
| FOSTER Samuel Henry.   Royal Oak, Crabbs Cross. | 1928 – 33 |
| FOSTER Samuel Henry.   Bell Inn, Headless Cross. | 1934 – 36 |
| FOURT Elijah.   Warwick Arms. | 1882 – 90 |
| FOURT Emma (Mrs).   Cricketer's Arms, Beoley Road. | 1879 – 80 |
| FOURT Francis.   Cricketer's Arms, Beoley Road. | 1888 – 90 |
| FOURT Francis.   Warwick Arms. | 1891 – 98 |
| FOURT Henry.   Cricketer's Arms, Beoley Road. | 1900 |
| FOURT Thomas B.   Cricketer's Arms, Beoley Road. | 1872 – 78 |
| FOWKES Thomas.   Malt Shovel. | 1841 – 54 |
| FOWKES Thomas.   Fox and Goose / Royal Hotel. | 1822 – 50 |
| FOWLER Alfred.   Bristol Inn. | 1921 – 24 |
| FOWLER Kenneth Reginald H.   Unicorn Hotel. | 1934 – 36 |
| FRANCIS Emma (Mrs).   Bell Inn, Britten Street. | 1888 – 95 |
| FRANCIS Edwin.   Bell Inn, Britten Street. | 1868 – 86 |
| FRANCIS J.   Bell Inn, Headless Cross. | 1898 – 99 |
| FRANCIS James.   New Inn, Mount Pleasant. | 1854 – 55 |
| FRANCIS William.   Vine Inn. | 1850 |
| FRANCIS William.   Fox and Goose / Royal Hotel. | 1854 – 55 |
| FREE Edmund.   Beehive Inn. | 1868 – 79 |
| FREE Elizabeth (Mrs).   Beehive Inn. | 1880 – 86 |
| FREE Sarah Ann (Miss).   Beehive Inn. | 1887 – 90 |
| FULLWELL Reuben.   Unicorn Tap. | 1884 – 88 |
| FUTRILL Alfred Edwin.   Jubilee Oak. | 1932 – 33 |
| | |
| GAMSON Henry.   Old Briton. | 1884 – 90 |
| GANDERTON John.   Cross and Bowling Green. | 1841 |
| GANDERTON William.   Cross and Bowling Green. | 1850 – 55 |
| GARDNER Elizabeth (Mrs).   Black Boy. | 1841 – 54 |
| GARDNER William.   Royal Oak, Prospect Hill. | 1835 – 60 |
| GARFIELD (or CORFIELD) Edwin.   Old Briton. | 1910 – 12 |

| | |
|---|---|
| GARLICK James.   Golden Cross / Railway Inn. | 1890 – 91 |
| GASCOIGNE T.   Forester's Arms. | 1900 – 06 |
| GATHERCOLE Frank.   Royal Hotel. | 1897 – 98 |
| GATHERCOLE Frank.   White Hart. | 1900 – 01 |
| GATHERCOLE James.   White Lion, Astwood Bank. | 1897 – 1900 |
| GATHERCOLE T (Frank)?   Fox & Goose / Royal Hotel. | 1896 |
| GEARING R. R.   Unicorn Hotel. | 1926 – 27 |
| GEE John.   New Inn / Nevill Arms. | 1855 |
| GIBBS John.   Star and Garter. | 1850 |
| GIBBS John Frederick.   Old Briton. | 1908 |
| GLOVER George Henry.   Queen's Head, Queen Street. | 1921 – 28 |
| GLOVER George Henry.   Fountain Inn. | 1932 |
| GLOVER Lewis.   Royal George. | 1892 – 1900 |
| GLOVER Minnie (Mrs).   Cross and Bowling Green. | 1926 – 33 |
| GODSON L.   Golden Lion. | 1903 – 07 |
| GODSON William E.   Shakespeare Tavern. | 1916 – 30 |
| GOODALL William E.   Cricketer's Arms, Beoley Road. | 1891 – 93 |
| GOODE Francis.   Village Inn. | 1908 |
| GOODYEAR William.   Red Lion, Astwood Bank. | 1872 – 95 |
| GOOSTRY Ralph Edgar.   Unicorn Hotel. | 1940 |
| GORTON Laurie (Miss).   White Lion, Astwood Bank. | 1896 |
| GOUCHER Rowland.   Oddfellow's Arms, Astwood Bank. | 1940 |
| GRAY William Oliver.   Lamb and Flag. | 1888 |
| GREAVES Seymour.   Plough and Harrow. | 1850 |
| GREEN Edward.   Cricketer's Arms, Headless Cross. | 1888 |
| GREEN John.   Fleece Inn, Evesham Street. | 1908 – 09 |
| GREEN Josiah.   Fox Inn. | 1868 – 91 |
| GREEN Rowland.   Nevill Arms. | 1873 – 75 |
| GREEN Thomas.   Nevill Arms. | 1900 |
| GREEN Thomas.   Royal Oak, Prospect Hill. | ? |
| GREY Reuben.   Lamb and Flag. | 1878 – 82 |
| GRIFFIN William.   Shakespeare Tavern. | 1932 |
| GRIFFIN William.   Forester's Arms. | 1936 |
| GRIFFITHS Leslie George.   Railway Tavern, Hewell Road. | 1940 |
| GRIMES Thomas Owen.   Queen's Head, Queen Street. | 1932 |
| GROVE Horace Esme.   Railway Tavern, Hewell Road. | 1934 |
| GROVE Horace Esme.   Fleece Inn, Evesham Street. | 1936 – 40 |
| GUEST Elizabeth (Mrs).   Railway Tavern, Hewell Road. | 1897 |
| GUEST George Frederick.   Rising Sun. | 1887 |
| GUEST George Frederick.   White Lion, Red Lion Street. | 1888 – 90 |
| GUEST George Frederick.   Railway Tavern, Hewell Road. | 1890 – 96 |
| GUEST John.   Rising Sun. | 1841 – 64 |
| GUEST John.   Queen's Head, Bromsgrove Road. | 1868 |
| GUEST Maria (Mrs).   Rising Sun. | 1866 – 84 |
| GUISE John.   Queen's Head, Queen Street. | 1883 – 87 |
| | |
| HADEN Beatrice (Mrs).   Jubilee Oak. | 1921 – 32 |
| HADEN Benjamin.   Oddfellow's Arms, Astwood Bank. | 1902 – 17 |
| HADEN B. (Mrs).   Oddfellow's Arms, Astwood Bank. | 1918 |
| HADEN (Mrs).   Railway Inn / Golden Cross. | 1905 |

| | |
|---|---|
| HADEN William Francis.   Unicorn Tap. | 1890 – 96 |
| HADEN William Francis.   Railway Inn / Golden Cross. | 1896 – 1904 |
| HADGKISS Jessie (Mrs).   Rose and Crown, Webheath. | 1909 – 19 |
| HADGKISS Walter.   Crown Hotel, Prospect Hill. | 1893 – 97 |
| HADGKISS Walter.   Vine Inn. | 1900 |
| HADGKISS Walter J.   Fountain Inn. | 1901 – 06 |
| HADGKISS Walter J.   Rose and Crown, Webheath. | 1906 – 08 |
| HALFORD John Albert.   Nag's Head. | 1912 – 14 |
| HALFORD William.   Rose and Crown, Feckenham. | 1896 – 97 |
| HALL Charles.   Royal Oak, Crabbs Cross. | 1940 |
| HALL Herbert.   Gate Hangs Well. | 1921 – 34 |
| HANDS James.   Britannia Inn. | 1864 |
| HANSON John.   Lamb and Flag. | 1921 – 28 |
| HANSON John.   Cricketer's Arms, Beoley Road. | 1932 – 40 |
| HARBERT Henry.   Red Lion, Bradley Green. | 1841 – 50 |
| HARBON Francis.   Old Briton. | 1884 |
| HARBRIDGE Walter William.   Nag's Head. | 1900 – 04 |
| HARMAN Benjamin.   Royal George. | 1880 – 87 |
| HARRIS Benjamin.   New Inn / Nevill Arms. | 1860 – 65 |
| HARRIS James E.   Fountain Inn. | 1912 |
| HARRIS Job.   Fleece Inn, Crabbs Cross. | 1868 |
| HARRIS Thomas.   Old Briton. | 1913 |
| HARRISON Thomas.   Queen's Head, Bromsgrove Road. | 1893 – 96 |
| HARRISON William.   Lygon Arms. | 1864 |
| HARVEY F.   Rose and Crown, Webheath. | 1920 |
| HARVEY (Mrs).   Rifleman Inn. | 1886 |
| HARVEY Thomas.   Rifleman Inn. | 1881 – 85 |
| HARWOOD Walter.   Fox and Goose / Royal Hotel. | 1872 – 75 |
| HAWKES A. G.   Lygon Arms. | 1950's |
| HAWTHORN John B.   Alma Tavern. | 1884 – 87 |
| HAWTHORN Thomas.   Crown Inn, Astwood Bank. | 1855 |
| HAYES Thomas.   Alma Tavern. | 1884 |
| HAYNES Benjamin.   Crown Inn, Astwood Bank. | 1868 |
| HEMMING David.   White Swan. | 1903 – 10 |
| HEMMING Henry.   Crown Inn, Astwood Bank. | 1841 – 54 |
| HEMMING Henry.   White Lion, Astwood Bank. | 1850 – 62 |
| HEMMING Sarah (Miss).   The Magpie, Tardebigge. | 1800 – 12 |
| HEMMING William C.   Brewer's Arms. | 1923 – 28 |
| HERBERT Samuel.   Golden Cross / Railway Inn. | 1875 – 90 |
| HERMAN Alfred C.   Dog and Pheasant. | 1880 – 85 |
| HERMAN Caroline (Mrs).   Dog and Pheasant. | 1886 – 91 |
| HEWITT Lionel Preston.   Hungry Man. | 1940 |
| HEYNES Robert.   Dog and Pheasant. | 1872 – 74 |
| HEYNES Robert G.   Shakespeare Tavern. | 1893 – 96 |
| HEYNES Robert G.   Bell Inn, Headless Cross. | 1900 – 01 |
| HICKEN Alfred.   Village Inn. | 1897 – 1906 |
| HICKS William.   Red Lion, Bradley Green. | 1876 – 80 |
| HIGGS Paul.   Jubilee Oak. | 1868 |
| HILL John George.   Fox and Goose, Foxlydiate. | 1841 |
| HILL George.   Brewer's Arms. | 1920 – 23 |

| | |
|---|---|
| HILL William.   Bristol Inn. | 1868 – 73 |
| HIRST John Edward.   White Hart. | 1908 – 34 |
| HIRST W.   White Hart. | 1903 – 07 |
| HOBBIS Beniah.   Golden Salmon. | 1880 – 81 |
| HOBBS Charles Alfred.   Rifleman Inn. | 1911 – 15 |
| HOBDAY John Frederick.   Lamp Tavern. | 1899 – 1901 |
| HOBDAY John Frederick.   Eagle Inn. | 1904 – 14 |
| HOBDAY Joseph.   Red Lion, Hunt End. | 1855 – 68 |
| HOBSON Nellie Isabelle.   Unicorn Hotel. | 1919 – 21 |
| HODGETTS Mary (Mrs).   Alma Tavern. | 1879 – 80 |
| HODGETTS Walter Thomas.   Nevill Arms. | 1932 – 40 |
| HODGETTS William.   Alma Tavern. | 1875 – 78 |
| HOLBECHE Emma (Mrs).   Woodland Cottage. | 1899 – 1905 |
| HOLBECHE John.   Royal George. | 1871 – 74 |
| HOLBECHE John.   Fleece Inn, Evesham Street. | 1881 |
| HOLBECHE John.   Rose and Crown, Feckenham. | 1889 – 92 |
| HOLBECHE John.   Crown Inn, Astwood Bank. | 1893 – 94 |
| HOLLINGTON Joseph.   King's Arms. | 1868 – 77 |
| HOLLINGTON Sarah (Mrs).   King's Arms. | 1878 – 87 |
| HOLLINGTON William.   Railway Tavern, Hewell Road. | 1868 – 81 |
| HOLMES Emma (Mrs).   Cricketer's Arms, Headless Cross. | 1896 – 1916 |
| HOLMES Frederick K.   Cricketer's Arms, Headless Cross. | 1893 – 95 |
| HOLMES John James.   Railway Tavern, Hewell Road. | 1936 |
| HOLYOAKE William.   Crown Hotel, Prospect Hill. | 1875 – 80 |
| HOPCROFT Amy Belle (Mrs).   Brook Inn. | 1932 – 40 |
| HOPCROFT Benjamin.   Brook Inn. | 1875 – 78 |
| HOPCROFT Benjamin.   Brook Inn. | 1912 – 32 |
| HOPCROFT Mary (Mrs).   Brook Inn. | 1879 – 82 |
| HOPKINS D.   Royal Hotel. | 1905 – 08 |
| HOPKINS Edward.   Scale and Compass. | 1920 – 27 |
| HOUGHTON Charles Henry.   Bell Inn, Headless Cross. | 1866 – 96 |
| HOUGHTON Ann (Mrs).   Bell Inn, Headless Cross. | 1897 – 98 |
| HOUGHTON David.   Old Briton. | 1860 – 80 |
| HOUGHTON Elizabeth (Mrs).   White Hart. | 1897 |
| HOUGHTON James Edward.   Bristol Inn. | 1882 – 94 |
| HOUGHTON James Edward.   White Hart. | 1895 – 96 |
| HOUGHTON Reuben.   Eagle Inn. | 1872 – 74 |
| HOWARD John.   Scale and Compass. | 1911 – 13 |
| HUBBARD Ernest.   Rose and Crown, Webheath. | 1921 – 23 |
| HUBBARD Ernest.   Fox and Goose, Foxlydiate. | 1923 – 25 |
| HUMPHREYS Elizabeth (Mrs).   Brook Inn. | 1854 – 68 |
| HUMPHREYS Richard.   Brook Inn. | 1841 |
| HUMPHREYS William.   Brook Inn. | 1872 – 73 |
| HUNT Frederick.   Nevill Arms. | 1908 – 20 |
| HUNT H.   White Hart. | 1822 – 23 |
| HUNT John.   Navigation Inn, Tardebigge. | Circa. 1800 |
| HUNTLEY Peter.   Britannia Inn. | 1875 – 76 |
| HUTTON John.   Hollybush. | 1841 |
| HYDE Thomas.   Unicorn Hotel. | 1891 – 1917 |
| | |
| IRELAND Thomas.   Crown Hotel, Prospect Hill. | 1822 – 23 |

| | |
|---|---|
| JACKSON Thomas.   Vine Inn. | 1864 |
| JAKEMAN Charles H.   Golden Lion. | 1900 – 02 |
| JAKEMAN John.   Volunteer's Arms. | 1891 – 1903 |
| JAKEMAN John.   Lamb and Flag. | 1904 – 15 |
| JAMES A.   Bristol Inn. | 1914 |
| JAMES Herbert.   White Lion, Astwood Bank. | 1917 – 28 |
| JAMES James.   Rose and Crown, Feckenham. | 1841 – 50 |
| JAMES Martha (Mrs).   Rose and Crown, Feckenham. | 1854 – 82 |
| JAMES Richard.   Golden Salmon. | 1860 – 74 |
| JAMES William Henry.   Scale and Compass. | 1890 – 1904 |
| JAMES William Henry.   Red Lion, Astwood Bank. | 1905 – 19 |
| JEFFRIES (Mrs).   Hollybush Inn. | 1890 |
| JEFFRIES Walter.   Hollybush Inn. | 1875 – 89 |
| JEFFS F. W.   Alma Tavern. | 1934 |
| JENNINGS David.   Forester's Arms. | 1912 – 27 |
| JENNINGS Frank Shakespeare.   Rifleman Inn. | 1906 – 10 |
| JENNINGS William Henry.   Royal Oak, Crabbs Cross. | 1924 – 27 |
| JENNINGS William Henry.   Forester's Arms. | 1928 – 36 |
| JENNINGS William Henry.   Warwick Arms. | 1936 |
| JOHNS Alice (Mrs).   Lord Nelson, Church Green. | 1864 – 68 |
| JOHNS Thomas.   Lord Nelson, Church Green. | 1860 |
| JOHNS Samuel.   Hollybush Inn. | 1855 |
| JOHNSON Benjamin.   Fleece Inn, Evesham Street. | 1892 – 94 |
| JOHNSON Frederick.   Scale and Compass. | 1868 |
| JOHNSON George Farmer.   Scale and Compass. | 1855 – 64 |
| JOHNSON Joseph.   Scale and Compass. | 1854 |
| JOHNSON Mary (Mrs).   Scale and Compass. | 1887 – 89 |
| JOHNSON Sarah (Mrs).   Cross and Bowling Green. | 1860 – 64 |
| JOHNSON Thomas.   Scale and Compass. | 1866 |
| JOHNSON Walter.   Scale and Compass. | 1872 – 86 |
| JOHNSON William Henry.   Eagle Inn. | 1892 – 96 |
| JOHNSTON John.   Plough and Harrow. | 1873 – 74 |
| JONES George Ernest.   Park Inn. | 1928 – 36 |
| JONES Henry.   Plough and Harrow. | 1892 |
| JONES Richard Warner.   Lamb and Flag. | 1916 – 20 |
| JONES Samuel.   Forester's Arms. | 1888 – 1900 |
| JONES Samuel.   Gate Hangs Well. | 1900 – 02 |
| JUGGINS Frank.   Fox and Goose, Foxlydiate. | 1926 – 28 |

David Jenning's two Forester's Arms tokens.

| | |
|---|---|
| KENDAL George.    Gate Hangs Well. | 1916 – 19 |
| KENNEDY Edward.    Foxlydiate Hotel. | 1940 |
| KEYTE Charles.    Eagle Inn. | 1890 – 91 |
| KIBLER Thomas.    Fleece Inn, Evesham Street. | 1928 |
| KIBLER William.    Alma Tavern. | 1891 – 1905 |
| KINGS L.    Eight Bells. | 1921 |
| KNIGHT Maria (Mrs).    Eagle Inn. | 1868 |
| KNIGHT William.    Eagle Inn. | 1860 – 64 |
| | |
| LADDS James.    Fleece Inn, Crabbs Cross. | 1870 |
| LAIGHT Charles.    Jubilee Inn. | 1896 |
| LAIGHT Charles Valentine.    Royal George. | 1912 – 14 |
| LAIGHT George.    Lygon Arms. | 1876 – 95 |
| LAIGHT George.    Rose and Crown, Feckenham. | 1898 – 1901 |
| LANDER Joseph.    Crown Hotel, Prospect Hill. | 1888 – 92 |
| LAUGHER Henry.    Fox and Goose / Royal Hotel. | 1860 – 68 |
| LAWFORD Horace Alfred.    King's Arms. | 1936 |
| LEA Benjamin.    Cricketer's Arms, Headless Cross. | 1872 – 73 |
| LEASON ?    Bell Inn, Headless Cross. | 1913 – 14 |
| LEDBURY William.    Bird in Hand, Walford Street. | 1841 – 68 |
| LEE Thomas.    Bell Inn, Pudding Bag Lane. (Parsons Road)? | 1868 |
| LEES Frederick Arthur.    King's Arms. | 1911 – 14 |
| LEWIS Alfred.    Eight Bells. | 1891 – 1903 |
| LEWIS Alfred Harden.    Queen's Head, Bromsgrove Road. | 1892 |
| LEWIS Ann (Mrs).    Beehive Inn. | 1860 – 64 |
| LEWIS Ann Amelia (Mrs).    Eight Bells. | 1904 – 06 |
| LEWIS Charles H.    Oddfellow's Arms, Astwood Bank. | 1928 – 36 |
| LEWIS James.    Beehive Inn. | 1850 – 55 |
| LEWORTHY Clifford.    Hollybush Inn. | 1917 |
| LEYSTER Mary (Mrs).    Woodbine Cottage. | 1873 – 82 |
| LOCKE Alfred.    Bell Inn, Headless Cross. | 1925 – 27 |

The Eight Bells, Feckenham – now a private house.

| | |
|---|---|
| MACEY Sidney.    White Lion, Astwood Bank. | 1895 |
| MADDOCKS Joseph.    Fleece Inn, Crabbs Cross. | 1914 |
| MALINS William Henry.    Greyhound Inn. | 1879 – 1914 |
| MANNING Ralph.    Plumber's Arms. | 1936 – 40 |
| MANSELL Frank Richard.    Fountain Inn. | 1934 |
| MANSON Edward.    Village Inn. | 1940 |
| MARIES Albert.    Golden Salmon. | 1892 |
| MARIES Albert.    Horse and Jockey, Evesham Street. | 1893 – 94 |
| MARIES George Frederick.    Fox Inn. | 1904 – 14 |
| MARIES George Frederick.    Rifleman Inn. | 1932 – 40 |
| MARIES James.    Printer's Arms. | 1841 – 50 |
| MARIES Myra (Mrs).    Fox Inn. | 1916 – 21 |
| MARIES Richard Henry.    Railway Inn / Golden Cross. | 1927 – 32 |
| MARSH William Ronald.    Queen's Head, Queen Street. | 1940 |
| MARSHALL Elizabeth.    Rose and Crown, Feckenham. | 1893 – 96 |
| MARSHALL William.    Red Lion, Bradley Green. | 1884 – 96 |
| MARSHALL William.    King's Arms. | 1921 – 24 |
| MARSON Malcolm Stuart.    Hungry Man. | 1936 |
| MARTIN Ronald B.    Scale and Compass. | 1916 – 19 |
| MARTIN W.    Fleece Inn, Evesham Street. | 1927 |
| MASON Albert Victor.    Jubilee Oak. | 1915 – 16 |
| MASON Thomas.    Red Lion, Red Lion Street. | 1924 – 27 |
| MASTERS Edgar John.    Eight Bells. | 1907 – 20 |
| MASTERS John Thomas.    Black Horse. | 1874 – 1909 |
| MASTERS John W.    Black Horse. | 1932 – 40 |
| MASTERS Mary Jane (Mrs).    Black Horse. | 1928 – 31 |
| MASTERS William.    Black Horse. | 1868 – 73 |
| MASTERS William Frederick.    Black Horse. | 1910 – 27 |
| MATLEY James.    Alma Tavern. | 1871 – 74 |
| MATTS William Harry.    Railway Inn / Golden Cross. | 1932 |
| MAXWELL David H.    Lamb and Flag. | 1890 |
| MAXWELL (Mrs).    Fleece Inn, Evesham Street. | 1910 – 11 |
| MAYNE R. N.    Unicorn Hotel. | 1919 |
| Mc LAND George.    Bristol Inn. | 1874 – 76 |
| MEALING Joseph.    Nevill Arms. | 1904 – 08 |
| MEASURES Alfred Holman.    Sportsman's Arms. | 1928 |
| MELEN George.    Crown Hotel, Prospect Hill. | 1888 |
| MENCE John.    Unicorn Hotel. | 1822 – 23 |
| MERRY David.    Gate Hangs Well. | 1891 – 1900 |
| MILLINGTON Edwin.    Village Inn. | 1891 – 96 |
| MILLS Clarence Charles.    Royal Oak, Crabbs Cross. | 1906 – 20 |
| MILLS George.    White Hart. | 1884 – 90 |
| MILLS George.    Lygon Arms. | 1896 |
| MILLS Harriet (Mrs).    Royal Oak, Crabbs Cross. | 1921 – 23 |
| MILLS James.    Bell Inn, Headless Cross. | 1855 |
| MILLS James.    Bell Inn, Britten Street. | 1860 – 64 |
| MILLS James Ambrose.    Old Briton. | 1900 – 07 |
| MILLS James Ambrose.    Crown Hotel, Prospect Hill. | 1911 – 23 |
| MILLS John Henry.    Royal Oak, Crabbs Cross. | 1868 – 79 |
| MILLS Joseph.    Royal Oak, Crabbs Cross. | 1841 – 55 |
| MILLS Mary (Mrs).    Royal Oak, Crabbs Cross. | 1860 – 66 |
| MILLS Matthew.    Royal Oak, Crabbs Cross. | 1894 – 1905 |
| MILLS Reuben.    Hart Inn. | 1872 |
| MILLS Reuben.    Golden Salmon. | 1875 – 78 |
| MILLS Reuben.    Nag's Head. | 1879 – 98 |

| | |
|---|---|
| MILLS Sarah (Mrs).    Nag's Head. | 1899 – 1900 |
| MILLWARD Albert Alfred.    Sportsman's Arms. | 1922 – 27 |
| MILLWARD Albert Alfred.    Oddfellow's Arms, Astwood Bank. | 1927 |
| MILLWARD Ann (Mrs).    Folly Inn, Headless Cross. | 1850 |
| MILLWARD Emma (Mrs).    Rising Sun. | 1920 – 27 |
| MILLWARD Frank H.    Jubilee Inn. | 1925 – 28 |
| MILLWARD G.    Fleece Inn, Evesham Street. | 1895 |
| MILLWARD George.    Oddfellow's Arms, Astwood Bank. | 1897 – 1901 |
| MILLWARD Harry James.    Rose and Crown, Feckenham. | 1883 – 88 |
| MILLWARD Harry James.    Fleece Inn, Evesham Street. | 1888 – 90 |
| MILLWARD Harry James.    Golden Salmon. | 1891 |
| MILLWARD Harry James.    Oddfellow's Arms, Astwood Bank. | 1891 – 96 |
| MILLWARD James.    Folly Inn, Headless Cross. | ? |
| MILLWARD John.    White Swan. | 1921 |
| MILLWARD John Gough.    Rising Sun. | 1893 – 1919 |
| MILLWARD Stephen George.    Horse and Jockey, Evesham Street. | 1895 – 96 |
| MILLWARD Stephen George.    Fox Inn. | 1898 – 1903 |
| MILLWARD Samuel.    Shakespeare Tavern. | 1860 – 84 |
| MOGG George.    Brewer's Arms. | 1854 – 75 |
| MOGG R. J.    Woodland Cottage. | 1898 – 99 |
| MOLE David.    Bell Inn, Pudding Bag Lane. (Parsons Road) ? | ? |
| MOORE George.    White Swan. | 1854 – 64 |
| MOORE John.    White Lion, Red Lion Street. | 1835 – 41 |
| MOORE (Mrs).    White Lion, Red Lion Street. | 1845 |
| MOORE Oliver.    Woodbine Cottage. | 1893 – 94 |
| MOORE Stephen.    White Lion, Red Lion Street. | 1850 |
| MORGAN George.    White Hart. | 1873 – 74 |
| MORRIS Hector Charles.    Alma Tavern. | 1932 |
| MORRIS Joseph.    Plough and Harrow. | 1868 |
| MORRIS Thomas.    Acorn Inn. | 1850 |
| MORRIS Thomas.    Crown Inn, Crabbs Cross. | 1880 |
| MORRIS William.    Crown Inn, Crabbs Cross. | 1841 – 55 |
| MORRIS William James.    Rifleman Inn. | 1922 – 28 |
| MORTON George.    Oddfellow's Arms, Windsor Street. | 1897 – 1908 |
| MORTON Henry.    Woodbine Cottage. | 1904 – 08 |
| MOSS Frederick Henry.    White Lion, Red Lion Street. | 1933 – 34 |
| MOSS Frederick Henry.    Star and Garter. | 1936 – 40 |
| MOYTHAN Ambrose.    Plymouth Arms. | 1869 – 79 |
| MUNSLOW Alfred.    Hollybush Inn. | 1918 |
| MUSTIN Emma.    Fountain Inn. | 1871 – 72 |
| MUSTIN George.    Royal George. | 1860 – 68 |
| | |
| NASH Joshua.    Dog and Pheasant. | 1892 – 96 |
| NEALE William.    Vine Inn. | 1868 |
| NESS John Howard.    Jubilee Inn. | 1928 – 36 |
| NEWBERRY Thomas.    Woodman Inn, Astwood Bank. | 1895 |
| NEWBERRY William M.    Woodman Inn, Astwood Bank. | 1896 – 1901 |
| NEWMAN H C.    Foxlydiate Hotel. | 1939 |
| NOKES Alfred Edwin.    Rifleman Inn. | 1887 – 95 |
| NORCOTT Archibald.    Woodman Inn, Astwood Bank. | 1889 – 91 |
| NORTHALL Henry.    Alma Tavern. | 1940 |
| | |
| OAKLEY James.    Fleece Inn, Evesham Street. | 1861 – 64 |
| ONIONS Joe.    Plough and Harrow. | 1940 |
| OWEN Henry.    Seven Stars. | 1909 – 19 |

| | |
|---|---|
| PAGE Thomas.   Red Lion, Red Lion Street. | 1854 |
| PALMER Jesse.   Golden Lion. | 1892 – 96 |
| PALMER William Thomas.   Park Inn. | 1916 – 19 |
| PARKER Samuel Richard.   Golden Salmon. | 1885 – 90 |
| PARKER Samuel Richard.   Shakespeare Tavern. | 1891 – 93 |
| PARKINSON John William.   Beehive Inn. | 1891 – 1904 |
| PARRY James.   Red Lion, Hunt End. | 1930 – 40 |
| PARSONAGE Henry.   Golden Lion. | 1872 – 88 |
| PARSONAGE Henry (Mrs).   Golden Lion. | 1889 – 91 |
| PARSONS George.   Woodland Cottage. | 1841 – 73 |
| PARSONS Thomas.   Woodland Cottage. | 1874 – 75 |
| PARTRIDGE Alfred.   Oddfellow's Arms, Windsor Street. | 1911 – 36 |
| PENTYCROSS Edwin.   Queen's Head, Bromsgrove Road. | 1897 – 1905 |
| PERKINS Albert.   Crown Inn, Astwood Bank. | 1872 – 80 |
| PERKINS Edward Joseph.   Red Lion, Astwood Bank. | 1932 – 40 |
| PERKINS Joseph Alexander.   White Lion, Astwood Bank. | 1888 – 94 |
| PERKINS Joseph Alexander.   White Lion, Astwood Bank. | 1900 – 05 |
| PERKINS Sarah Ann (Mrs).   White Lion, Astwood Bank. | 1880 – 81 |
| PERKS Edward.   Crown Hotel, Prospect Hill. | 1902 – 08 |
| PERKS W. E.   Fleece Inn, Evesham Street. | 1891 |
| PERRY A. G.   Woodbine Cottage. | 1890 |
| PHILLIPS John.   Nevill Arms. | 1887 – 99 |
| PINCHBECK Leonard.   Royal Oak, Crabbs Cross. | 1936 |
| PINFIELD David.   Forester's Arms. | 1883 – 87 |
| PINFIELD David.   King's Arms. | 1888 – 1910 |
| PINFIELD James.   Britannia Inn. | 1855 – 60 |
| PINFIELD John.   Britannia Inn. | 1873 – 74 |
| PINFIELD John.   Fleece Inn, Evesham Street. | 1875 – 81 |
| PINFIELD John.   Golden Salmon. | 1883 – 84 |
| PINFIELD Richard.   Cherry Tree, Headless Cross. | 1850 – 55 |
| (Billing's Directory for 1855 gives <u>Binfield</u> Richard, Apple Tree). | |
| PINFIELD William.   Cherry Tree, Headless Cross. | 1841 |
| PINFIELD – WELLS Edwin.   White Lion, Red Lion Street. | 1902 – 28 |
| PINFIELD – WELLS Edwin Arthur.   Volunteer's Arms. | 1883 – 90 |
| PINFIELD – WELLS Edwin Arthur.   Brewer's Arms. | 1892 – 1901 |
| PINFIELD – WELLS Elizabeth (Mrs).   Brewer's Arms. | 1901 – 18 |
| PINFIELD – WELLS L.   Volunteer's Arms. | 1904 – 08 |
| PINFIELD – WELLS (Mrs).   White Lion, Red Lion Street. | 1929 – 32 |
| PINFIELD – WELLS William.   Hart Inn. | 1904 |
| PLANT Charles.   Warwick Arms. | 1868 |
| POLLARD Ernest.   Railway Inn / Golden Cross. | 1936 – 40 |
| POLLETT Ernest.   Warwick Arms. | 1940 |
| POOLE Mary Ann (Mrs).   Eagle Inn. | 1888 – 89 |
| POOLE Matthias.   Bell Inn, Headless Cross. | 1907 – 08 |
| POOLE William.   Eagle Inn. | 1875 – 87 |
| POWELL Eliza (Mrs).   Fox and Goose, Foxlydiate. | 1868 |
| POWELL Thomas.   Lamb and Flag. | 1850 – 55 |
| POWELL Thomas.   Fox and Goose, Foxlydiate. | 1860 – 64 |
| POWELL Samuel.   White Lion, Astwood Bank. | 1864 – 74 |
| PRICE C.   Golden Lion. | 1892 |
| PRICE John.   Dog Inn, Ipsley Street. | 1854 – 55 |
| PRICE Thomas.   Lygon Arms. | 1860 |
| PYE Thomas Francis.   Alma Tavern. | 1906 – 31 |

| | |
|---|---|
| RALPH Joseph.   Seven Stars. | 1875 |
| RALPH Levi.   Seven Stars. | 1876 – 84 |
| RALPH Levi.   Woodbine Cottage. | 1895 – 1903 |
| RANDALL John.   Village Inn. | 1919 – 25 |
| READER James.   Cross and Bowling Green. | 1868 – 78 |
| READING William Henry.   Baker's Arms, Astwood Bank. | 1883 – 90 |
| REASON William.   Fox and Goose / Royal Hotel. | 1887 – 90 |
| RICHARDS Ann.   White Lion, Astwood Bank. | 1841 |
| RICHARDS T.   Railway Tavern, Hewell Street. (Road). | 1850 |
| RICHARDS Thomas.   White Lion, Astwood Bank. | 1830's |
| RICHARDSON William.   Fleece Inn, Evesham Street. | 1912 – 21 |
| RICHARDSON William.   Nag's Head. | 1924 – 25 |
| RICKARDS George.   Red Lion, Red Lion Street. | 1855 |
| RICKARDS George.   Lamp Tavern. | 1860 – 80 |
| RICKARDS Joseph.   Warwick Arms. | 1854 – 55 |
| RICKARDS Joseph.   Warwick Arms. | 1872 – 76 |
| RICKARDS Keziah (Mrs).   Lamp Tavern. | 1881 – 99 |
| RICKARDS Thomas.   Sportsman's Arms. | 1854 – 98 |
| RIGBY Joseph.   Old Briton. | 1914 |
| ROBERTS Frederick.   Golden Cross / Railway Inn. | 1870 – 75 |
| ROBERTS John R.   Hollybush Inn. | 1912 – 16 |
| ROUNTREE Hugh.   Fleece Inn, Evesham Street. | 1872 – 75 |
| ROUNTREE Hugh.   Fox and Goose / Royal Hotel. | 1875 – 83 |
| ROUSE Jane (Mrs).   Baker's Arms, Astwood Bank. | 1872 – 82 |
| ROUSE Richard.   Baker's Arms, Astwood Bank. | 1854 – 68 |
| ROWBERRY William J.   Shakespeare Tavern. | 1898 – 1900 |
| ROWBOTHAM George.   Alma Tavern. | 1936 |
| RUDGE James.   Rifleman Inn. | 1868 – 80 |
| RUSSELL William.   Scourer's Arms. | 1909 – 12 |
| RUSSELL William F.   Wagon and Horses. | 1912 – 40 |
| RYLAND Thomas.   Lamb and Flag. | 1884 – 88 |
| | |
| SALISBURY Charles Frederick.   Royal George. | 1908 – 09 |
| SALLIS Frederick William.   Plough and Harrow. | 1936 |
| SANDERS Oliver.   Crown Inn, Feckenham. | 1850 – 54 |
| SANDERS Sarah.   Crown Inn, Feckenham. | 1841 |
| SAUNDERS William.   Bell Inn, Headless Cross. | 1903 – 06 |
| SAVAGE Alan.   Why Not. | 1925 – 40 |
| SAVAGE George.   Lamb and Flag. | 1891 – 93 |
| SAVAGE George.   Cricketer's Arms, Beoley Road. | 1894 – 96 |
| SAVAGE John.   Cross and Bowling Green. | 1898 – 1901 |
| SAVAGE Thomas.   Why Not, Ridgeway, Cookhill. | 1868 – 98 |
| SAVERY George Joseph.   Fox Inn. | 1892 – 97 |
| SEALEY Bernard.   Red Lion, Red Lion Street. | 1896 – 99 |
| SEALEY Howard.   Nag's Head. | 1932 – 34 |
| SEALEY John.   Woodman Inn, Webheath. | 1855 – 83 |
| SEALEY Walter.   Fountain Inn. | 1921 – 24 |
| SHAKELS James.   Lygon Arms. | 1940 |
| SHAKLES P. F.   Warwick Arms. | 1927 – 34 |
| SHELTON Elizabeth (Mrs).   Woodland Cottage. | 1911 – 14 |
| SHELTON Emma (Mrs).   Lamp Tavern. | 1904 – 13 |
| SHELTON Florence (Mrs).   Railway Inn / Golden Cross. | 1909 – 24 |
| SHELTON Frederick.   Park Inn. | 1899 – 1904 |
| SHELTON Frederick.   Railway Inn / Golden Cross. | 1906 – 08 |
| SHELTON Harry.   Lamp Tavern. | 1902 – 03 |

| | |
|---|---|
| SHELTON John.    Railway Inn / Golden Cross. | 1924 |
| SHELTON William Frederick.    Woodland Cottage. | 1905 – 10 |
| SHEPHERD George.    Park Inn. | 1921 – 24 |
| SHEPHERD George Herbert.    Royal Hotel. | 1903 – 04 |
| SHINTON John.    Greyhound Inn. | 1846 – 73 |
| SHINTON John.    Fox and Goose, Foxlydiate. | 1872 – 78 |
| SHINTON John (Mrs).    Fox and Goose, Foxlydiate. | 1879 – 83 |
| SHRIMPTON Harriet (Mrs).    Queen's Head, Queen Street. | 1904 – 20 |
| SHRIMPTON Henry.    Star and Garter. | 1885 – 86 |
| SHRIMPTON Henry (Junior).    Star and Garter. | 1887 – 1908 |
| SHRIMPTON Simeon.    Queen's Head, Queen Street. | 1860 – 64 |
| SHRIMPTON Simeon.    Queen's Head, Queen Street. | 1888 – 1903 |
| SIMPSON Philip Alan.    Unicorn Hotel. | 1924 – 25 |
| SKIDMORE David.    Fleece Inn, Evesham Street. | 1922 – 26 |
| SKINNER Thomas.    Alma Tavern. | 1892 |
| SLATTER James.    Lamb and Flag. | 1883 |
| SMALLWOOD Charles.    Queen's Head, Queen Street. | 1868 – 76 |
| SMALLWOOD Elizabeth.    Red Cow. | 1864 – 70 |
| SMALLWOOD George.    Red Cow. | 1835 – 61 |
| SMITH Alfred.    White Swan. | 1889 – 1900 |
| SMITH Alfred.    Wagon and Horses. | 1901 – 12 |
| SMITH Alfred.    Royal Hotel. | 1912 – 36 |
| SMITH Alfred.    Nag's Head. | 1916 – 23 |
| SMITH Ann (Mrs).    Vine Inn. | 1875 – 80 |
| SMITH Arthur Leonard.    Plough and Harrow. | 1893 – 1906 |
| SMITH Ernest.    Red Lion, Astwood Bank. | 1897 – 98 |
| SMITH Ernest.    Royal Hotel. | 1940 |
| SMITH George.    Horse and Jockey, Evesham Street. | 1860 – 68 |
| SMITH Helen (Mrs).    Horse and Jockey, Evesham Street. | 1871 – 79 |
| SMITH Henry.    (Old) Horse and Jockey, Ipsley Street. | 1860 |
| SMITH Henry.    Red Lion Inn, Astwood Bank. | 1896 |
| SMITH James Frederick.    King's Arms. | 1928 |
| SMITH John Frederick.    Old Briton. | 1892 – 1900 |
| SMITH John H.    Royal George. | 1914 – 15 |
| SMITH John H.    Fleece Inn, Crabbs Cross. | 1916 |
| SMITH Joseph.    Vine Inn. | 1871 – 75 |
| SMITH Samuel.    Plough and Harrow. | 1860 – 64 |
| SMITH T.    Royal George. | 1905 – 07 |
| SMITH Thomas William.    Horse and Jockey, Evesham Street. | 1904 |
| SMITH William Thomas Mortiboy.    Woodman Inn, Astwood Bank. | 1892 – 94 |
| SMITH William Thomas Mortiboy.    Royal Hotel. | 1900 – 02 |
| SNELGAR Reginald.    Talbot Hotel. | 1932 – 36 |
| SOOBROY F.    White Hart. | 1902 |
| SPENCER Alfred.    Cricketer's Arms, Beoley Road. | 1900 |
| SPIERS George.    Woodbine Cottage. | 1884 – 88 |
| SPIERS John Thomas.    Fox Inn. | 1922 – 34 |
| SPROSEN Frederick Richard.    Lygon Arms. | 1898 – 1936 |
| SPROSEN (Mrs).    Lygon Arms. | 1936 |
| SPROSEN W.    Lygon Arms. | 1897 |
| STALWORTH William Henry.    Plumber's Arms. | 1892 – 1910 |
| STANLEY Albert Henry.    Scourer's Arms. | 1926 – 28 |

| | |
|---|---|
| STANLEY Charles Henry.   Railway Tavern, Hewell Road. | 1911 – 17 |
| STARKEY Robert Charles Walter.   Talbot Hotel. | 1940 |
| STEPHENS H.   Eight Bells. | 1930 – 32 |
| STEVENS Harry.   Rising Sun. | 1932 |
| STEVENS Thomas.   Woodland Cottage. | 1921 – 40 |
| STEVENS William J.   Nag's Head. | 1925 – 31 |
| STEWARD John.   Royal George. | 1875 – 76 |
| STINTON Alfred.   Unicorn Hotel. | 1864 – 90 |
| STOKES Elizabeth M. (Mrs).   Jubilee Oak. | 1940 |
| STOKES Ernest.   Jubilee Oak. | 1933 – 36 |
| STORRS Josiah.   Queen's Head, Queen Street. | 1876 – 82 |
| STOREY H.   Gate Hangs Well. | 1903 – 06 |
| STREET Reuben.   Nag's Head. | 1934 – 36 |
| STUBBS Rowland.   Unicorn Tap. | 1860 – 82 |
| STUBBS Rowland.   Unicorn Tap. | 1888 – 89 |
| STURGES James.   Eagle Inn. | 1928 – 40 |
| STYLER Enoch.   Scale and Compass. | 1907 – 08 |
| STYLER James.   Eagle Inn. | 1916 – 27 |
| STYLER (Mrs).   Scale and Compass. | 1909 – 10 |
| STYLER Thomas.   Royal Oak, Crabbs Cross. | 1880 – 83 |
| STYLER W.   Eight Bells. | 1933 – 36 |
| STYLER William.   Lygon Arms. | 1868 |
| STYLER William.   Black Boy. | 1872 – 73 |
| SUCH Edward.   Scourer's Arms. | 1891 – 1900 |
| SUCH Elizabeth (Mrs).   Scourer's Arms. | 1901 – 04 |
| SUMMERS Frederick S.   Lamb and Flag. | 1900 – 01 |
| SUMMERS Francis Theodore.   Woodman Inn, Astwood Bank. | 1922 – 40 |
| SUTOR Emma (Mrs).   Woodman Inn, Astwood Bank. | 1888 – 90 |
| SUTOR Henry.   Woodman Inn, Astwood Bank. | 1872 – 81 |
| SWALLOW John.   Star and Garter. | 1909 – 14 |
| SWANN Charles.   Alma Tavern. | 1883 |
| | |
| TALBOT William.   Plumber's Arms. | 1884 – 91 |
| TAY Tobias.   Red Lion, Red Lion Street. | 1835 |
| TAYLOR Samuel.   Plymouth Arms. | 1854 – 69 |
| THEAY Thomas.   Lamp Tavern. | 1913 – 36 |
| THOMPSON John.   Shakespeare Tavern. | 1888 – 89 |
| THOMPSON Thomas G. Hastings.   Vine Inn. | 1921 – 25 |
| THORNTON Christiana (Mrs).   Britannia Inn. | 1895 – 1908 |
| THORNTON Christiana (Mrs).   Nag's Head. | 1909 – 11 |
| THORNTON Joseph.   Britannia Inn. | 1880 – 86 |
| THORNTON Reuben.   Golden Salmon. | 1879 |
| THORNTON William.   Britannia Inn. | 1887 – 94 |
| TIMSON Harry.   Hollybush Inn. | 1923 – 31 |
| TOLLEY William.   King's Arms. | 1855 – 64 |
| TOMKINS Henry.   Cricketer's Arms, Beoley Road. | 1924 – 28 |
| TOWERS G.   Village Inn. | 1907 |
| TOWNSEND George.   Red Lion, Hunt End. | 1850 – 54 |
| TREVOR William John.   Hollybush Inn. | 1908 – 11 |
| TUNKS William.   Railway Inn / Golden Cross. | 1936 |

| | |
|---|---|
| UNITT Lewis.   Wagon and Horses. | 1872 – 78 |
| UNITT William.   Wagon and Horses. | 1854 – 68 |
| UNITT William.   Wagon and Horses. | 1879 – 1900 |
| | |
| VANN Emma (Mrs).   Rose and Crown, Webheath. | 1925 – 40 |
| VANN Harry.   Rose and Crown, Webheath. | 1924 |
| | |
| WADE (Mrs).   Lamb and Flag. | 1889 – 90 |
| WAKEMAN Sarah (Mrs).   Bell Inn, Astwood Bank. | 1864 – 68 |
| WAKEMAN Susan (Miss).   Bell Inn, Astwood Bank. | 1872 – 82 |
| WALL George.   Woodbine Cottage. | 1891 – 92 |
| WALKER George.   White Hart. | 1867 – 68 |
| WALKER George E.   Crown Inn, Astwood Bank. | 1895 – 1930 |
| WALKER Henry.   Woodman Inn, Astwood Bank. | 1903 – 21 |
| WALKER Henry.   Crown Inn, Astwood Bank. | 1932 – 44 |
| WALKER John.   Bell Inn, Astwood Bank. | 1883 – 92 |
| WALKER Susannah (Mrs).   Bell Inn, Astwood Bank. | 1893 – 1913 |
| WALTERS Grace Mary (Mrs).   Oddfellow's Arms, Windsor Street. | 1940 |
| WALTON James.   Fox and Goose / Royal Hotel. | 1835 |
| WARD George.   Fountain Inn. | 1916 |
| WARD Vernon James.   Bell Inn, Headless Cross. | 1928 – 33 |
| WARDLE Jane (Mrs).   Nag's Head. | 1872 – 78 |
| WARDLE George.   Nag's Head. | 1860 – 68 |
| WARING Francis.   Seven Stars. | 1886 – 96 |
| WARNER Frank.   Woodland Cottage. | 1916 – 20 |
| WARNER Jonah.   Queen's Head, Bromsgrove Road. | 1886 – 88 |
| WATTON Ernest.   Royal Oak, Crabbs Cross. | 1889 – 92 |
| WEAVER William.   British Workman. | 1875 – 77 |
| WEBB Ann (Mrs).   White Lion, Astwood Bank. | 1886 – 87 |
| WEBB Bernard.   Queen's Head, Bromsgrove Road. | 1916 – 40 |
| WEBB Felix.   White Lion, Astwood Bank. | 1882 – 85 |
| WEBB Henry James.   Rising Sun. | 1888 – 92 |
| WEBB James.   Red Lion, Red Lion Street. | 1860 – 86 |
| WEBB Mary (Mrs).   Red Lion, Red Lion Street. | 1887 – 90 |
| WEBB Stephen.   Crown Inn, Astwood Bank. | 1860 – 64 |
| WELLS E.   Old Briton. | 1891 |
| WELSBOURNE John.   Vine Inn. | 1854 – 61 |
| WHARRAD Charles.   Royal George. | 1901 – 04 |
| WHEILDON Adrian Richard.   Unicorn Hotel. | 1928 – 30 |
| WHELE Jesse.   Fountain Inn. | 1873 – 1900 |
| WHITE Thomas.   Cross and Bowling Green. | 1940 |
| WHITEHEAD Sam.   Eight Bells. | 1940 |
| WHITEHOUSE William.   Hollybush Inn. | 1891 – 1903 |
| WHITEHOUSE William H.   White Lion, Astwood Bank. | 1932 – 36 |
| WHITMORE Alfred.   Village Inn. | 1889 – 90 |
| WHITMORE John.   Village Inn. | 1872 – 81 |
| WHITMORE Maria (Mrs).   Village Inn. | 1882 – 88 |
| WILKES Albert.   Sportsman's Arms. | 1899 – 1918 |
| WILKINSON Ann (Mrs).   Park Inn. | 1864 – 89 |
| WILKINSON John.   Park Inn. | 1890 – 98 |
| WILKINSON Jonas.   Park Inn. | 1890 – 98 |
| WILKINSON Jonas.   Park Inn. | 1854 – 55 |
| WILKINSON Joseph. (Jonas) ?   Park Inn. | 1850 |
| WILKINSON Matthew.   Park Inn. | 1837 |
| WILKS Mary (Mrs).   Alma Tavern. | 1868 |

| | |
|---|---|
| WILKS William.   Alma Tavern. | 1864 |
| WILLIAMS Richard.   Red Lion, Red Lion Street. | 1850 |
| WILLIS Herbert.   Red Lion, Red Lion Street. | 1822 – 23 |
| WILLIS John.   Hart Inn. | 1868 |
| WILLIS William.   Printer's Arms. | 1880 – 82 |
| WILLIS William.   White Swan. | 1883 – 88 |
| WILSHAW Charles Joseph.   Warwick Arms. | 1900 – 26 |
| WILSON John Thomas.   Village Inn. | 1926 – 36 |
| WINDLE Thomas.   Woodman Inn, Astwood Bank. | 1882 – 87 |
| WINDRIDGE James Edwin.   Fleece Inn, Crabbs Cross. | 1921 |
| WOOD Albert Edward.   Rifleman Inn. | 1928 |
| WOOD Alfred James.   Bell Inn, Headless Cross. | 1921 – 25 |
| WORTH Harvey.   Cricketer's Arms, Beoley Road. | 1920 – 21 |
| WRIGHT Catherine (Mrs).   Fleece Inn, Evesham Street. | 1884 – 87 |
| WRIGHT John.   Black Horse. | 1850 – 55 |
| WRIGHT John.   Fleece Inn, Evesham Street. | 1882 – 84 |
| WRIGHT Stephen.   Railway Inn / Golden Cross. | 1925 – 27 |
| WRIGHT William.   Seven Stars. | 1897 – 98 |
| | |
| YALLOP Robert.   Railway Tavern, Hewell Road. | 1882 – 86 |
| YALLOP Mary (Mrs).   Railway Tavern, Hewell Road. | 1887 – 89 |
| YARNALL William.   Fox and Goose, Foxlydiate. | 1850 – 55 |
| YARNALL William.   Queen's Head, Bromsgrove Road. | 1860 – 64 |
| YATES Albert Edward.   Lamb and Flag. | 1936 |
| YATES Albert Edward.   Talbot Hotel. | 1946 |
| YATES Frederick.   Jubilee Inn. | 1918 – 24 |
| YATES John.   Golden Salmon. | 1882 |
| YEOMANS Emma Caroline (Mrs).   Cross and Bowling Green. | 1912 – 25 |
| YEOMANS William Wilson.   Cross and Bowling Green. | 1902 – 08 |
| YOUNG Annie (Miss).   Bell Inn, Britten Street. | 1915 – 21 |
| YOUNG Edgar.   Bell Inn, Britten Street. | 1926 – 51 |
| YOUNG Florence (Miss).   Bell Inn, Britten Street. | 1923 |
| YOUNG Francis.   Jubilee Oak. | 1891 – 1915 |
| YOUNG Henry.   Jubilee Inn. | 1868 – 95 |
| YOUNG Henry.   Bell Inn, Britten Street. | 1896 – 1914 |
| YOUNG Thomas.   Bell Inn, Britten Street. | 1924 |
| YOUNG William H.   Horse and Jockey, Evesham Street. | 1880 – 92 |
| YOUNG William Henry James.   Lamb and Flag. | 1894 – 99 |
| YOXALL Robert.   Greyhound Inn. | 1874 – 78 |

Village Inn, Beoley.

# THE FOLLOWING ARE BEER RETAILERS THAT CANNOT BE ASSIGNED TO NAMED PUBS, THEIR OTHER TRADES ARE AS LISTED IN THE DIRECTORIES

| | |
|---|---|
| ADAMS Richard.   Windsor Street. | 1855 |
| ALLEN James.   Redditch. | 1835 |
| AUBURY Robert.   Astwood Bank. (Needle stamper). | 1841 |
| AVERY George.   Evesham Street. (Shopkeeper). | 1854 |
| AVERY Richard.   Alcester Street. | 1850 |
| AVERY Sarah.   Evesham Street. (Needle and fish-hook maker). | 1855 |
| | |
| BAKER Gerard.   Astwood Bank. (Boot and shoe maker). | 1860 – 68 |
| BALLARD William.   Redditch. | 1850 |
| BARTLEET W.   Britten Street. | 1850 |
| BAYLIS Benjamin.   Redditch. (Needle maker and shopkeeper). | 1854 |
| BAYLIS Charles.   Redditch. (Needle maker). | 1854 |
| BEAUMONT William Leaming.   Feckenham. | 1936 – 40 |
| BLACKSHAW Kate.   24 Edward Street. (Ale stores). | 1901 |
| BOGG Richard.   Cookhill. | 1841 |
| BROOKS Samuel.   Headless Cross. | 1876 – 77 |
| BROWN Allan Charles.   Alcester Street. (Grocer and painter). | 1854 – 68 |
| BROWN Family.   Evesham Street. (Brewers and Maltsters). | From 1841 |
| BROWN John.   Redditch. (Baker). | 1850 – 54 |
| BROWN Joseph.   Redditch. (Painter and plumber). | 1835 – 41 |
| BROWN Samuel.   Prospect Hill / Chapel Green West. | 1850 – 55 |
| BUTLER Edward.   Evesham Street. | 1851 |
| | |
| CHAMBERS James.   Prospect Hill. (Plumber and painter). | 1841 – 54 |
| CHARMAN George.   Windsor Street. | 1850 |
| CLARK Amelia (Miss).   Church Green. | 1864 |
| COOK George.   Mount Pleasant. | 1860 – 68 |
| COOK William.   Mount Pleasant. | 1860 – 68 |
| CROMAR Ellen (Mrs).   9 Albert Street. | 1908 – 28 |
| CROW John.   Redditch. | 1835 |
| CROW Thomas.   Headless Cross. | 1860 – 64 |
| | |
| DAVIES William.   Redditch. | 1835 |
| DAVIS Emanuel.   Redditch. | 1841 |
| DAVIS John.   Mount Pleasant. (Evesham Street). | 1841 |
| DIPPLE Emma (Mrs).   24 Edward Street. (Ale stores). | 1896 – 99 |
| DIPPLE W. H.   24 Edward Street. | 1895 |
| DUGGINS Mary (Mrs).   Edward Street. | 1864 |
| | |
| EADES John.   Bates Hill. | 1860 |
| EAVES James.   Red Lion Street. (Dairyman and Shopkeeper). | 1873 |

| | |
|---|---|
| EDWARDS William.   Walford Street. | 1872 – 74 |
| EMMS William.   Webheath. | 1841 |
| ENGLISH Henry.   Feckenham. | 1873 |
| | |
| FIELD John.   Beoley Lane. (Road). | 1841 |
| FIGGETT Charles.   Redditch. | 1835 |
| FISHER George.   Evesham Street. | 1855 |
| FISHER George.   Walford Street. (Shopkeeper). | 1860 – 64 |
| FISHER George.   Herbert Street. (Part of George Street). | 1868 |
| FRANCIS George.   Redditch. | 1854 |
| | |
| GALE Ann (Mrs).   Red Lion Street.   (Grocer). | 1864 |
| GALE Ann (Mrs).   Edward Street. | 1868 |
| GOLDY Harry.   24 Edward Street. | 1891 – 93 |
| GREEN Edward.   Headless Cross. | 1887 – 88 |
| GREEN John.   Beoley Road. | 1868 |
| GREEN Joseph.   Redditch. | 1854 |
| GREEN Rowland.   Astwood Bank. (Needle finisher and Carrier). | 1855 – 64 |
| GWYNN Jonathan.   Walford Street. | 1876 – 77 |
| | |
| HARMAN Benjamin.   Headless Cross. | 1878 – 80 |
| HARRIS Ann (Mrs).   Beoley Road. | 1850 |
| HAWTIN Richard.   Edward Street. | 1860 |
| HEALEY Charles.   Unicorn Hill. | 1860 |
| HILL Emma (Mrs).   Evesham Street. | 1868 |
| HOLLINGTON William.   Crabbs Cross. (Cattle dealer). | 1841 |
| HOUGHTON Henry.   Astwood Bank. (Needle stamper). | 1860 |
| HOUGHTON Reuben.   Headless Cross. | 1876 |
| HOUGHTON William Henry.   Headless Cross. | 1864 |
| | |
| IRESON Ambrose.   Headless Cross. (Forester's Arms)? | 1860 |
| | |
| JAMES Charles.   Headless Cross. | 1880 |
| JEFFS Thomas.   Feckenham. (Cow-keeper). | 1850 – 73 |
| | |
| KNIGHT Solomon.   Astwood Bank. | 1868 |
| | |
| LAYTON Richard.   Ipsley Street. (Butcher). | 1860 |
| LEWIS Amelia (Mrs).   24 Edward Street. (Shopkeeper). | 1872 – 86 |
| LEWIS George.   Headless Cross. | 1878 |
| LEWIS Henry.   24 Edward Street. (Shopkeeper). | 1860 – 68 |
| | |
| MALINS R. H.   Edward Street. | 1894 |
| MENCE Arthur.   24 Edward Street. (Shop and Ale Store). | 1887 – 90 |
| MERRY Hannah (Mrs).   Peakman Street. | 1868 |

MILLWARD James.      Walford Street. (Shopkeeper).                         1855
MORGAN Thomas.       Herbert (George) Street.                              1864
MORRALL Jabez Yardley.   Headless Cross.                                   1879 – 85
MOUNTFORD William Henry.   Bates Hill and Prospect Hill.
(Hairdresser, butcher and palm-maker).                                     1864 – 68

OAKLEY George.    Redditch.                                                1835 – 41
OAKLEY James.     Redditch.                                                1854

PAYNE Elizabeth E. (Mrs).   24 Edward Street.                              1921
PERKS William.    Headless Cross.                                          1876 – 79
POOL Leonora (Mrs).     Headless Cross. (Beer maker).                      1868
POOL Owen.    Headless Cross.                                              1864
POOL Thomas.   Herbert (George) Street.                                    1868
PRESCOTT Thomas.    Redditch.                                              1841

RICHARDS George.    Headless Cross. (Omnibus proprietor).                  1864
RICHARDSON Charles.    Cookhill. (Farmer).                                 1891 – 1900
RUSHTON Albert Edward.    Evesham Road, Headless Cross.                    1904

George Richards of Headless Cross, listed above as an 'Omnibus Proprietor' would have had a carriage similar to the one illustrated below. It was a general purpose vehicle used for both passengers and freight from early to late Victorian Era. Some were privately owned but many belonged to hotels, inns and coaching houses. Hotels with posting stables were used in stages of 10 to 15 miles with horses standing by, ready harnessed for change-over. The average pace was about 10 miles per hour and they were very punctual – people set their clocks by them.

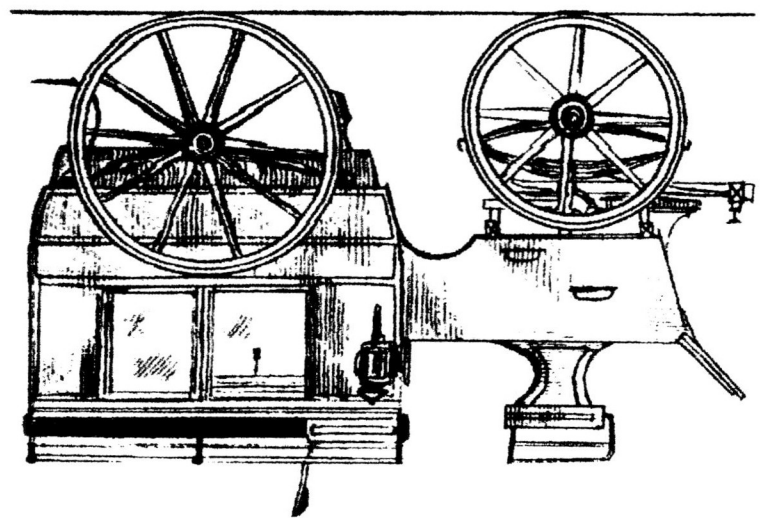

SALT John.   Headless Cross.                                               1854
SALT John.   Edward Street.                                                1855
SAULT John.  Headless Cross.                                               1884 – 86
SMITH Thomas.   Windsor Street.                                            1841 – 50
SMITH Thomas.   Headless Cross.                                            1889

| | |
|---|---|
| STANLEY Henry Morton.   Redditch. (Fish-hook maker). | 1841 |
| STANLEY John Joseph.   24 Edward Street. (Shopkeeper). | 1904 – 10 |
| STANLEY (Mrs).   24 Edward Street. (Shopkeeper). | 1914 |
| STEVENS Richard.   Prospect Hill. | 1850 – 54 |
| STEWARD Ann (Mrs).   Unicorn Hill. (Baker). | 1860 |
| STILES George.   Feckenham. | 1841 |
| STYLER Edward.   Feckenham. (Farmer). | 1850 – 64 |
| STYLER Mary (Mrs).   Headless Cross. | 1850 – 54 |
| | |
| TERRILL George.   Redditch. | 1835 |
| TOWNSEND Alfred.   Headless Cross. (Needle stamper). | 1855 |
| TRUSCOTT Cardew.   9 Albert Street. (Commission agent). | 1880 – 1904 |
| TRUSCOTT Emily Welsford (Miss).   9 Albert Street. | 1932 – 36 |
| | |
| WAGER Henry.   Redditch. | 1854 |
| WAKEMAN J.   Prospect Hill. | 1890 |
| WATSON James.   Church Green. (Grocer). | 1835 – 50 |
| WEBB William.   Evesham Street. (Fish-hook maker). | 1841 |
| WEDGEBURY Samuel.   Prospect Hill. | 1868 |
| WEETMAN Michael.   Headless Cross. (Blacksmith). | 1860 |
| WHARRAD Charles.   Headless Cross. (Shopkeeper). | 1860 |
| WHATELEY John.   Mount Pleasant. | 1841 |
| WHEELER Ann (Mrs).   Unicorn Hill. (Shopkeeper). | 1864 |
| WHEELER Ann (Mrs).   Red Lion Street. | 1868 |
| WHEELER William.   Astwood Bank. (Wood dealer). | 1841 |
| WHITCOOMB William.   Britten Street. | 1864 |
| WHITE James.   Redditch. | 1854 |
| WILKS Sarah (Mrs).   Britten Street. | 1868 |
| WILLIS William.   Headless Cross. | 1878 – 79 |
| WILSON John.   Walford Street. | 1882 – 83 |
| WILTSHIRE William.   Feckenham. (Shoemaker). | 1841 – 54 |
| WRIGHT Joseph W.   Headless Cross. | 1900 |

Morton Stanley's advert for his George Street fishing tackle business from the 1884 Kelly's Directory. The family no longer brewed or sold beer. They gave land in Headless Cross which is called Morton Stanley Park.

# BEER RETAILERS
# The 1830 Beer Act

The Act allowed anyone whose name was on the rate-payer's list to purchase a licence to brew beer for two guineas (£2.10p ).

Pub licensees and Beer Retailers are listed in directories such as Kelly's (every fourth year) and Redditch Needle District Almanack, but from the 1840's to the 1870's few pubs are mentioned by name. Licence holders were often engaged in other occupations and brewed beer for sale in their shops or on farms. Many later moved on to recognized pubs or converted their existing premises to pubs. They often held licences for only a very short space of time, appearing in the directory once or twice. Even some pub names were transitory, Thomas Morris opened the 'Acorn' in Crabbs Cross, opposite the 'Royal Oak' but only appears in the 1850 Kelly's Directory. The 'Turf Tavern' in 1855 later becoming known as the 'Fleece Inn.' William Emms in 1854 – 55 opened 'The Case is Altered' in Headless Cross which in later directories becomes the 'Gate Hangs Well.' Also in Headless Cross, Richard Pinfield opened the 'Apple Tree' in 1850 – 55. Elizabeth Billings brewed beer at the 'Elbows' Tardebigge in the early Victorian period, the inn sign was two bent arms (from the book – ' A Thousand Years in Tardebigge' by Margaret Dickens) but by the 1870's she had gone back to farming.

Early beer retailers who were later to become pub landlords were traced back through the directories using their name and location to connect them. This is fairly reliable in areas where there was only one beer retailer and only one inn but was extremely difficult in places like Walford Street which over the years had many beer retailers and at least six licensed premises.

The 1830 Act was modified in 1840 and repealed in 1869 but beerhouses continued to exist for many years afterwards.

A beer retailer's shop would have been much like the present day off-licence, having a licence to sell beer for consumption 'off' the premises. Beer would have been sold in bottles and also 'drawn from the wood', i.e. a wooden barrel, into a jug supplied by the customer.

One such establishment which existed in Redditch from Victorian times up to the 1920's was at 24 Edward Street. The licence holders were ……

| | |
|---|---|
| LEWIS Henry. | 1860 – 88. |
| LEWIS Amelia (Mrs). | 1872 – 86. |
| MENCE Arthur. | 1887 – 90. |
| GOLDY Harry. | 1891 – 93. |
| DIPPLE W. H. | 1895. |
| DIPPLE Emma (Mrs). | 1896 – 99. |
| BLACKSHAW Kate. | 1901. |
| STANLEY John Joseph. | 1904 – 10. |
| STANLEY (Mrs ). | 1914. |
| PAYNE Elizabeth E. (Mrs ). | 1921. |

It should be noted that a beer-house was not licensed for the sale of spirits.

Before coffee and tea became the national beverages that they are today, beer in its various forms was the normal daily drink. Therefore it is not surprising that there were a large number of beer retailers and public houses to cater for this huge market.

"Reports From Committees 1852 – 53 ; Select Committee of the House of Lords on Public Houses and the Sale of Beer." This states that the number of licences issued in 1850 to houses for the sale and consumption of intoxicating liquors had risen to 123,396.

The Licensing Act 1872. In an attempt to curb excessive drunkenness, Henry Bruce (Home Secretary in Gladstone's Liberal Government of 1867 – 74) carried through the Commons a Licensing Act which strictly limited the hours and places at which alcoholic liquor could be sold. As can be imagined this was an extremely unpopular measure and was the cause of some rioting.

Definitions:

MALT — Barley or other grain, prepared for brewing by steeping, germinating and kiln drying.

BEER — An infusion of malt by fermentation flavoured with hops. ( Now a general term for all kinds of similar brews ).

ALE — Generally paler kinds of beer, the malt not being roasted or burnt.

PORTER — Short for Porter's Ale because it was supposedly drunk, chiefly by London porters and the lower class of labourers.

STOUT — A stronger variety of Porter.

The bottling of beer only became popular in the 1860's when the tax on glass was reduced. Early bottles were corked by hand and later by machine. The screw stopper was introduced in 1885 and the crown cork top in 1908. Maltsters, wine and spirit merchants, agents for the large, out of town, breweries and other wholesale suppliers are not listed here : however, a few of their advertisements may be of interest.

P Spencer & Sons advertising match holder – striker – ashtray which would have stood on the bar in many of the towns pubs. They were manufacturers of ginger beer and other soft drinks.

# VICTORIAN ADVERTS (HALF SIZE) FOR BREWER'S AGENTS ETC. IN THE REDDITCH AREA

---

**MRS. JOHN THOMAS,**
AGENT FOR MESSRS. BASS & CO'S
CELEBRATED ALES AND STOUT.

Flower & Sons, Stratford-on-Avon.
Guinness's Extra Stout.
Northampton Brewery Co.
Arnold & Co's Wickwar Ales.

And the Unsurpassable ANGLO-BAVARIAN-ALES.

OFFICES BROMSGROVE ROAD, REDDITCH.

STORES: RED LION STREET.

N.B.—Families Supplied in Casks of 9 Gals. and Upwards
A carefully selected Stock, in good condition for immediate use, always on hand.

---

*The Needle District Almanack*

**HENRY DAVIS,**
CLIFTON HOUSE, REDDITCH

SOLE AGENT FOR

MESSRS. HENRY MITCHELL & CO., LTD.,
Brewers, and Wine and Spirit Merchants,

Cape Hill, Birmingham.

---

ADVERTISEMENT.

**THOMAS PEART,**
SOLE AGENT FOR
MESSRS. WORTHINGTON & CO'S
**CELEBRATED ALES**
(BY APPOINTMENT TO H.R.H. THE PRINCE OF WALES).
SOLE AGENT FOR
**G. TAYLOR'S CELEBRATED STOUT,**
HOCKLEY BREWERY, BIRMINGHAM,
AND
**WORTHINGTON & SONS,**
Wine and Spirit Merchants.
**IMPORTER OF CIGARS.**
N.B.—ALWAYS ON HAND A
**LARGE STOCK**  **OF CIGARS,**
IN FIRST-CLASS CONDITION.
Stores: Beneath the Park Road Assembly Room,
REDDITCH.

---

**J. D. MUNSLOW,**
AGENT FOR
**W. & A. GILBEY'S**
WINES AND SPIRITS;
AND
**WALKER & WALTON'S**
**BRITISH WINES,**
46 and 48, Evesham Street,
REDDITCH.
Sample Bottles at Wholesale Prices.
ESTABLISHED 1865.

---

**GEORGE MELEN,**
**MALTSTER, Etc.**

ALLSOPP & SONS'
BURTON ALES AND STOUT,
AND
GUINNESS & CO'S
EXTRA DUBLIN STOUT.

Stores:
HEWELL ROAD, REDDITCH.

# THE SHAKESPEARE BREWERY – WALFORD STREET

Barrel label.      Actual size.

This barrel label and others illustrated at reduced size, give some idea of the range of beers produced locally by Brown & Co. in the Walford Street brewery.

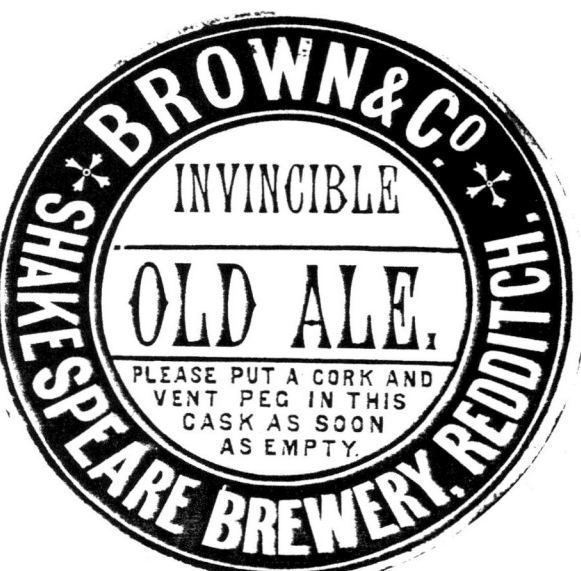

Brown's premises at 61 Evesham Street. The archway led to extensive outbuildings and to the brewery in Walford Street. W. & W. Brown were originally brewers and maltsters and also bakers but they later diversified into selling coal and lime. After brewing ceased with the onset of the First World War they added corn, seed and animal feed to the list.

The Shakespeare Brewery was taken over by H. T. Townsend whose family had been needle makers and who had married into the Brown family. Townsend was not a brewer, he was a bottler and brewers agent.

Brown's archway looking back into Evesham Street
and their advert from the 1910 Redditch Directory.

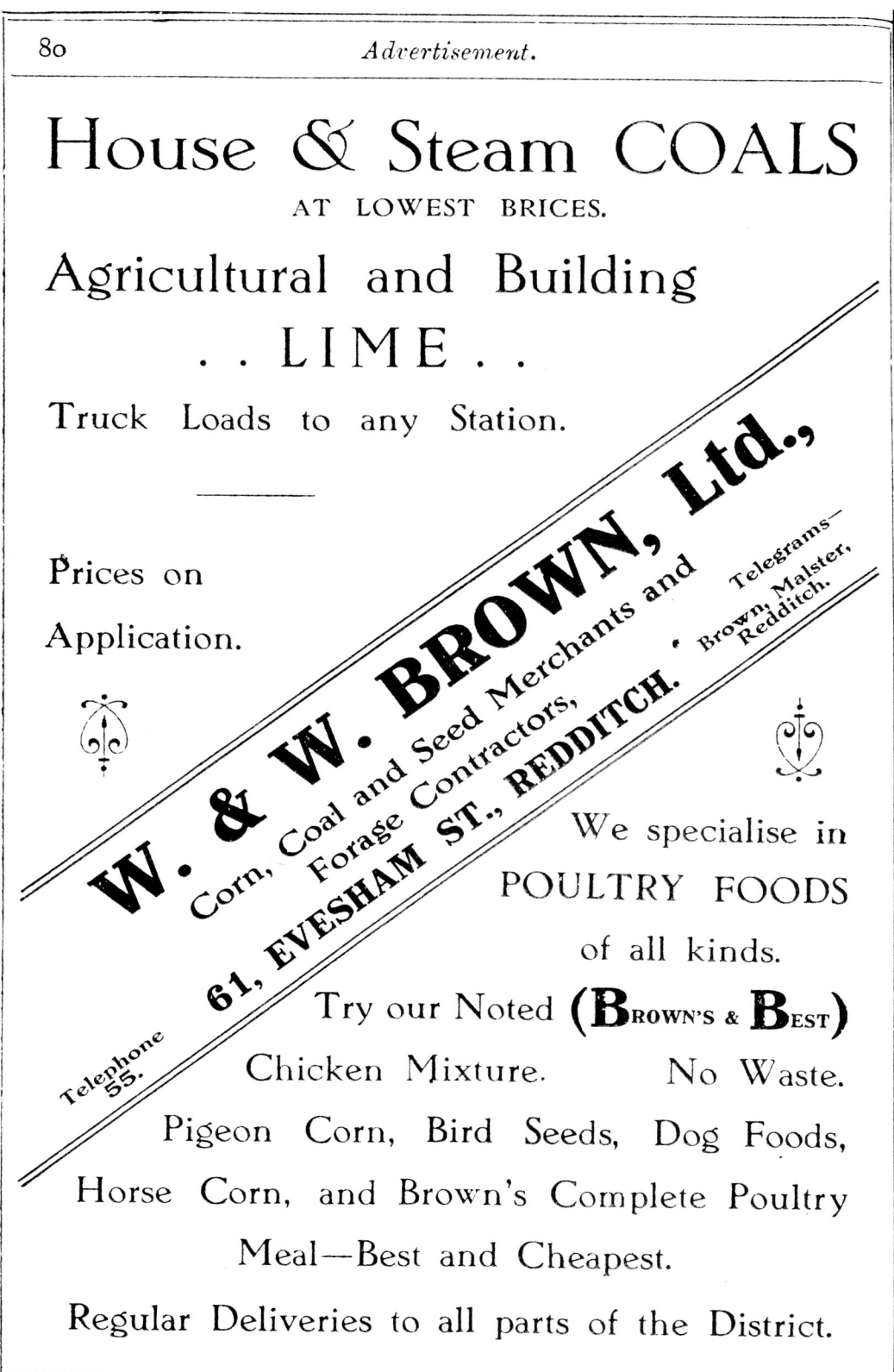

W. & W. Brown's advert from the 1923 Redditch and District Directory and Almanack.

A feature of the town centre skyline for many years the Shakespeare Brewery and Tavern. Below, the brewery again shortly before it and other buildings in the picture were demolished. In the foreground block paving has been laid in the new Royal Square. Brooms and shovels are still in evidence.

LEFT: One of Brown's beautifully embossed beer bottles bearing the portrait of a king with a flagon of ale and the legend "Invincible Ale a dish for a King."

BELOW: Three of H. T. Townsend's rather plain bottles in clear, brown and green glass.

## THE BROWN'S–TOWNSEND'S SHAKESPEARE BREWERY
Walford Street

Extract from the 1923 Redditch & District Business Review

**H. T. TOWNSEND, The Brewery, Walford Street, Bottler of Ales and Stouts, etc. Telephone No.: 204.**

As an old-established business, and as a purely local enterprise employing local labour, the above is well worthy of mention in our review of the prominent business concerns of Redditch and district.

It was founded, we understand, in the year 1878, and formerly known as Brown's Brewery, and carried on by Messrs. Brown & Co.

The present proprietor has been in possession for a period of fifteen or sixteen years, but was with the previous owners for twenty years.

Since assuming control, Mr. Townsend has, by enterprise and attention to all details of the business, obtained a large measure of support from Redditch and the surrounding district.

The premises utilised, known as The Brewery (though brewing is not carried on now), are very suitable for the business, and are fitted up and installed with up-to-date machinery and plant for carrying on an extensive business, scrupulous cleanliness and hygienic principles being observed throughout.

Worthington's and Ind Coope's Ales and Guinness' Stout are supplied in bottle, and also in casks of various sizes to suit the requirements of customers.

Mr. Townsend is sole district agent for Ind Coope's Ales, and also for Bulmer's Cider, both of which are supplied in cask and bottle.

Both the trade and the public will find that every attention is paid to their orders and requirements, and therefore no necessity exists to go outside the town for supplies in these lines.

# H. T. TOWNSEND
## THE BREWERY
## REDDITCH

Telephone REDDITCH 3004

### Retail

## *Price List*

GUINNESS, BASS and WORTHINGTON
BULMERS CIDER in Cask or Bottle
DOUBLE DIAMOND, ANSELL'S and M. & B. BOTTLED BEERS
MANNS, MACKESONS and WATNEYS
WINE AND SPIRIT MERCHANTS

Many popular beers were bottled and labelled by Townsend for sale in local pubs and off licences.

Down Littleworth, a small road opposite the shop in Evesham Street, was the malthouse and stables used by Townsend as a bottle store.